Illustrated Q&A 3.0

Thomas B. Calvert

Wordware Publishing, Inc.

Library of Congress Cataloging-in-Publication Data

Calvert, Thomas B.
Illustrated Q&A 3.0 / by Thomas B. Calvert.
p. cm.
Updated ed. of: Illustrated Q&A. 1987.
ISBN 1-55622-155-X
1. Data base management. 2. Q&A (Computer program)
I. Calvert, Thomas B. Illustrated Q&A. II. Title. Title:
Illustrated Q and A 3.0.
QA76.9.D3C362 1989
005. 369— dc20 89-25024
CIP

1506 Capital Avenue
Plano, Texas 75074

Printed in the United States of America

ISBN 1-55622-155-X

10 9 8 7 6 5 4 3 2
8911

All inquiries for volume purchases of this book should be addressed to Wordware Publishing, Inc., at the above address. Telephone inquiries may be made by calling:

(214) 423-0090

Contents

Contents (Cont.)

Contents (Cont.)

Recommended Learning Sequence

Recommended Learning Sequence (Cont.)

Module 1
ABOUT THIS BOOK

This book describes Q&A, a product developed and marketed by Symantec Corporation of Cupertino, California. It has features not previously found in word processing or database management software.

Q&A combines the features of word processing, spreadsheet, and database programs into one integrated package. Q&A adds another dimension — an artificial intelligence feature. Q&A's basic functions include:

- Word processing including a Spell Check feature
- File function including a file manager and form generator
- Report function to generate custom designed reports generator
- Query system operated through the Intelligent Assistant; and, for simplicity, called the Assistant.

The Write function in Q&A provides the word processing features. It allows you to create and edit documents, produce merge letters, combine text files, import files, and export files. All of the intricate features of sophisticated word processing software are incorporated into this portion of Q&A.

A Spell Check function permits you to automatically check the spelling in a document. An existing main dictionary is used to verify correct spelling for commonly used words. A user-created personal dictionary customizes the spelling checker to fit your specialized needs.

The File function provides the capability to design forms on your computer screen. The forms contain information separated into designated areas called labels. Each label is associated with information that is stored in databases. The data can be retrieved in all or in part to produce different information displays in various on-screen forms or in hardcopy reports. The same data can be retrieved almost instantly by the Assistant function.

The Report function permits you to retrieve information stored in databases and select, sort, and rearrange it to display and/or print in a predefined report format. Data entered in the File function is readily accessible for use in reports that you create.

The most impressive function is the built-in database query system provided by the Assistant. The Assistant understands any of your questions when posed in everyday language and terms. Reports can be created by the Assistant from any existing databases. In addition, any questions about your databases can be easily answered by the Assistant in a matter of milliseconds.

ORGANIZATION

This book is developed to fit the needs of a wide range of users. It is organized into small, easy-to-read modules. These modules are presented in alphabetical order to provide descriptions, applications, and illustrations that give thorough insight into how Q&A operates and how it can be used to solve practical, everyday problems. The alphabetical sequencing of functions in modular form make this book a ready reference tool for any user. Many examples of typical screens and menus are presented in the various sections in this book. The examples can be used to learn the steps necessary to use Q&A or can be used as patterns to design your own applications.

With fully descriptive examples you can practice with Q&A and take the mystery out of using the software. The recommended "hands-on" experimentation permits you to jump into this software and have fun learning to use it.

Each of Q&A's four major functions contain many features. Each module in this book describes a feature. The module name reflects in a few words the operation being described.

A Recommended Learning Sequence containing a list of all of the modules in this book, organized in a simple-to-complex order, is presented in the front of the book for use as an easy reference check list.

You can use the check list, whether you are a student or teacher, to plot your progress through the subject.

Appendixes contain useful reference information and exercises. The exercises can be used for self-instruction or the classroom.

HARDWARE AND SOFTWARE REQUIREMENTS

Q&A requires an IBM PC, IBM Personal System 2 (PS/2 Model), or a PC/XT, PC/AT, or any PC-compatible microcomputer having at least 512K or more of random access memory (RAM). Your computer system must be equipped with at least two floppy disk drives or one floppy disk drive and a hard disk drive. PC-DOS or MS-DOS 2.0 or a later version is required for IBM PCs. DOS 3.3 is required for PS/2 models.

One floppy disk drive and a hard disk drive is more advantageous than a two-floppy disk drive system. With a hard disk drive system you can copy all

Q&A files into a Q&A directory. When operating any Q&A function, files are easily retrieved as needed from the hard disk drive. With a two-floppy disk drive system, it is necessary to install system disks (e.g., #1, #2, etc.) in drive A individually as needed and a data disk in drive B. This means that you must constantly swap system diskettes in and out of drive A. In addition, if you create many large databases, you will be swapping data diskettes in and out of drive B.

If you are using Q&A in a PC network, the same hardware is acceptable. DOS 3.1 or a later version is required with at least 640K of RAM.

INSTALLATION

When using a dual floppy disk drive, it is necessary to format and use a diskette in drive B to store your data. Q&A will not operate on a dual disk drive system without a data diskette installed in drive B. Q&A program diskettes are used in drive A.

CREATING WORKING COPIES Never use your original distribution diskettes for day-to-day operation of Q&A. Always create working copies of each of the seven diskettes. Keep your original distribution diskettes as backups.

Working Copies for 5¼-Inch Floppy Disk System The following instructions describe how to create working copies of the diskettes for a two floppy disk drive system for 5¼-inch diskettes.

1. Cover the write-protect notch on each of the Q&A distribution diskettes with a protect tab. The protect tab is a small adhesive-backed plastic or paper strip. With this tab on the diskette, it cannot be overwritten or accidentally damaged in the computer disk drive.
2. Install a PC-DOS or MS-DOS system diskette in drive A.
3. Turn the computer power switch to ON. The computer boots the operating system and the DOS prompt (A) is displayed.
4. Format seven new double-density, double-sided diskettes in drive B using the FORMAT command. Refer to the documentation provided with your computer for instructions on how to format data diskettes. These diskettes do not require that the operating system be resident on the diskette (i.e., do not use the /S formatting option).
5. At the DOS prompt (A) remove the PC-DOS or MS-DOS diskette from drive A.
6. Install the first of the Q&A program diskettes into drive A.

7. Type **COPY A*.* B:** and press **Return**. A working copy of the program diskette is created.
8. Repeat Steps 6 and 7 for each of the remaining six Q&A program diskettes.
9. Ensure that the working copy diskettes are properly identified with labels denoting the contents.

Working Copies for 3½-Inch Disk Systems To make working copies on 3½-inch diskettes, you need four diskettes. Follow the same instructions as for copying 5¼-inch diskettes.

Ensure that the working copy diskettes are properly identified with labels denoting the contents of each diskette.

INSTALLING Q&A PROGRAMS ON A HARD DISK Q&A distribution diskettes (5¼- or 3½-inch diskettes) are installed on hard disk drive C (or D). The drive must be formatted and ready to accept data. Refer to documentation covering your computer and hard disk drive for instructions on how to format the drive.

You should create a separate directory on your hard drive for the Q&A files. Refer to your DOS manual for detailed instructions on how to make a directory using the MDIR command. Before attempting to perform the following installation procedure, be advised that Q&A Disk #4 must be the last diskette copied to the hard disk drive.

1 Cover the write-protect notch on each of the Q&A distribution diskettes with a protect tab. The protect tab is a small adhesive-backed plastic or paper strip. With this tab on the diskette, it cannot be overwritten or accidentally damaged in the computer disk drive.
2. Turn the computer power switch to ON.
3. Ensure that the C drive prompt (C) is displayed. Refer to the operations guide for your computer for instructions on how to preset the system to drive C.
4. Create a Q&A directory by typing: **MKDIR\QA** or **MD\QA**
5. Install the first of the Q&A program diskettes into drive A.
6. Type **COPY A:*.* C:** and press **Return**. The program diskette is copied to drive C.
7. Repeat Steps 5 and 6 for each of the program diskettes.

It is not necessary to copy the Tutorial diskette to the hard drive. Disk space can be saved by making a backup copy of the Tutorial diskette.

Installing Q&A software from 3½-inch diskettes is performed the same as described for 5¼-inch floppy diskettes except that there are only four diskettes to install.

CREATING A CONFIG.SYS FILE

For Q&A to operate properly, your root directory should contain a CONFIG.SYS file containing the following information:

Files = 20

Buffers = 2 or more (Buffers = 10 is preferable, but takes much more memory.)

If you have a CONFIG.SYS file with at least the recommended information, you do not need to go further in this topic.

CONFIG.SYS File on a Hard Disk

If you have a hard disk drive and want to create a CONFIG.SYS file, perform the following steps:

1. Turn on the computer power. At the prompt (C), type **CD\QA** and press **Return**.
2. Type **QAFILE** and press **Return**. Instructions are displayed on the screen. Since most hard disk drives are labeled "C:", at startup (booting) of the computer, type **C** in response to the Q&A prompt message.

   If your computer already has a CONFIG.SYS file meeting the minimum requirements, a message is displayed to inform you so.
3. To activate a new or changed CONFIG.SYS file, reboot your computer by turning the power switch off for a few seconds and then back on, or press the **Ctrl-Alt-Del** keys simultaneously.

CONFIG.SYS File on 5¼- or 3½-Inch Diskettes

1. Place a PC-DOS or MS-DOS in drive A and turn the computer power switch on.
2. Change to drive B by typing **B:** and press **Return**.
3. Place Q&A diskette 1 in drive B, type **QAFILES**, and press **Return**.
4. Type **A** and follow the instructions displayed on the screen.

START RUNNING Q&A WITH A HARD DISK

1. At the C prompt, type **CD\QA** and press **Return**.
2. At the C\QA prompt, type **QA** and press **Return**. The Q&A Main Menu is displayed.

START RUNNING Q&A FROM DISKETTES

1. Place a PC-DOS or MS-DOS diskette in drive A and turn your computer power on.
2. At the A prompt, remove the DOS diskette in drive A and place the Q&A System Disk 1 in drive A.
3. Place a blank formatted diskette in drive B.
4. At the A prompt, type **QA** and press **Return**. The Q&A Main Menu is displayed.

WHAT YOU SHOULD KNOW

You should be familiar with your computer, its keyboard, and the operating system commands which allow you to list a directory of your diskettes (or hard disk), format a disk, and copy, rename, and delete files.

In addition, you should be thoroughly familiar with how to set up directories and paths. Refer to the DOS manual for appropriate instructions. This is particularly important if you are using a hard disk drive. Your DOS manual also explains how to format diskettes for use as data diskettes.

You will also want a printer to make hard copies of forms, reports, and documents. Refer to Module 73 for a list of compatible printers.

If you have the required equipment and software, Q&A will operate on your computer system. Knowing about your computer, keyboard, and operating system software prepares you for using Q&A.

Turn to Module 2 to begin the learning sequence.

Module 2
SAMPLE SESSION

DESCRIPTION

This module guides you through several Q&A operations. You experience Q&A's word processing feature called the Write function. In this sample session you learn the basics of creating and saving a document file.

Next, you experiment with Q&A's *File* function. This powerful feature lets you create, save, and print structured files containing business or personal information, such as customer lists or telephone directories.

This module is intended to provide a quick overview. Q&A has many other useful features that are thoroughly described in the individual modules of this book.

GETTING STARTED

The instructions for installing the Q&A program on either hard disk or floppy disk systems are contained in Module 1. Once you have installed Q&A for your system, use the following step-by-step procedure to familiarize yourself with some of the useful features offered by Q&A.

1. With the Q&A program properly installed, type **QA** and press **Return** to display the Q&A Main Menu. This menu displays as follows:

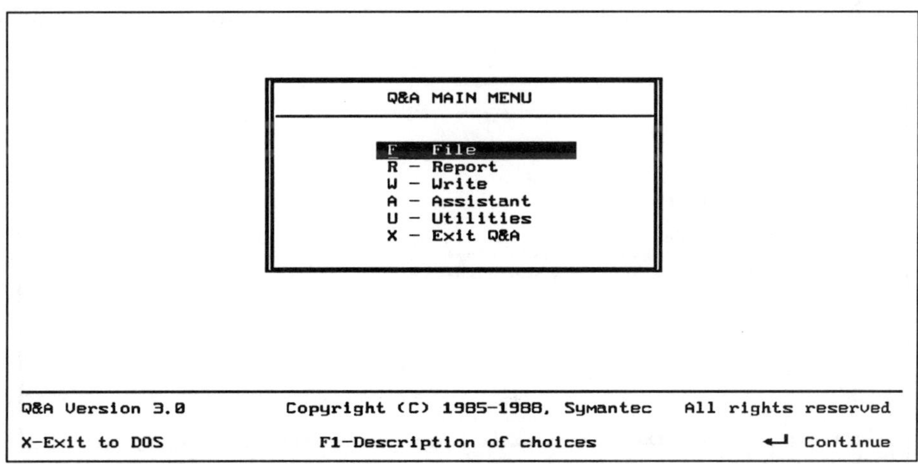

2. Notice the menu structure. Typing the indicated letter puts you into the selected Q&A function. For example, typing W and pressing Return places you into the Write function.
3. Insert a formatted floppy disk into your working drive. This is probably drive B if you are using a two-drive floppy system, or drive C if you are using a hard disk system.
4. Proceed to the following Sample Session.

SAMPLE SESSION

This session lets you experience Q&A's Write and File functions. Perform each step in the order indicated. Follow the directions carefully. Bold keys and text passages indicate those that are pressed or typed. In this session you also set the Automatic Execution to "Yes" to eliminate the need for pressing Return after each menu selection. Begin at the Q&A Main Menu and have fun!

NOTE

Control key sequences are shown Ctrl-#, where # is any character key. When this appears, press the Control and character key simultaneously.

1. At the Q&A Main Menu, the cursor is located at F - File. Type **W** and press **Return**. The Write Menu is displayed. The cursor is located at T - Type/Edit.
2. Press **Return** to display a Working copy (blank) screen for a new document.
3. Type **Dear Mr. Cook** and press **Return** twice. Then type the following paragraph letting the automatic word wrap feature end your lines for you.

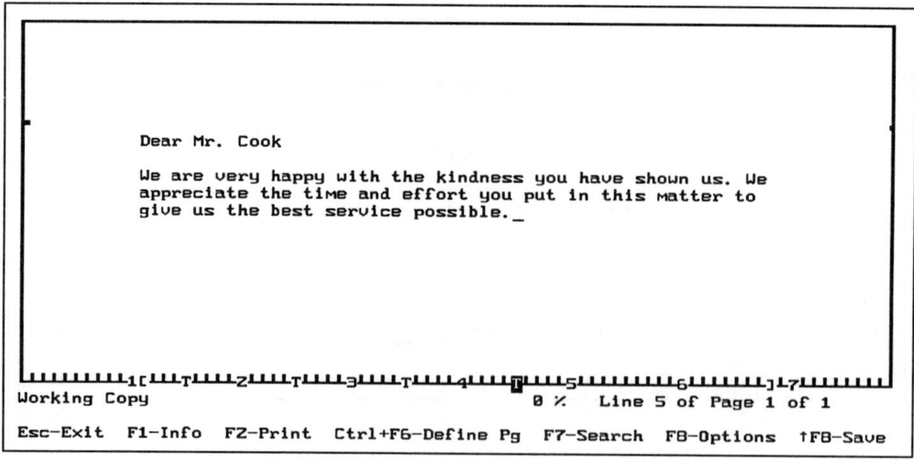

4. Press **Esc**. The Write Menu is displayed. Type **S**, press **Return**, and type the filename: **SAMPLE** in response to the "Document:" prompt and press **Return** to save the document to disk.

5. To print the letter, type **P** (Print) and press **Return**. Notice the Print Options Menu. Before continuing, make sure your printer is turned on and ready for printing.

```
                              PRINT OPTIONS

    From page............:   1          To page............:  1
    Number of copies......:  1          Print offset........: 0
    Line spacing..........:  >Single<   Double      Envelope
    Justify...............:  Yes >No<
    Print to..............:  >PtrA<  PtrB   PtrC   PtrD   PtrE   DISK
    Type of paper feed....:  Manual  >Continuous<  Bin1   Bin2   Bin3   Lhd
    Number of columns.....:  >1<   2    3    4    5    6    7    8
    Printer control codes.:
    Name of Merge File....:
  ______________________________________________________________________
                        Print Options for SAMPLE
 Esc-Cancel   F1-Info   Ctrl F6-Def Pg   F9-Save changes & go back   F10-Continue
```

6. Accept the defaults for the print options and press **F10** to print the document.

7. Press **Esc**. The Q&A Main Menu is displayed. The cursor is located at F - File.

8. To create a database, press **Return**. The File Menu is displayed.

9. Press **Return** to display the Design Menu. Type **D** and press **Return** to name a file.

10. Type **PHONE** and press **Return** to name the file. An extension ".dtf" is automatically added to the filename. A blank form is displayed for you to begin the design.

11. Move the cursor to the location where you want the Name field to appear, then type the information shown on the following screen for field names. Be sure to end each field with a colon (:), leave the appropriate number of blank spaces (noted in brackets), then end each field with a greater than symbol (>). Do not type the brackets or the numbers, They are shown only for illustration purposes to indicate how many blank spaces to key in setting up the area for the fields.

```
Name:                                   >
Address:                        >
City:               >   State:      >   Zip:      >
Phone:              >_

PHONE                                           0 %   Line 7 of Page 1 of 1
Esc-Cancel          F1-How to design          F8-Options          F10-Continue
```

12. Press **F10** when you have finished entering all of the labels. "Saving design" is displayed at the bottom of the screen. The Format Spec screen is displayed.
13. Accept the default for "information types" and press **F10**.
14. Press **Esc**. Notice that the Main Menu is displayed and the form is saved to disk as PHONE. The cursor is located at F - File.
15. Press **Return**. The File Menu is displayed.
16. Type **A** and press **Return**. A message is displayed at the bottom of the screen requesting the name of the file in which you want to enter data.
17. Type **PHONE** and press **Return**. The first form of the file is displayed with the cursor located at the first field.
18. Type the information shown in the following screens to create two forms. Press **F10** after completing the first form and to move to a blank screen for creating the second form.

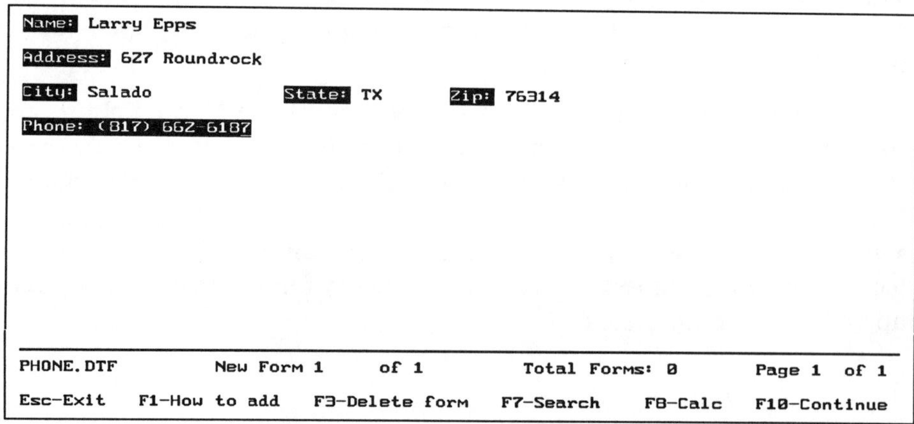

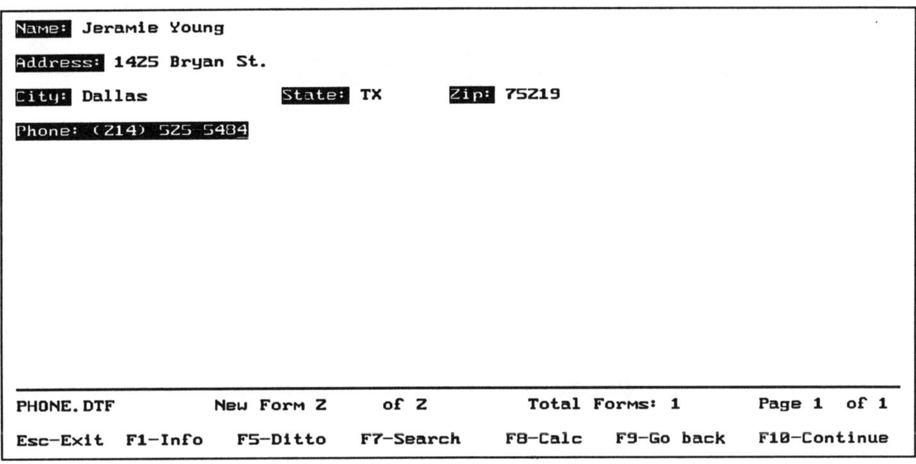

19. After completing both forms, press **Shift-F10** to save the completed forms to disk. The File Menu is displayed.
20. Press **Esc** to return to the Q&A Main Menu.
21. Type **U** and press **Return**. The Utilities Menu is displayed.
22. Type **S** and press **Return**. The Set Default Directories screen is displayed.
23. Press **Tab, Down Arrow,** or **Return** to move the cursor to Automatic Execution. Use **Right Arrow** or **Left Arrow** to move the cursor to Yes.
24. Press **F10** to save the setting.
25. Press **Esc** to return to the Main Menu.
26. Type **X** to exit from Q&A and return to DOS.

Here you have learned a few techniques in word processing and creating databases. These unique features, as well as many others, are described in the modules ahead in greater detail.

27. Turn to Module 58 to continue the learning sequence.

Module 3
ADVANCED ADJECTIVES LESSON

DESCRIPTION

Teaching the Assistant advanced *adjectives* provides the additional capability for comparisons to be made as a result of your inquiries to the Assistant. You actually must teach the Assistant additional adjectives that denote comparative value.

Adjectives have three *degrees of comparison:* positive, comparative, and superlative. For example:

Positive	*Comparative*	*Superlative*
fast	faster	fastest

If you teach the Assistant the positive degree, it can determine what you mean if you ask for the "fastest" or the highest comparative value. Adjectives taught to the Assistant are directly related to individual fields on forms for a specified database.

At the Q&A Main Menu, selecting A displays the Assistant Menu. Entering T displays a prompt message requesting the name of the file about which you plan to teach the Assistant. Entering the filename and pressing Return displays the Basic Lessons Menu. Selecting 5, Advanced lessons, displays the Advanced Lessons Menu. Selecting 3, Advanced vocubulary: adjectives, displays the screen on which adjectives can be entered.

The screen displayed by Q&A for you to enter advanced adjectives requests a high value and a low value for each numeric or money field. The numeric and money fields are displayed with pound (#) signs filling the information blank. If there are no number or money fields on the form, the Assistant displays a message indicating that condition.

```
Will you use adjectives in your questions about the highlighted
field?  If YES, type them in the blanks below.  If NO press F8 to
select other fields that have adjectives, or F10 to continue.   If
you're NOT SURE, press F1 for examples and explanation.

High value:  <                 >   Low value:   <                 >
             <                 >                <                 >
             <                 >                <                 >
             <                 >                <                 >
```

When viewing this screen, remember that it is not necessary to assign adjectives to every numeric or money field. For example, you would not want to assign adjectives for a telephone number or Zip code.

It is not absolutely necessary to assign opposite values. That is, you can assign a low value adjective and not assign a high value adjective for a field. The reverse is also true. You are allowed to assign up to four high and four low value adjectives for each numeric and/or money field on the screen. Pressing F6 moves the cursor to the previous field (highlighting the field). Pressing F8 moves the cursor to the next field. After entering adjectives on the screen, pressing F10 completes the operation and the Advanced Lessons Menu is displayed.

Typical adjectives known to the Assistant are:

Low Value		*High Value*
big	bigger	biggest
bottom		top
few	fewer	fewest
great	greater	greatest
high	higher	highest
large	larger	largest
less		least
many	more	most
low	lower	lowest
minimum		maximum
small	smaller	smallest

An important thing to remember is that some numeric adjectives are better defined as verbs to the Assistant. Refer to Module 4 to better understand this distinction.

The ability to define to the Assistant relative degrees of size, importance, or other attributes related to fields on a form enables you to design an attributes matrix. The terms contained within this definition for each field add to the power and potential by which the Assistant can retrieve information for you. You are creating the level of intelligence and relevance used by the Assistant when it is time for it to perform a task for you. The advanced adjectives lesson should be an important part of your training of the Assistant.

TYPICAL OPERATION

In this illustration, teach the Assistant some advanced adjectives for a specific file and then exit to the Q&A Main Menu. Begin at the Q&A Main Menu.

1. Type **A**. The Assistant Menu is displayed.
2. Type **T**. A prompt message is displayed requesting the name of the file for which you want to provide instruction to the Assistant.
3. Type **INVNTRY** and press **Return**; the Basic Lessons Menu is displayed.
4. Type **5**. The Advanced Lessons Menu is displayed.
5. Type **3**. The form design for the specified database is displayed. This is the screen on which you enter adjectives related to specific fields.

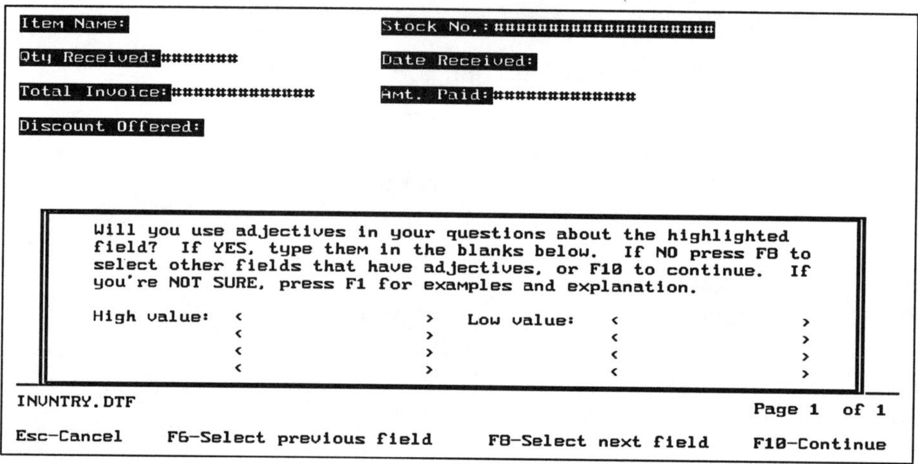

The cursor is located on the first High value for the amount paid field. You can type adjectives in all uppercase, initial uppercase, or lowercase characters.

6. Press **F8** to highlight the Qty Received field. Type **best** and press **Return**. The cursor moves to the first field for Low value.
7. Type **worst** and press **Return**. The cursor moves to the second field for High value.
8. Press **F8**. The next field area, Total Invoice, is highlighted. The cursor is located at the first high value for that field.
9. Type **large** and press **Return**. The cursor moves to the first field for Low value.

You can continue entering adjectives by repeating Steps 8 and 9 for the next field on the form, or proceed to Step 10.

10. Press **F10**. The Advanced Lesson Menu is displayed.
11. Press **Esc**. The Basic Lessons Menu is displayed.

12. Press **Esc**. The Assistant Menu is displayed.
13. Press **Esc**. The Q&A Main Menu is displayed.
14. Turn to Module 4 to continue the learning sequence.

Module 4
ADVANCED VERBS LESSON

DESCRIPTION

Teaching the Assistant advanced *verbs* provides the "action" words for the Assistant on which to base decisions when you are requesting information. Typical verbs that you may want to teach are:

advance	decrease	demote
earn	hire	increase
identify	pay	promote
terminate	train	work

When requesting the Assistant to "do something," the verbs permit the Assistant to comply with the request. For example, in a customer file you can ask the Assistant to "discount" all purchases made by customers contained in a specific database. "Purchases" would be a field label on a form in the database. You can also ask the Assistant to "increase" the quantities shipped to customers.

Q&A has no difficulty with verbs having regular verb endings. *Regular verb endings* include the form "s, es, en, ed," and "ing." However, irregular verb forms are not recognized as regular verbs. In the case of irregular verb forms, each form must be specified if you want each verb form used.

Verbs taught to the Assistant are directly related to individual fields on forms for a specified database. Verbs must be different from field names and different from assigned alternate field names.

At the Q&A Main Menu, selecting A displays the Assistant Menu. Typing T displays a prompt message requesting the name of the file about which you plan to teach the Assistant. Entering the name of the file and pressing Return displays the Basic Lessons Menu. Selecting 5, Advanced lessons, displays the Advanced Lessons Menu. Selecting 4, Advanced vocabulary: verbs, displays the screen on which verbs can be entered.

When viewing this screen, remember that it is not necessary to assign verbs to every field. You are at liberty to assign verbs to only those fields that may be used in a future request.

Pressing F6 moves the cursor to the previous field (highlighting the field). Pressing F8 moves the cursor to the next field. After entering verbs on the screen, pressing F10 completes the operation and the Advanced Lessons Menu is displayed.

APPLICATIONS

It is important to define to the Assistant the action words related to possible requests for data that you may make. Of course, there are many words already in the vocabulary used by the Assistant. However, you can add additional verbs that relate better to your line of business or home activity. The advanced verbs feature is simply another option available to you to completely customize Q&A to your needs.

The advanced verbs lesson is one of the basic steps in teaching the Assistant what it needs to know. This module and lesson for the Assistant should be an important part of your training of the Assistant.

TYPICAL OPERATION

In this illustration, teach the Assistant some advanced verbs for a specific file and then exit to the Q&A Main Menu. Begin at the Q&A Main Menu.

1. Type **A**. The Assistant Menu is displayed.
2. Type **T**. A prompt message is displayed requesting the name of the file for which you want to provide instructions to the Assistant.
3. Type **CUSTOMER** and press **Return**. The Basic Lessons Menu is displayed.
4. Type **5**. The Advanced Lessons Menu is displayed.
5. Type **4**. The form design for the specified database is displayed. This is the screen on which you enter verbs related to specific fields.

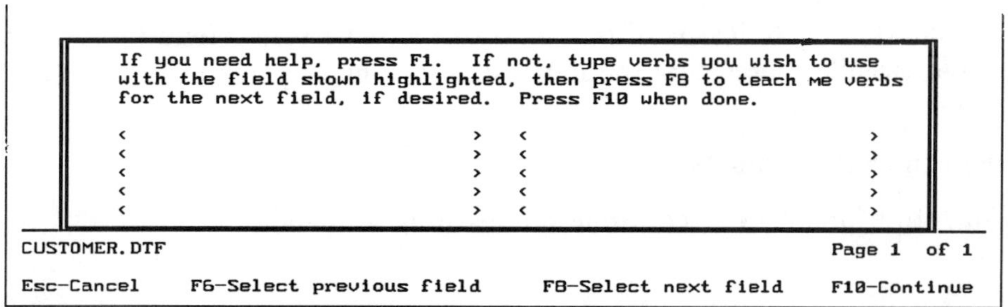

The cursor is located on the first field on the form (Company Name:). The field area is highlighted.

6. Type the verb that you want to assign to the field. For this example, type **requires**. The verb "requires" can be used when making inquiries to have the Assistant list all companies that "require" a discount for all invoices paid within 30 days after receipt.
7. Press **Tab** to move the cursor to the next available blank for entering another verb associated with the Company Name field.
8. Type **requests**. The verb "request" can be used when making inquiries to have the Assistant list all companies that "request" discounts, information, specifications, etc. related to their orders.

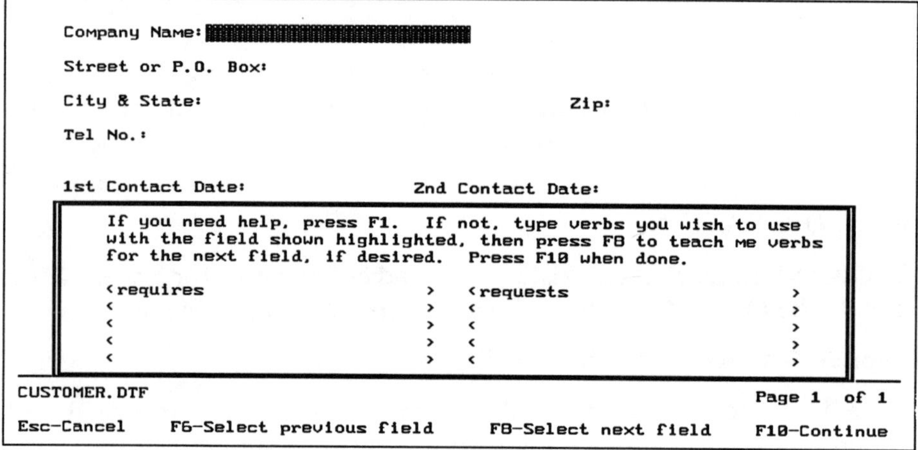

9. Press **F8** to select the next field. Determine if you want to assign a verb to that particular field. If so, repeat the appropriate steps above as often as necessary to assign verbs to the database.
10. Press **F10** when you have finished assigning verbs to the data base. The Advanced Lessons Menu is displayed.

You can continue with lessons from the Advanced Lessons Menu by referring to applicable modules describing the individual lessons or you can exit to the Q&A Main Menu.

11. Return to the Main Menu.
12. Turn to Module 19 to continue the learning sequence.

Module 5
ALTERNATE FIELD NAMES LESSON

DESCRIPTION

This module describes how to teach alternate field names to the Assistant. *Alternate field names* are synonyms for a field label. You can use different words (alternate words) of your choice for each field label. You specify to the Assistant the synonyms to use for field names contained on forms in your databases. By designating a single alternate name or several alternate names for each field on a form, you can refer to fields by "nicknames" when asking the Assistant to perform some task.

Predefined field names (labels) are designated when you design a form. These names, assigned at design time, are the names used by the Assistant when reports are produced. Any messages pertaining to the names are also displayed using these exact names.

At the Q&A Main Menu, selecting the Assistant function displays the Assistant Menu. Typing T displays a prompt message requesting a filename. Entering a filename and pressing Return displays the Basic Lessons Menu.

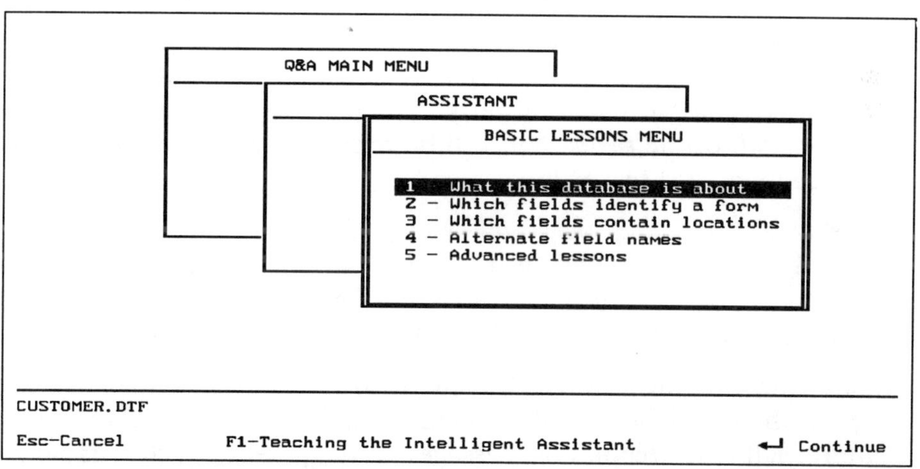

Selecting 4, Alternate field names, displays the alternate field names screen. The screen contains a window displayed over the top of the form design for the specified file.

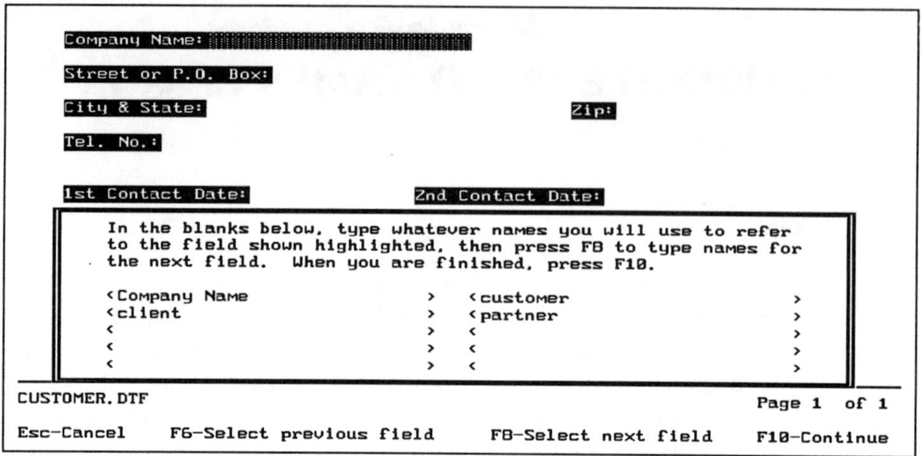

The first name on the screen is the name of the field label and is the official name for the field. Pressing F8 moves the cursor to the next field on the form. You can type an alternate field name for each field on the form. Several alternate names can be typed for each field label on the form. It is not absolutely necessary to assign alternate field names at all.

Pressing F6 moves the cursor to the previous field. Use the Return, Tab keys and Shift and Tab to move the cursor between the alternate field name entries in the window.

PRECAUTIONS As with adjectives and verbs, do not assign duplicate field names to fields which are related. For example, if you have defined field names for "electrical parts" and "mechanical parts," you cannot define an alternate name of "part" for both of the fields. You will be warned if you attempt to assign the same alternate name for two fields.

If two fields are assigned the same name, the first occurrence assumes a predesignated name. The second field is nameless unless you assign an alternate name. If a name is not assigned to this second field and it is a selected field in a report, it is automatically designated the name of "No Name."

In addition, note that the first name displayed on the screen for each field is the name used as the field label. The field name is the name used by the Assistant as the column heading for reports or messages. You can reassign that name just by retyping it on the alternate field names screen. However, if you replace it, be sure to enter it later in the list to ensure that it can be used by the Assistant.

It is recommended that you retype the official field name (first name on the alternate field name list) in all uppercase letters. Then, all report column headings and messages are emphasized.

Pressing F10 completes the lesson for the Assistant. The alternate field names entered on the screen are saved for the Assistant to use in the future.

APPLICATIONS

It is often helpful to define alternate field names for field labels contained on forms in your databases. As you create more forms and add to your databases, it becomes increasingly difficult to remember the exact name of a field label. If you assign alternate field names and teach them to the Assistant, you will minimize problems in retrieving information. Several possibilities are predefined before a query is performed for a field on a form.

Today in many businesses trade jargon is used. The alternate field name feature permits you to use the jargon of your trade. One example of a trade using business jargon is the banking industry. Alternate field names allow you to use your business jargon daily while using Q&A, but on reports submitted to customers, you can use more formal vocabulary.

TYPICAL OPERATION

In this illustration, teach the Assistant some alternate field names for a field label on a form. Begin at the Q&A Main Menu.

1. Type **A**. The Assistant Menu is displayed.
2. Type **T**. A prompt message is displayed requesting the name of a file for which you want to provide instruction to the Assistant.
3. Type **CUSTOMER** and press **Return**, the Basic Lessons Menu is displayed.
4. Type **4**. The form design for the specified database is displayed. The alternate field names screen is displayed in a window over the form. The cursor is located at the first field label. The field label is highlighted. In this example, the "Customer" can be defined by several alternate names. The first entry in the alternate field name screen is Company Name. The cursor is located on the first blank available for entering an alternate field name.
5. Type **Client** and press **Return**. The cursor moves to the next blank in the window.
6. Type **Patient** and press **Return**. The cursor moves to the next blank in the window.

7. Type **ID Number** as the last alternate field name entered for the first field on the form.

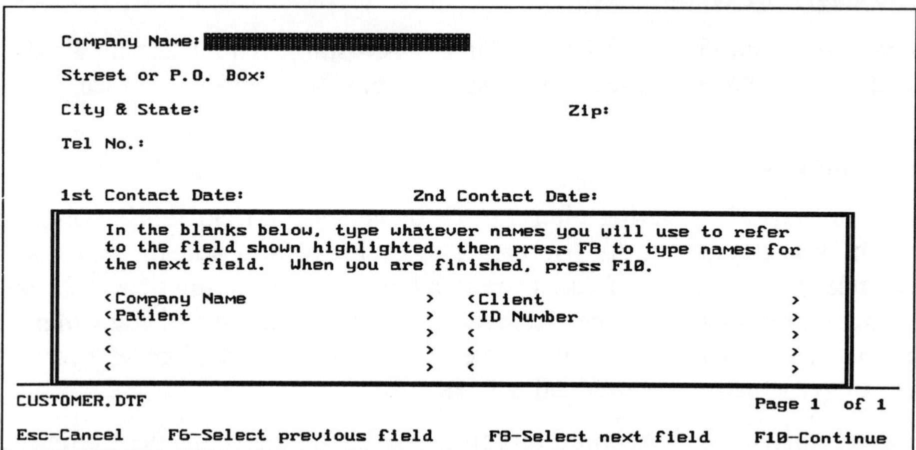

```
Company Name:
Street or P.O. Box:
City & State:                                 Zip:
Tel No.:

1st Contact Date:                  2nd Contact Date:

In the blanks below, type whatever names you will use to refer
to the field shown highlighted, then press F8 to type names for
the next field.  When you are finished, press F10.

<Company Name                    >  <Client                        >
<Patient                         >  <ID Number                     >
<                                >  <                              >
<                                >  <                              >
<                                >  <                              >

CUSTOMER.DTF                                             Page 1  of 1
Esc-Cancel   F6-Select previous field   F8-Select next field   F10-Continue
```

8. Press **F10** when you have completed assigning alternate names to the field. The Basic Lessons Menu is displayed.
9. Return to the Main Menu.
10. Turn to Module 90 to continue the learning sequence.

Module 6

ASSIGN/CHANGE FORM INFORMATION TYPES

DESCRIPTION

Each field on a form must have an *information type* assigned to it. If an information type is not assigned, Q&A automatically assigns an information type of "T." The "T" type designates "text."

Assigning information types is an important step in designing a form. After forms are designed, information is entered into each field to create a completed form. A collection of completed forms comprise one of your data bases.

The information type for a field determines what kind of data can be entered into the blank field. The information type also determines how data is formatted in the field. For example, date information can be formatted in several different ways (e.g., 10 January, 1990 or 01/10/90).

After designing a form (laying out the form) on the screen, the next step in the design process is to assign an information type for each field. Designing a form (layout) is described in Module 37.

Assigning or even changing information types on a form is accomplished immediately after form layout. Pressing F10 displays the Format Spec screen for the form.

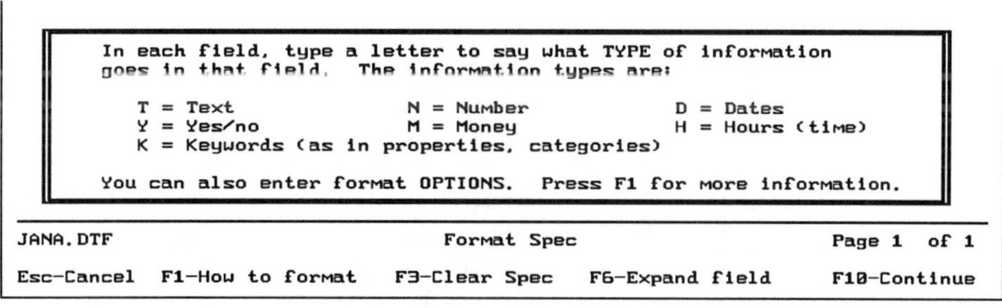

The default information type for each field is T (text) when first displayed on the Format Spec screen.

Assigning or changing information types is done by moving the cursor or pressing Tab to move to the appropriate field and typing the Information Type Code. The following table lists each information type, the associated code, and a description of its use.

Information Type

Code	Description
D	Date information (e.g., 10 Jan 1990 or January 10, 1990)
H	Hour time
K	Keyword field (Refer to Module 55 for use of these fields.)
M	Money field
N	Numeric field to contain quantities or numbers used in calculations. Refer to Module 8 for instructions on using calculations in reports.
T	Text or alphabetical data.
Y	Yes or
N	No responses when queried by the Assistant.

If you want, you can specify information type options that control the layout of a form in any format that you need.

Information Type

Code	Description	Options	Option Code
D	Date	Justify Right	JR
		Justify Left	JL
		Justify Center	JC
H	Time	Justify Right	JR
		Justify Left	JL
		Justify Center	JC
K	Keyword	Justify Right	JR
		Justify Left	JL
		Justify Center	JC
		Uppercase	U
M	Money	No. of decimals	0 to 7 (to right of decimal)
		Insert commas	C
		Justify Right	JR

Code	Description	Options	Option Code
		Justify Left	JL
		Justify Center	JC
N	Number (arithmetic operations only)	Insert commas	C
		Justify Right	JR
		Justify Left	JL
		Justify Center	JC
T	Text	Justify Right	JR
		Justify Left	JL
		Justify Center	JC

An example of a detailed information type depicting options is:

```
Amount Received: N,3,JR,C
```

The number (N) represents an amount received that is three decimal digits (3), right justified (JR), and with commas (C) inserted in the number.

APPLICATIONS

Specifying an information type for each field on a form ensures that you get the wanted results from Q&A. For calculations to be performed correctly, dates and times to be entered properly on reports, and fields to be tagged as keyword fields, fields must be identified by the kind of data being entered.

Fields properly identified by the kind of information being entered becomes a convenience to you. Only text, numbers, etc. can be valid entries in appropriately identified fields.

TYPICAL OPERATION

In this illustration, access the File function and layout a simple form. Then, assign an information type to each field on the form. Begin at the Q&A Main Menu.

1. Select the File Menu.

2. Type **D** to display the Design Menu.
3. Type **D** again, and notice the cursor moves to the filename prompt requesting you to enter the name of a new file.

NOTE

To change information types for an existing file, type R in this step instead of typing D. This allows you to change (redesign) an existing form.

4. Type **INVNTRY** and press **Return**. A blank screen is displayed.
5. Type the field names shown in the following illustration, leaving the specified number of blanks for the data shown in brackets (e.g., [35]). The numbers shown in brackets are for illustration purposes only. Do not type the brackets or the numbers shown on the sample screen.

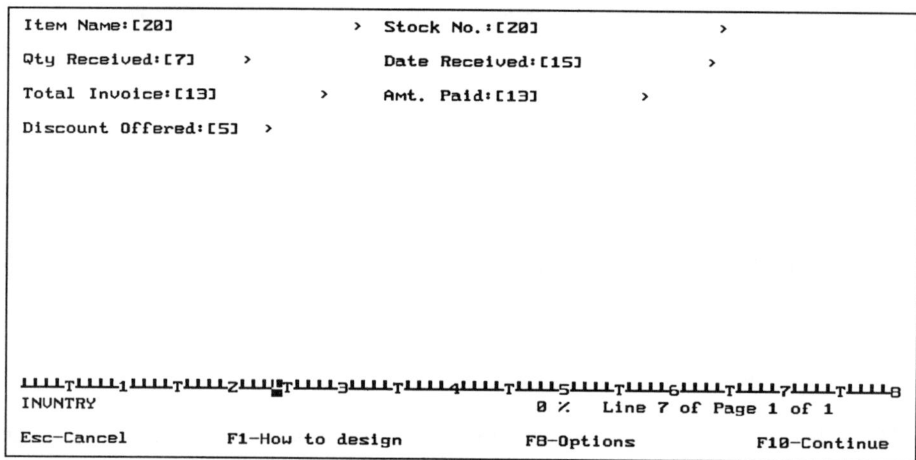

6. Press **F10**. "Saving Design" is displayed at the bottom of the screen. The Format Spec screen for the form is displayed. Notice that each field is identified with an information type code of T (text). The cursor is located at the first character position in the first field.

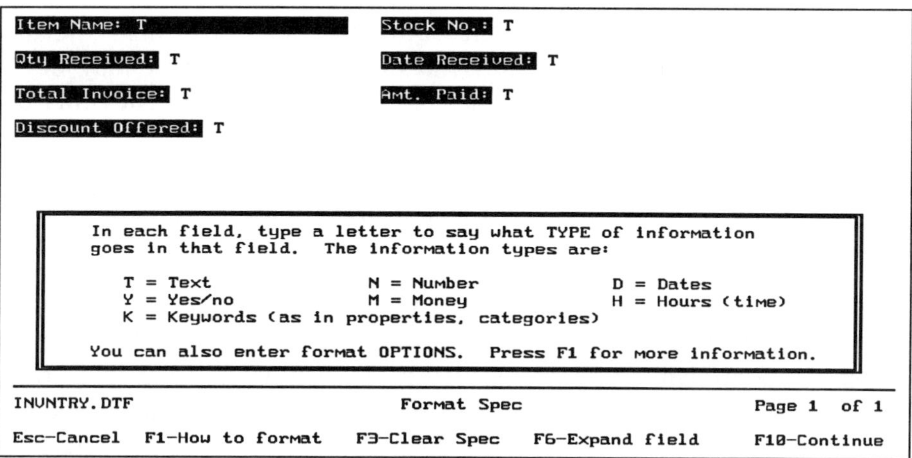

7. At the first field, press **Return**. This field is a text field, so "T" is the correct information type to use.

8. Press **Tab** to move the cursor through the fields on the form. At each information type code that is displayed, either leave it as T (for text) or change it according to the following table:

Item Name	**T**
Stock No.	**N**
Qty Received	**N**
Date Received	**D**
Total Invoice	**M**
Amount Paid	**M**
Discount Offered	**Y**

9. Press **F10**. The Global Format Options screen is displayed.

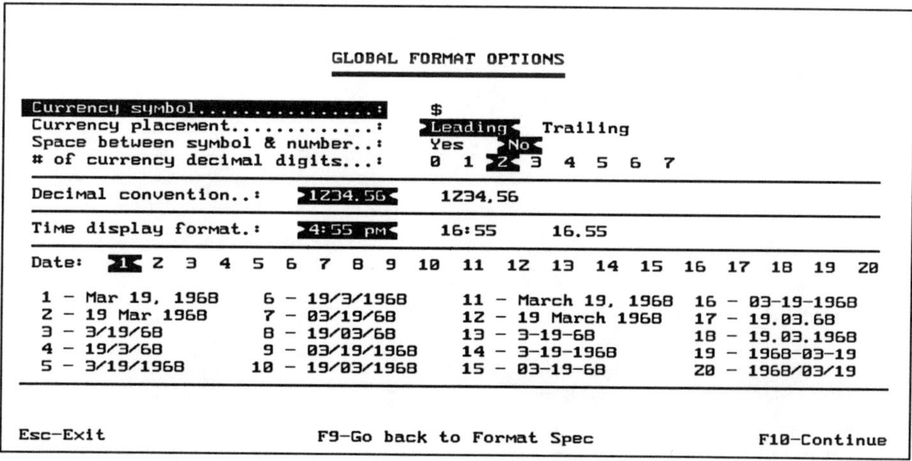

10. Press **Tab** and the arrow keys to move the cursor through the available options. The highlight indicates the option chosen. You may accept the default options highlighted on the screen or choose any of the other options.

Notice that any of the date format options must match the number of blank spaces allocated on the form design screen for that option. If you want to use the Date format option 11, your form design must contain 14 spaces allocated for the date field.

11. Press **F10**. The assigned information types for the file are saved and the File Menu is displayed. If you exit from this form design and later return to it from the Redesign a file feature on the Design Menu, you will notice that the information type codes are no longer displayed. They have been replaced with other codes (e.g., AA, AB, etc.). These codes are Q&A internal codes and must remain in place. Do not remove or change them.
12. Press **Esc**. The Q&A Main Menu is displayed.
13. Turn to Module 33 to continue the learning sequence.

Module 7
BLOCK SELECTION

DESCRIPTION

A *block of text* is a string of characters, words, paragraphs, or pages. You select and mark blocks of text when working with many of the features in the Write function. When a block of text is selected, it is identified from the rest of the text in a document. On a monochrome monitor, a selected block is highlighted in inverse video. On a color monitor, a selected block is displayed in a different color from the text around it. Once selected, the text can be moved, copied, deleted, or printed.

To select a block is a simple operation. For example, if you are selecting a block of text to copy it to another location in the same document, place the cursor at the first character of the block and press F5. This operation initiates the block selection operation. The message: "Use the arrow keys to select the text you want to copy then press F10." is displayed at the bottom of the screen. Move the cursor across characters, words, etc. to identify and highlight the block of text being selected. Stop the cursor at the last character of the chosen block of text and press F10 to complete the block selection.

The following is a brief overview of how to select blocks of text for typical functions:

To copy a block of text within a document: Press F5, select the block of text, and then press F10.

To copy a block of text to another document: Press Alt-F5, select the block of text, and then press F10.

To make another copy of the selected block of text within the same document: Press Shift-F7.

To move a block of text within a document: Press Shift-F5, select the block of text, move the cursor, and then press F10.

To move a block of text to another document: Press Alt-F5, select the block of text, and then press F10.

To delete a block of text: Press F3, select the block of text, and then press F10.

To print a block of text: Press Ctrl-F2 and press F10.

Each of these functions and more are described in other modules contained in this book.

Q&A has a feature in the Write function that is not found in most word processing software. This feature permits you to press function or control keys several times in succession to repeat an operation on consecutive blocks of text. For example, if you are selecting a block of text to copy within the same document, pressing F5 the first time initiates the copy function; pressing F5 a second time selects the word on which the cursor is positioned. Pressing F5 a third time selects the entire sentence in which the word is located. Pressing F5 a fourth time selects the entire paragraph. You can continue by pressing F5 until the entire document is selected.

The following table is a summary of ways in which you can block select text after initiating a block function (ex., F5 for copy).

Key	Action
Cursor control keys PgDn,PgUp	All text located between the first arrow keys, Home, End character selected (initial cursor location) and the subsequent location of the cursor is block selected.
Character keys (A,a - Z,z)	All text located between the first cursor location and the first occurrence of the character key pressed is block selected.
Spacebar	Next word is selected.
Return	Remainder of the paragraph is selected.

APPLICATIONS

Once you select a block of text, you identify and mark characters, words, paragraphs, or pages. Selection of a block of text is a prerequisite to performing other Write functions such as move, copy, delete, or print.

TYPICAL OPERATION

In this illustration, select a block of text for another Write function (copy, move, etc.). Begin at the Q&A Main Menu.

1. Open a new document and type the following text:

```
This exercise is a practice session using the block
selection feature of Q&A.  It is similar in many ways to
the techniques used by other word processing software.
Characters, words, paragraphs, etc. can be selected and
highlighted for moving, copying, deleting, or printing.

Working Copy                                0 %   Line 5 of Page 1 of 1
Esc-Exit  F1-Info  F2-Print  Ctrl+F6-Define Pg  F7-Search  F8-Options  ↑F8-Save
```

2. Press the **Up** and **Left Arrows** to move the cursor to the first character in the second sentence (It is similar . . .).
3. Press **F5**. The block selection is initiated. The character "I" is highlighted and the following mes sage appears at the bottom of your screen.

Use the arrow keys to select the text you want to copy, then press F10.

4. Press **Right Arrow** to move the cursor to the end of the sentence. Place the cursor on the period (.). Characters and words are highlighted as you move the cursor.

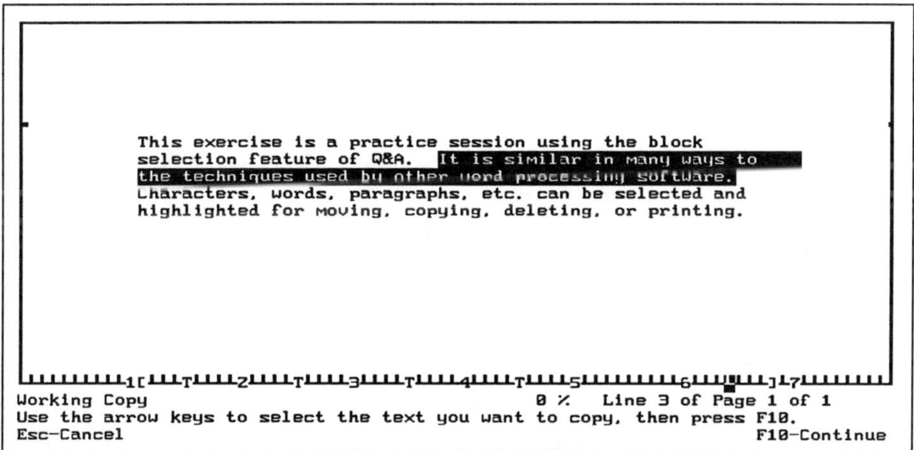

5. Press **F10**. The block selection operation is ended.

You have completed the block selection practice. At this point you can proceed with another function. You can move, copy, delete, or print the selected text.

Refer to the following modules to perform any of the functions identified.

Module 18 to copy a block of text within a document.

Module 17 to copy a block of text to another document.

Module 25 to delete a block of text.

Module 66 to print a block of text.

6. Press **Esc** to cancel the block selection. The highlight on the text and the message at the bottom of the screen disappears. Block selection can be canceled anytime by pressing Esc.
7. Press **Esc** to return to the Write Menu.
8. Press **Esc** to exit from the Write Menu. A prompt message is displayed warning you that the Working Copy of the document has not been saved. The cursor is located at N - No.
9. Type **Y** to return to the Q&A Main Menu without saving the document.
10. Turn to Module 17 to continue the learning sequence.

Module 8
CALCULATE IN A REPORT

DESCRIPTION

An additional option available when producing a report is the capability to perform calculations within the report. You can perform calculations on any report columns that contain numbers. The results of the calculations can also be included in the report.

Refer to Module 79 for instructions on how to design/redesign a report. Column calculation codes are designated on the Column/Sort Spec screen described in Module 79. Column calculation codes are indicated on the Column/Sort Spec screen immediately following sort codes. Refer to Module 86 for information about sort codes and corresponding definitions.

The following column calculations can be performed in a report.

Description	*Calculation Code*
Column total*	T
Average value of column *	A
A count of entries in column*	C
Column's minimum value*	MIN
Column's maximum value*	MAX
Column subtotal**	ST
Column subaverages**	SA
Column subcounts**	SC
Column subminimum values**	SMIN
Column submaximum values**	SMAX

* Printed at bottom of the column
** Printed at column breaks

When performing calculations using every value contained in a column, the result of the calculation is located at the bottom of the column. The calculation code used to produce a total at the bottom of the column is the T code.

Various subcalculations can be performed using only specific numbers in a column. The results produced by these calculations are positioned at column breaks when the value in a sorted column changes.

Subcalculations are canceled by entering the code CS to the Column/Sort Spec in appropriate fields. This cancellation prevents Q&A from displaying or printing subcalculations (e.g., subtotals and subcounts).

APPLICATIONS

Performing calculations in your reports enhances your ability to display information and makes your reports more useful. The calculation codes provide a wide range of capability. The way in which you enter calculation codes is relatively simple. Q&A automatically performs the operations as you have specified.

The simplest calculation is to perform column totals. More difficult are subcalculations at column breaks. Probably most complicated is canceling subcalculations.

TYPICAL OPERATION

In this illustration, enter calculation codes on the Column/Sort Spec screen. Review Module 79 and couple the information presented in this module with the tasks required to design a form. After completing the Column/Sort Spec screen in Module 86, you can easily incorporate calculation functions. Begin at the Q&A Main Menu.

1. Select the Report Menu.
2. Type **D** to select Design/Redesign a report. A prompt message is displayed requesting the name of the database to use in creating the report.
3. Type **CUSTOMER** and press **Return**. The CUSTOMER database was created in a previous module. A prompt message is displayed requesting the name that you want to give the report being created.
4. Type **SALES** and press **Return**. The Retrieve Spec screen for the specified database is displayed.

```
Company Name: _

Street or P.O. Box:

City & State:                                 Zip:

Tel. No.:

1st Contact Date:               2nd Contact Date:

Product Area:

Yearly Sales (K):             Credit Rating:




CUSTOMER.DTF                 Retrieve Spec for SALES                 Page 1  of 1

Esc-Cancel  F1-How to retrieve   F3-Clear Spec   F6-Expand field    F10-Continue
```

5. Press **F10**. The Column/Sort Spec screen for the specified database is displayed.

6. Press **Tab** to move the cursor to any field designated to appear in a report as a sorted column.

7. Press **End**. The cursor moves to the end of the field.

8. If you have previously entered a sort code, immediately following the sort code (i.e., AS or DS), type a comma (,), a space, and the calculation code. If you have not entered a sort code, just type a comma (,), a space, and the calculation code. Select a calculation code from the table previously listed at the beginning of this module.

In the "Yearly Sales" field, values contained on forms in this field are reflected in column 4 of the report. The values are sorted in descending order (as designated by the sort code DS) and column 4 in the report is totaled (as designated by the sort code T).

9. Repeat Steps 6 and 7 until you have entered all of the codes for calculations that you want performed in a report.

10. Press **F10** twice. A message is displayed indicating that the report design has been saved to disk. The message also gives you the opportunity to print or not print the report.

11. You can choose to exit and not print the report or to continue on the Print Options Menu and print the report. To exit, type **N**. The Report Menu is displayed. Press **Esc**. The Q&A Main Menu is displayed.

    To print the report refer to Module 72 for instructions on how to print a report. The Print Options Menu is displayed and you may proceed to print the report.

12. Turn to Module 26 to continue the learning sequence.

Module 9
CENTER/UNCENTER TEXT

DESCRIPTION

Centering a word or group of words on a line in a document is a feature that is used often when creating letters, contracts, and memorandums. Q&A has an automatic line-centering feature that centers a single character, word, or group of words within the set margins.

Centering text can also apply when designing a report or customizing a file. The procedures for centering text in these instances differ from centering text in a document.

Centering a line of text may be performed while creating a new document or editing an existing document in the Q&A Write function. The line may already exist or it may be one that you have just created.

An existing line is centered by positioning the cursor at any location on the line and pressing F8. The Options Menu is displayed. Simply type C (Center line). An existing line of text is automatically centered; a line being typed is centered as you type it.

Should you want to remove the line-centering feature from a line, just position the cursor at any location on the line and press F8. The Options Menu is displayed. Then, type U (Uncenter line). The line moves to the left margin.

APPLICATIONS

Centering a line is used most often to position document headings or table headings on a text page. The alternative to Q&A's automatic line-centering feature is to center text manually. This less productive method requires counting characters, moving the cursor, backspacing, etc. Overall, manual centering is extremely time consuming and often unreliable.

There are occasions when you want the text in a document to appear ragged on the right and left. Centering individual lines allows you to easily accomplish this effect as in the following illustration.

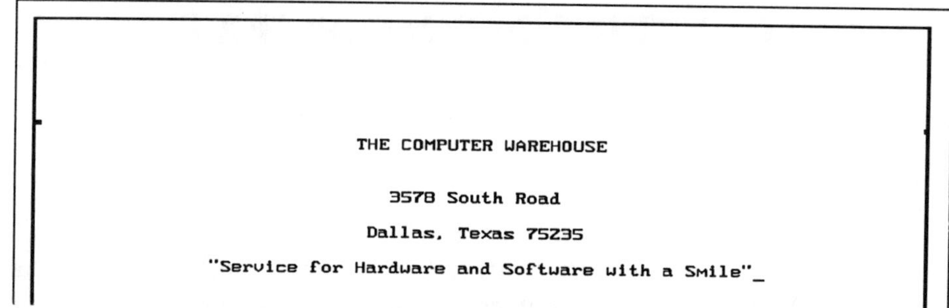

Later, if you want to change either the document margins or the number of characters on any centered line, Q&A always keep the lines centered.

TYPICAL OPERATION

In this example, type and center a line using the automatic line-centering feature. Next, type and center a second line. Begin at the Q&A Main Menu.

1. Type **W** to select the Write Menu. The cursor is located at T - Type/Edit.
2. Press **Return** to open a new document.
3. Type the following text and leave the cursor at the end of the line as follows:

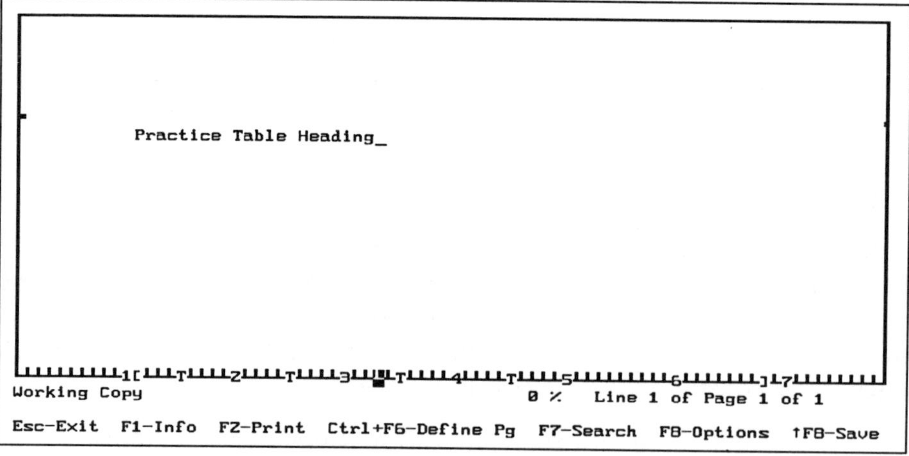

4. Press **F8**. The Options Menu is displayed in a window over the text.

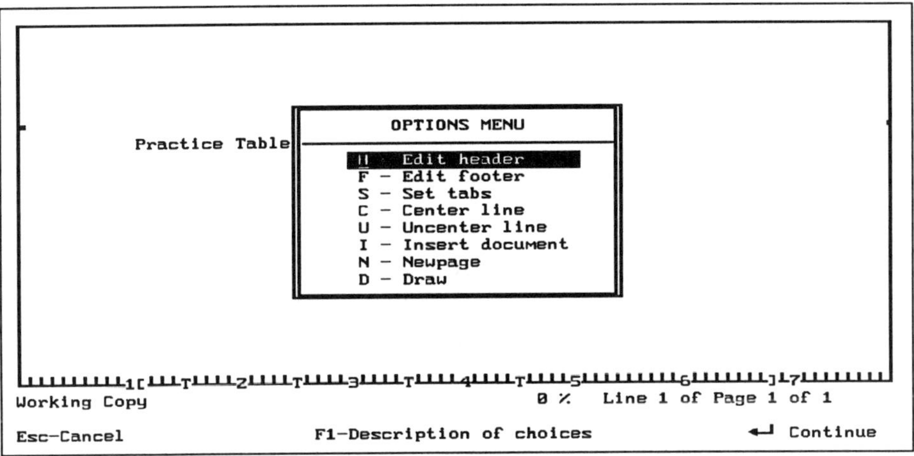

5. Type **C** to center the line. The cursor is located at the end of the centered line.

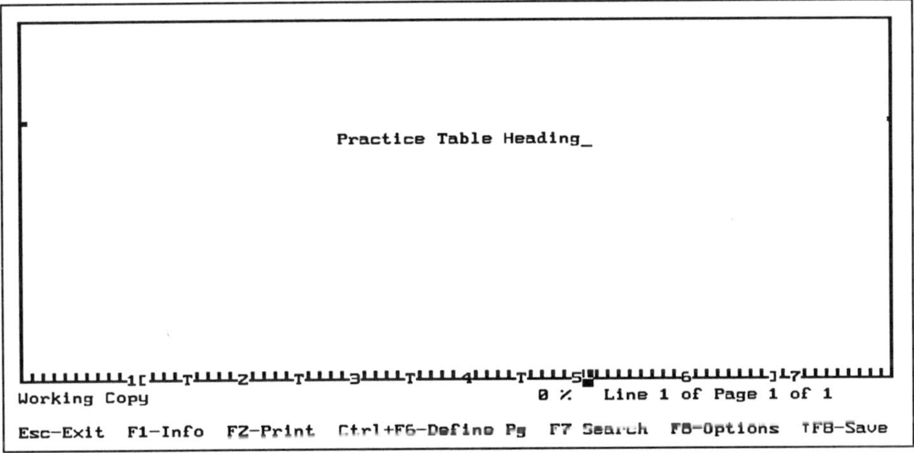

6. Press **F8** to uncenter that same line. Make sure that the cursor is located at any place on the line. The Options Menu is displayed.
7. Type **U**. The centering is undone. The typed line moves back to the left margin and the cursor returns to its initial position on the line.
8. Press **Esc** twice to exit from the Write Menu. A prompt message is displayed warning you that the Working Copy has not been saved. The cursor is located at N - No.
9. Type **Y** to return to the Q&A Main Menu without saving the document.
10. Turn to Module 63 to continue the learning sequence.

Module 10
CHANGE THE SCREEN PALETTE

DESCRIPTION

Various combinations of screen foreground and background colors displayed can be selected while working on forms in the Q&A File function. You can choose and set the different screen color combinations (called *palettes*) and designate them for different databases.

The Change Palette function is accessed starting at the Q&A Main Menu by selecting the File function. When the File Menu is displayed, selecting D displays the Design Menu. Choosing C displays a prompt requesting a filename.

After entering a valid filename, the Customize Menu is displayed.

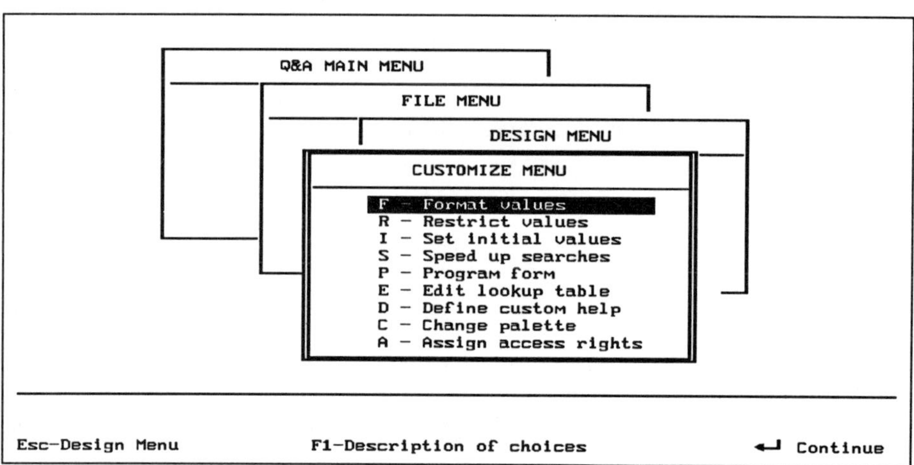

Choosing C, displays the first form in the specified database.

You can browse through the available colors by pressing F8 to move forward through the colors or by pressing F6 to move back through the colors. There are seven color combinations available.

Pressing F10 selects the palette that you want to remain in effect for the specified file. The selected colors remain set for a specified database until you change them. While setting the Change Palette feature, you can retrieve existing forms that you have designed and change the palette to test what is most suitable for your needs.

Pressing Esc returns you to the File Menu.

APPLICATIONS

Highlighting fields on forms in color is useful for helping you to identify where data is to be entered or in determining where data is located. For example, you can highlight all fields in which you are entering data. These are the variable fields, that is, fields of different lengths in which unlike data is entered.

On the other hand, you can also highlight the names for fields on a form. The field names are the standard or constant items which you have designated for certain areas on the form. For example, field names on a form such as Customer name, address, phone number, etc. can be highlighted in a color.

TYPICAL OPERATION

In this example, select a file for which you want to change the palette, access the Customize Menu, and change the color combination on the displayed form. Begin at the Q&A Main Menu.

1. At the Q&A Main Menu, the cursor is located at F - File. Press **Return**. The File Menu is displayed.
2. Type **D**. The Design Menu is displayed.
3. Type **C**. A prompt message is displayed requesting the name of the file that you want to customize.
4. Type a filename (ex., CUSTOMER, EMPLOYEE, etc.) and press **Return**. The Customize Menu is displayed. The File is displayed on the screen with the field names highlighted and the background in a solid color.
5. Type **C**. Press **F6** to move backward, or press **F8** to move forward through the available colors. Step through the various colors to view the seven palettes. An example is:

NOTE

You can type information in the field blanks to see which colors suit you best. When you are finished viewing the choices, Pressing F10 saves the palette colors, but does not save the samples that you typed.

```
Company Name:
Street or P.O. Box:
City & State:                              Zip:
Tel No.:

1st Contact Date:              2nd Contact Date:
Product Area:
Yearly Sales (K):               Credit Rating:

CUSTOMER.DTF                Palette 6  of 7             Page 1  of 1
Esc-Cancel     F6-Previous palette     F8-Next palette     F10-Continue
```

6. Press **F10** when you find the color selection that you like best. The color selection is set and the Customizing Menu is displayed. Each time you access this database, the color selection displays until you change it using this same procedure.
7. Return to the Main Menu.
8. Turn to Module 30 to continue the learning sequence.

Module 11
CLEAR A DOCUMENT

DESCRIPTION

If you start creating a document and then decide to quit for any reason, you may abandon your work without saving the document. This process is called *clearing* the document. If the document was previously saved on disk from a previous edit session, the saved version remains unaffected on the disk.

At any point while creating or editing a document you may decide to clear the document. Pressing Esc displays the Write Menu. Selecting the Clear function by pressing C causes Q&A to question whether you positively want to discard the document and/or any editing changes that you have made.

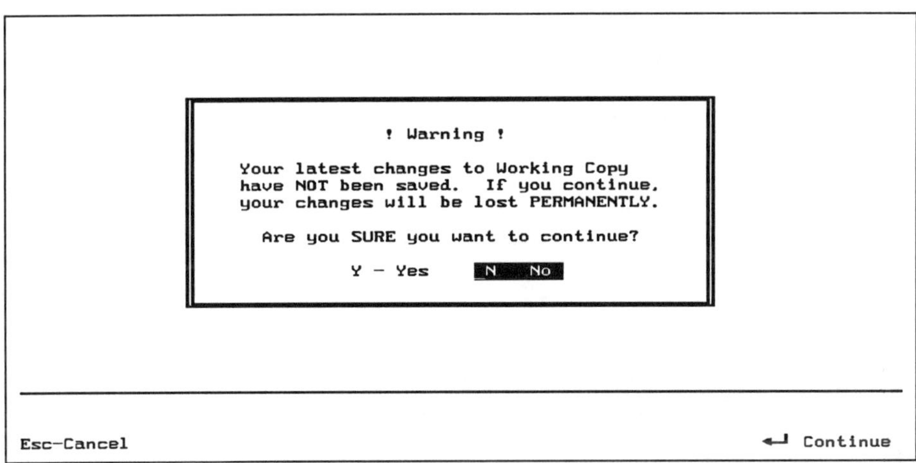

You may return to the Write Menu and save the document by pressing Return, or you can proceed to clear the document by typing Y. If you clear the document, any text created or changes that you made are lost forever and are unretrievable. A blank screen (a new Working Copy) for a new document is displayed after clearing a document.

APPLICATIONS

Clearing a document is often useful for a number of reasons. At times you may only want to review a document that is currently saved on disk. After review, you can easily clear it from the screen. Then, you are ready to begin a new document without having to return to the Main Menu or to the Write Menu.

In an editing session with an existing document, you may accidentally delete text that you intended to keep in the document. By the same token, you may add text or make extensive changes which are really not wanted. By clearing the current document and reopening the original version previously saved on the disk, you can conveniently start over again.

If you open a document other than the one you intended to open, clearing the displayed document is an easy way to begin again.

TYPICAL OPERATION

In this illustration, begin with the Q&A Main Menu. Enter the Write function and begin an edit session in a Working Copy of a new document. Clear the document by exiting from the edit session to the Write Menu. At the Write Menu, select the Clear function. After the document is cleared, exit from the Write function and return to the Q&A Main Menu.

1. At the Q&A Main Menu, type **W**. The cursor is located at T - Type/Edit.
2. Press **Return**. A Working Copy (blank screen) is displayed for a new document.
3. Type the following text:

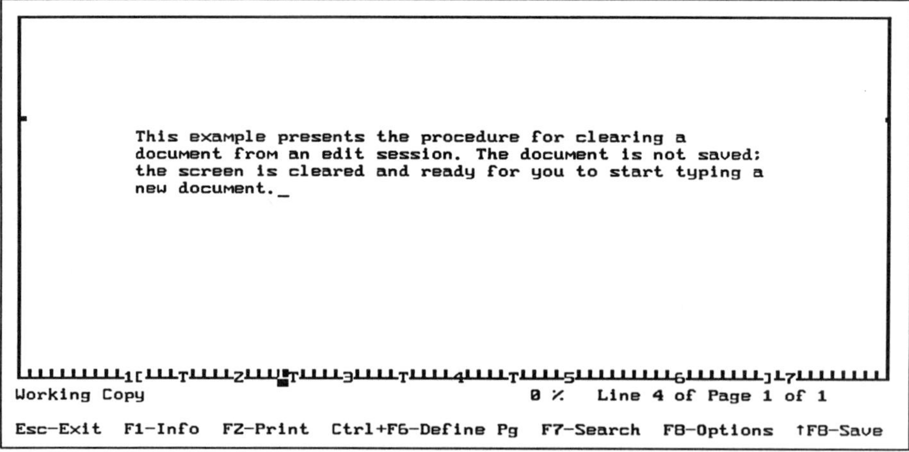

4. Press **Esc** to clear the document. The Write Menu is displayed.

5. Type **C** to execute the Clear function. A prompt message is displayed warning you that the Working Copy of the document has not been saved. The cursor is located at N - No.
6. Type **Y** to proceed with clearing the document. The cursor moves to Y - Yes in the prompt message and the document is cleared. A blank screen (new Working Copy of a document) is displayed.
7. Press **Esc** to return to the Write Menu.
8. Press **Esc** again to return to the Main Menu.
9. Turn to Module 89 to continue the learning sequence.

Module 12
CLEAR A MACRO

DESCRIPTION

Clearing a macro is the process of erasing a previously defined macro from the computer's memory. Therefore, any macro that you want to clear must reside in the computer's memory when the clear operation is performed. If the macro that you want to clear is saved on disk, it must first be retrieved from the disk. Retrieving the macro from disk places it into the computer's memory.

Another procedure can also be used to erase a previously defined macro. The process is called *undefining a macro.* It involves redefining a macro by not specifying any keystrokes for the macro. In other words, the macro is redefined as blank (or no keystrokes).

If a macro has been saved to disk, clearing the macro from the computer's memory during an edit session does not delete or erase the macro from its storage place on the disk.

CLEAR A MACRO While in any Q&A function (for example, the Write function) you can clear any macro resident in the computer's memory. If the macro is saved on disk and has not been used in the current session with Q&A, you can retrieve the macro from disk by using the Get Macro function. Refer to Module 81 for instructions on how to retrieve a macro from disk.

CAUTION

Pressing Shift-F2 simultaneously displays the Macro Menu Box. Selecting C clears *all* macros currently resident in the computer's memory. There is no warning message issued that all of the macros are cleared as soon as you type C.

NOTE

For key sequences connected by a hyphen (such as Shift-F2, you hold the first key while you type a second key.

After clearing a macro, the identifier consisting of a single key or two-key combination can be used to identify another macro.

UNDEFINING A MACRO This process is an alternate way to erase a macro resident in the computer's memory. Follow the same procedures as described in Module 24 for defining/redefining a macro. The only exception is that you redefine the macro to "no keystrokes." As soon as the small flashing square is displayed awaiting the keystrokes comprising the macro, simply press Shift-F2. The macro is cleared just as if you had used the Clear selection on the Macro Menu Box.

Also, as with the Clear selection, the macro identifier now can be used to distinguish another macro.

APPLICATIONS

The applications for clearing a macro are quite obvious. Once in a while it's necessary to just "clean house." You may want to erase all of those infrequently used macros stored to disk. You may need to free a macro identifier so you can create a new macro that is important to your work. Either of the procedures described are excellent ways to clear a macro.

TYPICAL OPERATION

In this example, enter the Write function and display a Working Copy (blank screen) for a new document. Create a macro identified by Ctrl-P, use the macro, and then clear it from the computer memory. Begin at the Q&A Main Menu.

1. Type **W**. The Write Menu is displayed. The cursor is located at T - Type/Edit.

2. Press **Return**. A Working Copy (blank) screen for a new document is displayed.

3. Press **Shift-F2**. The Macro Menu is displayed. The cursor is located at D - Define Macro.

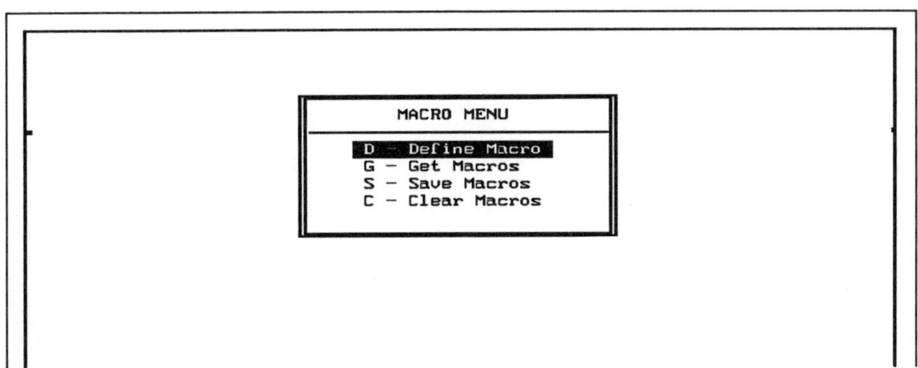

4. Press **Return**. A prompt message is displayed at the bottom of the screen requesting the macro identifier.
5. Press **Ctrl-P**. A small flashing square is displayed at the bottom right of the screen, informing you that the macro key sequence can be entered.
6. Type **CUSTOMER NAME:** and press **Return**.
7. Press **Shift-F2**. A prompt message is displayed requesting the name of the file to which the macro is to be saved. The macro is not saved for this exercise.
8. Press **Esc**. The macro remains in the computer's memory.
9. Move the cursor to an open area on the screen and press **Ctrl-P**. The macro keystrokes "CUSTOMER NAME:" are repeated and displayed on the screen.
10. Press **Shift-F2**. The Macro Menu is displayed.
11. Type **C**. The macro is cleared from the computer's memory. To test this, press **Ctrl-P**. Notice that the macro no longer exists; no keystrokes are automatically typed.
12. Press **Esc** to return to the Write Menu.
13. Press **Esc** to exit from the Write Menu. A prompt message is displayed warning you that the Working Copy has not been saved. The cursor is located at N - No.
14. Type **Y** to return to the Q&A Main Menu without saving the document.
15. Turn to Module 83 to continue the learning sequence.

Module 13
COLUMN HEADINGS/WIDTH FOR A REPORT

DESCRIPTION

This module describes how to customize column headings and widths in a report. Q&A automatically uses the field labels in your databases as column headings. These field labels are centered above each column in the report and each column is evenly spaced across the screen or printed page. In addition, Q&A precisely formats each column to hold the information contained in the fields.

Fortunately, Q&A is extremely flexible. You can set column headings and/or widths to your own choosing for all reports for all databases.

Beginning at the Q&A Main Menu and selecting the Report function displays the Report Menu. Selecting S on the Report Menu initiates a prompt message requesting the name for the database in which you want to change column headings and/or widths. After typing the valid name for a database, the Column Headings/Width Spec screen for the specified database is displayed. You then have a choice of three options for each field on the form: (1) to enter a new column width expressed in numbers, (2) to enter a new column heading, or (3) to enter a new column width and new column heading. After changing column headings and/or widths, pressing F10 returns you to the Report Menu. Pressing Esc displays the Q&A Main Menu.

If you need to use a multi-line heading, you can use a heading containing up to three lines. To use a multi-line heading, type an exclamation mark (!) to indicate where the heading is to be broken to the next line.

If you are entering a new column heading in a field that is too small to hold the information, move the cursor to the field and press F6. An editing line is displayed at the bottom of the screen which allows you to enter the entire heading. Once you type the heading, press Return and an arrow displays where the extra character(s) would display.

If the column widths for a report having numeric columns are not wide enough for the number entries, asterisks are displayed where the number should appear. If this happens, you can change the column width for any of those columns.

You can also use a number as a column heading in a report by entering a colon and a number in any field on a form in the Column Headings/Width Spec Screen. An example is: :25; this produces a column heading (or title) of the literal "25."

Remember, if you change column headings or widths, the change is effective for all reports related to the specified database. Even the reports generated by the Assistant are affected by the changes you make by following the instructions in this module.

APPLICATIONS

Again, you hold absolute control over anything that Q&A does. You control the exact format of any report created by Q&A. This versatility is unprecedented. The capability to format reports to meet your needs is a powerful tool. Being able to customize column headings and column widths allows you the utmost control over report formats.

TYPICAL OPERATION

In this illustration, enter the Report function and select the option to set new headings. After setting a new heading for the first column on a report, return to the Q&A Main Menu.

1. At the Q&A Main Menu, the cursor is located at F - File. Type **R**. The Report Menu is displayed.
2. Type **S**. A prompt message is displayed requesting the name of the file for which the global options are to be set.
3. Type **CUSTOMER** and press **Return**. The Global Options Menu is displayed. The cursor is located at C - Set column.

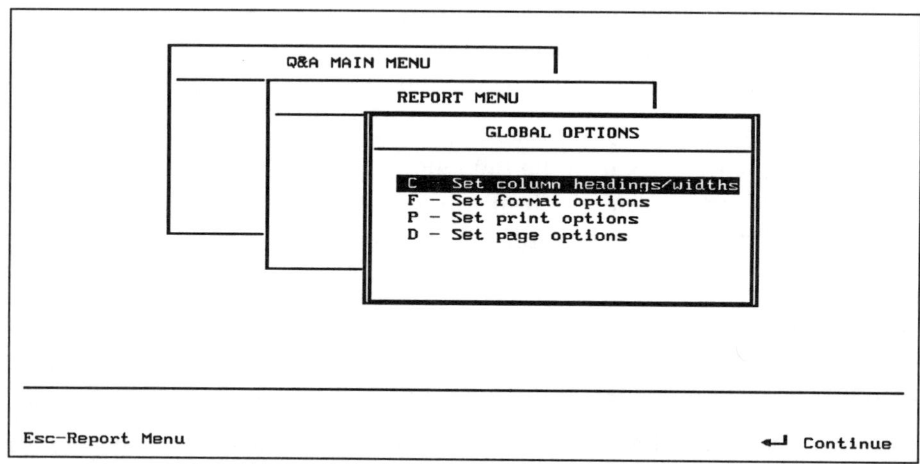

4. Press **Return**. The Column Headings/Width Spec screen for the specified file is displayed.

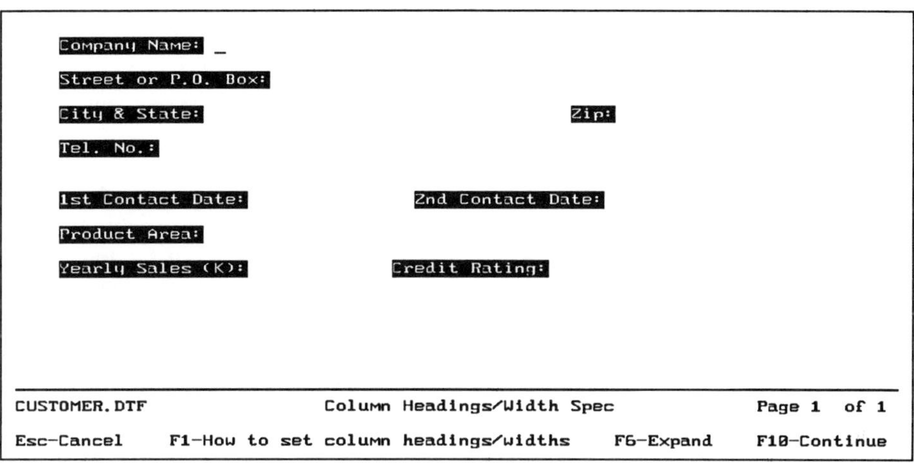

5. Press **Tab** to move the cursor to any field on the screen and choose any one of the following three options:

   a. Type the new width for the column. A maximum of 80 is allowable.

   b. Type the new heading.

   c. Change the column width and heading. Type the new width for the column followed by a colon (:) and the new heading.

6. Repeat Step 5 for other fields on the form for which you want a column heading different than the actual field name indicated on the form. For example, the following form indicates that the first field is to hold a 25-character customer name.

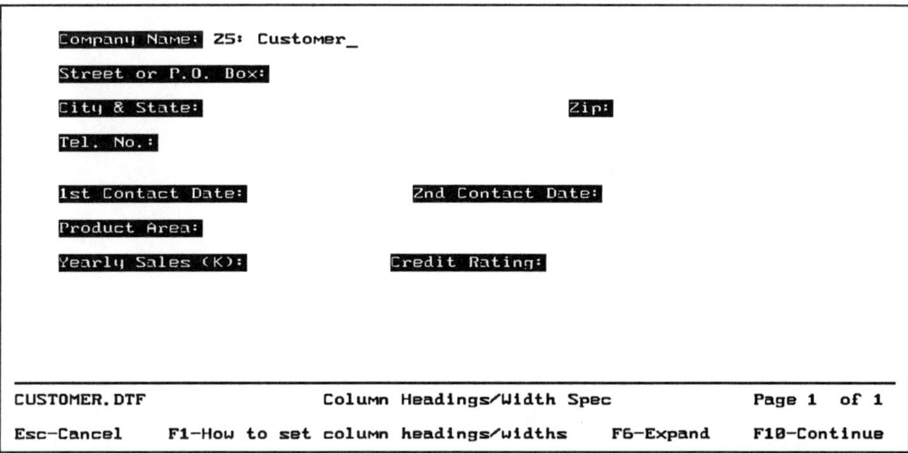

NOTE

If you want to change the name of a field, but the space provided on the form is too small, press F6 and a special edit line is displayed at the bottom of the screen where you can type the over-sized column name.

7. Press **F10**. The Global Options Menu is displayed.
8. Return to the Main Menu.
9. Turn to Module 8 to continue the learning sequence.

Module 14
COPY AN ENTIRE DATABASE TO ANOTHER DATABASE

DESCRIPTION

Copying an entire database to another database is a simple process. There are two procedures performed when copying a database. First, the design of the original database must be copied. Then, the data contained in all or selected forms in the database is copied into the copied design.

If you are interested in only copying selected forms in the database, refer to Module 16.

Copying a database design is a file operation. From the Q&A Main Menu, access the File Menu. Selecting C (Copy) causes a prompt message requesting you to enter the name of the database design that you want to copy. As with many other functions that require the name of a document or file, if you do not know the exact filename, you can just leave a blank in response to the filename prompt and press Return to access a list of files. The names of all databases stored to disk are listed on the screen when you press Return.

After entering the name of the database and pressing Return, the Copy Menu is displayed. Typing D initiates copying only the database design (i.e., form design). A prompt message is displayed requesting the name that you want to assign to the new database. Enter the filename and press Return. When the design of the database is copied, the Copy Menu is displayed.

Copying a database and all of its forms compresses the receiving database file. It takes far less disk space to copy the data rather than making a backup of the database. This procedure is an alternative to making a backup copy. Backup is a selection on the File Menu.

APPLICATIONS

The capability to copy only the design of a database can certainly speed up the process of creating a new database design. This is especially true when many of the fields in the existing database design are similar to what you want in a new database.

TYPICAL OPERATION

In this illustration, copy an entire database to another one. At the Copy Menu, copy all of the forms in an existing database to another existing database. Begin at the Q&A Main Menu.

1. The cursor is located at F - File. Press **Return** to enter the File function. The File Menu is displayed.
2. Type **C** to initiate copying the design of the database. A prompt message is displayed requesting you to enter the name of the source database to be copied.
3. Type **INVNTRY** and press **Return**. The Copy Menu is displayed.

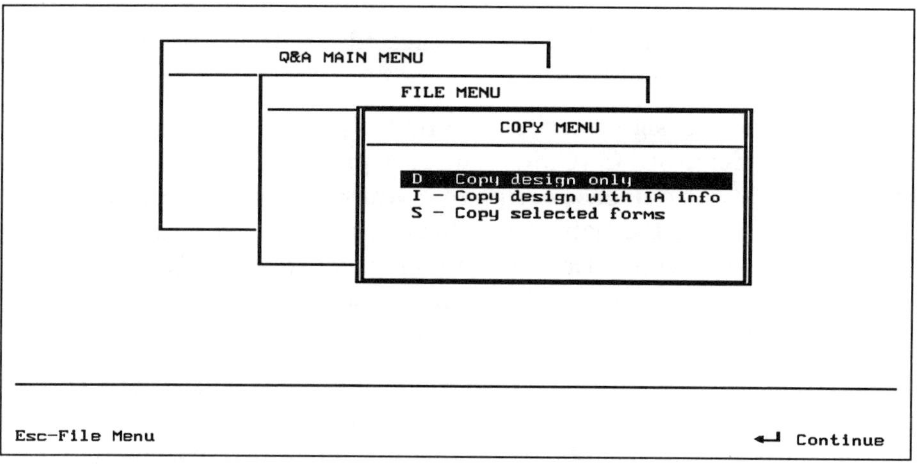

4. Type **D**, then type **STOCK** and press **Return**. The operation to copy the form design takes several minutes. Then, the Copy Menu is displayed.
5. Type **S**, a prompt message is displayed requesting the name of the file that contains the information to be copied.
6. Type **INVNTRY** and press **Return**. The Retrieve Spec screen for the database is displayed.
7. Press **F10**. The Merge Spec screen for the database is displayed.
8. Press **F10**. The entire source database (named INVNTRY) is copied to another database (named STOCK). The File Menu is displayed.
9. Turn to Module 16 to continue the learning sequence.

Module 15
COPY A FORM DESIGN

DESCRIPTION

Any existing form design can be copied to enable you to create a new database with an existing form layout. When copying the form design from a database, the copied result is a new but empty database.

Copying form design is started from the Q&A Main Menu. Accessing the File function by entering F and pressing Return displays the File Menu. Selecting C on the File Menu initiates a prompt message requesting the name of the database to be copied. Entering the filename and pressing Return displays the Copy Menu. Selecting D on the Copy Menu initiates a prompt message requesting the name of the new database. After entering the filename and pressing Return, the copy operation is initiated. A message is displayed informing you that the copy operation is in progress.

At either prompt message, if you need to see the names of existing files saved to disk, use the Spacebar or Del key to delete the filename displayed. Press Return to display a list of all files saved to disk.

A form design can also be copied by using information from the Assistant. This option is displayed on the Copy Menu.

Selected forms or an entire database (including form design and all forms) can be copied. Refer to Module 16 for instructions on how to copy selected forms from one database to another. Refer to Module 14 for instructions on how to copy an entire database to another database.

APPLICATIONS

This form design copy feature enables you to copy a complete form design, that is, field labels, information types, form layout, etc. Form information in the database is not copied. This capability is particularly useful if you want to create similar database designs.

Once a form design is copied, it can easily be redesigned to fit a new requirement you may have. Refer to Module 40 for complete information on redesigning a form; this is the module you will want to use after copying a form design.

TYPICAL OPERATION

In this illustration, initiate the copy function, specify the name of the database to be copied, enter the name of the new database, and press Return to complete the copy operation. Begin at the Q&A Main Menu.

1. The cursor is located at F - File. Press **Return** to enter the File function. The File Menu is displayed.
2. Type **C**. A prompt message is displayed requesting the name of the file to be copied. To see names of existing files saved to disk, delete the filename displayed at the prompt message using the Spacebar or Del keys. The following screen is displayed.

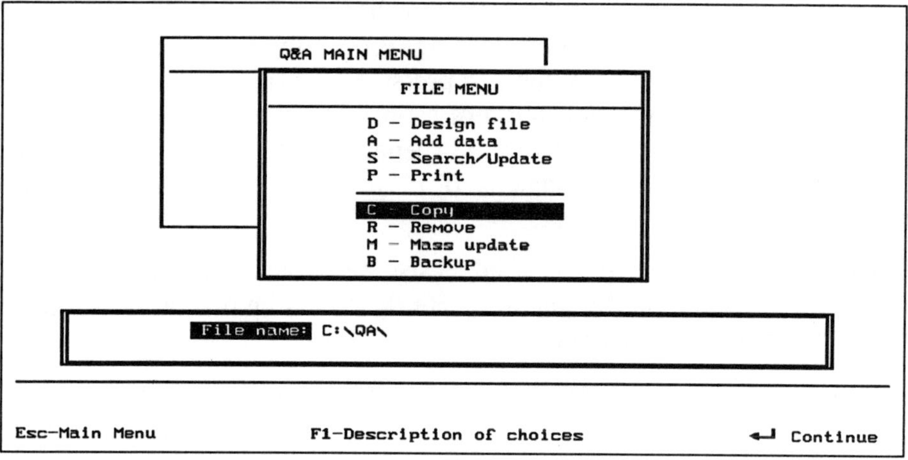

3. Type **CUSTOMER** and press **Return**. The Copy Menu is displayed.

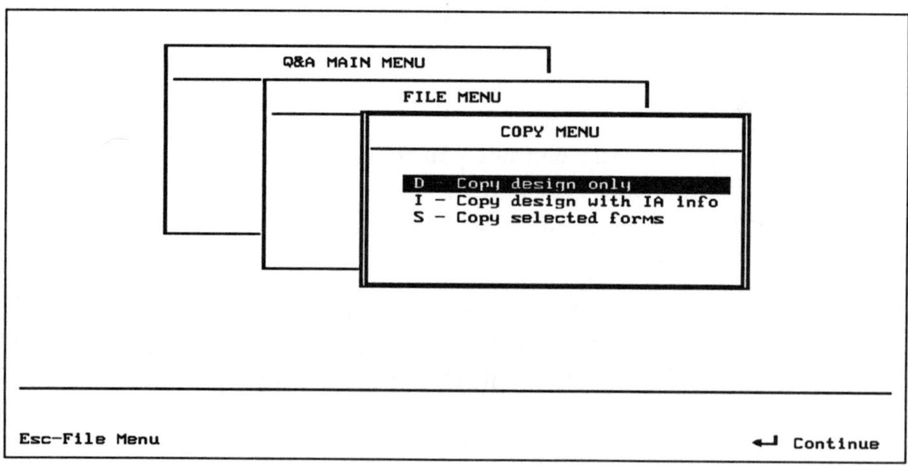

4. Type **D**; a prompt message is displayed requesting the name of the new database.

5. Type **PROSPECT** and press **Return**.

NOTE

If you attempt to copy a form design to an existing filename, a warning message is displayed. You have the choice of (Y) to write over the existing file or (N) to return to the filename prompt where you can type a different name.

A message is displayed informing you that the form design is being copied. For large databases, copying takes several minutes. The form design is copied to the specified database. The Copy Menu is displayed.

6. Return to the Main Menu.

7. Turn to Module 40 to continue the learning sequence.

Module 16

COPY FORMS FROM ONE DATABASE TO ANOTHER DATABASE

DESCRIPTION

Q&A allows you to copy selected forms that were created in one database to another database within Q&A. Using this feature you can create new databases containing forms from existing databases. You have the options to copy all information contained on specified forms, copy only specified information from all of the forms, or copy specified information from selected forms.

Copying a single form or many forms is not difficult. From the Q&A Main Menu, access the File Menu. Select C (Copy). A prompt message requests you to enter the name of the database which contains the forms to be copied.

After entering the name of the database and pressing Return, the Copy Menu is displayed.

Typing S (Copy selected forms) initiates the copying of selected forms. Enter the filename and press Return. The Retrieve Spec screen is displayed. The *retrieve specifications* designate which forms in the database you want to copy. For example, you can specify that forms containing customers having the last name of Brown be selected. Likewise, you can specify forms containing a certain Zip code be selected. After entering the retrieve specifications and pressing F10, the Merge Spec screen is displayed.

The *merge specifications* permit you to sort forms in a specified order. This sort feature is strictly optional and can be bypassed when copying forms. After entering merge specifications and pressing F10, the specified forms are copied to the designated database.

Several restrictions apply when copying a file from one database to another. These include:

1. The destination database must be an existing database.
2. The labels and information types in the destination database must match those in the original database.
3. Fields being copied to the destination database must exist in the destination database.

The DOS COPY command can also be used to copy an entire database to another database. When this method is used, you do not have the alternative of selecting which forms that you want copied. The entire database is copied. To copy an entire database using the DOS COPY command, use the following command form at the DOS prompt:

```
A>COPY a:database1.* b:database2.*
```

In this message:

a is the disk drive containing the original database. If a hard disk drive is being used, this letter is c or d. In this case, the complete path should be specified.

database1 is the source or original database.

b is the destination disk drive. If you are using more than two floppy disk drives or a hard disk drive, this letter can be: c, d, e, etc.

database 2 is the name of the new (or copy) database.

CAUTION

Be sure that labels and information types in the destination database are compatible with the database being copied.

APPLICATIONS

The ability to copy forms from one database to another allows you to transfer all forms to another database. You can also use this feature to perform assembly operations. That is, you can copy forms from various databases to a single database where you are appending the forms in the file as you copy them. This feature can be used even if the forms that you are copying do not meet the current needs. You can copy the forms to another database and then modify them as required. All of this eliminates the need to recreate the forms just to get them into another database.

This feature can also be used to copy an entire database to produce a backup copy of your data. Having a backup copy of an extensive database is imperative.

TYPICAL OPERATION

In this illustration, initiate the copying of selected forms. Designate that all forms in the database are to be copied in the order of appearance in the existing database. Begin at the Q&A Main Menu.

1. The cursor is located at F - File. Press **Return** to enter the File function. The File Menu is displayed.
2. Type **C** to begin the copy operation. A prompt message is displayed requesting the name of the file to be copied. To see the names of existing files saved to disk, delete the displayed filename at the prompt message using the Spacebar or Del key. A screen is displayed showing the files saved to disk.
3. Type **CUSTOMER** and press **Return**. The Copy Menu is displayed.
4. Type **S**. A prompt message is displayed requesting the name of an existing destination database.
5. Type **CUSTOMER** and press **Return**. The Retrieve Spec screen for the forms being copied is displayed.

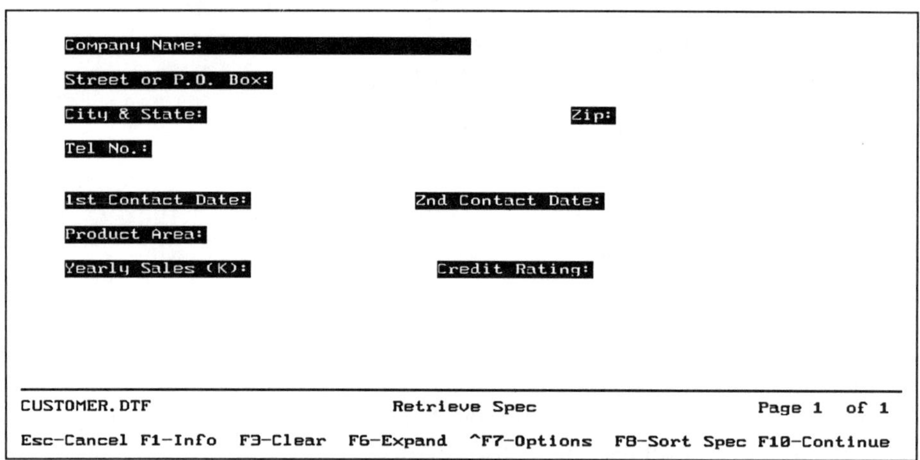

Company Name:
Street or P.O. Box:
City & State: Zip:
Tel No.:
1st Contact Date: 2nd Contact Date:
Product Area:
Yearly Sales (K): Credit Rating:

CUSTOMER.DTF Retrieve Spec Page 1 of 1
Esc-Cancel F1-Info F3-Clear F6-Expand ^F7-Options F8-Sort Spec F10-Continue

NOTE

The Retrieve Spec screen displays the same information as the form design for the database, except the screen name, "Retrieve Spec" is displayed at the bottom of the screen.

6. Press **F10**. The Merge Spec screen is displayed.

NOTE

The Merge Spec screen displays the same information as the form design for the database, except the screen name, "Merge Spec" is displayed at the bottom of the screen.

In this example, you are copying an existing database and overwriting onto the same filename. You can create another database having the same fields as the CUSTOMER database if you want. Refer to Module 37 for instructions on how to create a new form design.

At the Retrieve Spec screen, you can type retrieve specifications. Only those forms having the specified information will be retrieved for the copy operation. If no retrieve specifications are indicated, all forms in the database are copied.

On the Merge Spec screen, you can select individual fields in the database to be copied to the new database. Fields to be copied are selected by typing numbers in field locations to correspond to the fields in the destination database. The destination database must contain the fields selected to be copied. It is also important to ensure that the same number of character positions and information type codes exist in the destination database.

If no Merge Spec information is specified, the field data from the source database is copied to corresponding fields in the destination database.

7. Press **F10**. If no forms are found that meet the retrieve specifications, Q&A informs you with a message. A prompt message allows you to continue by typing "Y"; or, you can type "N" and attempt to repeat the copy operation.

When the copy operation is completed, the File Menu is displayed.

8. Turn to Module 57 to continue the learning sequence.

Module 17
COPY TEXT TO ANOTHER DOCUMENT

DESCRIPTION

In Module 7, you learned how to select a block of text so another Write function could be performed with that text. Copying text to another document is a function that can be performed by using a selected block of text. Once a block of text is selected, you can easily copy the text to a new document or any other document stored on disk.

The copy operation must occur while you are in an edit session with the document containing text to be copied. The cursor is placed at either the beginning or at the end of the block of text to be copied. Pressing Ctrl-F5 initiates the copy process. Moving the cursor to highlight the text being copied and pressing F10 selects the text for copying.

After you have selected the block of text, pressing F10 activates Q&A to prompt you for the name of the file where you want the text copied.

Be sure to designate the directory path correctly (ex., C: \ QA \ DOC). Entering the name of the file and pressing Return completes the copy operation. The cursor is displayed in the original document at its original location.

If you cannot remember the names of the documents stored on disk, press Return at the prompt to display a list of those stored.

NOTE

A copy cannot be made to another document having the same name as the current document. If you attempt to copy from one document to another, each having the same name, a warning message is displayed.

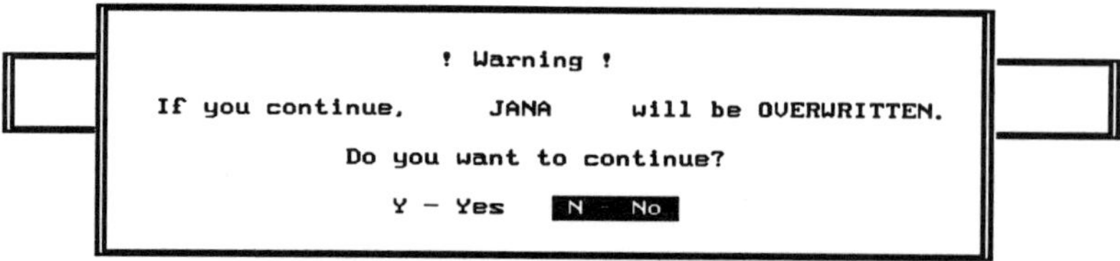

An entire document currently stored on disk can be copied (or imported) into a new or existing document during an edit session.

Refer to Module 50 for instructions on how to copy an entire existing document into a new or existing document.

APPLICATIONS

To eliminate the need to retype text that already exists, copy text from one document to another. You may generate text that is frequently used in other documents. This is particularly true in legal documents such as contracts, affidavits, leases, and powers of attorney. Many documents used in today's modern offices fall within the same category. There will be many occasions when you can "lift" text contained in other documents to create a new version of a document.

TYPICAL OPERATION

In this example, copy a block of text from one document to another document. Exit from the edit session without saving the document to disk. Begin at the Q&A Main Menu.

1. Type the following text:

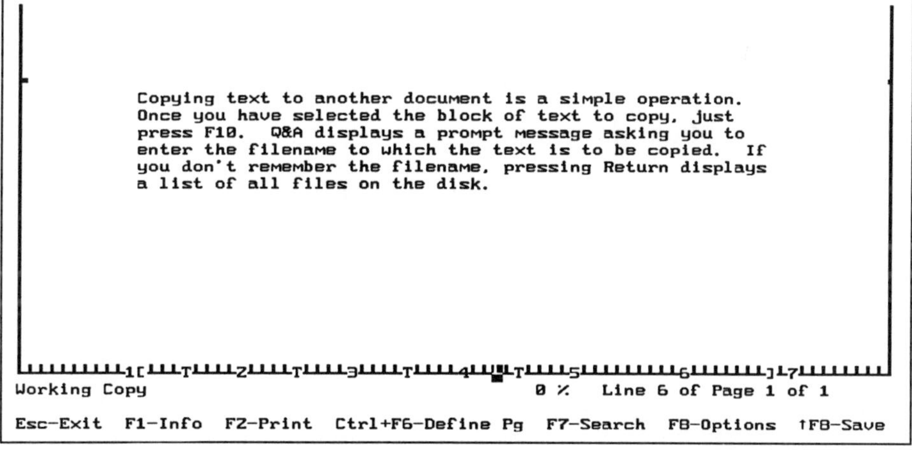

2. Press the arrow keys to position the cursor on the first character at the beginning of the text. In this case, the first letter is C in the word "Copying." You may also locate the cursor on the last character of the block of text to be copied.
3. Press **Ctrl-F5**.

4. Press **Right Arrow** to move the cursor to the last character in the first sentence.
5. Press **F10**. A prompt message is displayed requesting the name of the document to which you want the text copied.

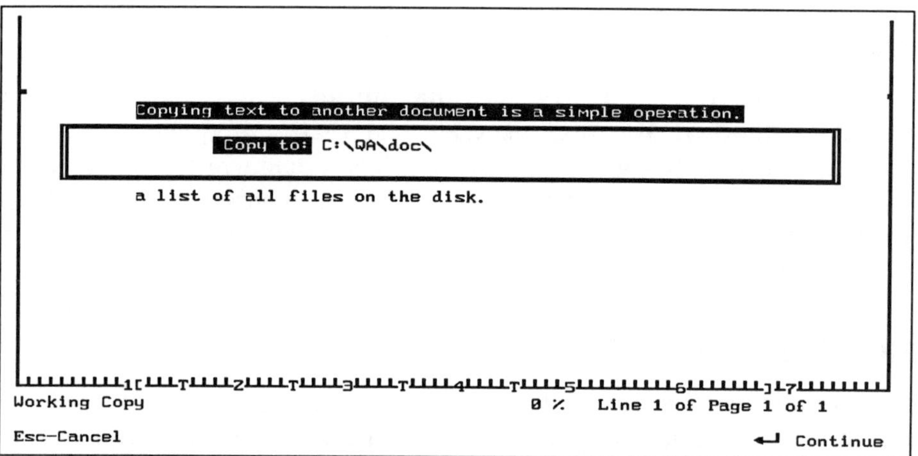

6. Type the name of the receiving document. If you cannot remember the name of a particular document, press Return and a list of the names of all files on the disk is displayed.
7. Press **Return**. The copy operation is completed and the cursor is located in the original document at the last displayed location.
8. Return to the Main Menu without saving.
9. Turn to Module 18 to continue the learning sequence.

Module 18
COPY TEXT WITHIN A DOCUMENT

DESCRIPTION

Copying text is accomplished by selecting (highlighting) the text being copied and pressing F10. Choosing the text to be copied is done by locating the cursor at the beginning of the text, pressing F5, and moving the cursor through the text. As you move the cursor through the text, it is highlighted. Pressing F10 defines the block of text. The cursor is then moved to the location where you want the text copied. The operation is completed by pressing F10.

The marked text is duplicated following the cursor position. Text following the copied text moves down the screen. It is not replaced by the copied text. The selected block of text remains at its original location in the document.

To make multiple duplicates of blocks of text, the Shift-F7 keys can be pressed. The block of text remains defined as long as you are editing or creating the current document or until you define another block of text for copying, deleting, or moving.

This means that during the creation of a document you may at any time repeat the copy operation exactly as last defined by the block selection by pressing Shift-F7.

APPLICATIONS

Copying blocks of text to other locations within a document lets you transfer text that is repetitive information to one or more other locations within the same document.

This useful copy feature eliminates the need of retyping text that already exists. This application is especially helpful when you are creating tabular information for a form that you are creating. Anytime your basic text is repetitive in content or layout, it is to your advantage to use the copy feature.

TYPICAL OPERATION

In this example, type a paragraph of text, then copy the first sentence of the paragraph to any location on the screen. Begin at the Q&A Main Menu.

1. Open a new document and type the following text:

```
This text is written to provide information that can be
used to copy or duplicate several times within a single
document.  The copy operation which involves copying text
from one location to another within a single document is
extremely simple and useful.  Try your luck at doing this.
```

2. Use the arrow keys to move the cursor to the first character of the paragraph.
3. Press **F5**. The first character in the sentence is highlighted. A message is displayed at the bottom of the screen indicating for you to use the arrow keys to move through the text to select it for copying.
4. Press **Right Arrow** to move the cursor through the first sentence and thus highlight it. The highlighting indicates that the sentence is selected as a block to be copied.
5. Press **F10**. A message is displayed at the bottom of the screen telling you to move the cursor to the location where you want the text copied.
6. Move the cursor to any location on the screen and press **F10**. Notice that the highlighted text is duplicated and the cursor is positioned at the beginning of the copied block of text. A typical result is shown:

```
This text is written to provide information that can be
used to copy or duplicate several times within a single
document.  The copy operation which involves copying text
from one location to another within a single document is
extremely simple and useful.  Try your luck at doing this.

This text is written to provide information that can be
used to copy or duplicate several times within a single
document.

Working Copy                                    0 %   Line 7 of Page 1 of 1
Esc-Exit  F1-Info  F2-Print  Ctrl+F6-Define Pg  F7-Search  F8-Options  ↑F8-Save
```

The copied text is stored in memory and can be duplicated numerous times in the document by pressing F10. The text remains in memory until you perform another copy operation. Another copy operation replaces the text stored in memory with the latest text copied.

7. Return to the Q&A Main Menu without saving the document.
8. Turn to Module 60 to continue the learning sequence.

Module 19
CREATE A REPORT

DESCRIPTION

Reports can be created (or generated) by typing a request to the Assistant. When creating a report you must provide the Assistant with certain specific information. For example, you must specify the following:

- The fields on existing forms that are to be column headings on the report. For example, you may specify Last Name, City, Zip, or some other selection criteria.
- Selection criteria pertaining to the forms from which you want information extracted. For example, you may specify that you want all customers having the last name of Smith to be selected.
- How you want the forms sorted. You may want information reported to be sorted by largest account to smallest account (i.e., descending order by dollar amount).
- Which columns are to appear in a report. That is, you can specify column restrictions. Refer to Module 39 which describes how to define to the Assistant specific column information.

PREREQUISITES It is important to remember that before you can ask the Assistant to create a report, you must first teach the Assistant about your database. The following lessons must be completed before attempting to create a report:

- Database Lesson (Module 22).
- Form Fields Lesson (Module 39).
- Location/Name Fields Lesson (Module 56).
- Alternate Field Names Lesson (Module 5).
- Units of Measure Lesson (Module 90).
- Advanced Adjectives Lesson (Module 3).
- Advanced Verbs Lesson (Module 4).

Creating a report is initiated from the Q&A Main Menu by selecting A to access the Assistant. The Assistant Menu is displayed. Selecting A - Ask me to do something, places the Assistant into the "do something" mode. A prompt message requests the name of the file (database) with which you want the Assistant to work. The request box is displayed and you can enter your report request.

If you use vocabulary with which the Assistant is unfamiliar, a message is displayed telling you that the Assistant does not understand. You will be given an opportunity to change the request or you can instruct the Assistant to proceed.

APPLICATIONS

Creating reports simply by typing a request to the Assistant to retrieve and display information is extremely useful. At any time, information contained in vast databases can be retrieved and displayed in specified formats.

With your own on-line inquiry system ready to display any information needed simply at your request, you have instant recall of data when needed.

TYPICAL OPERATION

In this illustration, request the Assistant to create a report (displayed on the screen) of information contained in a specific database. Begin at the Q&A Main Menu.

1. Type **A** to display the Assistant Menu.
2. Type **A**. A prompt message is displayed requesting the name of the file for which you want a report created.
3. Type **CUSTOMER** and press **Return**. The following screen is displayed and the Assistant is ready to perform a task for you.

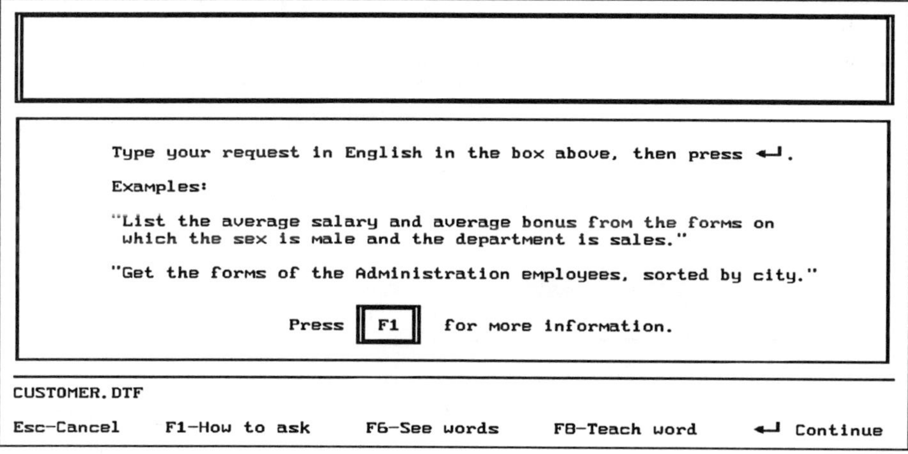

4. Type **LIST CLIENTS** and press **Return**. "Working" is displayed at the bottom of the screen. The following screen, indicating that the Assistant required additional information, is displayed.

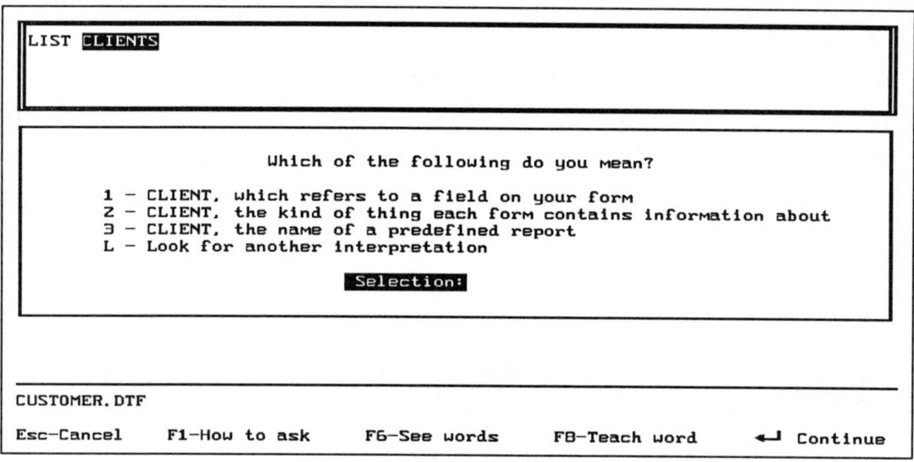

5. Press **Esc**. A blank request screen is displayed.
6. Type **LIST CUSTOMERS** and press **Return**. Type **1** and press **Return**. The following screen is displayed.

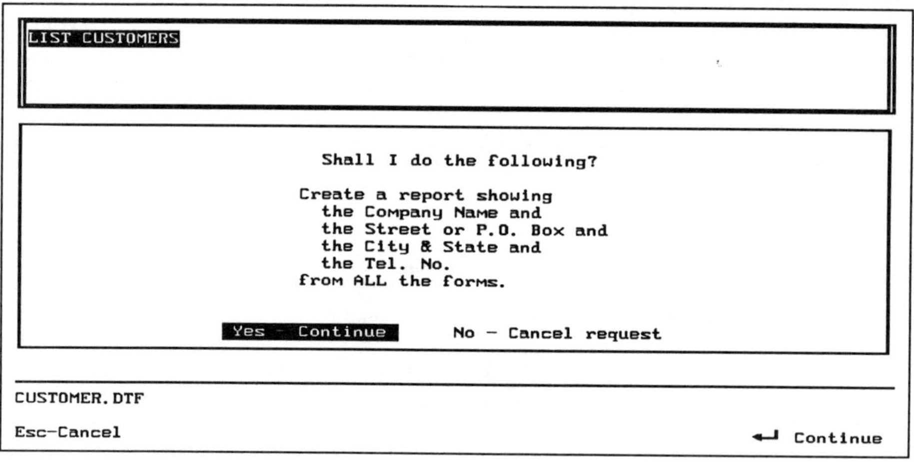

7. Press **Return** to display the report. The following is a typical report showing results.

```
LIST CUSTOMERS

        COMPANY NAME
-------------------------
Jackson & Jackson
Harrison & Jones
BJ Company
R. M. Johnson
Bebeco, Inc.
Autocratics & Associates
Finley & Company

CUSTOMER.DTF
******************************  END OF REPORT  ******************************
Esc-Cancel      F2-Reprint       { → ← ↓ ↑ PgUp PgDn }-Scroll       F10-Continue
```

8. Press **Esc**. The screen is cleared; only the blank request box is displayed at the top of the screen. If you want to request another report, it can be entered at this point.
9. Return to the Q&A Main Menu.
10. Turn to Module 64 to continue the learning sequence.

Module 20
CURSOR MOVEMENT

DESCRIPTION

This module describes the various ways in which the cursor is moved. The cursor lets you know the location on the screen where text entry or menu selection is made.

Once you have loaded Q&A and entered a document edit session in the Write function or other Q&A feature, movement of the cursor becomes critical. The cursor is the intensified flashing bar. Whether you are doing word processing, designing a form, or requesting infor mation from the Assistant, you must move the cursor to perform the operations.

The following table lists the keypad keys used for moving the cursor. When using the keypad for cursor movement, ensure that Num Lock is pressed in.

NOTE

For key sequences connected by a hyphen (such as Ctrl-Right Arrow), you press and hold the first key while you press the second key.

Key	Action — Moves the cursor . . .
Up Arrow	up one line
Down Arrow	down one line
Right Arrow	right to the next character
Ctrl-Right Arrow	right to the next word
Left Arrow	left to the next character
Ctrl-Left Arrow	left to the next word
PgUp	to first character of the previous screen
Ctrl-PgUp	to first character of the previous page
PgDn	to first charcter of the next screen
Ctrl-PgDn	to first character of the next page
Home (pressed 1 time)	to the first character of the line
Home (pressed 2 times)	to the first character of the screen
Home (pressed 3 times)	to the first character of the page
Home (pressed 4 times)	to the first character of the document
Ctrl-Home	to the first character of the document
End (pressed 1 time)	to the last character of the line
End (pressed 2 times)	to the last character of the screen
End (pressed 3 times)	to the last character of the page
End (pressed 4 times)	to the last character of the document
Ctrl-End	to the last character of the document
F9	to scroll up
Shift-F9	to scroll down

The keypad keys are referred to as navigation keys in Q&A. As you practice moving the cursor within a document, file, etc., you will be able to use combinations of keys to move the cursor across an entire document. Time saved by using these key combinations is appreciable over many days of working with Q&A.

There are also other keys that cause cursor movement. These include:

Key	Action — Moves the cursor . . .
Spacebar	one space to the right
Tab	to the right one tab setting
Return	one line down

APPLICATIONS

Cursor movement within a document is a vital word processing feature. In the Q&A Write function, the cursor can be moved in any direction in the document. Text can be entered after positioning the cursor at any location on the screen.

The ability to move the cursor in any direction within a document or file is an absolute necessity. Furthermore, the ability to move the cursor long distances saves time. There are several keys that expedite cursor movement. These include Home, End, and F9.

TYPICAL OPERATION

In this illustration, begin at the Q&A Main Menu and enter into the Write function. Enter at least one page of any text information. Refer to the list of cursor movement keys presented in this module. Try each key (or combination) to see the results. Exit from the document and return to the Q&A Main Menu without saving the document to disk.

1. At the Q&A Main Menu, type **W** to display the Write Menu.

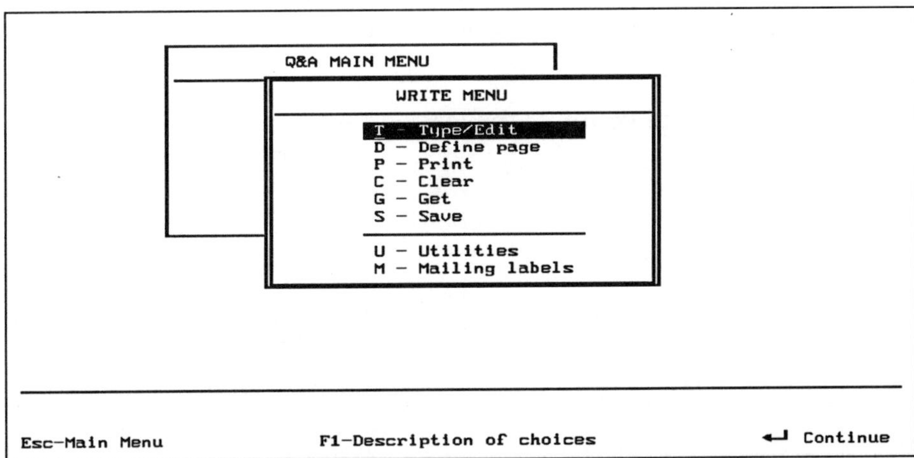

2. Type **T**. A Working Copy (blank) screen of a new document is displayed.

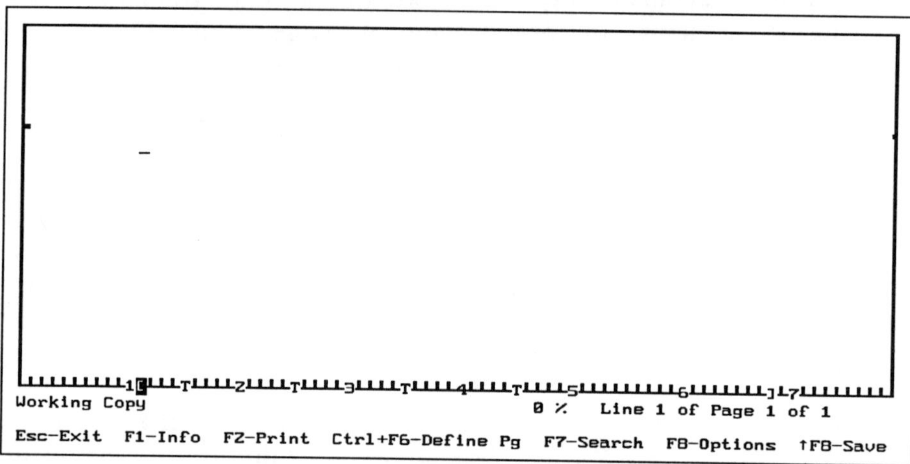

3. Type any text into the Working Copy of the document. Type one paragraph of text that you can easily enter.
4. Experiment using the cursor movement keys. Start at the top of the list presented in the Description paragraph of this module. Practice using each of the keys (or combinations) to see the results.
5. Press **Esc** twice to exit from the practice document. A prompt message is displayed warning you that the Working Copy has not been saved. The cursor is located at N - No.
6. Type **Y** to display the Q&A Main Menu. The document is not saved to disk.

WARNING

Always be sure to exit from Q&A through the menu network. Never just turn your computer power off; you could damage your Q&A software and lose the document.

7. Turn to Module 41 to continue the learning sequence.

Module 21
CUSTOMIZE A FILE

DESCRIPTION

After you have completed basic form design, you have the option to customize that design. Customizing a file can encompass one or all of several options. Most customizing options are described in this book within separate modules. However, the purpose of this module is to tie together the options for customizing a file. It also presents some of the more advanced techniques available to customize a file.

Customizing a file involves any of the following basic operations. Where a separate module exists in this book describing a customizing operation, refer to the applicable module.

Change Palette	Module 10
Create Custom Help	Module 46
Create Indexed Fields (Speedy Fields)	This Module
Edit Lookup Table	Module 30
Field Format Values	Module 6
Programming Words/Statements	Modules 75 and 76
Predetermined Form Values	This Module
Restrict Field Values	This Module
Assign Access Rights	Appendix D

CHANGE PALETTE Changing the palette involves changing the colors and physical presentation of forms displayed on the screen. Changing the palette in no way affects a printed form.

A complete description of how to change the palette is presented in Module 10.

CREATE CUSTOM HELP Operations involved in the File function, and particularly items related to forms, can be directly related to help information that you can create yourself. Module 46 describes how to create customized on-line help. You can actually create help messages directly related to fields on forms in one of your databases.

CREATE INDEXED FIELDS This customizing option permits you to identify, on a database form design, the fields upon which you want to place definite restrictions. Forms containing these identified fields are placed in an indexed file. When you request a search, the speed of the search process is significantly increased. The procedure for creating indexed fields or speedy fields is described in this module.

EDIT LOOKUP TABLE You have at your fingertips the ability to create a lookup table for use with the programming word LOOKUP. This table can contain specific values that can be recalled when using the LOOKUP command to automatically enter field information on forms. Module 30 describes how to create and edit a lookup table.

FIELD FORMAT VALUES You can streamline the appearance and functionality of forms by redefining information types for fields. Particularly for advanced users, the capability to format each field of information exactly as you want it is a valuable function. For example, you can justify or center field information, make it all uppercase letters, or format dates and numeric information as desired. Refer to Module 6 for a description of advanced methods for assigning information types to fields.

PROGRAMMING WORDS AND STATEMENTS Your forms can be enhanced by including programming statements in fields on forms. The programming statements can contain special functions and expressions that perform calculations automatically. This ensures your improved speed and productivity with Q&A. Modules 75 and 76 describe how to use special programming words and statements.

PREDETERMINED FORM VALUES By specifying to Q&A the fields on which you plan to place restrictions, searching speed is increased. These specified fields are placed in an indexed file, thus making a search for data more rapid. This module describes the procedure for automatically entering common values into fields on a form.

RESTRICT FIELD VALUES Forms can be customized to restrict values that can be entered. This technique improves overall database accuracy. Module 6 describes how to assign/change the information types for fields on a form (e.g., text of number). This module describes some advanced techniques that can be used to restrict values that can be entered into fields.

The following table lists Restrict Value symbols and definitions for the symbols.

EXACT MATCH RETRIEVAL SYMBOLS

Symbol	Definition
x	equal to the value of x
=x	equal to the value of x
/x	not equal to the value of x
=	empty
/=	not empty
x;y;z	x, y, or z in one field

RANGE RETRIEVAL SYMBOLS

Symbol	Definition
< >x	greater than the value of x
<x	less than the value of x
< > =x	greater than or equal to the value of x
< =x	less than or equal to the value of x
< >x..< =y	greater than the value of x and less than or equal to the value of y
< >x;< =y	greater than the value of x and less than or equal to the value of y
< >x;< =y	greater than the value of x or less than or equal to the value of y

TEXT AND CHARACTER RETRIEVAL SYMBOLS

Symbol	Definition
?	any single character
..	any group of characters
< > 3x..	begins with the value of x
..x	ends with the value of x
x..y	begins with the value of x and ends with the value of y
..x..	includes the value of x
..x..y..z	includes x, y, and z in that order

ASSIGN ACCESS RIGHTS Access rights to a database is controlled through the Assign access rights option on the Customize Menu. Through the access rights option you can assign access rights or declare sharing mode for a database. Network aspects of using Q&A in a multi-user environment are discussed briefly in Appendix D.

Customizing a file is relatively simple. At the Q&A Main Menu, enter the File function. On File Menu, select Design File option and the Design Menu is displayed. Choose Customize a File on the Design Menu. A prompt message is displayed requesting the name of the file which you want to customize. After entering a filename and pressing Return, the Customize Menu is displayed. Select the custom file feature that you want and press Return. Add the custom feature wanted from the Customize Menu and press F10. Repeat the process as necessary to add all of the custom features that you want. When finished press Esc at the Customize Menu and the Design Menu is displayed. Press Esc several times to return to the Q&A Main Menu.

APPLICATIONS

Use of the customizing features permits adding forms with greater ease, faster, and with fewer data-entry errors. Most of the applications for customizing features are described in each individual module previously mentioned.

Of the customizing features discussed in this module, two primarily either improve your speed at working with forms or improve Q&A processing time. These two features are creating indexed fields and predetermined form values.

The customizing feature to restrict field values improves overall accuracy of data entry.

TYPICAL OPERATION

In this illustration, enter the File function, and customize a file by restricting a field value. Begin at the Q&A Main Menu.

1. At the Q&A Main Menu, the cursor is located at F - File. Press **Return**. The File Menu is displayed.
2. Type **D**. The Design Menu is displayed.
3. Type **C**. A prompt message is displayed requesting the name of the file which you want to customize.
4. Type **CUSTOMER** and press **Return**. The Customize Menu is displayed.
5. Type **R**. The Restrict Spec screen for the specified file is displayed. The Restrict Spec screen is similar to the design form.

```
Company Name:
Street or P.O. Box:
City & State:                                  Zip:
Tel No.:

1st Contact Date:                   2nd Contact Date:
Product Area:
Yearly Sales (K):                     Credit Rating:


CUSTOMER.DTF                     Restrict Spec                  Page 1  of 1
Esc-Cancel   F1-How to restrict values   F6-Expand field        F10-Continue
```

6. Use the arrow keys or press **Tab** to move the cursor to the "1st Contact Date" field, and type **Feb 26,1990**. Data entry into the field is now restricted to dates after the specified date of Feb 26, 1990.

You can enter as many restrict values as wanted on a form. Just move the cursor to the field where you want to enter a restrict value and type the restrict value.

7. Press **F10**. The restrict values are saved. The Customize Menu is displayed.
8. Return to the Main Menu.
9. Turn to Module 10 to continue the learning sequence.

Module 22
DATABASE LESSON

DESCRIPTION

This lesson is used to teach the Assistant about your individual databases. Through this lesson you instruct the Assistant that you want it to review the contents of specific databases. The Assistant searches through each form to become acquainted with the field labels and information. The database lesson is essential before you can request the Assistant to perform any task related to a database.

Beginning at the Q&A Main Menu and selecting the Assistant function initiates the lesson by displaying the Assistant Menu. Typing T displays a filename prompt. Entering a filename and pressing Return, displays the Basic Lessons Menu.

Selecting option 1 ("What this database is about") displays a screen over the first form in the database.

If a form contains a field label "Company Name," an associative word, "Customer," could be entered. Be sure that you think of most likely words that could be used when referring to the fields on the form.

After entering words or phrases that are closely associated with the fields on the form, pressing F10 completes the lesson; the Basic Lessons Menu is displayed. Pressing Esc twice returns you to the Q&A Main Menu.

APPLICATIONS

Teaching the Assistant everything you can about your databases ensures maximum performance when requesting that tasks be performed. With many definitions related to individual fields on a form, you are more certain to have the most correct retrievals made by the Assistant. Take the time to carefully think through the possible words and phrases that describe information on a form.

TYPICAL OPERATION

In this illustration, teach the Assistant about a database. Enter possible words and phrases associated with a database and then exit the lesson. Begin at the Q&A Main Menu.

1. At the Q&A Main Menu, the cursor is located at F - File. Type **A**. The Assistant Menu is displayed.
2. Type **T**. A prompt message is displayed requesting you to enter the filename of the file for which you want to provide instruction to the Assistant.
3. Type **CUSTOMER** and press **Return**. Press **Return** to accept the default to begin. The Basic Lessons Menu is displayed. The cursor is located on selection "1 - What this database is about."
4. Press **Return**. The database lesson screen is displayed.

```
"Each form contains information about a particular _________."

Are there any words or phrases that could be used to complete
the above sentence?  If YES, type them in the blanks below.
If NO, press F10 to continue.  If you're NOT SURE, press F1
for more explanation.

                    <                              >
                    <                              >
                    <                              >
                    <                              >
                    <                              >
                    <                              >
                    <                              >
                    <                              >
                    <                              >
                    <                              >
                    <                              >

CUSTOMER.DTF
Esc-Cancel              F1-Examples and explanation              F10-Continue
```

5. Type words or phrases related to the fields on the form. For this practice session, enter the following words for the "Company Name" field. Press **Return** after each entry.

   Customer

   Client

   Patient

   Business

   Jobber

The results are:

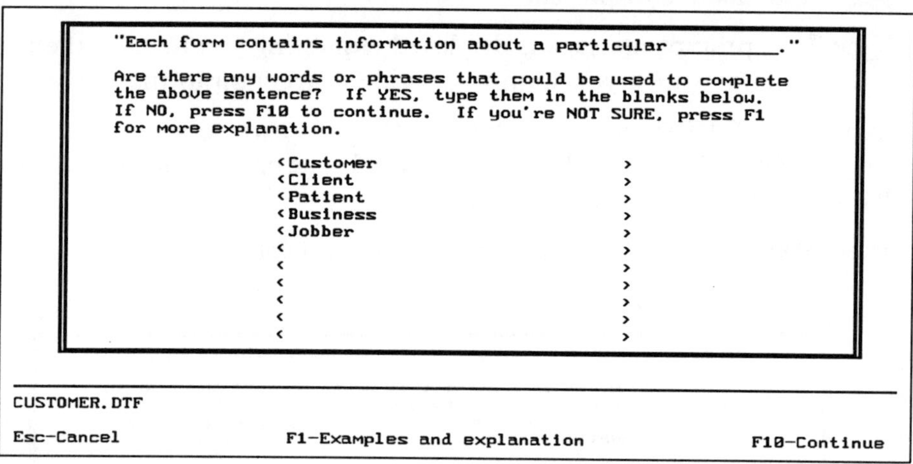

6. Press **F10** to complete the lesson and display the Basic Lessons Menu.
7. Return to the Main Menu.
8. Turn to Module 39 to continue the learning sequence.

Module 23
DEFAULT DIRECTORY

DESCRIPTION

The Global Defaults feature of Q&A permits you to set default directories, set Automatic Execution, Network ID, and Install Alternate Programs on the Q&A Main Menu.

SETTING DEFAULT DIRECTORIES Location of program files is controlled by Q&A; you cannot specify the directory for program files. Selection of the drive depends on the number and type of disk drive(s) supported by your computer system. Your computer system may have two to four floppy disk drives or one to two floppy disk drives and one to two hard disk drives. When you specify the disk where files are to be stored, Q&A later finds and retrieves the files or documents as needed. After you are finished with your work on documents or databases, they are stored on the disk(s) specified in the default directory.

The default settings for Q&A directories for a floppy disk drive system are set as follows:

Document files	Drive B:/ (the root directory)
Database files	Drive B:/ (the root directory)

If you install Q&A on a hard disk drive system, all files are automatically set to reside on drive C root directory at initial installation. You can change file default settings anytime for any computer disk system configuration.

As you are working with your Q&A files, it is not necessary to specify drive/path parameters when referring to a file. Q&A uses the drive/path parameter setting contained in the default directory. You can change the default setting to suit your needs.

Refer to the DOS manual for your computer for instructions on how to define and use directories and paths.

Changing default directories is a Utility function. From the Q&A Main Menu, the Utilities Menu is accessed by typing U. The Set Default Directories screen is displayed by typing S.

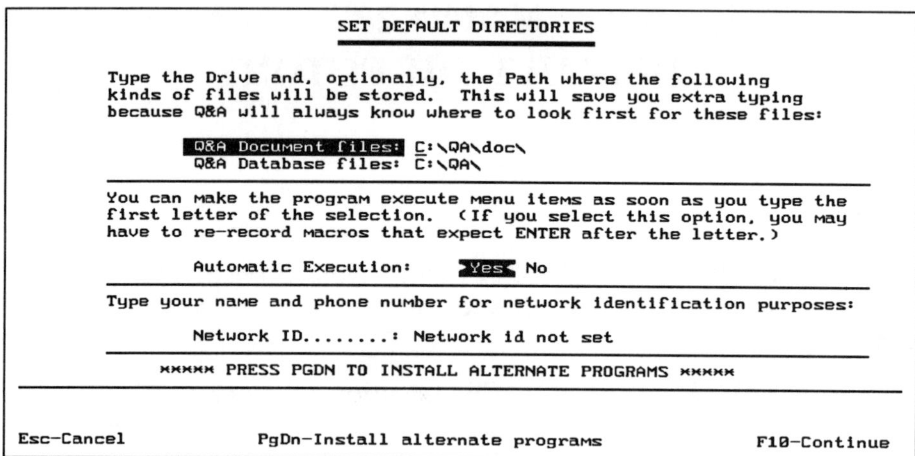

The Set Default Directories screen consists of two screens. Pressing the PgDn key displays the Alternate Programs screen.

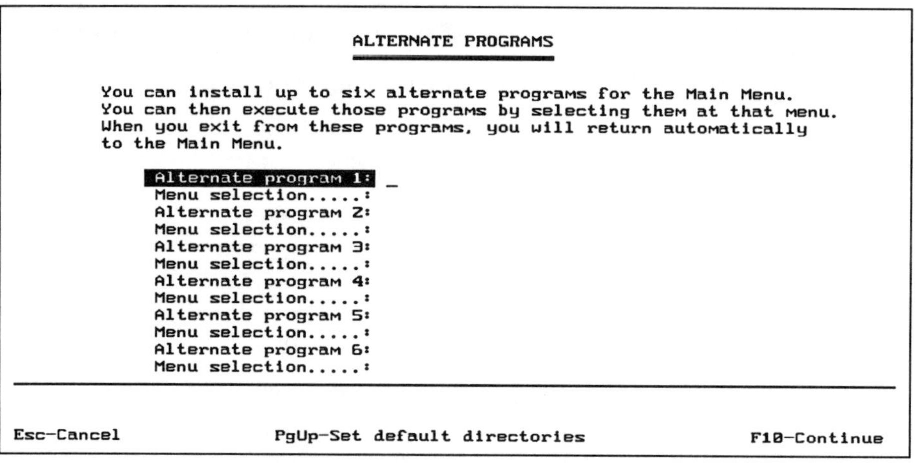

After entering the desired disk drive and pressing Return at each of the selection locations on the screen, pressing F10 sets the new default settings.

SPECIFYING NETWORK ID Users on a local area network (LAN) can enter their name and phone number using the Set Default Directories screen. This is not necessary if you use only a personal computer not linked with other users on a network. The default directory feature provides flexibility if you have a hard drive system. There may be occasions when you want document files or even database files to be stored on individual diskettes rather than the hard drive. You can easily designate the resident location of your files.

SETTING AUTOMATIC EXECUTION Selecting functions within Q&A is done by typing an alphabetical character and pressing Return.

You can set the Automatic Execution to "Yes" and eliminate the need to press Return at each menu selection. Simply typing the menu selection character executes the selection.

Setting Automatic Execution to "Yes" speeds up overall use of Q&A. You do not need to press Return after making each function selection.

SETTING ALTERNATE PROGRAMS An additional global default that can be set by hard disk users is Alternate Programs. Alternate Programs can be compared to User Exits that can be accessed from an applications program, typically on mainframe computer system software. Up to six DOS programs or Q&A macros can be installed on the Q&A Main Menu.

After setting the default directory and alternate programs, you can easily access these alternate programs from the Q&A Main Menu. Upon completing a selected program, you can return to the Q&A Main Menu. However, Q&A macros set program location in accordance with how they are programmed.

The alternate programs specified must be stored on the hard disk where the Q&A software resides. Any macros installed on the Q&A Main Menu must also be stored in the file QAMACRO.ASC which must also be resident on the same hard disk.

APPLICATIONS

The ability to select the specific drive on which you want files to reside permits you to configure the Q&A system to operate on a combination of hard/floppy disk drives or on multiple floppy disk drives.

If you have an extended memory board, you can designate that your working files reside in RAM memory, thus rapidly improving the overall performance of Q&A. One word of caution: if you store your files in RAM memory while working with Q&A, do not forget to copy them to a diskette or your hard drive.

TYPICAL OPERATION

In this example, the default directory for a hard drive system is changed to ensure that document files are saved on disk drive B in a directory named QADOC. This permits storing of the files on a diskette for archive purposes. They can be copied from drive B to drive C to continue using them as working copies if desired. In addition, Automatic Execution is set to "Yes." Begin at the Q&A Main Menu.

1. Type **U**. The Utilities Menu is displayed.

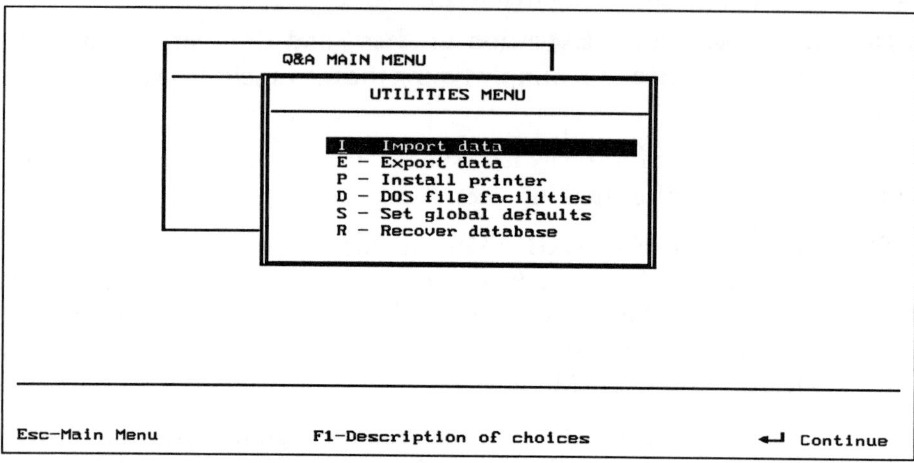

2. Type **S**. The Set Default Directories screen is displayed.
3. At "Q&A Document files:" type **B:\QADOC**.

NOTE

In step 4, you change the Automatic Execution default to Yes. If you have followed the Sample Session steps in Module 2, your Automatic Execution is already set to Yes. Skip to step 5 to continue the Typical Operation.

4. Press **Tab, Down Arrow,** or **Return** to move the cursor to Automatic Execution. Use **Right** or **Left Arrow** to move the cursor to Yes.
5. Press **PgDn** to display the Alternate Programs screen. This step is to allow you to view this important option.
6. Press **F10** to record the settings just made.
7. Press **Esc** to return to the Q&A Main Menu.
8. Turn to Module 34 to continue the learning sequence.

Module 24
DEFINE/REDEFINE A MACRO

DESCRIPTION

A macro is a set of operations and/or keystrokes predefined to Q&A, identified by a special sequence of keys, and invoked by pressing those keys. A macro functions when a specified single key or two-key combination is pressed. This can be done anytime at any location within any of the Q&A functions as long as Q&A is awaiting text entry. Do not attempt to invoke a macro in response to a prompt message or as a menu selection.

The macro function in Q&A, especially as applied to the word processing function, can be compared to user-defined keys so popular in other word processing software. The macro capability of Q&A is a very powerful feature.

DEFINING A MACRO Creating a macro involves the process of defining each keystroke that you want implemented by the macro. Once defined, a macro remains "filed" in your computer's memory until you are ready to use it. A macro can be defined that only involves a single keystroke or it can encompass thousands of keystrokes. The real essence of using a macro is achieved when one single macro represents a multitude of keystrokes.

A macro file containing all macros that you have created can be used with the Write, File, Report, and Assistant functions of Q&A. A macro can be defined at anytime while in any Q&A function.

Pressing Shift-F2 displays the Macro Menu.

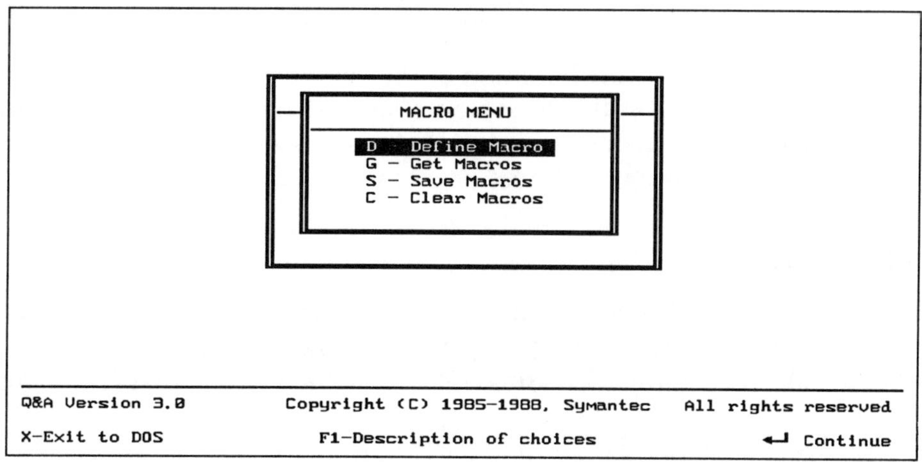

Typing D activates macro definition. From this point, the key sequences typed identify the macro (name the macro). You can type any character or press any function key in combination with Shift, Ctrl, or Alt to produce a two-key combination as a macro identifier.

The sequence of actual keystrokes for the defined macro are typed. Shift-F2 is pressed to complete the macro definition.

There are some cautions that should be observed when identifying macros. Two-key combination identifiers can be used. That is, Ctrl, Alt, Shift plus a character key, function key, or keypad key can be used to identify a macro.

Beware of assigning a single character key as a macro identifier. Each time you type that single character key, the macro is activitated and the predefined sequence of keystrokes is produced. Often the results are unwanted or even disastrous.

Do not define, as macro identifiers, keys which are used for other purposes by Q&A. Typical keys in this category are the function keys and special keys that perform routine operations (e.g., Tab key and Return).

Certain keys cannot be used alone as identifier keys for a macro. These include Shift, F9, Ctrl, Num Lock, Scroll Lock, and Caps Lock.

REDEFINING A MACRO An existing macro can be redefined at any time. This applies whether or not the macro has been saved to disk. Not only can you reidentify the macro identifier keys which invoke the macro, but also you can entirely restructure the key sequence of the macro itself.

The process of redefining a macro is almost exactly the same as that used to define a macro. The only exception is that when you enter the macro identifier keys, Q&A asks if you want to redefine the existing macro. The prompt is displayed at the bottom of the screen.

That key is already defined. Do you want to redefine it? (Y/N)

An answer of Y (yes) permits redefinition of the macro. You must retype the entire macro. You cannot position the cursor on displayed text created from invoking the macro and type over characters or insert characters or keystrokes. Concluding steps are identical to those used to define a macro.

APPLICATIONS

Macros are defined and used primarily to save time and effort. Not only is it possible to eliminate repetitive typing when working with word processing documents, but also when creating files or documents that function as spreadsheets. Macros are invaluable for retaining keystroke sequences for calculations that are used frequently.

Sophisticated macros can simplify making requests to the Assistant. If you use the Assistant frequently and make repetitive requests, defining macros to handle these requests enhances your productivity.

TYPICAL OPERATION

In this example, a macro is defined to produce repetitive information within a document. Enter the Write function and begin an edit session with a new document named DEFMAC. Identify the macro, define the keystroke sequence and then use the macro to produce desired repetitive results. Exit from the Working Copy of the document without saving it to disk. Begin at the Q&A Main Menu.

1. Type **W**. The Write Menu is displayed. The cursor is located at T - Type/Edit.
2. Press **Return**. A Working Copy (blank screen) for a new document is displayed.
3. To define a macro, press **Shift-F2**. The Macro Menu Box is displayed.

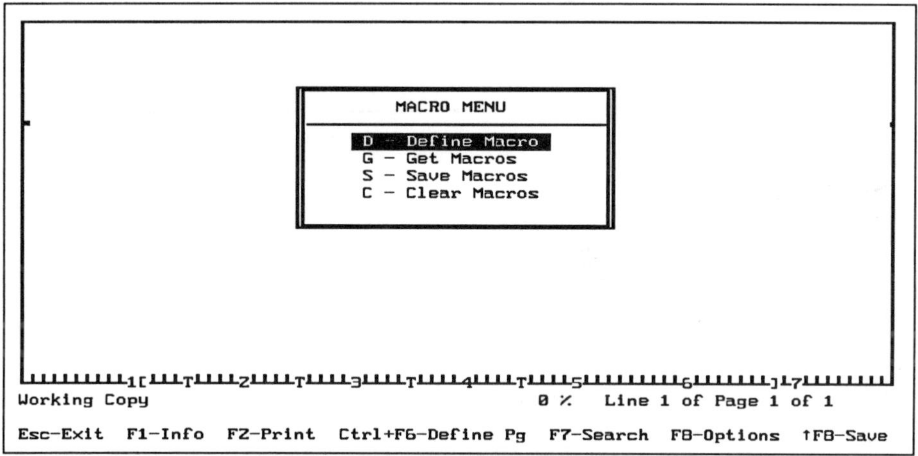

4. Type **D**. A prompt message is displayed at the bottom of the screen asking for the macro identifier that you want to assign to the keystroke sequence.

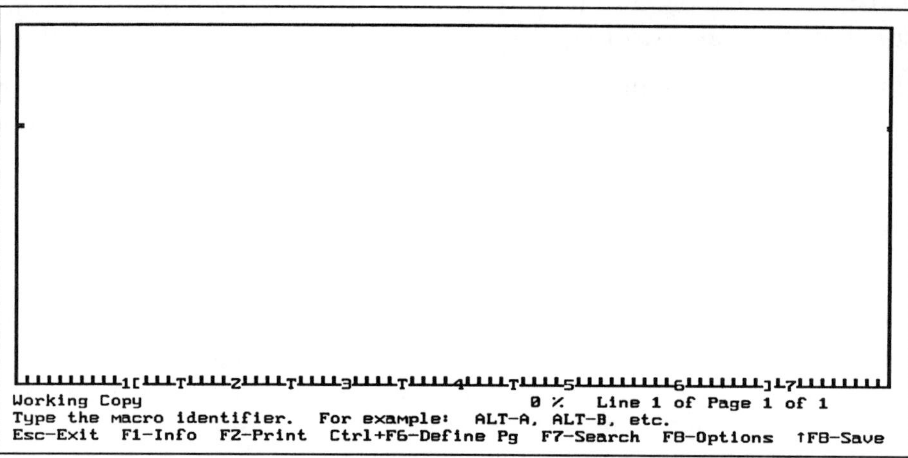

5. Press **Alt-A**. A small flashing square is displayed at the bottom right of the screen, informing you that the macro key sequence can be entered. If you attempt to define the macro definition keys and they are already used for another macro, a message is displayed informing you that the keys are already defined. You can redefine the current macro to other keystroke sequences.

6. Type the following key sequence:

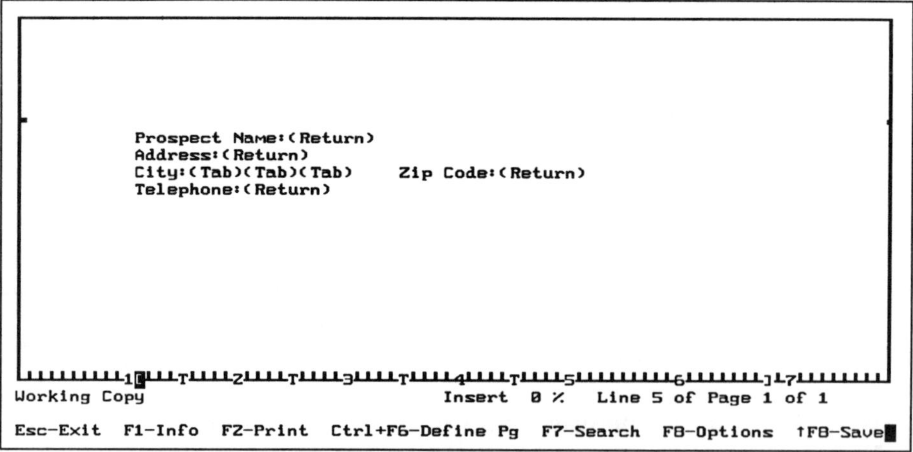

7. Press **Shift-F2**. The flashing box at the bottom of the screen disappears. A prompt message is displayed requesting the name of the file to which the macro is to be saved.

8. Type **QAMACRO.ASC** and press **Return**. The macro is defined and saved to the file named QAMACRO.ASC.
9. Use any of the cursor movement keys to position the cursor in any open area on the screen.
10. Press **Alt-A**. Note that the entire sequence of keystrokes is performed.
11. Press **Alt-A** again. The text (programmed keystrokes) are repeated and the cursor is positioned at the end of the text.
12. Press **Esc** to exit from the edit session. The Write Menu is displayed.
13. Press **Esc**. A prompt message is displayed warning you that the Working Copy of the document has not been saved. The cursor is located at N - No.
14. Type **Y**. The Q&A Main Menu is displayed without saving the document.

NOTE

The macro has not been saved; however, it remains in the computer's memory as long as you do not reboot or turn the computer power off.

15. Turn to Module 12 to continue the learning sequence.

Module 25
DELETE TEXT

DESCRIPTION

There are a variety of ways to delete text in a Q&A Write document. To completely erase or eliminate displayed text is to *delete text*. This applies whether the text is a single character, word, line, or large block of text. The following table outlines the deletion options that are available to you.

Operation	Key Sequence
Delete character (at cursor location)	Del
Delete character (with cursor at right of character)	Backspace
Delete last character typed	Backspace
Delete block of text (with cursor at first character in block)	F3 and move arrow keys to last character in the block, then press either F3 or F10
Delete line (with cursor anywhere on the line}	Shift-F4
Delete word (with cursor at first letter)	F4
Delete word and space following (with cursor anywhere on word)	F4

Pressing Del or Backspace performs deletion in Q&A documents or files. Either key deletes characters in the path of the cursor as it moves to the left. The text to the right of the cursor moves with the cursor as it deletes text. Text deleted by the Del or Backspace keys cannot be restored.

Characters deleted by other keys can be restored by pressing Shift-F7.

Blocks of text can also be restored if accidently deleted. When you delete, copy, or move a block of text, that text is stored in memory. Pressing Shift-F7 restores the text. When you copy, move, or delete a subsequent block of text, it replaces the text previously stored. Thereafter, only the latest text stored in memory is available to restore.

There is a limit to the amount of text that can be retored. Only about one full page of text can be restored. If you identify a block of text that is too large to restore, Q&A warns you that the block is too large.

Suppose that during an edit session, you have deleted lines, words, and blocks of text. Then you decide that you want to start the session over with the original document. You can do this provided the document being worked with was recalled from disk when the edit session was started. You can clear the Working Copy of the document in the editor. None of the changes made during the edit session, including the deletions, are saved to disk. The original text in the document previously saved on disk can be recalled into an edit session.

APPLICATIONS

The delete function is used to erase text during the creation of text or while editing a document in an edit session. The variety of ways available to delete characters, words, lines, or large blocks of text (paragraphs or pages) makes Q&A an extremely sophisticated word processor.

TYPICAL OPERATION

In this example, enter the Write function in an edit session with a Working Copy of a document. Delete a single character, a word, a word and the blank space following the word, a line, and finally a block of text. Exit from the edit session without saving the document to disk. Begin at the Q&A Main Menu.

1. Type **W** to display the Write Menu. The cursor is located at T - Type/Edit.
2. Press **Return** to open a Working Copy of a new document. A Working Copy (blank) screen of a new document is displayed.
3. Type the following text:

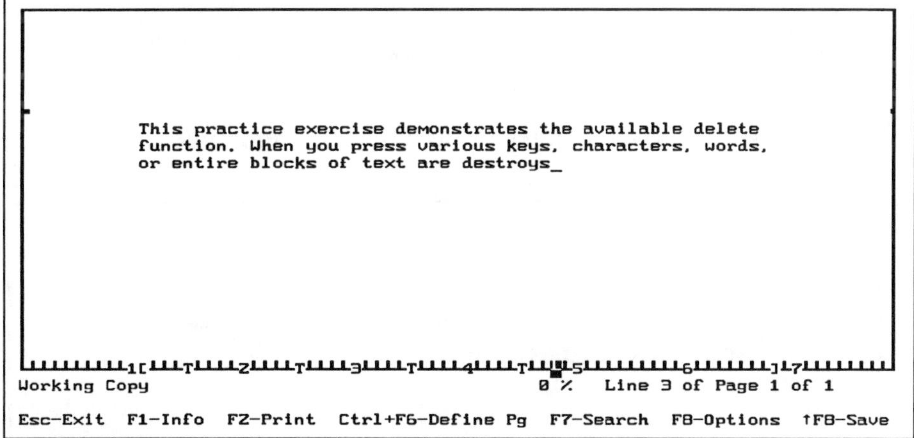

4. Press **Backspace** once to delete the character "s." It can also be deleted by pressing the Left Arrow to move the cursor to the character and pressing Del.
5. Press **Left Arrow** to move the cursor to the character "d" in the word "destroy."
6. Press **F4** to delete the entire word.

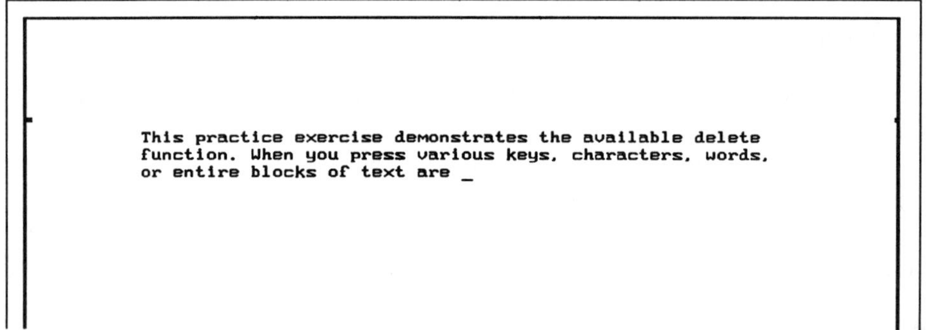

7. Press **F3**. The blank space is highlighted and the following prompt appears at the bottom of the screen:

```
This practice exercise demonstrates the available delete
function. When you press various keys, characters, words,
or entire blocks of text are █

Working Copy                                  0 %   Line 3 of Page 1 of 1
Use the arrow keys to select the text you want to remove, then press F10.
Esc-Cancel                                                   F10-Continue
```

8. Press **Left Arrow** several times to highlight the remainder of the line.

```
This practice exercise demonstrates the available delete
function. When you press various keys, characters, words,
or entire blocks of text are
```

9. Press **F10**. The highlighted characters are deleted and the message is removed. The cursor moves up to the end of the previous line.
10. Press **Shift-F4** to delete the entire line. The screen displays:

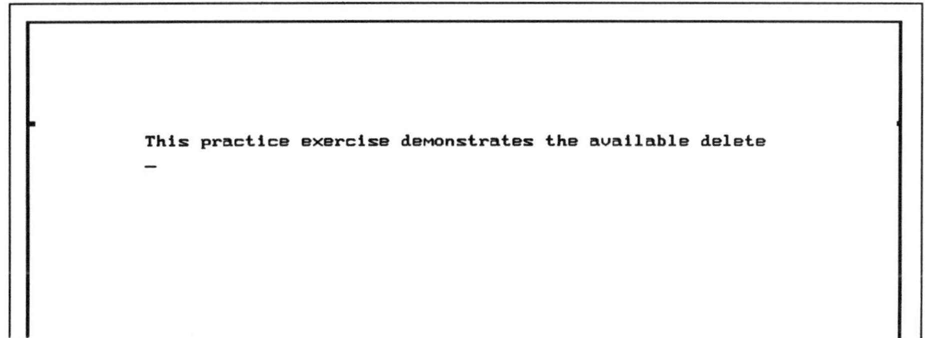

11. Press **Up Arrow** to move the cursor to the first character in the first word of the text.
12. Press **F3** and notice the same prompt message that displayed in Step 7.
13. Select the text to delete by pressing **Right Arrow** to highlight all of the text. Text is highlighted as the cursor moves through it.
14. Press **F10** to delete the selected block of text (highlighted). The cursor is located at its initial position.
15. Restore the line of text just deleted by pressing **Shift-F7**. The line of text is restored.
16. Press **Esc** to return to the Write Menu.
17. Press **Esc** to exit from the Write Menu. A prompt message is displayed warning you that the Working Copy of the document has not been saved. The cursor is located at N - No.
18. Type **Y** to return to the Q&A Main Menu without saving the document.
19. Turn to Module 9 to continue the learning sequence.

Module 26
DERIVED COLUMNS IN A REPORT

DESCRIPTION

Derived columns are created in a report to produce data that is not actually contained in any field on a form (database). You can create derived column information by performing calculations from existing form data. You can create up to four derived columns in a report. Calculations can be performed in derived columns by creating formulas designed to produce the desired results.

From the Q&A Main Menu, entering the Report function through the Report Menu and selecting D generates a prompt message requesting the name of a database for which you want to create derived columns. After entering a valid filename, a list of reports for database is displayed. You can enter the name of an existing report or a new report name at the prompt. Afterwards, the Retrieve Spec screen is displayed for the specified database. After entering retrieve specifications or pressing F10 to retrieve all forms in the database, the Column/Sort Spec screen is displayed. Upon completing the Column/Sort Spec screen and/or pressing F8, the Derived Columns screen is displayed.

```
                                DERIVED COLUMNS

Heading:
Formula:
Column Spec:

Heading:
Formula:
Column Spec:

Heading:
Formula:
Column Spec:

Heading:
Formula:
Column Spec:

CUSTOMER.DTF          Derived Columns for customer                 Page 1 of 4
Esc-Cancel      F1-Info      F9-Go back to Column/Sort Spec      F10-Continue
```

The Derived Columns screen is completed by typing in the heading for each of the four derived columns, typing the formula for calculations, and typing a specification for the derived column. It is necessary to press the Tab key or Return after each entry.

Formulas are created by using column numbers that you designated on the Column/Sort Spec screen. For example, if you designated five columns (#1, #2, #3, #4, #5) to be reflected in a report, a calculation might be formulated by any of the following expressions:

Formula	Description
#2 * #1	The value in column 2 times the value in column 1
#5 − #1	The value in column 5 minus the value in column 1
#3/(#2 + #3)	The value in column 3 divided by the sum of values contained in columns 2 and 3.

Q&A uses a precedence of order when calculating expressions in formulas. The order of precedence in which calculations are performed are as follows (first calculated to last calculated): parentheses ( ); multiplication (*) and division (/); addition (+) and subtraction (−); less than (<) and greater than (>), less than or equal to (< =), and greater than or equal to (> =); NOT; and AND OR.

Derived columns can also reference other derived columns. This technique can be used to produce running subtotals.

When finished entering derived column information, pressing F10 displays the Report Print Options Menu. You can then print the report or you can press F9 to return to the Column/Sort Spec screen.

APPLICATIONS

The capability to produce derived columns enables you to produce any kind of report to meet specific needs. Not only are four derived columns available in each report, but there is the capability to perform calculations in each or among each other.

As previously mentioned, derived columns can be referenced within each other to produce running subtotals. This technique can also be used to create a series of averages for fields on forms.

TYPICAL OPERATION

In this illustration, enter the Report function and retrieve all forms in the database, then complete the Column Heading/Width Spec screen and the Derived Columns screen. Proceed to the Print Options screen and print the report on the screen or exit to the Main Menu. Begin at the Q&A Main Menu.

1. Select the Report Menu.

2. Type **D**, then type **CUSTOMER** and press **Return**. A list of Report Names for the CUSTOMER database is displayed.
3. Type **CUSTOMER** again. The Retreive Spec screen for the specified database is displayed.
4. Press **F10**. The Column/Sort Spec screen is displayed.
5. Press **Tab** to move the cursor to the field that you want to designate as the first column in the report and type **1**.
6. Repeat Step 5 for each field chosen as a column on the report. Type the appropriate column number (e.g., 2, 3, etc.) for each field selected. Ensure that you designate both "Commission" fields as 13 and 14 respectively for this exercise.
7. Press **F8**. The Derived Columns screen is displayed.

```
                              DERIVED COLUMNS

Heading: _
Formula:
Column Spec:

Heading:
Formula:
Column Spec:

Heading:
Formula:
Column Spec:

Heading:
Formula:
Column Spec:

CUSTOMER.DTF            Derived Columns for CUSTOMER              Page 1 of 4
Esc-Cancel      F1-Info       F9-Go back to Column/Sort Spec      F10-Continue
```

8. Type the heading, in the Heading blank, for the first derived column and press **Return**. If you are typing a multiline heading, separate each line by an exclamation mark (!) (for example: TOTAL COMMISSIONS!MAR 89).
9. Type a formula, if applicable, in the Formula blank for the first derived column and press **Return** (for example, #13 + #14).
10. Type a specification for the derived column in the Column Spec blank and press **Return**.

```
                         DERIVED COLUMNS

Heading: TOTAL COMMISSIONS!MAR 89
Formula: #13 + #14
Column Spec: 9,ST

Heading: _
Formula:
Column Spec:

Heading:
Formula:
Column Spec:

Heading:
Formula:
Column Spec:

CUSTOMER.DTF          Derived Columns for CUSTOMER             Page 1 of 4
Esc-Cancel       F1-Info      F9-Go back to Column/Sort Spec    F10-Continue
```

The column specification "9 ST" designates that the column is defined as the ninth column on the report and subtotals and totals are to appear in the report.

The first entry in the Column Spec blank is a number which always identifies which column the derived column is to be on the report. For example, a column specification can consist of the column number, calculating, breaking, or sorting codes.

11. Repeat Steps 8, 9, and 10 for each derived column wanted.
12. Press **F10**. The Report Print Options Menu is displayed.
13. To return to the Column/Sort Spec screen, press **F9**. Complete entries on the menu and press **F10** to print the report.
14. Return to the Q&A Main Menu.
15. Turn to Module 52 to continue the learning sequence.

Module 27
DOS FILE FACILITIES

DESCRIPTION

The DOS File Facilities function lets you perform basic DOS file functions without having to exit from Q&A. From the Q&A Main Menu, you select the Utilities Menu which contains, as one of the options, DOS File Facilities. Selecting the DOS File Facilities option on the Q&A Main Menu gives you access to common DOS functions including List files, and Rename, Delete and Copy a file.

This menu-integrated method of performing DOS file functions directly from Q&A is a valuable time-saving tool. It provides you with ready access to other DOS functions without having to exit from Q&A, then having to reload and enter Q&A again.

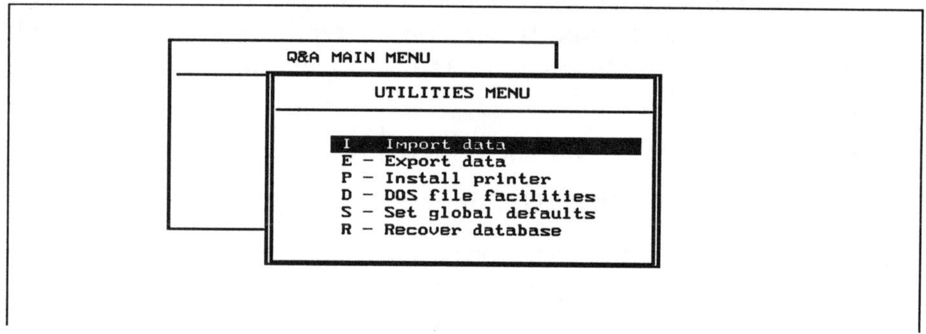

Any of the DOS file functions can be chosen from the DOS File Facilities screen.

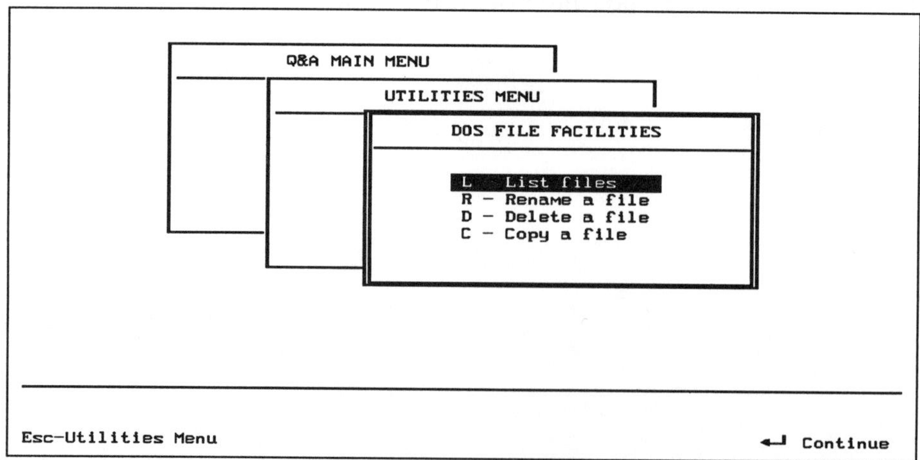

Each of the selectable functions has a specific use. To display the filenames contained on a disk or a directory, you can use the List files function. It displays the filenames for all files contained on a disk drive and directory.

To rename a file, you can use the Rename a file function. It permits you to change the name of an existing file saved to the disk to any other filename as long as the name conforms to file naming conventions. Refer to your DOS manual for information on file naming conventions.

The Delete a file function permits you to erase any file from the disk. Once the file is deleted it cannot be retrieved by conventional means.

Any file can be copied onto the same disk or another disk. The destination file must not have the same filename if you are copying the file to the same disk.

Once you have chosen a function from the DOS File Facilities screen, a prompt message is displayed requesting appropriate information. For example, if you select Rename a file, Delete a file, or Copy a file, the message requests the filename.

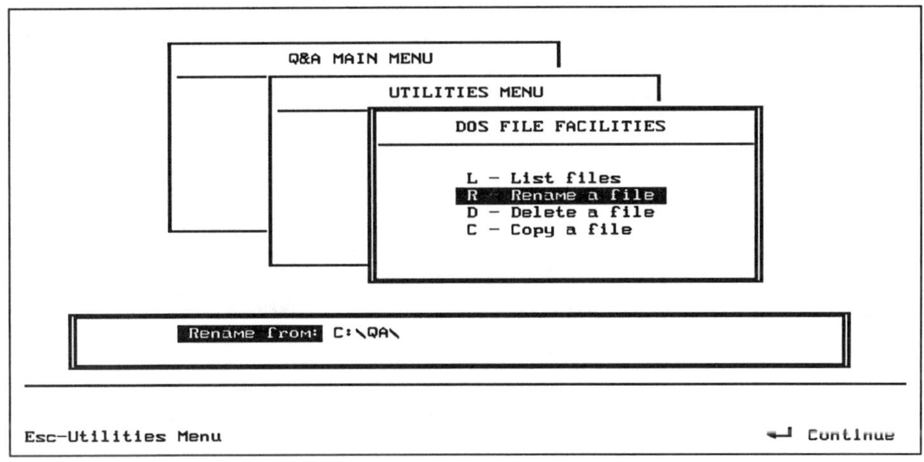

If you select List files, the message requests you to specify a drive or directory name.

Once you have responded to the prompt message, pressing Return invokes the operation.

If you are copying or renaming a file, a prompt message requests you to specify the new filename.

When the DOS File Facility that you have requested has been completed, the Utilities Menu is displayed. Return to the Q&A Main Menu by pressing Esc.

Databases that you create within Q&A are stored on disk in two files. One database file has a file extension of .DTF; the other file has a file extension of .IDX. Files with DTF extensions are the only files that are listed on the Q&A File and Report lists. Files with IDX extensions are used internally by Q&A. When you delete a database file, both files (DTF and IDX) are deleted.

APPLICATIONS

Listing files in a drive or directory is one of the most frequently used functions that you will perform while trying to manage your growing databases. As you build your databases, the number of files created can become extensive.

Files are usually named to reflect the contents of the file. If you need several versions of the same file, you can copy the file as many times as necessary. Copying a file can be one way of making a backup for a database. You can rename a file to make the name more descriptive of the contents. You can rename each file using the same base name and a different filename extension or you can use a completely different filename for each file. If the latter option is chosen, the filename extension applied to each is not revelant. Another method for distinguishing files of different names is by including a date within the filename to reflect the origination date.

TYPICAL OPERATION

In this illustration, use the DOS File Facilities screen to list files contained on a disk, then rename an existing file. Begin at the Q&A Main Menu.

1. Type **U**. The Utilities Menu is displayed.
2. Type **D**. The DOS File Facilities Menu is displayed. The cursor is located at L - List files.
3. Press **Return**. A prompt message is displayed at the bottom of the screen requesting the "Drive/Path:."
4. Press **Return** to list files contained on the default drive. You could change the drive/path by typing over the displayed drive and/or path. Filenames are listed.
5. Press **Esc** twice to remove the prompt message and return to the DOS File Facilities menu.

6. Type **R**, a prompt requesting the name of the file is displayed at the bottom of the screen The prompt reads "Rename from:." You can press Return to list files contained on the default drive or you can change the drive/path by typing over the displayed drive and/or path.
7. Type any valid filename and press **Return**. A prompt message, "Rename as:" is displayed.

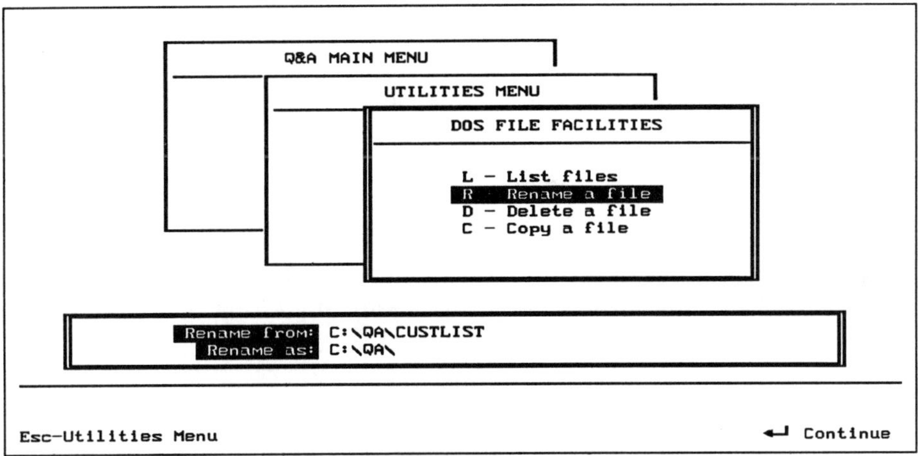

8. Type a different filename (ex., CUSTOMER) and press **Return**. The file is renamed to the designated filename and extension. The Dos File Facilities Menu is displayed when the operation is completed.

CAUTION

If you attempt to rename a file to a name already existing, a warning message is displayed informing you that the file already exists.

The Delete and Copy functions of the DOS File Facility operate the same way the Rename function does. You may choose to practice these functions now or go to the next module in the Recommended Learning Sequence.

9. Press **Esc**. The Utilities Menu is displayed.
10. Press **Esc**. The Q&A Main Menu is displayed.
11. Turn to Module 31 to continue the learning sequence.

Module 28
DRAW LINES AND BOXES

DESCRIPTION

To create special effects and enhance the appearance of documents, forms, spreadsheets, or reports, you can draw lines and boxes in any of these files. Q&A's drawing feature facilitates drawing of horizontal, vertical, and diagonal lines.

If the contents of a document are created in the Write function with lines and boxes integrated with the text, the document may be copied to a report or a form. The lines and boxes then may be displayed or printed in the form or report.

Drawing is initiated through the Draw function on the Options Menu. The Options Menu is displayed by pressing F8 while in a Working Copy of a document.

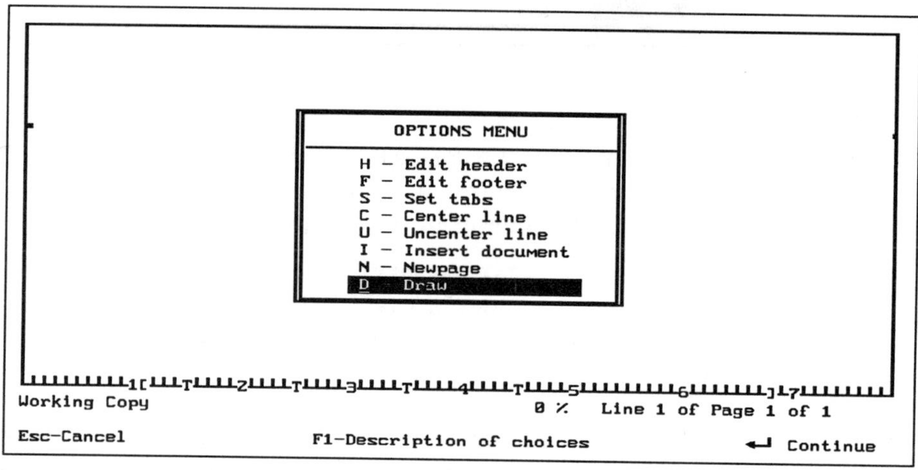

Selecting D on the menu puts you in the "Draw" mode.

Lines are drawn using the cursor control keys on the keypad. The arrow keys draw vertical or horizontal lines. Home/PgDn and PgUp/End draw diagonal lines. To draw double horizontal and vertical lines, press and hold the Shift key while pressing the arrow keys. Pressing the NumLock key produces the same result while drawing with the arrow keys. To prevent connecting individual drawings to each other, press F10 after completing each individual entity.

To erase any line or box drawn, press F8 and use the cursor keys to move in the same path as the displayed lines. This action erases the drawing. Some experimentation with your particular equipment is necessary.

Lines appearing on the screen can be over typed with other characters. If you insert text or even other drawn line segments on the same line of type, the drawn line segments are affected in the same way as if they were a string of characters.

A printer not rated as a graphics printer prints lines and boxes using dashes and vertical bars. Some computer monitors do not display graphics characters; however, this does not prevent you from using the drawing feature of Q&A.

The drawing feature can also be used when designing or redesigning a form. Lines or boxes can be drawn only around single-line fields. They cannot be drawn around multi-line fields.

APPLICATIONS

The lines and boxes feature is easily adaptable to producing simple graphics. For example, organization charts can be created relatively fast. There is no limit to the complexity of a chart that can be drawn.

Simple graphics consisting of lines and boxes can be produced for visual presentations as well. Let your imagination be your guide. If you create and use various forms and reports in your work, the capability to generate forms and reports with boxed information is valuable and impressive.

The drawing feature can be used to draw organization charts, programming flowcharts, forms of all kinds, and questionaires. With the capability to draw diagonal lines, you can use your imagination to create just about any kind of illustration.

TYPICAL OPERATION

In this illustration, enter the Write function, create a new document, and use the Draw function. Exit from the document and do not save the document to disk. Begin at the Q&A Main Menu.

1. Open a new document. Press **Return** at least two times to move down from the top of the screen. Type the following lines centered on the screen, pressing **Return** four times after the second line. Remember to use the Options Menu to select line centering for each line typed.

```
                         PRESIDENT

                      J.R. Smith, Jr.

1[   T    2    T    3    T    4    T    5         6       ]7
Working Copy                            0 %  Line 5 of Page 1 of 1
Esc-Exit  F1-Info  F2-Print  Ctrl+F6-Define Pg  F7-Search  F8-Options  ↑F8-Save
```

2. Press **Tab** once and type the following lines. Double space between each line and place at least four line spaces between each item typed.

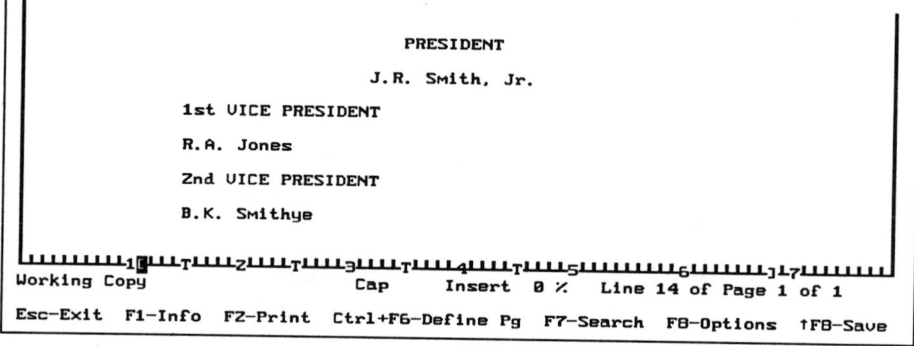

3. Press the arrow keys to move the cursor to the location as shown:

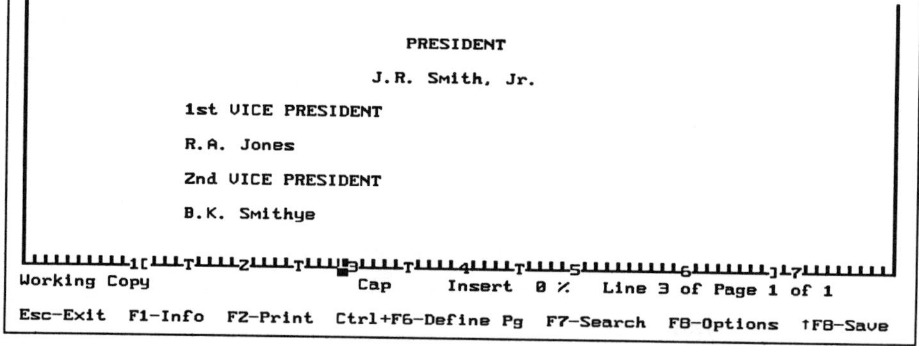

4. Press **F8**. The Options Menu is displayed.
5. Type **D** (Draw) and press **Return**. The draw mode is invoked.
6. Press the arrow keys to draw a box around PRESIDENT and J. R. Smith, Jr.
7. Press **F10** when finished drawing the first box.

8. Use the same sequence of moving the cursor, pressing **F8**, typing **D**, and drawing using the cursor control keys to construct boxes around the other two groups of words. Press **F10** after drawing each individual box.

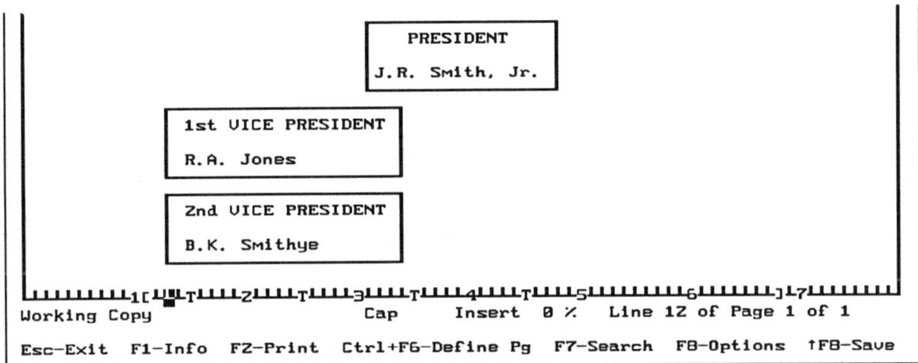

Now, again using the same techniques described in Step 8, connect the boxes to produce results as shown in the following illustration.

NOTE

If you made a mistake while drawing, press F8 and use the cursor control keys to track over the line in error, thus erasing it as you go. To start drawing again, press F8.

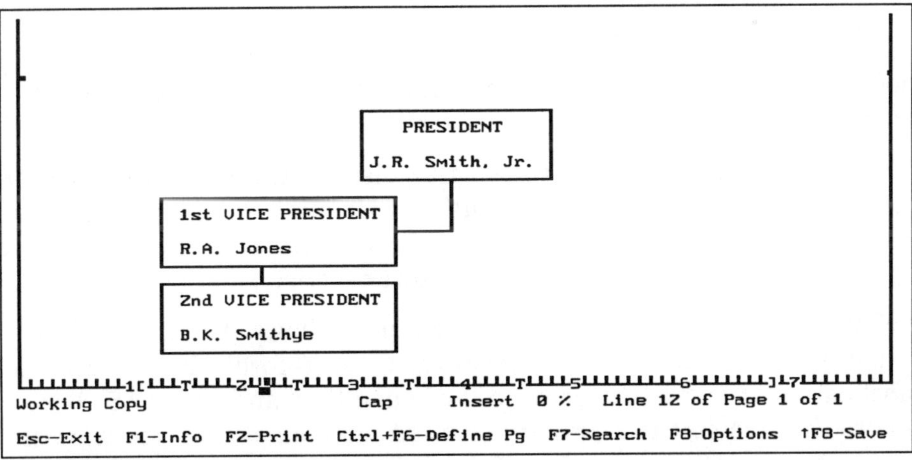

9. When you have completed drawing lines, press **F10** or **Esc** to exit from the draw mode.
10. Return to the Main Menu without saving the document to disk.
11. Turn to Module 47 to continue the learning sequence.

Module 29
EDIT A FORM

DESCRIPTION

Editing a form includes retrieving a form (or several forms) and changing any of the information contained in the fields.

Retrieving the form(s) that you want to edit is the first step. Starting at the Q&A Main Menu, the cursor is located at F - File. Pressing Return displays the File Menu. Typing S on the File Menu results in a prompt message requesting the name of the file. After entering the name of the file and pressing Return, the Retrieve Spec screen for the file is displayed.

Press F10 if you are retrieving all forms in the file. Otherwise, specify the retrieve criteria by using the arrow keys to move the cursor to the first field for which you want to designate a retrieve specification. Enter retrieve information and press F10. Using the arrow keys, move the cursor to any appropriate field for which you want to specify retrieve criteria. Again, enter any additional retrieve information. For example, if you want to retrieve all forms containing the Company name of Smith, move the cursor to the Company Name field and type Smith.

Additionally, if you want to retrieve all forms having a company name of Smith and located in San Antonio, Texas, enter the second retrieve specification of San Antonio, Texas, in the address field.

After specifying retrieve criteria, pressing F8 displays the Sort Spec screen for the file. If you want to display the forms in ascending or descending order, as determined by a particular field, the Sort Spec screen is used. Refer to Module 86 for detailed instructions for specifying sort criteria.

A brief summary of how to specify sort criteria follows. Move the cursor to the field that you want to sort. For example, to sort forms by a name field in alphabetical order, move the cursor to the Name field and type 1AS. The one (1) designates that the sort is a primary sort. AS designates that you want the sort performed by ascending order. Specifying DS designates a descending order sort is requested.

APPLICATIONS

Editing forms is a vital part of keeping your databases updated. The ability to choose specific forms for updating is even more valuable. This means that you do not spend extra time searching through every form in the database. Designating a retrieve specification (e.g., company, customer, city, zip code, last name, etc.) and a sort specification (primary and/or secondary sort) leads you directly to your forms requiring revision or updating.

TYPICAL OPERATION

In this illustration, search and retrieve certain forms, update them appropriately, and save the updated file. Begin at the Q&A Main Menu.

1. At the Q&A Main Menu, the cursor is located at F - File. Press **Return**. The File Menu is displayed.
2. Type **S**, then type **CUSTOMER** and press **Return**. The Retrieve Spec screen for the file is displayed.

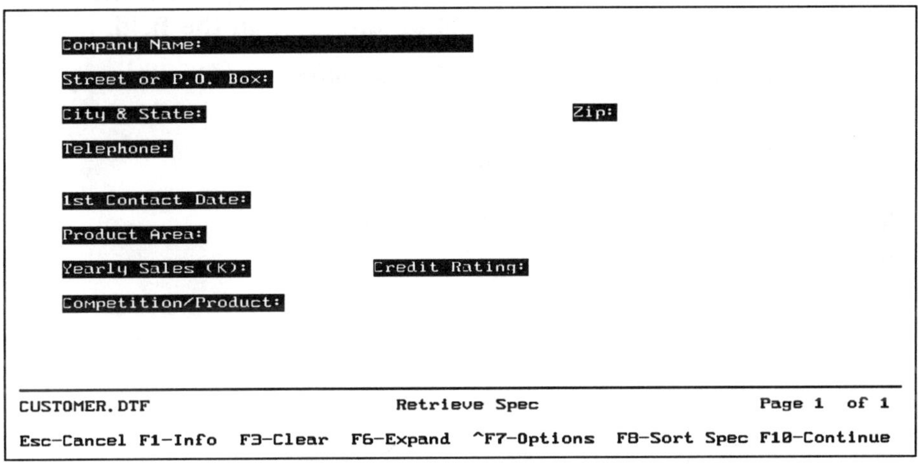

3. Use the **Arrow** or **Tab** keys to move the cursor to any field for which you want to designate a retrieve specification.

For example, if you want to retrieve all forms having the city DENVER, move the cursor to the City field and type DENVER. You can enter as many retrieve specifications as wanted in fields on a form.

4. Press **F8**. The Sort Spec screen is displayed. The screen looks the same as the Retrieve Spec screen except for the screen title.

5. Press the **Arrow** or **Tab** keys to move the cursor to any field for which you want to designate a sort specification.

For example, if you want to retrieve all of the forms having the city of DENVER with a specific Zip code sorted in descending order, type 1 DS in the Zip code field.

6. Press **F10** to begin the search. If no forms are found matching the retrieve and sort specifications, a prompt message is displayed.

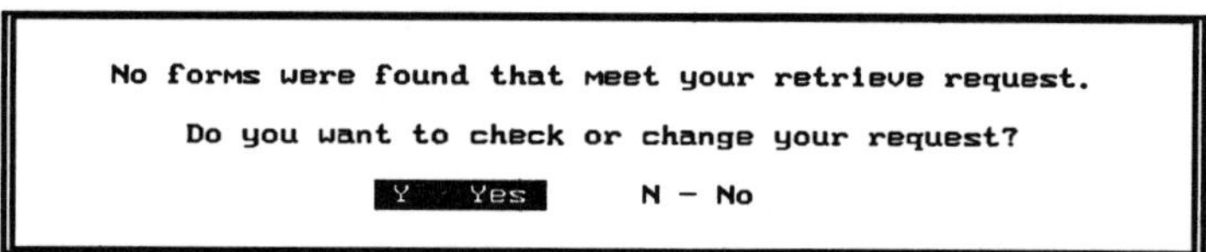

Otherwise, the first form meeting the retrieve and sort specifications is displayed.

7. Press the arrow or **Tab** keys to move the cursor to any field where a change is wanted and type over the information displayed in the field.
8. Press **F10** to display the next form. Repeat Step 7 to edit as many forms as you want.
9. Save the edited file. Return to the Main Menu.
10. Turn to Module 15 to continue the learning sequence.

Module 30
EDIT LOOKUP TABLE

DESCRIPTION

Lookup tables can be created to contain just about any reference information that you want to retrieve at some later time. These tables should contain only frequently used information. This module describes how to create an edit lookup table.

An edit lookup table is composed of a key column which contains the name of any item you are looking up. A key can be the name of a state if the edit lookup table is being used for postal rates. A key can be a part number, a person's name, or just about anything that you want — as long as it is the name of an item or person.

In addition to the key column, an edit lookup table contains a maximum of four data columns. Columns in the lookup table hold the various information related to each key.

Lookup tables are used in conjunction with the LOOKUP commands. There are three LOOKUP commands: Lookup, @LOOKUP, and @XLOOKUP. Refer to Module 76, Programming Words, for more details on LOOKUP.

You can create an edit lookup table for each database. The size of the lookup table is dependent upon the amount of memory in your computer. A 512K RAM system can accommodate a lookup table of about 600 lines or approximately 64,000 characters total. If a table is filling up as you create it, Q&A displays a warning message. After the display of the warning message, you may enter only about 1000 more characters.

At the Q&A Main Menu, select the File function by typing F. From the displayed File Menu, choose D to display the Design Menu. At the Design Menu, typing C displays a prompt message requesting the name of the database for which you want to create an edit lookup table. The Customize Menu is displayed. On the Customize Menu, choose E to enter the Edit Lookup Table function. A formatted table is displayed. After entering various "key" parameters and related values, pressing F10 saves the table and returns you to the Customize Menu. Pressing Esc a few times returns you to the Q&A Main Menu.

Once you have created a lookup table, there will be times when you want to add, change, or delete information. Remember the following tips for editing a table:

To delete a row — Press Shift-F4. Q&A deletes the row, moves the table up into the blank and creates a new blank row at the end of the table.

To insert a row — Position the cursor under the first character in the "Key" column, press the Ins (Insert) key and press Return. Q&A inserts a blank line in the table at the cursor position and moves all subsequent lines down.

To navigate within a table — Use the cursor navigation keys. However, if you are not in the insert mode, pressing Return moves the cursor to the beginning of the next line. If you are in the "insert mode" (Insert key pressed) and the cursor is located at the first character of the "Key" column, pressing Return inserts a blank row. Lookup tables can be constructed to contain freight rates (by zones), postal rates (by zones), weight or volume information by part numbers for a manufacturing operation, or standard delivery times for orders placed to certain vendors. Conversion factors used frequently in calculations are perfect candidates for inclusion in lookup tables.

TYPICAL OPERATION

In this illustration, enter the File function and create an edit lookup table. Begin at the Q&A Main Menu.

1. At the Q&A Main Menu, the cursor is located at F - File. Press **Return**. The File Menu is displayed.
2. Type **D**. The Design Menu is displayed. The cursor is located at D - Design a new file.
3. Type **C**. A prompt message is displayed requesting the filename for the file for which you want to create a lookup table.
4. Type **CUSTOMER** and press **Return**. The Customize Menu is displayed.
5. Type **E** to display the lookup table.

KEY	1	2	3	4

CUSTOMER.DTF   Lookup Table   Page 1 of 1

Esc-Cancel   F6-Expand   PgUp-Previous page   PgDn-Next page   F10-Continue

At the lookup table screen, you can type terms for "keys" and corresponding values in columns 1 through 4. It is not necessary to use every column; you can use only those needed to define lookup values. For example, you can place a list of cities or states in the Key column, sales tax information in column 1, postal zip codes in column 2, travel mileage from your location in column 3, etc.

Press Tab, cursor movement keys, and Return, to maneuver to locations where you want to type keys or values.

A typical table containing city sales taxes could appear as follows:

KEY	1	2	3	4
Little Rock	.07			
N. Little Rock	.065			
Sherwood	.04			
Jacksonville	.075			
Cabot	.075			
Maumelle	.075			
Lonoke	.055			
Conway	.05			

CUSTOMER.DTF Lookup Table Page 1 of 1

Esc-Cancel F6-Expand PgUp-Previous page PgDn-Next page F10-Continue

6. Press **F10**. The prepared edit lookup table for the specified database is saved. The Customize Menu is displayed.
7. Return to the Main Menu.
8. Turn to Module 75 to continue the learning sequence.

Module 31
EDITING A MACRO FILE

DESCRIPTION

Macro files are created in the Write function. A macro is a text file that can be edited just as though it were a document. Q&A requires that each macro conform to a specified definition. This definition can be compared to the syntax required in computer program commands.

Each macro has a start code, an identifier, keystroke actions, and an end code. The start code is <begdef>. The identifier is any character or function key on the keyboard. The identifier can be entered with Ctrl, Alt, or Shift. The macro text file contains all of the actions that you want the macro to perform. The end code is <enddef> and defines the end of the macro sequence. The Left Arrow (<) and Right Arrow (>) symbols specify to Q&A that the enclosed keystrokes represent special keys or codes. If the arrows are omitted, Q&A interprets the keystrokes literally and considers them as part of the text.

If you use keyboard keys such as Up Arrow, Backspace, Return, Shift, they must be enclosed within Left Arrow (<) and Right Arrow (>) symbols. The following table lists the keys and key combinations that are used with Shift, Unshift, Alt, and Ctrl.

Key	Shift	Unshift	Alt	Ctrl
A			<alta>	<ctrla> *
B			<altb>	<ctrlb>
C			<altc>	<ctrlc> *
D			<altd>	<ctrld> *
E			<alte>	<ctrle> *
F			<altf>	<ctrlf> *
G			<altg>	<ctrlg> *
H			<alth>	<bks> *
I			<alti>	<tab> *
J			<altj>	<ctrlent>
K			<altk>	<ctrlk>
L			<altl>	<ctrll>
M			<altm>	<enter> *
N			<altn>	<ctrln>
O			<alto>	<ctrlo>
P			<altp>	<ctrlp>
Q			<altq>	<ctrlq>

Key	Shift	Unshift	Alt	Ctrl
R			<altr>	<ctrlr>*
S			<alts>	<ctrls>*
T			<altt>	<ctrlt>*
U			<altu>	<ctrlu>
V			<altv>	<ctrlv>*
W			<altw>	<ctrlw>*
X			<altx>	<ctrlx>
Y			<alty>	<ctrly>*
Z			<altz>	<ctrlz>*
1			<alt1>	
2			<alt2>	
3			<alt3>	
4			<alt4>	
5			<alt5>	
6			<alt6>	
7			<alt7>	
8			<alt8>	
9			<alt9>	
0			<alt0>	
-			<ctrl->	
=				
[				<esc>*
]				<ctrl]>
;				
'				
`				
\				
,	<caps,>			
.	<caps.>			
/				
Esc	<esc>*	<esc>*		
Tab	<capstab>*	<tab>*		
Bksp	<bks>*	<bks>*		<ctrlbks>*
Enter	<enter>*	<enter>*		<ctrlent>
*				<ctrlprt>*
F1	<capsf1>*	<f1>*	<altf1>	<ctrlf1>
F2	<capsf2>*	<f2>*	<altf2>	<ctrlf2>*
F3	<capsf3>*	<f3>*	<altf3>	<ctrlf3>
F4	<capsf4>*	<f4>*	<altf4>	<ctrlf4>
F5	<capsf5>*	<f5>*	<altf5>*	<ctrlf5>*
F6	<capsf6>*	<f6>*	<altf6>	<ctrlf6>*
F7	<capsf7>*	<f7>*	<altf7>	<ctrlf7>
F8	<capsf8>*	<f8>*	<altf8>	<ctrlf8>
F9	<capsf9>*	<f9>*	<altf9>	<ctrlf9>
F10	<capsf10>*	<f10>*	<altf10>	<ctrlf10>
Home	<home>*			<ctrlhom>*

Key	Shift	Unshift	Alt	Ctrl
PgUp		<pgup>*		<ctrlpgu>*
Right Arrow		<rgt>*		<ctrlrgt>
Spacebar				
Left Arrow		<lft>*		<ctrllft>
End		<end>*		<ctrlend>*
Down Arrow		<dn>*		
PgDn		<pgdn>*		<ctrlpgd>*
Ins		<ins>*		
Del		<del>*		
-				
+				

* These keys are used by Q&A. Avoid using these keys as identifiers. If no key code is shown, type the key or key combination within the macro definition; otherwise, special key coding is required.

If you use a key combination that is used by Q&A, a message is displayed warning you before you are allowed to proceed.

APPLICATIONS

An individual macro can be used to produce certain results within a Write document. A complete macro file can also be created to produce specified results when working in a Write document. The identifiers (i.e., keystrokes used in combination with Alt, Ctrl, Shift, or Unshift) are the keystroke sequences that initiate the macro to perform the defined operation.

Editing a macro enables you to access the source file for the macro keystrokes and modify the keystroke sequences. For example, names and addresses can be defined within macros. The complete body of a letter, customer notice, contract, or report can be programmed into a macro. Each time the macro is initiated by typing the identifier keystrokes, the full text defined in the macro is typed automatically for you within the Write document with which you are working. By editing the macro file, you can easily modify the keystroke sequences without having to completely recreate a new macro containing the new keystroke sequences that you want.

TYPICAL OPERATION

In this illustration, identify the steps necessary to create a macro. Define a macro that produces a notice to inform a customer base of a rate change for services. Edit the macro file. Begin at the Q&A Main Menu.

1. At the Q&A Main Menu, the cursor is located at F - File. Type **W**. The Write Menu is displayed. The cursor is located at T - Type/Edit.
2. Type **T**. A Working Copy (blank) screen for a new document is displayed.

3. Press **Shift-F2**. The Macro Menu is displayed.
4. Type **D** and a message at the bottom of the screen requests the macro identifier.
5. Press **Alt**, type **A**, and press **Return**. Alt-A is the identifier for the macro. When you are working within a document, each time you press Alt with the character A, the macro is invoked. A combination of keys used by Q&A for other purposes was not used.
6. Type the following text.

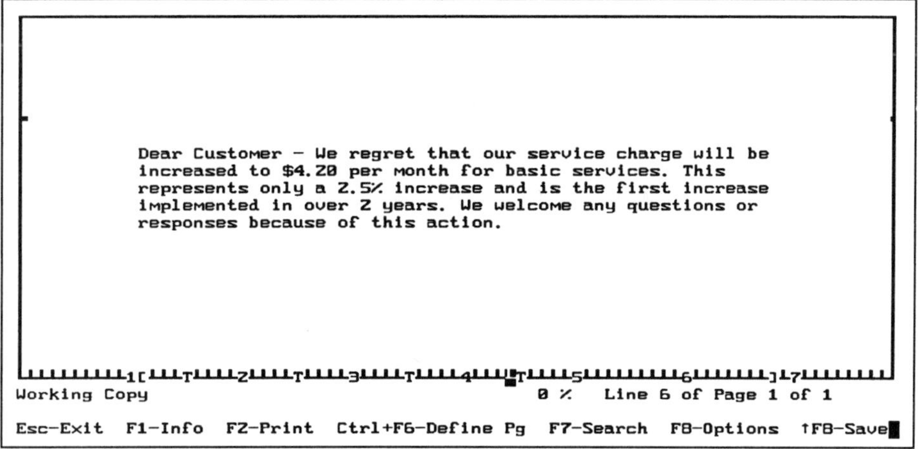

7. Press **Shift-F2**. A prompt message is displayed requesting the name to be assigned to the macro file.
8. Type **MACRO.TXT** and press **Return**. The macro is saved to the specified filename.
9. Press **Esc**. The Write Menu is displayed.
10. Press **Esc**. A prompt message is displayed warning you that the Working Copy of the document has not been saved. The cursor is located on N - No.
11. Type **Y**. The Q&A Main Menu is displayed. To edit the macro proceed to Step 12.
12. Type **W**. The Write Menu is displayed.
13. Type **G**. A prompt message is displayed requesting the name of the file to be edited.

14 Type **MACRO.TXT** and press **Return**. The Import Document Menu is displayed. The cursor is located on ASCII.

15. Press **Return**. The marco file is displayed on the screen. You can move the cursor to any location within the file and make editing changes. It is necessary to use the macro coding conventions as contained in the file (i.e., <sp> represents a blank space, <enter> represents a carriage return or line feed, etc.).

16. After you have made editing changes, press **Shift-F2**. The Macro Menu is displayed.

17. Type **S**. A message is displayed requesting the name of the file under which you want the macro to be saved. MACRO.TXT is the default displayed.

18. Press **Return**. The macro, with changes, is saved to disk.

19. Press **Esc**. The Write Menu is displayed.

20. Press **Esc**. The Q&A Main Menu is displayed.

21. Turn to Module 24 to continue the learning sequence.

Module 32
ENHANCE DOCUMENT TEXT

DESCRIPTION

Enhancing text in a document consists of identifying words or strings of text that you want printed in boldface, italics, superscript, subscript, strikeout, font, or underlined type. Enhancements can be used in any combination to improve the overall appearance of a document. This enhanced appearance is used primarily for emphasizing various types of text to a reader.

Text enhancements are made to a document during an edit session when creating a document, or during a later edit session to update the document. Of course, while in an edit session you are in the Type/Edit mode of the Write function of Q&A which is accessed through the Write Menu.

Begin by moving the cursor to the first character of any string of text that you want to enhance.

By pressing Shift-F6, type style selection is displayed at the bottom of the screen.

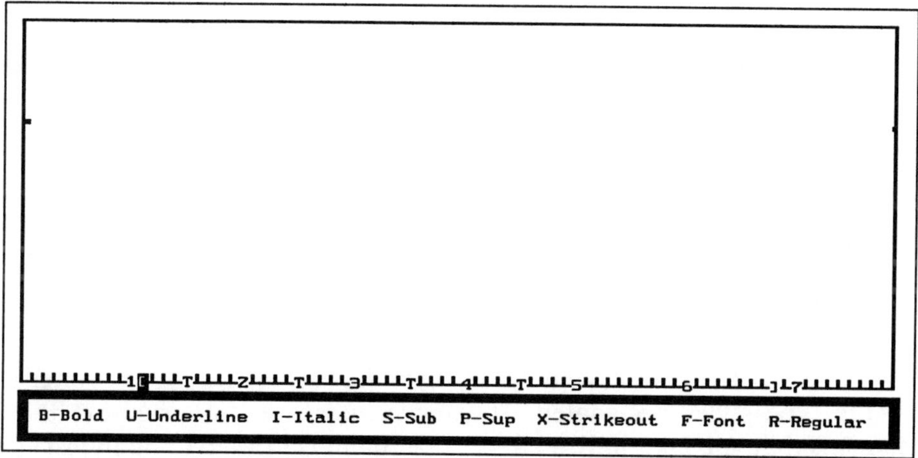

Select and type a code (B, U, I, S, P, X, F, or R) for the type style that you want. If you select F (fonts), the font menu is displayed at the bottom of the screen.

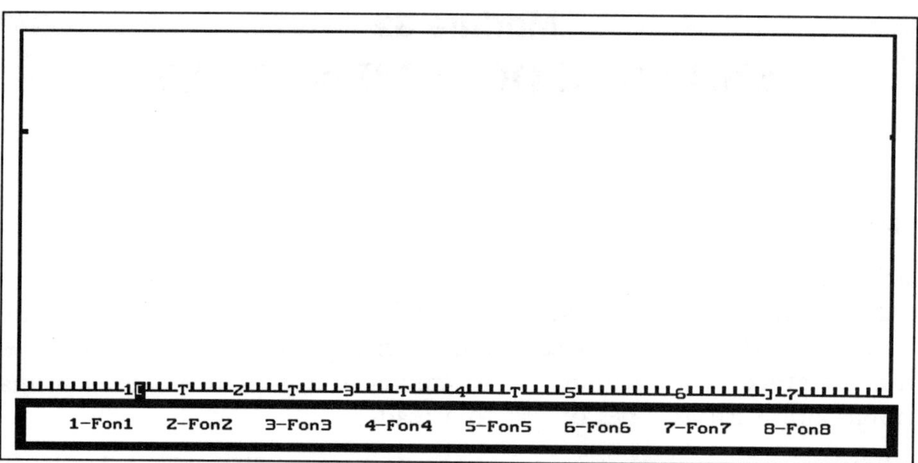

Fonts must be installed before you can assign them to text in a document. Refer to Module 73, Printer Installation, for instructions on how to install fonts.

If you edit text or add text to an enhanced text area, the new text is enhanced in the same way as the existing text.

Move the cursor to the last character of the string of text to be enhanced. Notice that the text selected is highlighted as you move the cursor. Pressing F10 completes the enhancement function.

If you want combinations of enhanced text (boldface, italics, etc.) all in the same document or in the same block of text, you must repeat the procedure for each type style wanted for each text string.

The enhanced text displays differently from the rest of the text on the screen. To verify whether or not text is enhanced in some way, move the cursor across it. On the status line at the bottom of the screen, each occurrence of enhanced text causes its status to display. That is, if text is italic, "Italic" is displayed on the status line as the cursor moves through it.

For text to print with the enhancements that you have specified, your printer must support the type styles designated. If your printer does not support the text enhancements that you have indicated, the document is printed in plain text. Laser printers usually support all forms of text enhancements. Most dot matrix printers support enhanced print features. Some daisy wheel printers support enhanced printing such as boldface, superscript, subscript, and underline. Refer to the user manual for your printer to verify enhanced print features available.

APPLICATIONS

Text printed with enhanced features is used to highlight or emphasize certain text in a document.

Boldface type or use of fonts is usually used to emphasize document titles, section headings, paragraph headings, notes, cautions, and warnings.

Italic type is used to designate quoted passages, titles of books, magazines, newspapers, names of ships, aircraft, and manned spacecraft. You may italicize words for emphasis, but italics are not normally used for this purpose.

Superscript type is used mostly in mathematical expressions. Subscripts are also used in mathematical expressions; however, they are more commonly used to designate footnotes within text.

Underlining text is another way to emphasize specified text. It is also used to designate book titles.

TYPICAL OPERATION

In this illustration, enter the Write function to create a sample document and enhance the text in the body of the document. Either print the document or just notice how enhanced text is displayed differently on the screen. Exit from the document without saving the document to disk. Begin at the Q&A Main Menu.

1. Open a new document and type the following text.

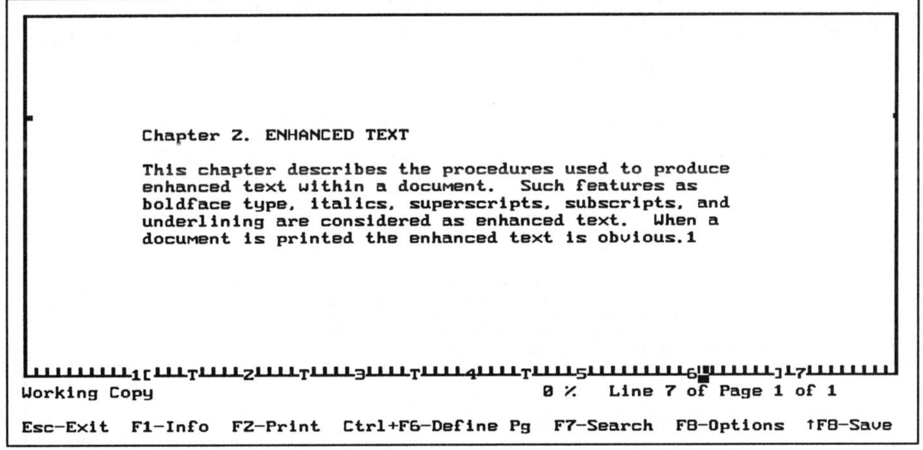

2. Move the cursor to the first character in the title and press. A list of text enhancement options is displayed at the bottom of the screen.

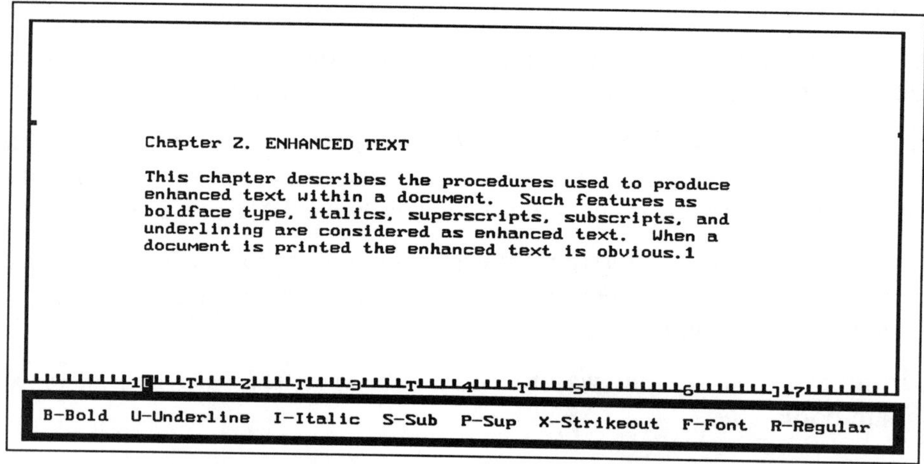

3. Type **B** (Boldface code). The first character is highlighted. A message is displayed at the bottom of the screen telling you to use arrow keys to select the text that you want boldfaced. If other enhancements are selected, the message corresponds to the selected enhancement.

4. Press **Right Arrow** to move the cursor to the end of the title line. Notice that the line of text is highlighted as you move the cursor to the right.

5. Press **F10**. The designated text is highlighted or enhanced on the screen in a different color to indicate it is boldface type. If you print the document, the chapter title is printed in boldface type.

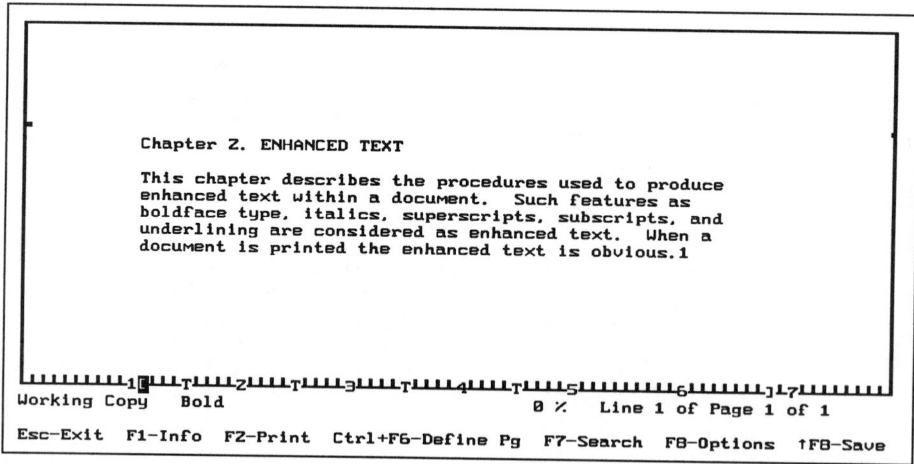

To enhance other text in the same paragraph, it is necessary to repeat the procedure. This time, designate a different type code.

6. Move the cursor to the numeral one (1) at the end of the paragraph, and press **Shift-F6**.
7. Type **S** (Subscript code). The number "1" is highlighted. The message displayed at the bottom of the screen requests that you use arrow keys to select text that is to be designated as superscript.
8. Press **F10**. Notice that the number 1 is now enhanced text (displayed in a different color). If you print the document, it appears properly as a subscript.

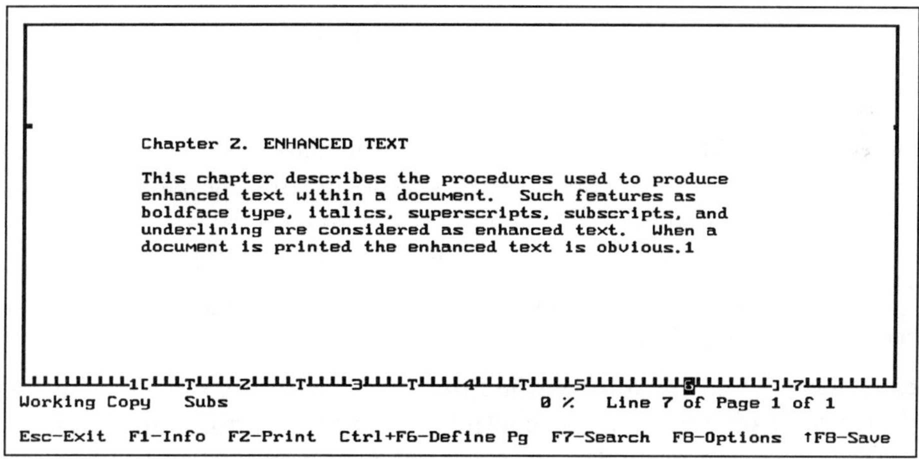

If you want, practice using each of the eight text enhanced print selections. Refer to Module 71 if you want to print the document to see the enhancements in a printed copy.

9. Return to the Main Menu without saving the document.
10. Turn to Module 53 to continue the learning sequence.

Module 33
ENTER DATA ON A FORM

DESCRIPTION

Entering data on a form involves typing information into each of the fields previously designed on a form. Module 37 describes how to design a form. *Field labels* are designated and an appropriate number of spaces are left for information related to the fields. In Module 6, you assigned an information type for each of the fields and set Global Format Options. Now, you are ready to enter information on the form and thus create a file or database.

The process is very easy. At the Q&A Main Menu, select F to display the File Menu. At the File Menu, select A and enter a filename for the database in which you want to add data to display the very first form. Adding data is accomplished just by typing information in the blank areas reserved for each field. After entering data in a field, pressing Tab or Return moves the cursor to the next field.

A field may be left blank just by not typing any information in that field and immediately pressing Return.

When designing a form, you specified the type of information for each field. As you enter data on forms, Q&A controls the type of information that you are allowed to enter. For example, you can only enter numbers and certain symbols in a field designed as a numeric field. This numeric field must be a field that is used for calculation. If you try to enter any information other than a date in a field designated for a date, or try to enter a date formatted differently than the design, a warning message is displayed.

This date can't be reformatted — is it a valid date? Is the field too small? You cannot always enter any information in any field; Q&A controls the type of information that you are allowed to enter based on the information type code entered when the form was designed.

EDITING A FORM As you are entering data in forms, you may need to return to a previous field and change an entry. The process is called *editing* the form. The following table lists the keys for moving the cursor so editing operations can be performed.

Key	Cursor Movement
Up Arrow	Up to next fields on the form
Down Arrow	Next line down
Right Arrow	Next character to right
Left Arrow	Previous character to left
Home (1st press)	First character in field
Home (2nd press)	First character, first field, of current form
F9	Previous form
F10	Next form
Tab	Beginning of next form
End (1st press)	Last character position of current field (can be a blank)
End (2nd press)	First character of last field
Shift-Tab	First character of previous field
Return	First character of next field
Ctrl-Home	First form in file (cursor located at first field, first character)
Ctrl-Left Arrow	Previous word in field
Ctrl-Right Arrow	Next word in field
Ctrl-End	Last form in file

DELETING A FORM Any form can be deleted at your discretion as you are entering data. Pressing F3 causes a prompt message to display:

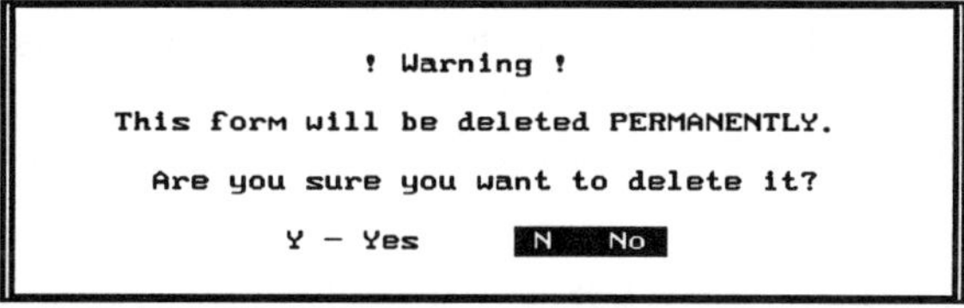

The cursor is located on N - No. Pressing Return permits you to cancel the delete request. Typing Y completes the delete operation. A blank form is displayed in place of a deleted form.

DUPLICATING FORM INFORMATION As you enter information on forms, you may find that most information on a previous form can be duplicated (copied) to save time. For example, if you are adding data to forms all requiring the same city, zip code, telephone area code, etc., you can duplicate those items from the previous form.

DUPLICATING FIELD INFORMATION Information from individual fields on a form can be copied from a previously displayed form. As you move the cursor to each field on a new form, you can press F5 at any field to automatically enter (duplicate) the same field information from the previous form. The cursor must be located in the field being copied. Field information can only be duplicated from the form immediately preceding the current form being displayed. If you have displayed several forms in succession using the F9 and F10 keys, the duplicate operation will not be successful.

DUPLICATING ENTIRE FORMS You can duplicate an entire form (previously displayed) by pressing Shift-F5. The entire form is copied to a blank form at the end of the current form file.

AUTOMATIC INSERTION OF DATE AND TIME The current date and/or time can be automatically typed into the date/time field by pressing the following keys:

Current date: Ctrl-F5

Current time: Alt-F5

This option is valid only if your computer has an internal clock that keeps the system date and time.

PRINTING A FORM CURRENTLY DISPLAYED While entering data on a form you can easily print a copy of any form currently displayed on the screen. With a selected form displayed on the screen, press F2. The File Print Options Menu is displayed. You can change values displayed or press F2 and print the displayed form. If you press the Esc key at the File Print Options Menu, a prompt message allows you to cancel the print operation or return to the File Print Options Menu.

PRINT ALL FORMS JUST ADDED Press Ctrl-Home to display the first form that you added during an edit session. Press Ctrl-F2 and the File Options Menu is displayed. You can change the values displayed or press the F10 key to begin printing of all forms added during an edit session. Printing can be stopped by pressing the Esc key or by pressing the F2 key to redefine the print options.

APPLICATIONS

Entering data on a form is the way in which you build a file or database. Designing a form allocates the space for data to be entered into one or many forms. Adding data onto the forms in each of the fields is the actual building of a form file. The file stays in the same order as you created it unless you specify otherwise (e.g., you can sort the forms into another order). Refer to Module 86 for information on sorting forms.

TYPICAL OPERATION

In this illustration, retrieve an existing form design (database), add information to fields on several forms, then save the forms. Begin at the Q&A Main Menu.

1. At the Q&A Main Menu, the cursor is located at F - File. Press **Return**. The File Menu is displayed.
2. Type **A**. A message is displayed at the bottom of the screen that prompts you to enter the name of the file in which you want to enter data.
3. Type **INVNTRY** and press **Return**. The first form of the file is displayed with the cursor located at the first field.
4. Type information into each field on the form. Press **Tab** or **Return** to move the cursor through the fields. At the last field press **F10** to move to the next form. Repeat Step 4 for as many forms as you want to complete.

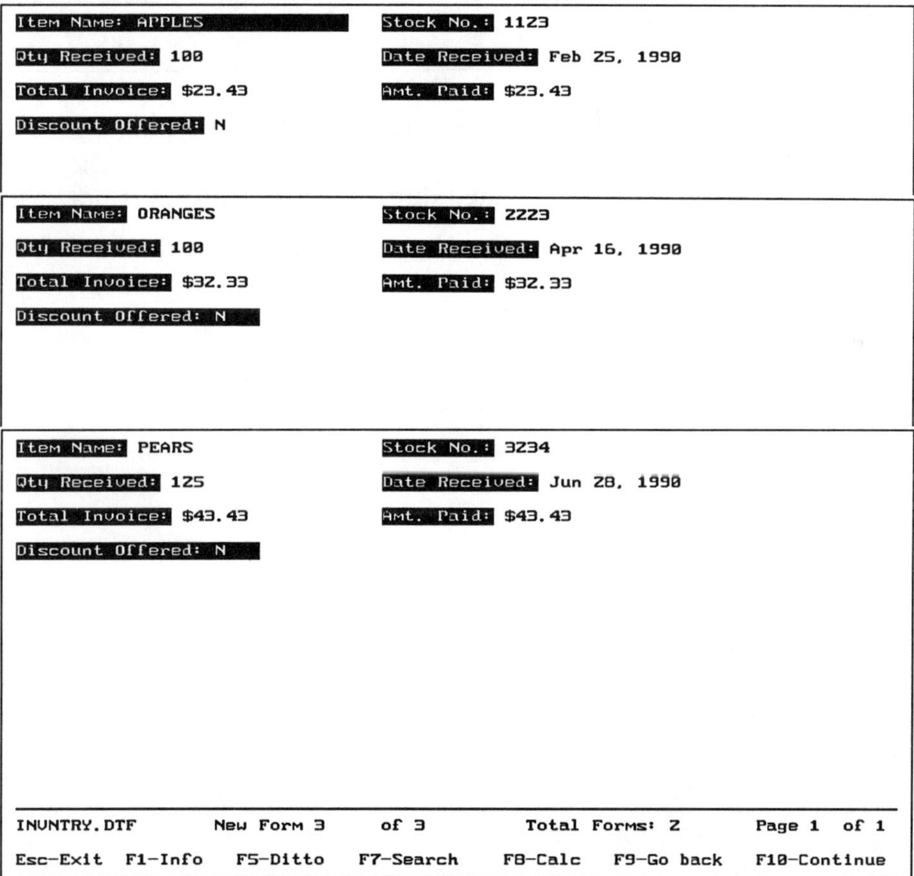

5. After you have entered data for the last form, press **F10** to display a blank form. If you press Esc while data is being entered on forms, a prompt message is displayed warning you that the form has not been saved.

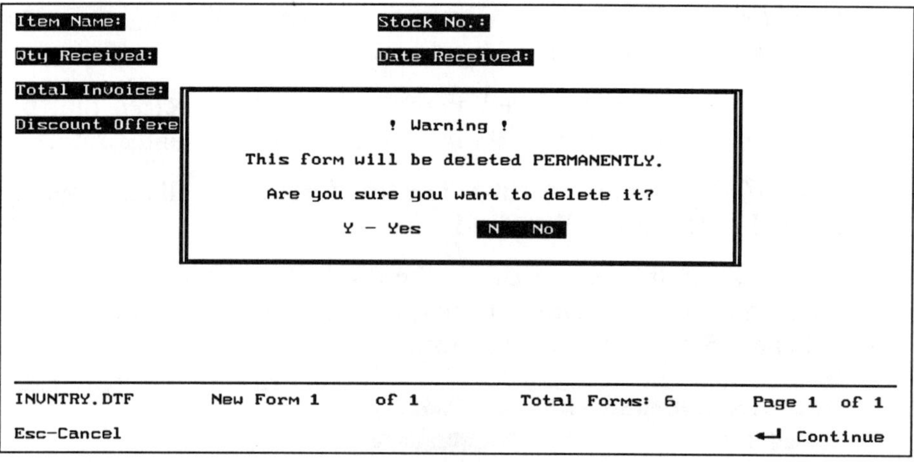

Typing N permits you to return to the form. Typing N and typing F10 saves the form and displays the next blank screen. Typing Y exits you from the form and displays the File Menu, the form created during the edit session is not saved.

6. Press **Shift-F10** to save the completed forms to disk. The File Menu is displayed.
7. Press **Esc**. The Q&A Main Menu is displayed.
8. Turn to Module 29 to continue the learning sequence.

Module 34
ENTER/EDIT DOCUMENT TEXT

DESCRIPTION

Entering or editing document text is a word processing operation and is performed in the Write function. The procedure for entering document text is performed in an *edit session* in a *Working Copy* of a document. An edit session is conducted through the *Type/Edit function*. The Type/Edit function can also be called an edit function or editor. Throughout this book, reference is made to "edit session" when discussing entering or editing text.

Editing document text consists of entering new text or making changes to existing text. Editing includes moving, copying, deleting, overtyping, or typing new information.

To begin an edit session in a new document, the Write function is selected at the Q&A Main Menu by typing W. The cursor is located at T - Type/Edit. An edit session is started by pressing Return at the Write Menu to invoke the Q&A editor. A Working Copy (blank) screen is displayed waiting for you to enter text. The designation "Working Copy" displayed at the bottom left of the screen indicates that the document is a new document that has not yet been named or saved to disk.

ENTERING TEXT At this point, you can begin typing to enter text. Q&A automatically wraps a word (called *word wrap*) to the next line if there is not enough space for it to fit at the end of any line. This means that you do not have to worry about hyphenating words.

While entering text you can type over existing text or insert text. As you are typing new text over a blank area on the screen you are actually typing over blanks. If you want to change text that was previously typed at the top of the screen, move the cursor to any location on that existing text and type over characters, words, etc. The old characters are replaced by the new ones that you type. This is called "overtyping" or "strikeover."

BASIC EDITING Simple editing functions include *Insert* and *Delete*. Text can be inserted simply by pressing the Ins key. The cursor displays as a highlighted square and the word "INSERT" appears on the status line at the bottom of the screen. Any text that you type is inserted at the cursor location. Text following the cursor moves to the right as you type the inserted characters. When finished typing the inserted characters, words, phrases, or paragraphs, press Ins to terminate the insert function.

If your computer has an internal clock, or if you have correctly set the date and time when you turned on your computer, you can embed the correct time and date into any document. The actual date and time does not display on the screen, but is printed when the document is printed.

Type: *@DATE(n)* for current date, and

@TIME(n) for current time.
Where: n = the display format (ex., if n = 1 the date format is: Sep 21,1989.

Standard U.S. and international date and time formats are:

Date formats:

1 - Jun 10, 1989	9 - June 10, 1989
2 - 10 Jun 1989	10 - 10 June 1989
3 - 6/10/1989	11 - 6-10-89
4 - 10/6/1989	12 - 6-10-1989
5 - 10/6/1989	13 - 06-10-89
6 - 06/10/1989	14 - 06-10-1989
7 - 10/06/89	15 - 10.06.89
8 - 10/06/1989	16 - 10.06.1989
	17 - 1989/06/10

Time formats:

1 - 3:45 pm   2 - 15:45   3 - 15:45

APPLICATIONS

Opening a document is the first step in creating a new document or editing an existing one. Entering text via the editor is the only means that you have of generating a document within Q&A. The editor is the door to creating text input that can be used by the other functions.

Editing text via the editor is also the only means that you have to make changes to existing documents. Entering/editing text is a simple operation, but a most important one.

TYPICAL OPERATION

In this example, begin at the Q&A Main Menu. Enter the Write function and begin an edit session. Enter text into a Working Copy of a new document. Perform simple edit functions including inserting characters and deleting characters. Exit from the document without saving it to disk.

At this time do not be concerned about setting margins or page layout. Let the default margin and tab settings remain in control. You will learn how to define page layout in Module 63.

1. At the Q&A Main Menu, type **W** to display the Write Menu. The cursor is located at T - Type/Edit.
2. Press **Return** to open a Working Copy (blank screen) for a new document.
3. Type the following text:

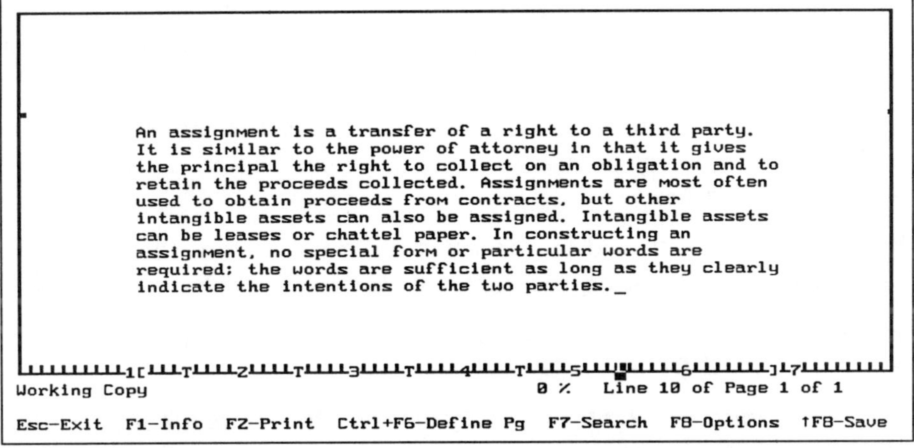

4. Use the arrow keys to move the cursor to the first character in the word "special" as shown:

```
An assignment is a transfer of a right to a third party.
It is similar to the power of attorney in that it gives
the principal the right to collect on an obligation and to
retain the proceeds collected. Assignments are most often
used to obtain proceeds from contracts, but other
intangible assets can also be assigned. Intangible assets
can be leases or chattel paper. In constructing an
assignment, no special form or particular words are
required; the words are sufficient as long as they clearly
indicate the intentions of the two parties.

Working Copy                          0 %   Line 8 of Page 1 of 1

Esc-Exit  F1-Info  F2-Print  Ctrl+F6-Define Pg  F7-Search  F8-Options  ↑F8-Save
```

5. Press **Del**. Notice that the character "s" is deleted. Each time you press the Del key the character at the cursor position is deleted.
6. Press **Del** enough times to delete the remainder of the word "special."
7. Press the arrow keys to move the cursor to the character "I" in the word "Intangible" as shown. Check to ensure that the keyboard is not in the insert mode. "Insert" should not be displayed below the ruler line at the bottom of the screen.
8. Type a lowercase letter **i**. Notice that typing over the capitalized letter with a lowercase letter replaces it with the lowercase letter. This illustrates the "overtype" feature.
9. The cursor is positioned at the letter "n" in the word "intangible." Press **Left Arrow** to reposition the cursor at the letter "i."
10. Press **Ins** to activate the insert mode. Notice the status line at the bottom of the screen; INSERT is displayed.
11. Type the phrase **For example,**. As you type, the letters are inserted into the text; following text moves forward in the document and the new words are entered.

```
An assignment is a transfer of a right to a third party.
It is similar to the power of attorney in that it gives
the principal the right to collect on an obligation and to
retain the proceeds collected. Assignments are most often
used to obtain proceeds from contracts, but other
intangible assets can also be assigned. For example, _
intangible assets can be leases or chattel paper. In
constructing an assignment, no form or particular words
are required; the words are sufficient as long as they
clearly indicate the intentions of the two parties.

Working Copy                          Insert  0 %   Line 6 of Page 1 of 1

Esc-Exit  F1-Info  F2-Print  Ctrl+F6-Define Pg  F7-Search  F8-Options  ↑F8-Save
```

Notice that the cursor is located at the end of the inserted string of text just typed.

12. Press **Esc** to return to the Write Menu.
13. Press **Esc** to exit from the Write Menu. A prompt message is displayed warning you that the Working Copy has not been saved. The cursor is located at N - No.
14. Type **Y** to return to the Q&A Main Menu without saving the document.
15. Turn to Module 82 to continue the learning sequence.

Module 35
EXPORT DATA

DESCRIPTION

The process of transferring Q&A File databases to another standard data format is called *exporting data.* Some common data formats are:

- Standard American National Standard Code for Information Interchange (ASCII)
- Data Interchange Format (DIF)
- dBASE-II
- dBASE-III.

Some application software readily accepts these formats. For example, Q&A File database can be transferred to DIF and then imported by Lotus 1-2-3.

Knowing the name of the data file that you plan to export and selecting U at the Q&A Main Menu displays the Utilities Menu. Selecting E (Export data) on the Utilities Menu displays the Export Menu.

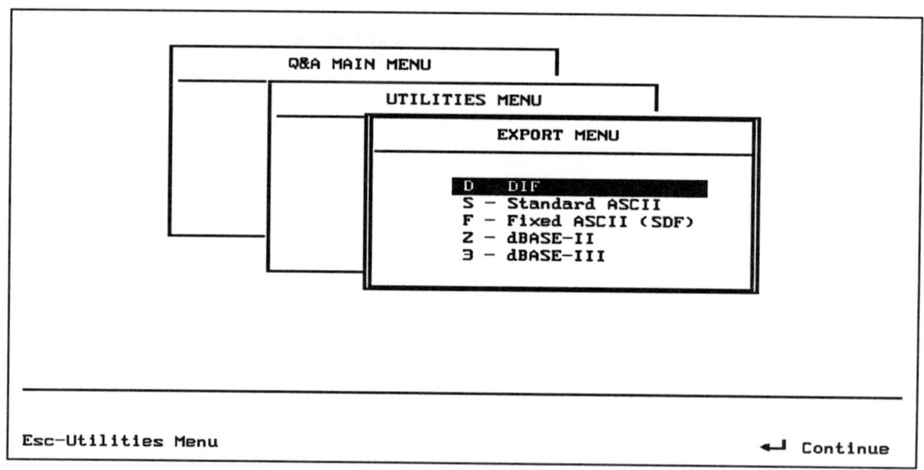

Upon selecting D, S, F, 2, or 3, a prompt message is displayed requesting you to enter the filename. Typing the filename and pressing Return causes display of another prompt message requesting the name of the file to which you want the data exported. Typing the filename and pressing Return causes a Retrieve Spec screen to display. The Retrieve Spec screen is a blank form from the specified file database. The screen permits you to identify all of the fields that you want retrieved.

As shown in the illustration, each field is identified with a number identifying the fields that are to be exported and the exact export order.

You can export a database without specifying a Merge Spec, just by pressing F10 when the Merge Spec screen is displayed. Information in the database is exported exactly in the order of the fields in the Q&A database.

When exporting to an ASCII file, the ASCII Options screen is displayed after exiting from the Merge Spec screen.

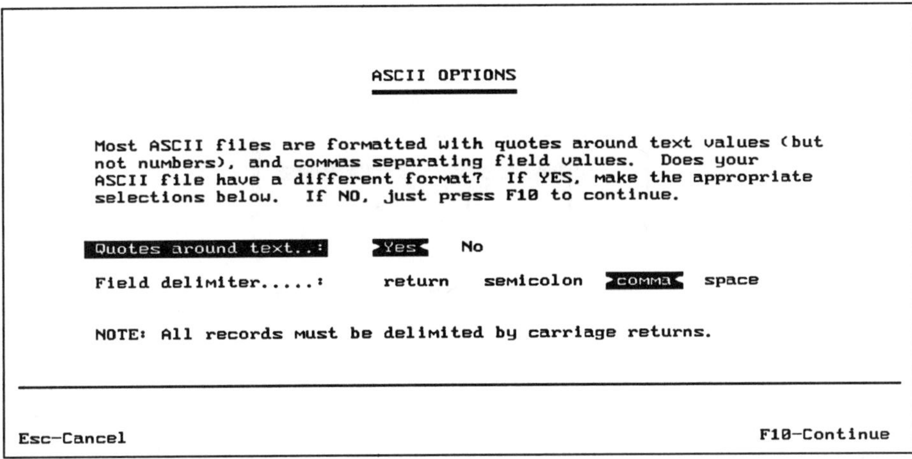

This screen allows you to customize the exported data to fit the import requirements of the accepting application program. Q&A has preset default values for defining ASCII export files. These default values are:

Quotation marks before and after values

Commas as field delimiters

Carriage return/line feed characters are record delimiters.

Pressing F10 at the ASCII Options screen invokes the export of the document. As each form is exported it is displayed on the screen. The Utilities Menu is displayed after the last form is exported.

APPLICATIONS

The ability to transfer or export data files to other application software is extremely convenient. Most computer-sophisticated businesses use a variety of software to perform different tasks. The ability to export data from one software application and import it into another widens your overall per formance and productivity.

TYPICAL OPERATION

In this illustration, access the Utilities Menu and select the choice to export data. Export an entire standard ASCII file accepting ASCII defaults provided by Q&A. After the file is exported, exit from the Utilities Menu to the Q&A Main Menu. Begin at the Q&A Main Menu.

1. Type **U**. The Utilities Menu is displayed.

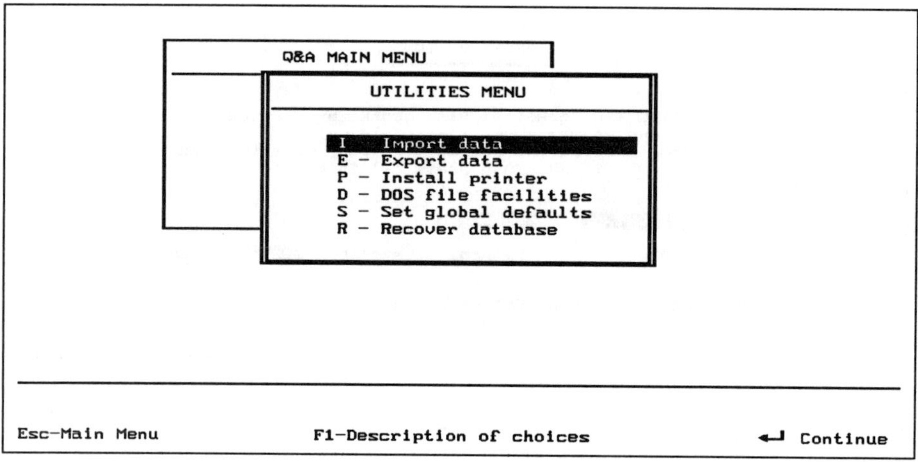

2. Type **E**. The Export Menu is displayed.

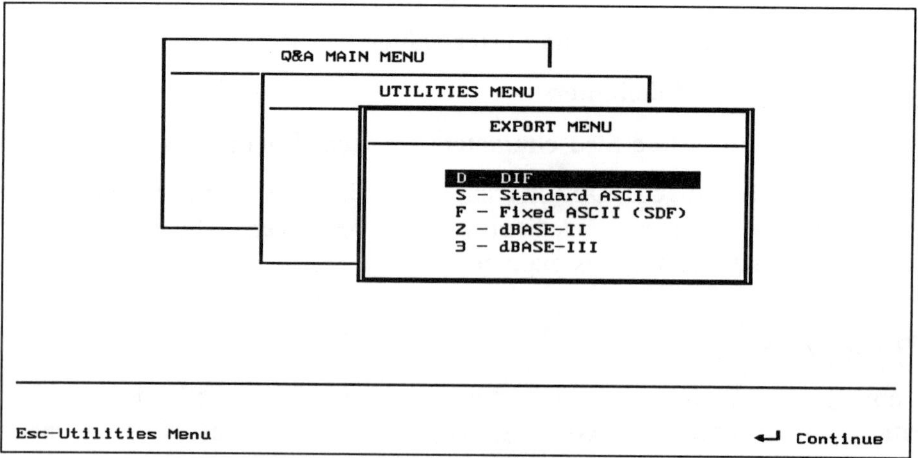

3. Type **S**. A prompt message is displayed requesting you to enter the name of the file that you want to export.
4. Type **CUSTOMER** and press **Return**. A prompt message is displayed requesting you to enter the name of the receiving file.
5. Type **CUSTLIST** and press **Return**. The Retrieve Spec screen for the specified database is displayed.

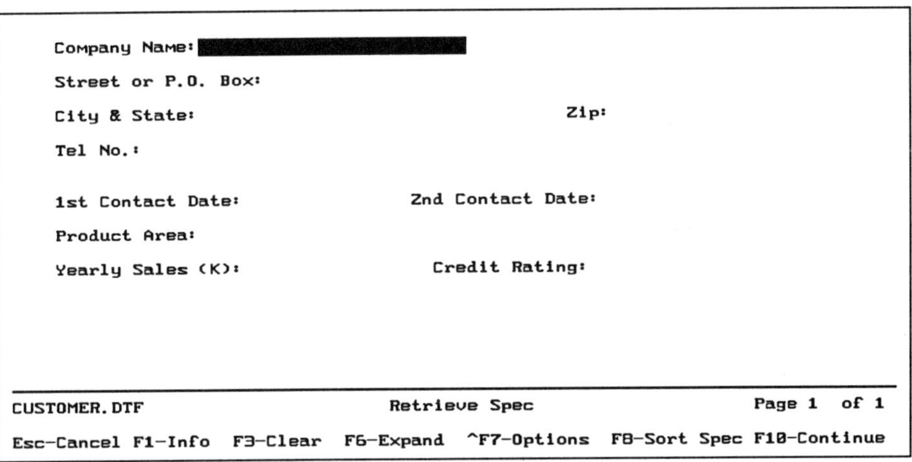

6. Press **F10**. The Merge Spec screen is displayed.
7. Press **F10**. All forms in the database are retrieved for the export operation. The ASCII Options screen is displayed.

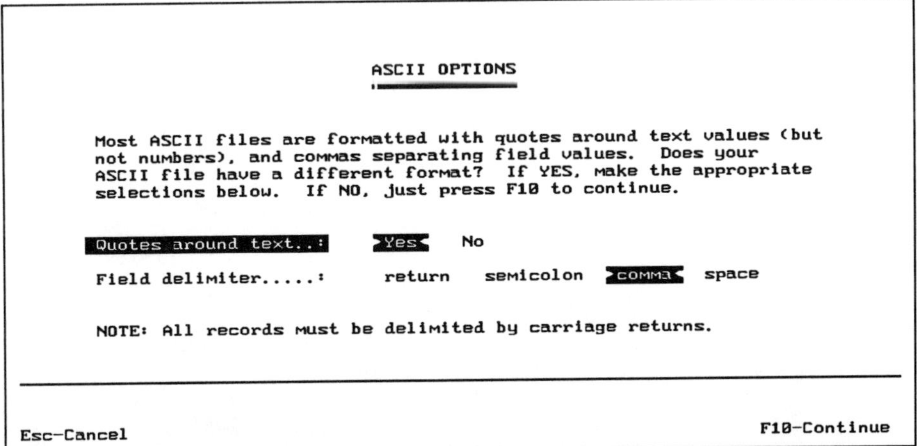

8. Press **F10**. The document is exported to the specified receiving file. Each form is displayed as it is exported. After display of the last form, the Utilities Menu is displayed.
9. Press **Esc**. The Q&A Main Menu is displayed.
10. Turn to Module 27 to continue the learning sequence.

Module 36
EXPORT A DOCUMENT

DESCRIPTION

Any Write document can be exported to another software package that accepts ASCII documents. *Exporting* means moving the document from under the control of Q&A and placing it under the control of another software package. For example, you can create a Q&A Write document and then decide to export (transfer) it to WordStar, Lotus 1-2-3, or another software package that accepts ASCII files as input.

There are two options available when exporting a document. One is to export a document without headers, footers, or pagination. You may often have documents in this category. Normally, these are straight text information and are exported to another software package that contains a text processing feature. Of course, the text can also contain tabular information.

The other option is to export a document with headers, footers, and pagination. This choice is selected by printing the document file to disk (or file). It actually produces a print file saved to disk. The print file can always be printed using the DOS print command.

EXPORTING TEXT ONLY From the Q&A Main Menu, access the Write Menu. If you are using floppy disk drives, ensure that the disk containing the file being exported is installed in the proper drive before proceeding further.

Type G (Get). Q&A displays a prompt message requesting the filename. Type the name of the file that you are exporting and press Return. The file is retrieved from disk and displayed on the screen.

Pressing the Esc key returns you to the Write Menu. To perform the export function, select U on the Write Menu. The Write Utilities Menu is displayed. Type E and press Return. The ASCII Menu is displayed. Select the appropriate type of export that is wanted. Choices include: Standard ASCII, Document ASCII, and Macintosh ASCII. A prompt message is displayed at the bottom of the screen requesting the name of the file being exported. The filename for the receiving file must have a different name from the current file.

Type a filename and press Return. An ASCII version of the document is created and stored to disk under the specified exported filename. This process exports a document without headers, footers, and pagination. This ASCII version of the document can be copied to a floppy diskette and easily imported by another software package.

EXPORTING TEXT WITH HEADERS, FOOTERS, AND PAGINATION From the Q&A Main Menu, access the Write Menu. Type G (Get). Q&A displays a prompt message at the bottom of the screen requesting the filename. Type the name of the file that you are exporting and press Return.

Press F2. The Print Options screen is displayed. At the "Print to" option on the screen select "DISK." Press F10. The Disk Print Menu is displayed. Select I for the IBM ASCII format or M for Macintosh ASCII format. A prompt message is displayed at the bottom of the screen requesting the name of the output file. The filename for the receiving export file must be a different name from the current filename. After the filename is typed and you press Return, the file is printed to disk under the specified filename. The input file (document) is displayed on the screen. This ASCII file contains all of the text, headers, footers, and pagination.

Either of the exporting options save the ASCII formatted file to disk. This file can now be imported by any other software package that accepts ASCII files. Refer to the instructions for importing documents for the specific software package that you are using.

APPLICATIONS

To export a document you must prepare the document so it can be accepted by another software package. This feature is useful if you create your document with a popular word processing software package and often need to transfer documents to other software applications (i.e., spreadsheets or database management systems, etc.).

You may decide to convert from the word processing software that you are presently using to Q&A or to another system. The ability to export your existing documents, to a different word processing or spreadsheet system is extremely valuable. Without such a feature, you can become locked into certain word processing, spreadsheet, or database systems. When choosing applications software, select those programs that are compatible with others.

TYPICAL OPERATION

In this illustration, prepare a Write document and export text only to an IBM ASCII file. Begin at the Q&A Main Menu.

1. Open a new document and type the following text:

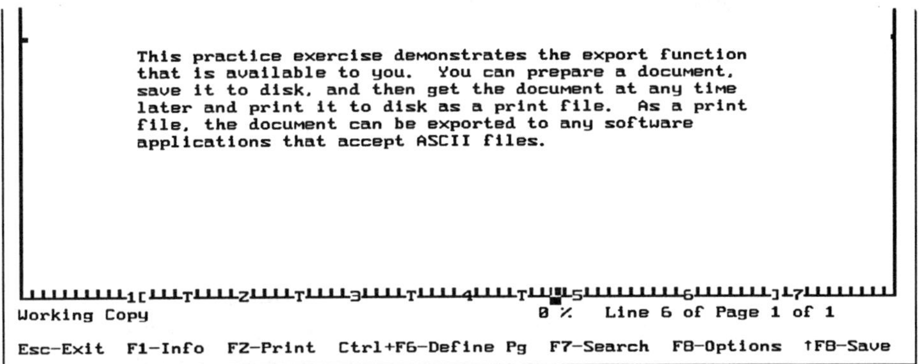

2. Press **Esc**, then type **S** (Save). A prompt message is displayed requesting a filename for the output document.
3. Type **EXPORT** and press **Return**. The document is saved to disk.

The Write Menu remains displayed. You could, at this point, exit from the Write function to perform other tasks. Later, upon returning, you may decide that you want to export the document. This is done by getting the document EXPORT and preparing an ASCII print file. The following steps describe the procedure necessary to export the file as an IBM ASCII file.

4. At the Write Menu, type **G**. A prompt message is displayed requesting a filename for the input document.
5. Type the filename **EXPORT** and press **Return**. The document is displayed.
6. Press **Esc**. The Write Menu is displayed.
7. Type **U**. The Write Utilities Menu is displayed.

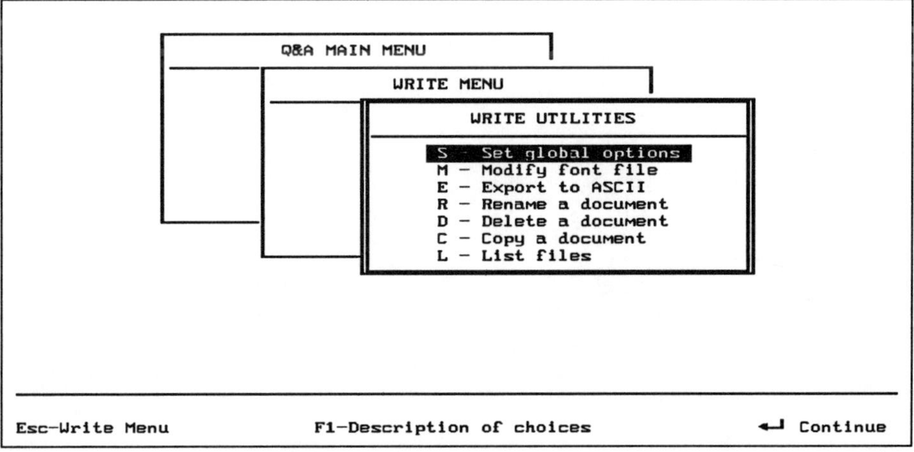

8. Type **E**. The ASCII Export Menu is displayed.
9. Type **S**. A prompt message is displayed requesting the name of the receiving file.
10. Type **EXPORT 1** and press **Return**. The file is exported to a disk file with the specified name, EXPORT1.

NOTE

Remember the filename given in this step must be a different filename than the current document or the document saved to disk. If you use the same document name, a prompt message is displayed. The cursor is located on N - No. Answering Yes causes the document file to be overwritten. Answering No displays the Write Menu; the export operation is aborted.

In this step, an ASCII formatted copy of the document named EXPORT1 is saved to disk. The original document EXPORT remains saved as a Write document. The ASCII Export Menu is displayed.

11. Return to the Main Menu.
12. Turn to Module 28 to continue the learning sequence.

Module 37
FORM DESIGN

DESCRIPTION

Form design involves creating a place or a file to enter data in a database at some later time. Designing a form is an easy task if you plan ahead. Determine what information you want included on the form. It helps to list the form items (called *>form labels*) and to actually count the number of characters (called the *information blank*) that are to be filled in. Also, determine and record whether the information for each form item is alphabetic, numeric, or alphanumeric. Such advanced planning will save you time.

Form design is started by accessing the File Menu from the Q&A Main Menu. Selecting the Design file function on the File Menu displays the Design Menu. The Design a new file selection on the File Menu causes a prompt message requesting you to enter the filename. Once you name the file, it becomes the database name with a file extension of ".dtf" attached to the filename. This filename extension is automatically assigned to each file created for designing a form. The database name is displayed at the bottom left of the screen.

The whole process of designing a form involves several procedures:

- Lay out the form
- Assign information types
- Set global Format Options.

In this module, form layout is described. Assigning information types and setting Global Format Options are described in Module 6.

With the form design screen displayed, use the arrow keys to locate the cursor where you want a field to begin. Type the label followed by a colon (:) or greater than (>) symbol. You can then count and leave the number of blanks required for the information. Follow the blank spaces allocated for information with a greater than (>) symbol. The greater than (>) symbol designates the end of the information; you cannot type past this point on the form when entering data. The colon and arrow characters are used to define exactly how much information can be typed in the field.

A single form can contain 10 screens of information. A field can contain a maximum of one screen page of information. Other limits are as follows:

Fields per record	2,182
Fields per screen page	218
Number of characters per record	16,780
Characters per field	1,678
Number of Records per file	16 million
File size	256 megabytes

The process of moving the cursor and typing the field labels is repeated until the entire form is designed. You can have more than one field on the same line on the screen. Pressing F10 completes the form design process. Then you are ready to assign information types. Refer to Module 6 for instructions.

APPLICATIONS

Designing a form is the process of building the structure in which you later fit database information. Forms are used to capture specific data that you use daily. By designing a form to contain certain information, only that information is retrieved from your database when requested. Forms are a means of selectively choosing what information you want from your database. When assigning the filename for a form, choose a name that reflects the contents of the file and one that is meaningful to you. Field names, labels, and lengths can all be custom tailored for your personal applications.

TYPICAL OPERATION

In this illustration, design a form which contains a prospective customer list. Enter pertinent information about each customer including company name, address, telephone number, individual to contact, date of first contact, type of product interest, prospective annual sales, competitor's products being used, credit rating, allowable discounts, and commissions. Free-form design is permitted; that is, you can place the form labels at any location desired on the screen. Begin at the Q&A Main Menu.

1. At the Q&A Main Menu, the cursor is located at F - File. Press **Return**. The File Menu is displayed.
2. Type **D** to display the Design Menu. The cursor is located at D - Design a new file.

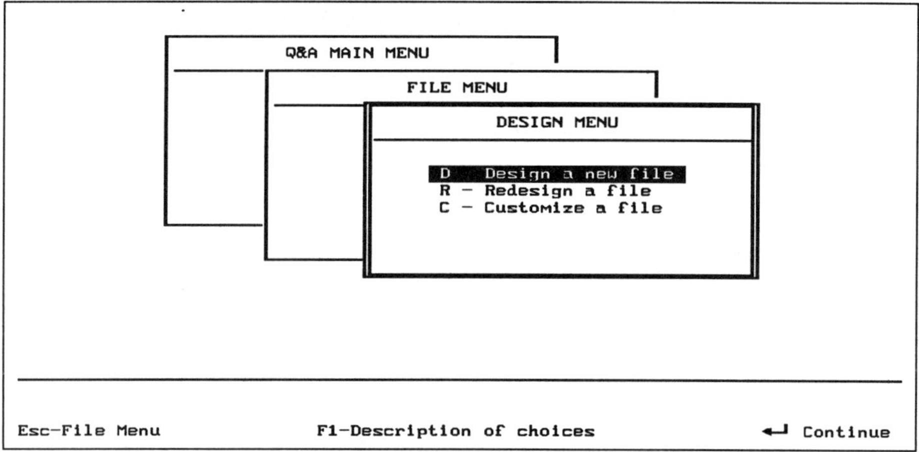

3. Press **Return**. A prompt message is displayed at the bottom of the screen requesting the name for the new file.

4. Type **CUSTOMER** and press **Return**; the filename extension ".dtf" is automatically added to the name. A blank form is displayed for you to begin form design. Move the cursor to the location where you want the customer's name to appear. It is recommended that you insert one blank line at the top of the screen. Then, press Tab before entering each field label to position the fields several spaces from the left side of the screen.

5. Type the label **Company Name:**. The label must be immediately followed by a colon (:). Determine how many characters you want to allow for the name of the company. For now, use 24 characters.

6. Press **Right Arrow** to move the cursor to the right 24 characters. Then, type a greater than (>) symbol.

NOTE

It is not necessary to enter extra spaces to ensure separation of the name of the company from the field name. Q&A automatically inserts a space after the colon for you.

Repeat Steps 5 and 6 to enter the following labels so that your screen resembles the following screen. Use the number of blanks shown in the brackets [ ] for this example. The numbers shown in the brackets are for illustration purposes only. Do not type the brackets and numbers while creating the example. If you do want more than a single space following each field label, include the extra spaces in the number count listed in brackets within the screen below.

You can draw boxes, center lines, or set tabs anytime during the form design process by pressing F8. The Options Menu is displayed.

```
     Company Name:[24]                         >

     Street or P.O. Box:[35]                                     >

     City & State:[30]                               > Zip:[10]       >

     Telephone:[15]              >

     1st Contact Date:[12]          > 2nd Contact Date:[12]          >

     Product Area:[35]                                      >

     Yearly Sales (K):[10]        > Credit Rating:[3]>

     Competition/Product:[36]                                   >_


LLLLTLLLL1LLLLTLLLL2LLLLTLLLL3LLLLTLLLL4LLLLTLLLL5LLLLTLLLL6LLLLTLLLL7LLLLTLLLL8
CUSTOMER                                         0 %   Line 17 of Page 1 of 1

Esc-Cancel          F1-How to design          F8-Options          F10-Continue
```

You can choose an option and proceed to implement that option. Boxes cannot be drawn around multi-line fields.

7. Press **F10** when you have entered all of the labels. "Saving design" is displayed at the bottom of the screen. The Format Spec screen is displayed. Since this module covers only the layout of a form, the other functions necessary to design a form are not described here.

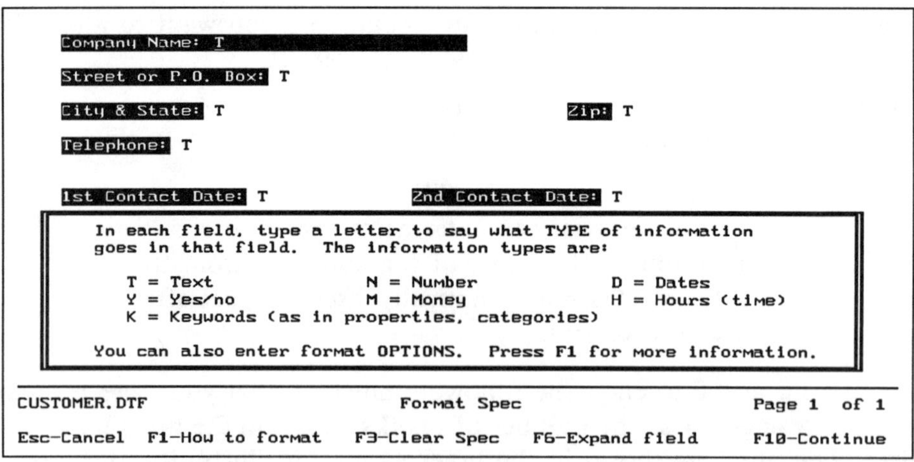

8. Press **Esc**. The Format Spec screen is removed from the screen; the blank form design is displayed.
9. Return to the Main Menu.
10. Turn to Module 59 to continue the learning sequence.

Module 38
FORM DESIGN/REDESIGN PRINT CRITERIA

DESCRIPTION

The *print criteria* for form design or redesign are actually the print specifications that you define for a form. The print specification identifies to Q&A which forms are to be printed and exactly where on the printed page the information contained in each field is to be printed.

Defining the *print specification* involves determining which forms are to be printed. This is called defining the retrieve specification. The *retrieve specification* tells Q&A which forms to retrieve from the database for printing. You can retrieve all forms in a database or you can selectively retrieve forms. Refer to Module 80 for instructions on how to retrieve specific forms.

Another item of importance is determining which fields are to be printed and where they are to appear on the printed page. This involves defining the field specification.

There are two specification styles available. One is called "Free-form" and the other is called "Coordinate." Each of the two styles is invoked from the Field Spec screen. If you want to print all fields on forms in a database press F10 at the Field Spec screen. The Print Options menu is displayed and you can proceed to perform the print operation. Refer to Module 69 for detailed instructions on printing forms.

From the Q&A Main Menu, entering the File function enables you to display the Print Menu. Design/Redesign a Print Spec is an option on the Print Menu. After specifying a filename, the Retrieve Spec screen for the specified file is displayed. You can specify exact retrieve specifications (refer to Module 80) or you can choose to retrieve all forms in the database. When finished identifying those forms to be retrieved, pressing F10 displays the Field Spec screen. Identification of which fields are to be printed is done on this screen. After tagging those fields to be printed, pressing F10 saves the print specification for later use. Successively pressing Esc moves you backward through the menus and eventually displays the Q&A Main Menu.

FREE-FORM STYLE The free-form style prints the data exactly as it is contained in each field followed by a printer carriage return. This style is extremely simple to use. On the Field Spec screen you just enter a character X or + in each field that you want printed. Entering X prints the data contained in the field and inserts a printer carriage return at the end of the data (moves the print head to the next line). The character + prints the data in the field and then skips a blank space and prints the next specified field.

You can specify the order in which fields are printed by identifying each field with a number and the character X or +. For example, using the CUSTOMER database, you can specify the following:

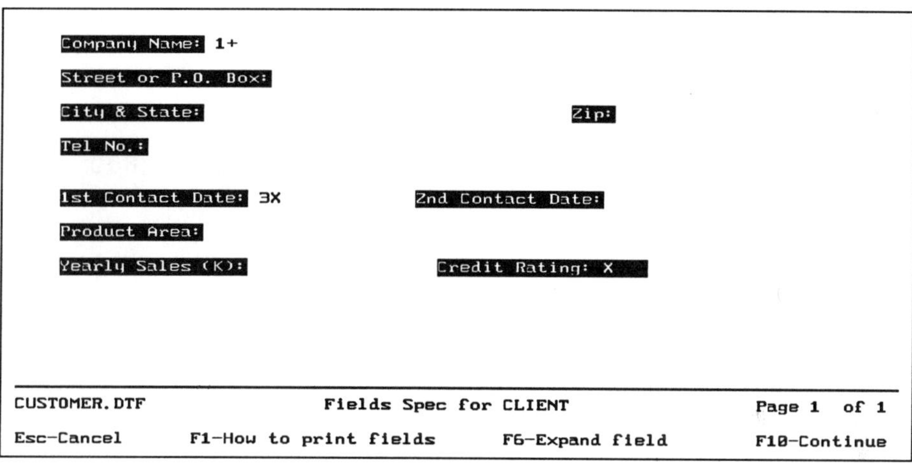

A typical printout is

```
Green and Wells, Inc. A
Dec 15, 1989
```

where the company name, Green and Wells, Inc., is printed followed by a space and their credit rating of A. The next line contains the third field specified on the Field Spec screen.

COORDINATE STYLE The coordinate style allows you to control exactly where printed field information is to appear on a printed page. This is done by specifying line and character position specifications. For example, 5,20 specifies that the field containing this specification is to be positioned on the printed page on line 5, character position 20. Again, using the CUSTOMER database, you can ensure that field information is printed exactly where you want it.

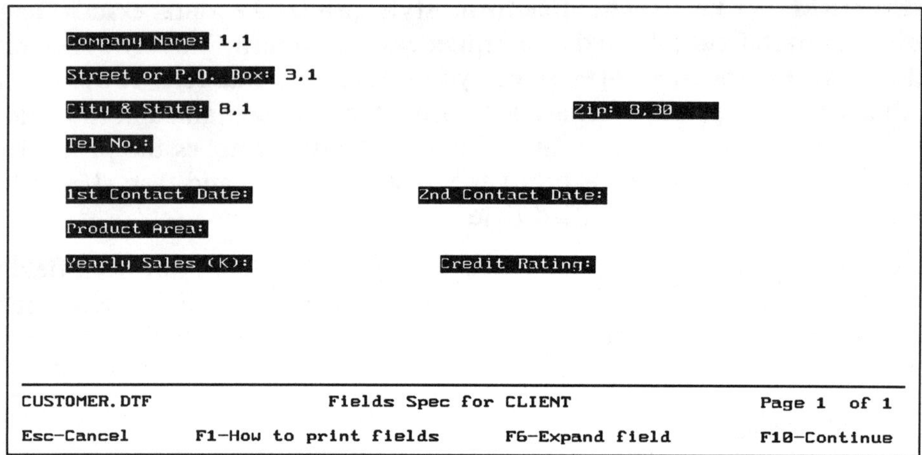

Typical results are: Character positions

```
 123456789012345678901234567890123456789012345678900

Rows
1   Wiley & Klingbiel
2
3    345 Bell Ave.
4
5
6
7
8   Azle, TX 74234
```

EXITING FROM DESIGN/REDESIGN PRINT SPECIFICATION OPERATION You can exit from the operation of designing/redesigning print specifications by pressing Esc anytime. When this is done, the Print Menu is displayed.

PRINTING FORMS After designing or redesigning the print specification for a database, printing is accomplished by following instructions presented in Module 69.

APPLICATIONS

The free-form style is excellent for creating mailing labels or for printing form information on blank paper. The option of specifying the order in which field data is to be printed is very useful. Even though the basic style is "free-form," you still maintain control of what and where it is printed.

The coordinate style is used primarily to print form data on preprinted forms or in a rigid format on paper.

TYPICAL OPERATION

In this illustration, enter the File function (Design/Redesign a file) and indicate at the Print Menu that you want to design a print specification for a database. Retrieve all forms in the database. Use the free-form style to produce a mailing label print specification. Begin at the Q&A Main Menu.

1. Select the File Menu. Type **P**; prompt message is displayed requesting the name of the file for which a print specification is to be designed or redesigned.
2. Type **CUSTOMER** and press **Return**. The Print Menu for the specified file is displayed. The cursor is located at D - Design/Redesign a spec.

If creating retrieve specifications, use Module 80 as reference to identify only those forms that you want retrieved.

3. Type **D**; a list of existing print specs for the database is displayed with a prompt message requesting the name you want to assign to the print specification.
4. Type **CLIENT** and press **Return**. The Retrieve Spec screen for the print spec is displayed.
5. Press **F10** to retrieve all forms in the database. The Field Spec for the specified database is displayed.

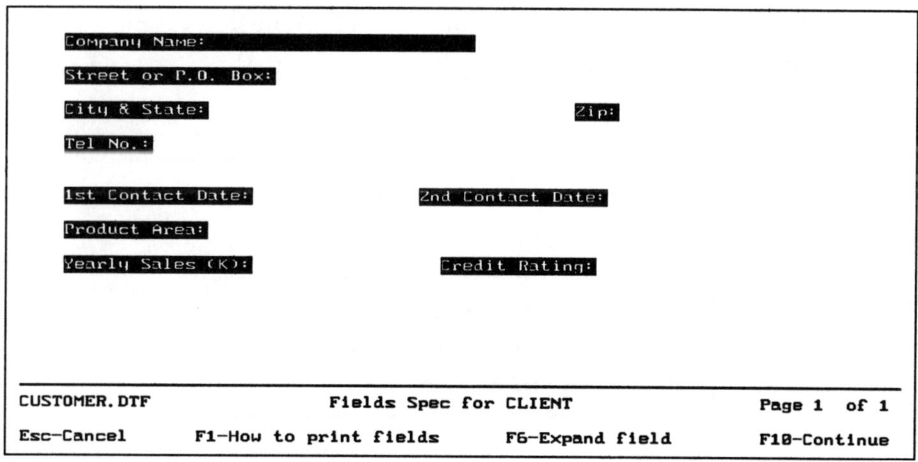

6. Type field specifications in each field to be printed on the mailing label. Use the free-form style. The results are:

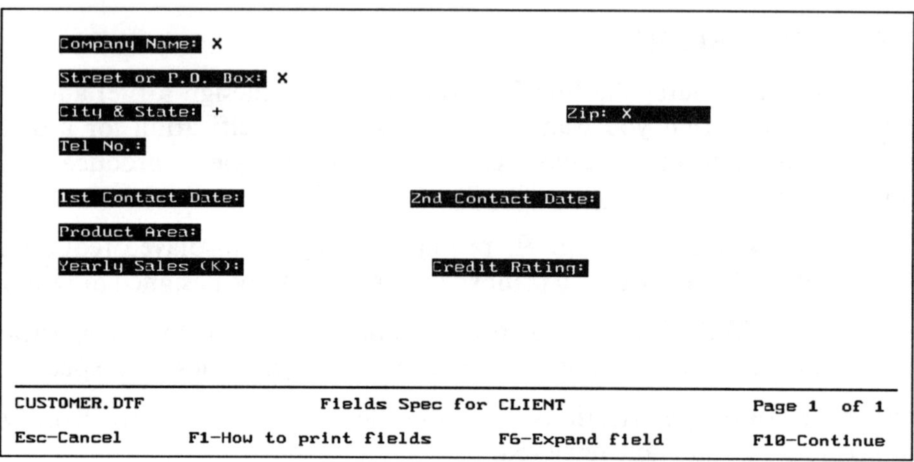

The typical results for a printed mailing label using this style is

Green & Wells, Inc.
23456 E. Avery
Oklahoma City, OK 56984

7. Press **F10**. The File Print Options Menu is displayed.
8. Accept the default values displayed on the screen (refer to Module 69 for instructions on how to use the Print Options Menu).
9. Press **F10**. The print specification is saved to disk. A prompt message is displayed.

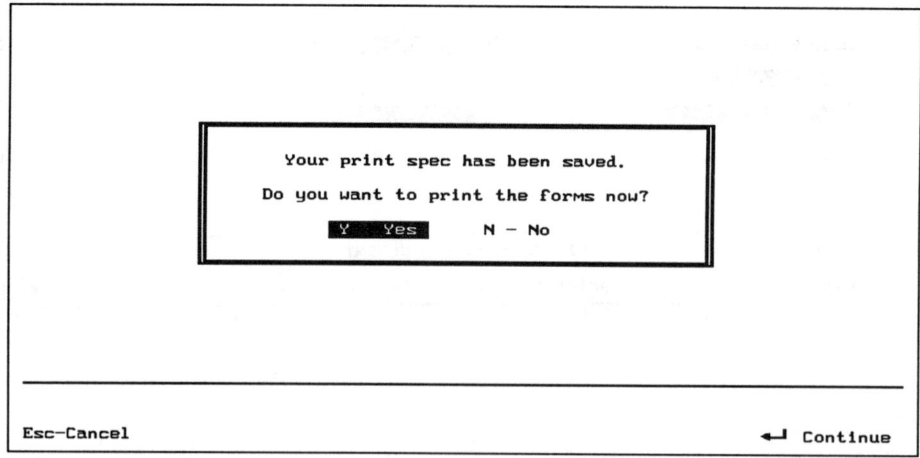

Typing Y prints all of the forms in the database. After the forms are printed, the Print Menu is displayed. Typing N displays the Print Menu.

10. Return to the Main Menu.
11. Turn to Module 69 to continue the learning sequence.

Module 39
FORM FIELDS LESSON

DESCRIPTION

For the Assistant to respond to many of your requests, you must teach the Assistant all that you can about your databases. An important lesson for the Assistant to learn is the individual fields contained on a form. This module, the form fields lesson, describes how to teach the Assistant about each field on a form.

The Assistant uses the information about fields on a form to provide you with concise reports. Each field that you identify in a form field lesson is used in a detailed report each time the report is requested.

At the Q&A Main Menu, selecting A displays the Assistant Menu. Entering T places the Assistant in the "learn" mode. Entering a valid filename and pressing Return in response to the prompt message displays the Basic Lessons Menu. Selecting option 2, "Which fields identify a form" displays the document.

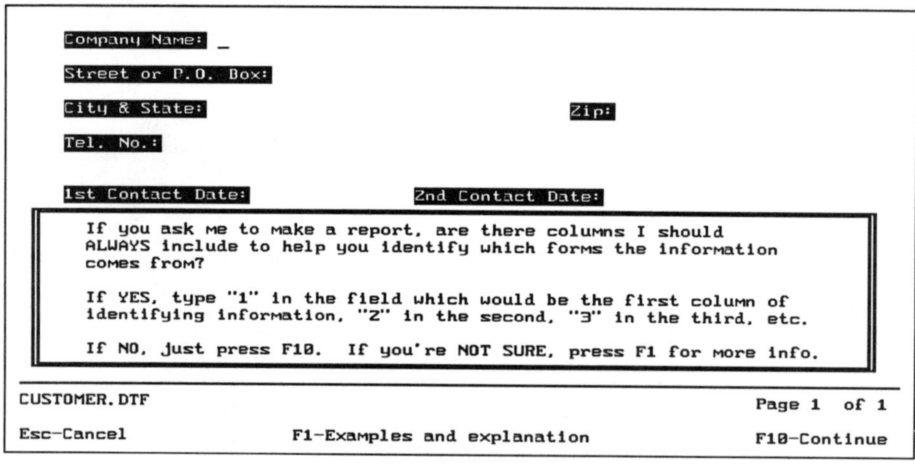

Typing a number in selected fields to represent corresponding columns wanted on a detailed report comprises the lesson to the Assistant.

After entering numbers in selected fields, pressing F10 completes the lesson and the Basic Lessons Menu is displayed.

APPLICATIONS

The Form Fields Lesson is important in that it is the way you identify to the Assistant which fields contained on a form are to be included in detailed reports. Once you identify those fields that are to be included in columns on a report, the information is saved and used by the Assistant each time you request a report pertaining to that database.

For example, if you want a report displaying customer names, addresses, and/or telephone numbers, those respective fields on the form for the Customer database are identified or "taught" to the Assistant. A field identified with "1" displays information contained in that field throughout the database in the first column in a report. A field identified with "29" displays information contained in that field throughout the database in the second column in a report.

Limit the number of fields identified on a form. It is recommended you use only one, two, or at the most three. Fields identified appear as columns in every detailed report. However, these are not the only columns that can appear on the report. For example, you may identify "Company Name" and "Address" as columns to appear on every report. If you ask the Assistant to list all customers and the amount of their purchases, a three-column report is prepared. "Company Name," if identified as "1," is the first column on the report. "Address," if identified as "2," is the second column. "Purchases," if identified as "3," is the third column on the report. Consequently, if only two fields were identified ("taught") to the Assistant, more columns can appear on a requested report depending upon the type of information requested.

Predefined reports can be prepared. Refer to Module 79 for detailed information on predefined reports. If predefined reports are requested, the layout of the predefined report supercedes the column structure taught to the Assistant in this lesson. This report could be a Customer List with specific columns designated within the layout of the report.

Fields identified for specific columns in a report from this lesson can be overridden. The request to override the identified columns for a specific request could be made as: List company names, addresses, and date of 1st contact with no identification columns. The wording "with no identification columns" tells the Assistant to ignore the columns identified by this lesson for a specific database. "With no identification columns" can be abbreviated as WNIC.

TYPICAL OPERATION

In this illustration, teach the Assistant which fields identify a form. Begin at the Q&A Main Menu.

1. Select the Assistant Menu. Type **T**. A prompt message is displayed requesting the filename of the file for which you want to provide instruction to the Assistant.
2. Type **CUSTOMER** and press **Return**. The Basic Lessons Menu is displayed.
3. Type **2**. The form design for the specified database is displayed. This is the screen used to identify numbers on fields which you want to appear as columns on a report.

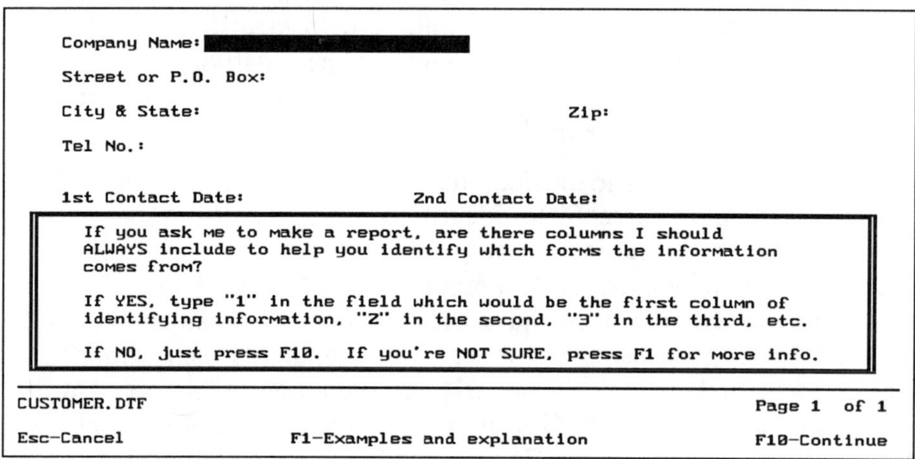

Company Name:

Street or P.O. Box:

City & State: Zip:

Tel No.:

1st Contact Date: 2nd Contact Date:

If you ask me to make a report, are there columns I should ALWAYS include to help you identify which forms the information comes from?

If YES, type "1" in the field which would be the first column of identifying information, "2" in the second, "3" in the third, etc.

If NO, just press F10. If you're NOT SURE, press F1 for more info.

CUSTOMER.DTF Page 1 of 1

Esc-Cancel F1-Examples and explanation F10-Continue

4. Type **1** at the first field (Company Name), **2** at the second field (Street or P.O. Box), and **3** at the third field (City). The cursor moves to the next field after you enter each number and press Return. The results are:

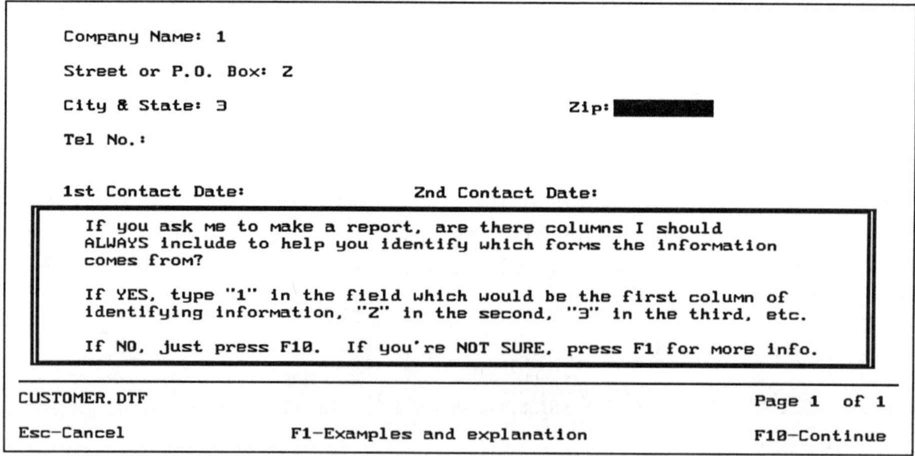

Company Name: 1

Street or P.O. Box: 2

City & State: 3 Zip:

Tel No.:

1st Contact Date: 2nd Contact Date:

If you ask me to make a report, are there columns I should ALWAYS include to help you identify which forms the information comes from?

If YES, type "1" in the field which would be the first column of identifying information, "2" in the second, "3" in the third, etc.

If NO, just press F10. If you're NOT SURE, press F1 for more info.

CUSTOMER.DTF Page 1 of 1

Esc-Cancel F1-Examples and explanation F10-Continue

5. Press **Return** until the cursor is located at the "Tel. No." field.
6. Type **4** and press **F10**. The Basic Lessons Menu is displayed.

You have identified columns to always appear on a report as columns 1 through 4 when querying the Assistant about this database.

If you should request a report about this database, the Company Name would always be the first column on the report, the Street or P.O. Box as the second column, the City as the third column, and the Tel. No. number as the fourth column. You can continue with lessons from the Basic Lessons Menu by referring to applicable modules describing the individual lessons or you can exit to the Q&A Main Menu.

7. Return to the Main Menu.
8. Turn to Module 56 to continue the learning sequence.

Module 40
FORM REDESIGN

DESCRIPTION

Form redesign involves taking a previously designed form (in a database) and changing it in some way to a design that you like even better.

One of the most important steps to take before attempting to redesign a form or database is to make a copy of the existing design. Of course, you will need to assign a different filename

to the copy. Redesigning a form can be compared to editing a document in word processing. Consequently, the same capabilities are available to you. That is, cursor movement, tab settings, etc., are all handled as if you are editing a Write document. You can even use the Draw feature to outline areas on a form with rules.

There are some important precautions to observe when redesigning a form. Q&A assigns an internal notation to each field called a field tag. The *field tags* are used to monitor locations of fields. The tags, such as AA, AB, AC, etc., must not be deleted unless you are deleting the entire field. Also, these tags must not be changed at any time.

Redesign can involve any or all of the changes subsequently described.

CHANGING A FIELD LABEL Changing a field label involves simply typing over the existing label. Characters in a label can be either deleted (by pressing the Del key) or inserted (by pressing the Ins key).

CHANGING FIELD LENGTH This involves changing the length (or blanks) of space allocated for the field information. Field length is changed either by inserting or by deleting spaces.

The colon (:) is used to end the field label and the Right (>) or Left Arrow (<) are used to denote the end of the field. Remember if you shorten the length of a field when redesigning a form, information contained in your original database may be lost. If the information for the field stored in the database contains more characters than exist on the redesigned form, the information placed on the form is truncated (cut off), thus causing you to lose characters of information.

MOVING A FIELD Any field can be relocated on a form just by retyping the field label (including the colon and the two character field tag at another location. Field tags are the Q&A assigned letters such as AA, AB, AC, etc.

It is important to delete the original location of the field label, including the colon (:) or left arrow (<), field tag, blank spaces allocated for the information, and the right arrow (>) denoting the end of the field.

An alternative procedure that may be followed to move a field is described in Module 60, Move Text in a Document.

ADDING A FIELD A field is added just by positioning the cursor where you want the field to begin and typing the label. It is recommended that you use the insert mode (press Ins) when adding fields. This prevents possible overtyping on existing fields.

Again, you must end the label with a colon (:) or left arrow (<), leave an appropriate number of blank spaces for field information, and end the field with a right arrow (>).

When adding a field, do not attempt to enter a field tag. Field tags are handled automatically by Q&A.

DELETING A FIELD Deleting a field is done by pressing the Del key. When deleting a field, delete the field label, the label ending code consisting of a colon (:) or less than symbol (<), the Q&A assigned field tag (AA, AB, AC, etc.), and the field ending greater than symbol (>).

CHANGING FIELD INFORMATION TYPE After redesigning a form, press F10. The Format Spec screen for the form is displayed. If you want to change the information type for a field, do it on this screen.

Valid information types are:

Field Tag	Information Type	Description
D	Date	Calendar date field
H	Hour	Time field
K	Keyword	Keyword field (used for special searching)
M	Money	Financial format. Used only in computations
N	Number	Quantity field. Used only in computations
T	Text	Text information only
Y	Yes/No	Yes/no or true/false. Used in queries

Changing the information type for a field is done just the same as when designing a new form and adding information types. The only difference is that when redesigning a form you type over existing information types to change them. Refer to Module 6 for complete instructions on assigning/changing information types.

If your form has financial, numerical, date, or time information types, use the Format Options screen to enter changes to these special fields.

APPLICATIONS

A form is usually redesigned to incorporate or delete some feature. For example, total number of fields on a form can be increased to include more information. Obsolete information contained in a database can be deleted by deleting the field from a form. The redesign feature gives you unlimited opportunities for enhancing your existing databases.

TYPICAL OPERATION

In this illustration, an existing form is redesigned, the design changes are made to a specified database and saved to disk. First make a backup copy of the form (database). Begin at the Q&A Main Menu.

1. Select the File Menu.
2. Type **D** to display the Design Menu.
3. Type **R**; a prompt message is displayed requesting the name of the file to be redesigned.
4. Type **CUSTOMER** and press **Return**. The Design screen for the specified file is displayed.

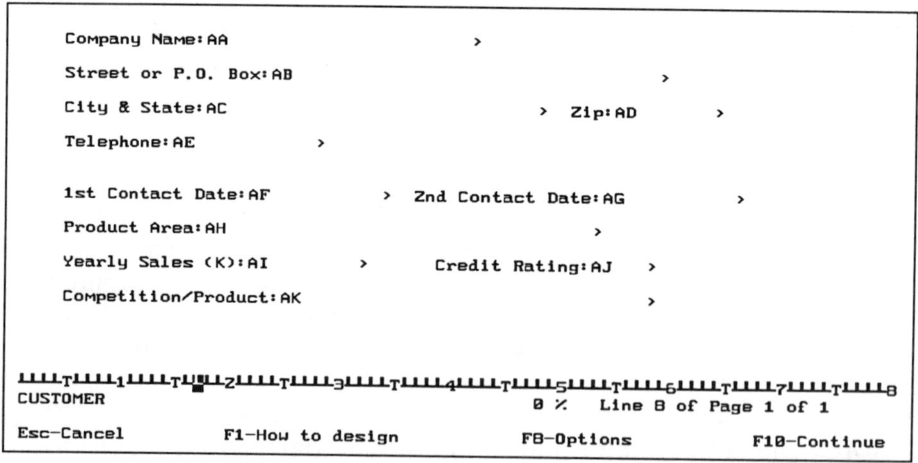

5. Press the arrow keys to move the cursor to the "Telephone" field. Place the cursor on the character "T."
6. Change the field label from "Telephone" to "Tel. No." by pressing **Ins** and typing over the label. Type **Tel. No.** and end the label with a colon (:). Press **Ins** to exit from the insert mode.
7. Press **Del** as required to delete the remainder of the previous label. The field code and number of spaces (15) for entry of the telephone number should remain unchanged.
8. Press the arrow keys to move the cursor to the field label Competition/ Product.
9. Press **Del** as required to remove the field label. Delete the label, the colon, the blanks allocated for the data (36), and the end of field code symbol (>).
10. Press **F10**. The Format Spec screen is displayed.

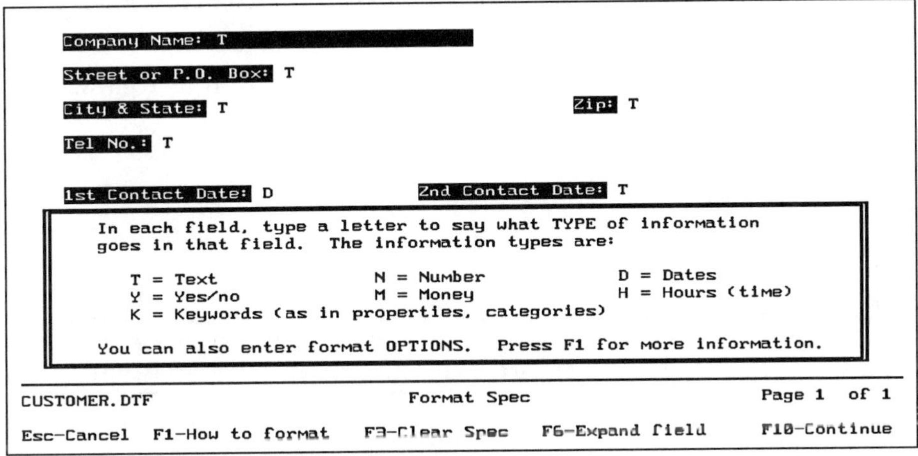

11. Type **D** in the "1st Contact Date" and "2nd Contact Date" fields and press **F10**. The Global Format Options Menu is displayed.

Since no new fields were added, there is no need to reassign any of the information types in this illustration.

12. Press **F10**. The File Menu is displayed.
13. Press **Esc**. The Q&A Main Menu is displayed.
14. Turn to Module 46 to continue the learning sequence.

Module 41
FUNCTION KEYS

DESCRIPTION

The function keys on your keyboard are programmed to provide a variety of quick and easy moves within Q&A functions. This module is provided primarily as a reference to these keys.

Function keys are defined in two places within Q&A:

- At the bottom of each screen display, and
- On the Function and Navigation Keys screen accessible through the F1 key.

These keys include the "F" keys and the cursor control keys located on the numeric keypad.

Keys are defined at the bottom of the Working Copy screen as follows:

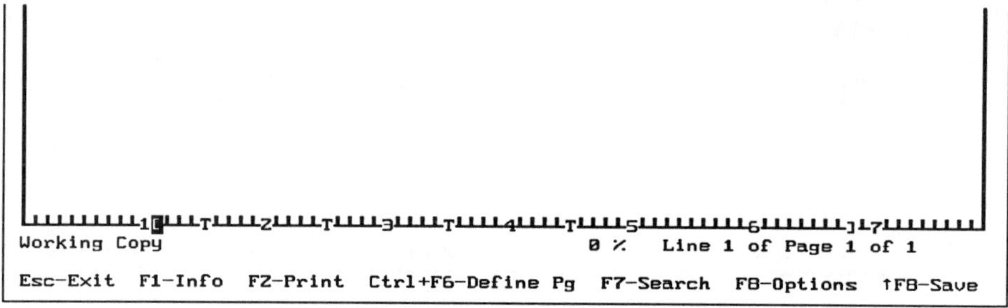

NOTE

For key sequences connected by a hyphen (such as Shift-F2), you press and hold the first key while you press the second key.

Function keys and their associated operations are as follows:

Key	Operation Performed
F1	Help
Ctrl-F1	Check word spelling
Shift-F1	Check spelling
F2	Print document
Ctrl-F2	Print text block
Shift-F2	Use macros
F3	Delete block

Key	Operation Performed
Ctrl-F3	Count words, lines and paragraphs
F4	Delete word
Shift-F4	Delete line
F5	Copy block
Alt-F5	Move block to file
Ctrl-F5	Copy block to file
Shift-F5	Move block
F6	Set temporary margins
Alt-F6	Add soft hyphen
Ctrl-F6	Define page
Shift-F6	Enhance text
F7	Search and replace
Shift-F7	Make multiple copies or restore/delete text
F8	Display Options Menu
Alt-F8	Print mailing labels
Ctrl-F8	Export document
Shift-F8	Save document
F9	Scroll screen up
Alt-F9	Calculate
Ctrl-F9	Assign Font
Shift-F9	Scroll screen down
F10	Continue

Refer to Module 20 for a complete description of how to use the cursor movement keys.

APPLICATIONS

Use of the function keys to perform various operations is a design concept used in Q&A to automate the functions that you may want to perform. It may seem as though there are too many function keystrokes to remember. After practice and continued use of the function keystrokes, you will become proficient using them.

TYPICAL OPERATION

In this illustration, display the Function and Navigation Keys screen. After viewing the screen, exit from the display and return to the Q&A Main Menu.

1. At the Q&A Main Menu, The cursor is located at F - File. Type **W**. The Write Menu is displayed. The cursor is located at T - Type/Edit.
2. Press **Return** to display a Working Copy (blank) screen for a Write document. Notice the function key assignments described at the bottom of the screen.

3. Press **F1**. The Function Key screen is displayed.

Key	Keystroke	Function	Key	Keystroke	Function
F1	Ctrl F1	Check spelling (word)	F2	Ctrl F2	Print text block
	Shift F1	Check spelling (doc)		Shift F2	Use macros
	F1	Info		F2	Print document
F3	Ctrl F3	Document statistics	F4	Ctrl F4	Delete to end of line
				Shift F4	Delete line (Ctrl Y)
	F3	Delete block		F4	Delete word (Ctrl T)
F5	Alt F5	Move block to file	F6	Alt F6	Hyphenate
	Ctrl F5	Copy block to file		Ctrl F6	Define Page
	Shift F5	Move block		Shift F6	Enhance text
	F5	Copy block		F6	Set temporary margins
F7	Alt F7	List fields	F8		
	Ctrl F7	Go to page/line		Ctrl F8	Export document
	Shift F7	Restore text		Shift F8	Save document
	F7	Search & Replace		F8	Options Menu
F9	Alt F9	Calculate	F10		
	Ctrl F9	Make font assignments			
	Shift F9	Scroll screen down			
	F9	Scroll screen up		F10	Continue

Esc-Cancel →PgDn-More←

4. Press **PgDn** to display the Navigation Key screen.

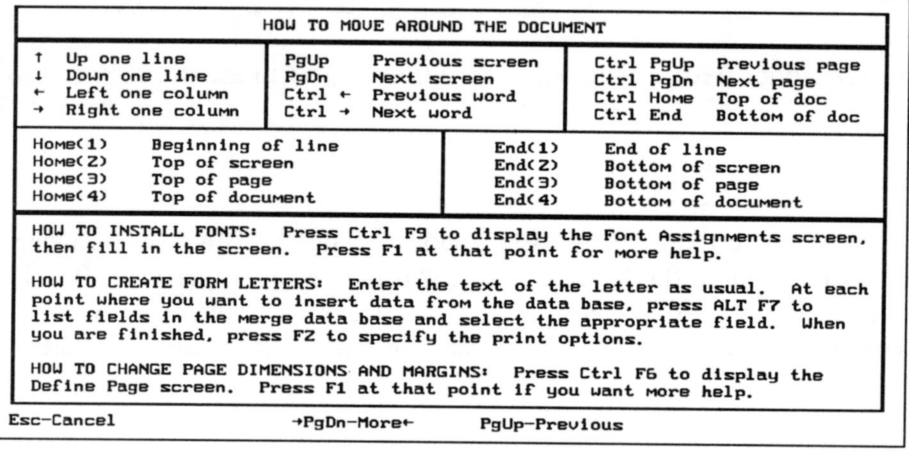

HOW TO MOVE AROUND THE DOCUMENT

↑	Up one line	PgUp	Previous screen	Ctrl PgUp	Previous page
↓	Down one line	PgDn	Next screen	Ctrl PgDn	Next page
←	Left one column	Ctrl ←	Previous word	Ctrl Home	Top of doc
→	Right one column	Ctrl →	Next word	Ctrl End	Bottom of doc

Home(1)	Beginning of line	End(1)	End of line
Home(2)	Top of screen	End(2)	Bottom of screen
Home(3)	Top of page	End(3)	Bottom of page
Home(4)	Top of document	End(4)	Bottom of document

HOW TO INSTALL FONTS: Press Ctrl F9 to display the Font Assignments screen, then fill in the screen. Press F1 at that point for more help.

HOW TO CREATE FORM LETTERS: Enter the text of the letter as usual. At each point where you want to insert data from the data base, press ALT F7 to list fields in the merge data base and select the appropriate field. When you are finished, press F2 to specify the print options.

HOW TO CHANGE PAGE DIMENSIONS AND MARGINS: Press Ctrl F6 to display the Define Page screen. Press F1 at that point if you want more help.

Esc-Cancel →PgDn-More← PgUp-Previous

5. Press **Esc**. The Working Copy (blank) screen for a new document is displayed. For this practice session, do not type any text on the screen.
6. Press **Esc** twice. The Q&A Main Menu is displayed.
7. Turn to Module 74 to continue the learning sequence.

Module 42
GET ACQUAINTED WITH THE ASSISTANT

DESCRIPTION

The Assistant is a unique feature of Q&A. It is a software robot that helps you get information from databases that you have created and stored to disk. It is not necessary to learn and use awkward computer commands to get immediate results. Commands are given by typing statements or questions just as you would if speaking to another person.

The Assistant can perform tasks that you would normally need to perform yourself in other database systems. Operations are performed from the Assistant function on the Q&A Main Menu. However, some operations can be performed within the File and Report functions.

Using the Assistant to perform procedures normally done in the File and Report functions greatly simplifies use of File and Report in Q&A.

Tasks easily handled by the Assistant function via the Q&A Main Menu include:

- Generating and printing special reports.
- Locating, sorting, and/or displaying existing forms in a database.
- Generating forms by filling in fields on designed forms from existing database information.

Tasks that can be handled by the Assistant via the File and Report functions include:

- Retrieving and displaying current date and time.
- Querying a database.

To have the capability to perform such tasks, the Assistant has its own vocabulary of approximately 400 words. All words used in any of your databases are known. All field labels, information types, and data are known to the Assistant. In addition, you can teach the Assistant new words; that is, you can add to its vocabulary. In fact, there are no language boundaries for the Assistant. Almost any language can be taught to the Assistant. The important factor is that you must first teach it the words that you plan to use. Refer to Modules 3 through 5, and 39, 56, and 90 for the procedure to use for vocabulary instruction.

Some restrictions apply to the capabilities of the Assistant. First, the Assistant knows only the vocabulary that you have taught it and the vocabulary derived from your databases. Do not use vocabulary that is unfamiliar to the Assistant. If you attempt to use unknown words, it stops and requests your help. Second, when making queries, base the structure of your questions on what is contained in your databases.

Accessing the Assistant function is accomplished by selecting A at the Q&A Main Menu. The menu is displayed as follows:

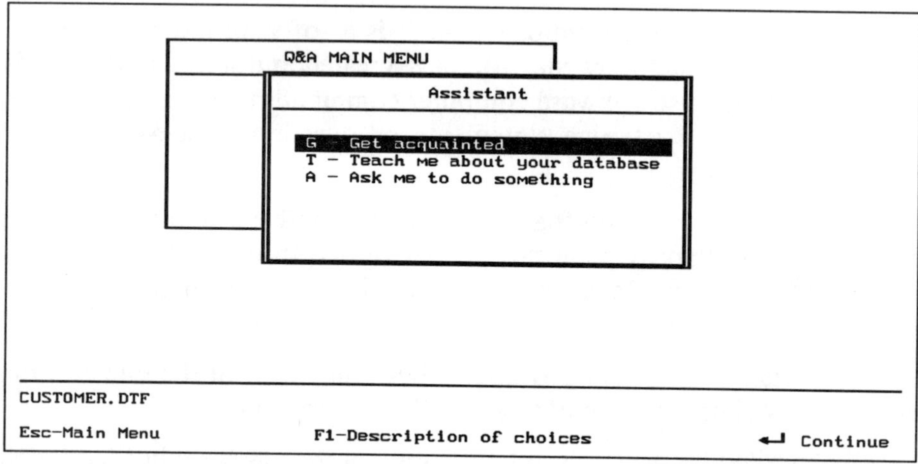

All functions performed by the Assistant are performed through this menu.

Selecting G on the menu displays overview information about the Assistant.

Typical information is:

- An example of database query about employees.
- A listing of typical requests.
- The steps to get acquainted.

The following are recommended to help you get acquainted:

- Online tutorial
- Q&A manual and quick reference card
- Practice session with a sample database

Selecting T at the Assistant Menu puts the Assistant into the "learn" mode. You can teach the Assistant about:

- Databases
- Fields on a form
- Fields containing locations

- Fields containing names of persons
- Alternate names of fields
- Units of measure
- Advanced adjectives for its vocabulary
- Advanced verbs for its vocabulary

Refer to the individual modules presented in this book which describe lessons for the Assistant. Lessons cover:

- What a database is about
- Which fields identify a form
- Which fields contain names of locations and people
- Alternate field names
- Units of measure
- Advanced vocabulary including adjectives and verbs.

Finally, a lesson is provided to allow you to update the Assistant.

Selecting A at the Assistant Menu puts the Assistant in the "do" mode. At this point you can make a request of the Assistant to perform a specific task.

Refer to various individual modules which describe procedures to use when requesting the Assistant to perform specific tasks.

APPLICATIONS

Uses for the abilities of the Assistant are almost unlimited. Until now there has never been a database system possessing such advanced aspects of "artificial intelligence." Having various tasks performed just as if they were done by another human proves invaluable when processing data. Retrieving information from voluminous databases can vastly improve your personal productivity. Whether you are using Q&A as a database system at home for personal matters or at your office. The advantage gained is your precious time.

TYPICAL OPERATION

In this illustration, practice entering the realm of the Assistant. Begin at the Q&A Main Menu and select the Assistant function. At the Assistant Menu, learn what you need to know about its operation by selecting the "Get acquainted feature."

1. Select The Assistant Menu. Type **G**. "Get acquainted" information is displayed.

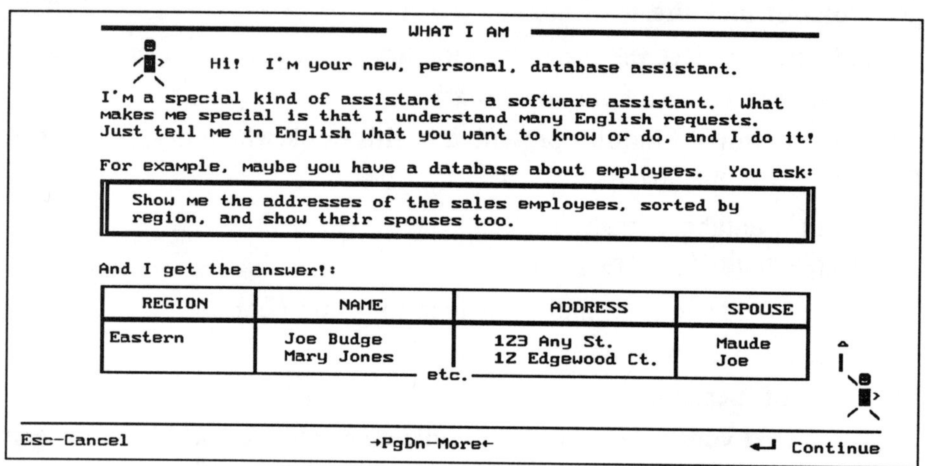

2. Press **PgDn** or **Return**. The next "Get Acquainted" screen is displayed.

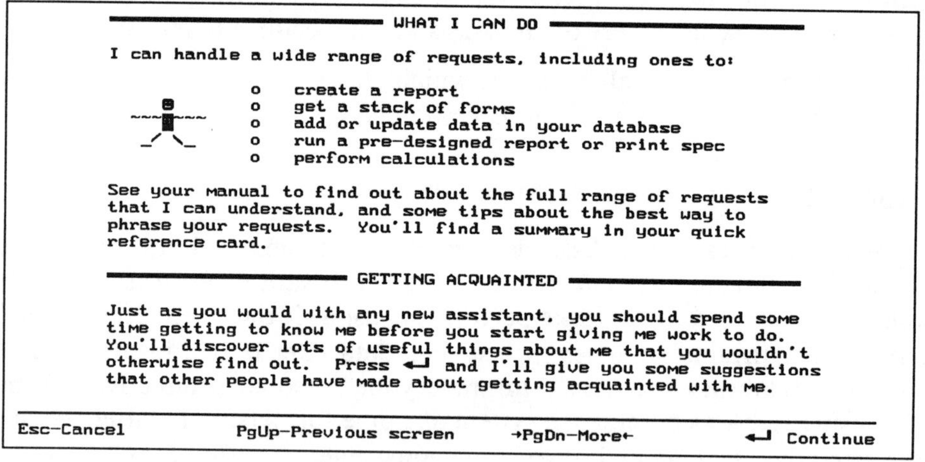

3. Press **PgDn** or **Return**. The next "Get Acquainted" screen is displayed.

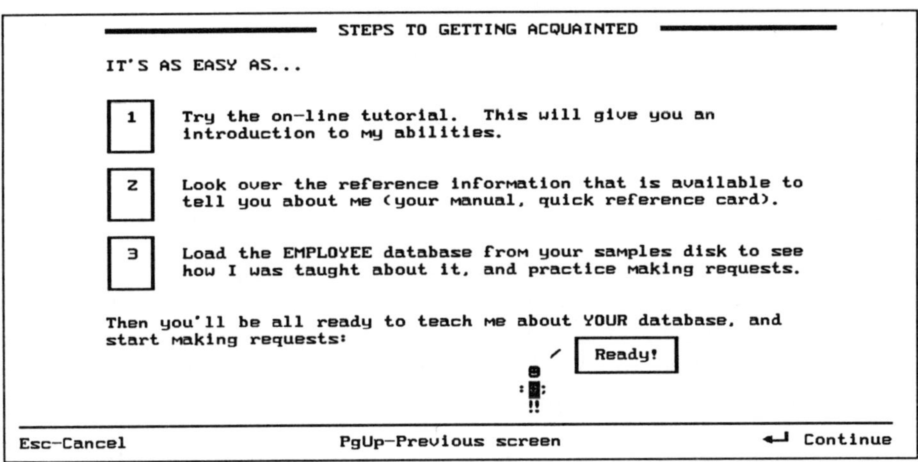

4. Press **PgDn** or **Return**. After the last screen, the Assistant Menu is displayed.
5. Press **Esc**. The Q&A Main Menu is displayed.
6. Turn to Module 48 to continue the learning sequence.

Module 43
GET A DOCUMENT

DESCRIPTION

To *get a document* is the process of bringing a document previously saved to disk into an edit session in the Write function. You can also retrieve any document that was created using Q&A or other compatible software such as WordStar, Lotus 1-2-3, Symphony, PFS:Write, IBM Writing Assistant, or any ASCII print file created from popular software applications.

Q&A can detect if you attempt to get a document from a compatible software application and automatically displays the Import Menu. Refer to Module 51 for importing these kinds of files.

Getting or retrieving a document is an extremely simple process. From the Q&A Main Menu, entering the Write function and typing G displays a message requesting you to enter the name of the document that you want to get. The message requests that you enter the correct directory path for placing the document there. For example: C: \ QA \ filename.

If you cannot remember the document name (file), pressing Return before entering a filename displays a list of all of the files stored on disk. Remember that many of the filenames may not be documents. Some are Q&A program files; others are macro files. Macro files have a filename extension of MAC. Program files have various filename extensions such as EXE, COM, etc. Refer to Module 74 for a complete description of Q&A program filenames.

Choosing the filename can be done in either of two ways:

- Type the filename in response to the prompt message.
- If you have chosen to display all of the filenames, use the Spacebar or arrow keys to move the highlighted selection bar to the file of your choice and press Return.

You are then in an edit session in the Type/Edit function with the retrieved document displayed on the screen. The cursor is located at the same position as the last time you were in an edit session with the document.

If you already have a Working Copy of a document displayed, Q&A prompts you with a warning message to allow you to save the document currently displayed before getting the newly specified document.

APPLICATIONS

Being able to retrieve documents and files that you have created and saved on disk is a necessity. Most documents, files, or databases that you create are saved to disk for later retrieval so updating and modification can be done.

TYPICAL OPERATION

In this example, get a previously saved document from disk. Begin at the Q&A Main Menu.

1. Select the Write Menu. Type **G** (Get).
2. Press **Spacebar** then press **Return** to display the file list for the default disk.

   A typical list is:

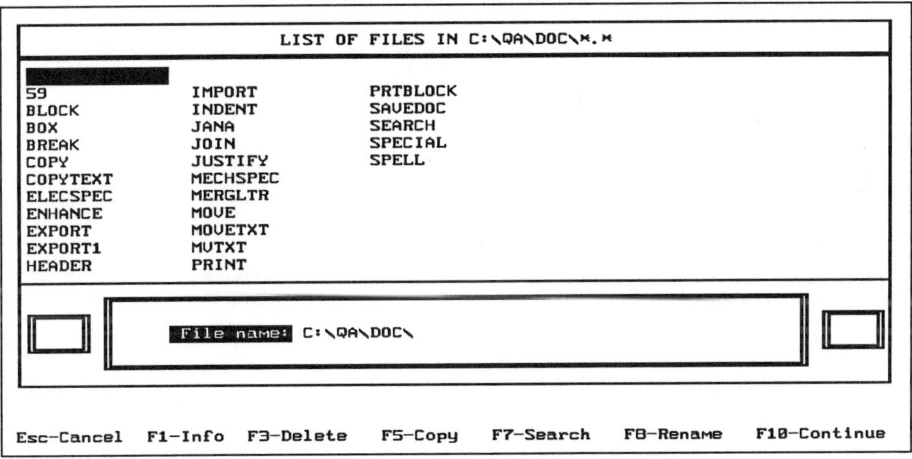

3. Type **MERGLTR** and press **Return.** The specified document is displayed.

```
February 9, 1990

*Company Name*

*Street*

*City & State*  *Zip*

Dear Sirs,

This letter is to inform you of our latest...

MERGLTR                                        0 %  Line 12 of Page 1 of 1
Esc-Exit  F1-Info  F2-Print  Ctrl+F6-Define Pg  F7-Search  F8-Options  ↑F8-Save
```

4. Return to the Main Menu without saving the document to disk.
5. Turn to Module 70 to continue the learning sequence.

Module 44
GLOBAL PARAMETERS

DESCRIPTION

Global parameters are the predefined values that can be set for various functions within Q&A. There are three major areas for which global parameters can be set.

- Default Directories and Alternate Programs
- Write Function Global Options
- Report Global Options

Default Directories — Q&A document default directories and Q&A database files directories are preset on the Default Directories screen. You may change these to route documents and files that are created to any disk drive that you choose.

In addition, an automatic execution feature can be selected to eliminate the need for pressing Return after typing menu selections (selections are the alphabetical characters on menus).

A network ID can also be entered on the Default Directories screen. This feature is convenient if you are operating in a PC network environment.

The following screen is the Set Default Directories screen:

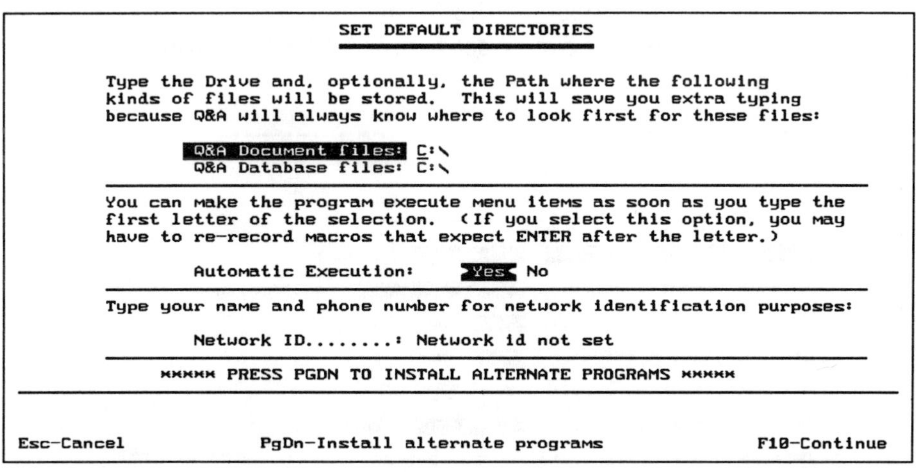

The Alternate Programs screen is accessible through the Set Default Directories screen.

From this screen, several alternate programs can be entered as menu selections to appear on the Q&A Main Menu. With this feature, you are actually modifying the Q&A Main Menu by adding additional selections that will invoke other software programs from the Q&A Main Menu. The screen is displayed by pressing PgDn at the Set Default Directories screen.

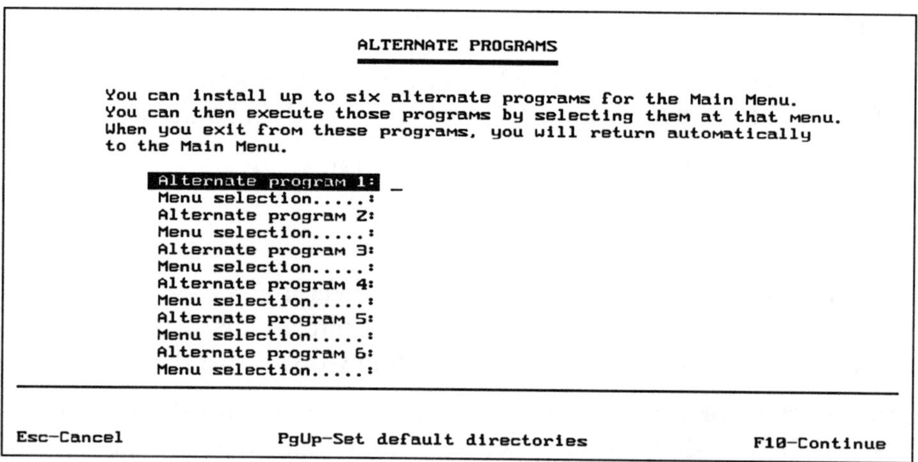

ALTERNATE PROGRAMS

You can install up to six alternate programs for the Main Menu.
You can then execute those programs by selecting them at that menu.
When you exit from these programs, you will return automatically
to the Main Menu.

Alternate program 1: _
Menu selection.....:
Alternate program 2:
Menu selection.....:
Alternate program 3:
Menu selection.....:
Alternate program 4:
Menu selection.....:
Alternate program 5:
Menu selection.....:
Alternate program 6:
Menu selection.....:

Esc-Cancel PgUp-Set default directories F10-Continue

These two screens are accesssed from the Q&A Main Menu by selecting the Utilities function which displays the Utilities Menu. Selecting the S option displays the Set Default Directories screen. The entering of required information on the screen is relatively self explanatory.

Write Function Global Options — The Write function Global Options are the document editing options that can be set for the Write Function. These are shown on the following screen.

EDITING OPTIONS

Default editing mode...: ▸Overtype◂ Insert
Default export type....: ▸ASCII with CR◂ ASCII without CR
Ghost cursor...........: ▸Yes◂ No
Show margins on screen.: ▸Yes◂ No
Automatic backups......: Yes ▸No◂
Decimal convention.....: ▸American◂ European
Default tab settings...: 5, 15, 25, 35
Spacing between columns: .25"

Editing options for all documents

Esc-Cancel F10-Continue

The screen is accessed from the Q&A Main Menu through the Write function. At the Write Menu, selection of the Utilities option displays the Write Utilities Menu. Set global options is the first option on the Write Utilities Menu.

Print defaults for new documents can also be set. The following screen displays all of the options that are available.

```
                              PRINT OPTIONS

    From page.............:   1            To page............:  9999
    Number of copies......:   1            Print offset.......:  0
    Line spacing..........:  >Single<    Double     Envelope
    Justify...............:   Yes  >No<
    Print to..............:  >PtrA<  PtrB   PtrC   PtrD   PtrE   DISK
    Type of paper feed....:   Manual  >Continuous<  Bin1   Bin2   Bin3   Lhd
    Number of columns.....:  >1<   2    3    4    5    6    7    8
    Printer control codes.:
    Name of Merge File....:

                       Print Options for New Documents
Esc-Cancel   F1-Info                                          F10-Continue
```

Document page defaults that can be set as global options are shown on the following screen.

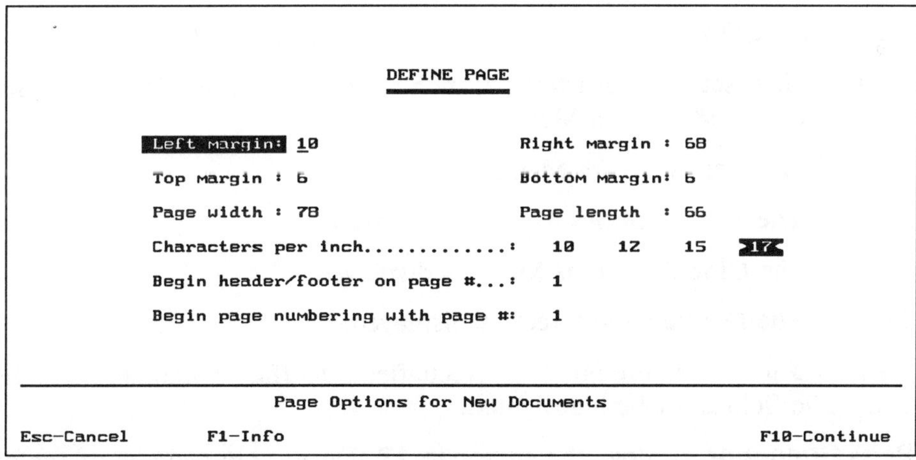

You can make any changes to the settings that you want. Refer to Module 63 for the procedures on how to define page layout settings.

Before proceeding to set global print options, it is important that you have properly installed your printer. That is, you must define the characteristics of your printer to Q&A. Refer to Module 73 for instructions on printer installation.

Afterwards, appropriate changes to the Print Options Menu. Refer to Module 71 for instructions on how to define Print Options for reports.

All of the settings you define are set as the default for page layout and print options for all documents and reports created in the future. The default settings remain as set until you change them.

Each time you enter the Type/Edit mode from the Write Menu to create a new document, these default settings govern page layout and options set for printing the document. The same is true for report parameters.

APPLICATIONS

Setting default directories is very important for routing documents and database files to appropriate disk drives on your computer system. Refer to the DOS manual for your computer for instructions on how to create directories on disk drives.

If you create Write documents that are all similar in page layout, setting global parameters to a standard format is quite convenient. In this manner, the tab settings, margin settings, and other page layout features are all standard for each of the documents that you create.

TYPICAL OPERATION

In this illustration, set the characters per inch parameter for new Write documents to 17. Begin at the Q&A Main Menu.

1. Type **W** to select the Write Menu.
2. Type **U**. The Write Utilities Menu is displayed.
3. Type **S**. The Global Options Menu is displayed.
4. Type **D**. The Define Page screen is displayed.
5. Press **Tab** to move through the screen fields to the "Characters per inch" field. The field must be highlighted.
6. Press **Spacebar** to move the cursor to **17**. Do not change any of the other screen defaults for this sample session.
7. Press **F10**. The global defaults are set. The Global Options screen is displayed.

8. Press **Esc** several times to move through the menus until the Q&A Main Menu is displayed.

NOTE

If you plan to print other documents, you may want to change this global option back to 10 characters per inch.

9. Turn to Module 23 to continue the learning sequence.

Module 45
HEADERS AND FOOTERS

DESCRIPTION

Placing document header and footer information on each page in a Write document readily identifies the document to a reader. *Headers* and *footers* are used to identify such items as chapter number and/or title, section number and/or title, revision or version number, release or creation date, security class, and page numbers.

You can use headers and footers individually or in combination within a document. If you choose to use only headers within a document, you cannot use footers only on some pages in the same document. You must be consistent throughout the document in usage. This usage restriction is imposed by the Q&A software.

While in an edit session with a document, headers and footers are created using the Options Menu. Pressing F8 while in the Working Copy of a document displays the Options Menu.

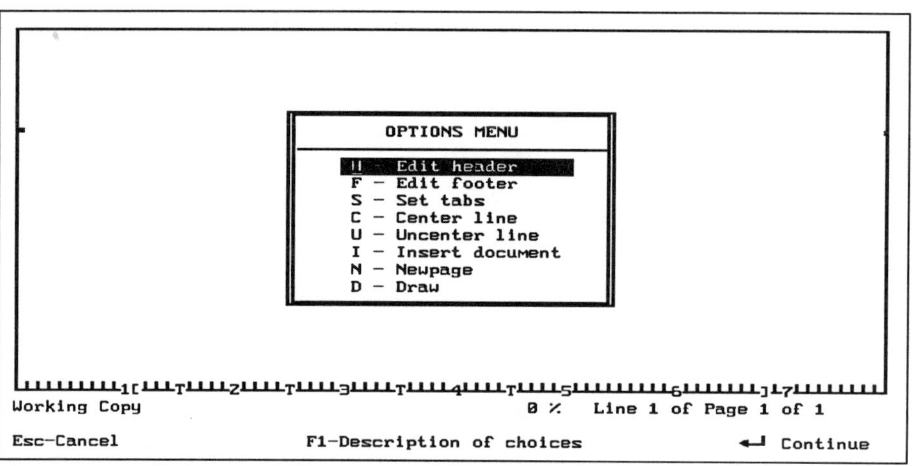

Typing either H (for header) or F (for footer) displays a window in which you can type appropriate information. A maximum of six lines can be typed for a header or for a footer. While typing the information you can insert or delete words or characters using the Ins or Del keys. Headers and footers are displayed (and printed) above and below the default line count for a document page. Pressing F10 completes the operation.

To edit existing headers and/or footers, follow the same procedure as if you were creating a header or footer. While editing a document, you cannot enter the screen area containing a header or footer unless you do so through the Options Menu.

Once entered, header and footer information is displayed on the screen as you page through a document.

The current time and date can be included anywhere in the text of the header, footer, or text of a document, provided your computer has an internal clock. The current date and/or time is not displayed in the document, but is printed when you direct it to your printer.

Type: *@DATE(n)* for current date, and
@TIME(n) for current time.

Where: n = the display format
(ex. if n=1, the date format is: Sep 21, 1989).

Standard U.S. and international date and time formats are available.

APPLICATIONS

Headers and footers enhance the general appearance of a document as well as add to its presentation of vital information. Readers are assisted in knowing the precise particulars about the document at a glance (e.g., chapter, title, version, or page number).

The header/footer feature is fully automatic once you enter the information. Take advantage of this feature often. Use it to your benefit to make your documents more attractive and useful.

TYPICAL OPERATION

In this example, header and footer information is entered into a new document. Enter a paragraph of text; then, enter a header and a footer. Begin at the Q&A Main Menu.

1. Select the Write Menu.
2. Press **Return** to display a Working Copy (blank screen) for a new document.
3. Type the following text:

```
     This is a practice document which illustrates how to add
     header and footer information in a document. It is an easy
     process. Just open an edit session in a document and
     proceed with the instructions described in this module._

Working Copy                                 0 %   Line 4 of Page 1 of 1
Esc-Exit  F1-Info  F2-Print  Ctrl+F6-Define Pg  F7-Search  F8-Options  ↑F8-Save
```

4. Press **F8** to display the Options Menu.
5. Type **H**. The header window is displayed at the top of the screen. The window is provided as a special area on the screen for you to enter header information.
6. Type the following header information. Center each line exactly as shown by pressing **F8**, then typing **C**.

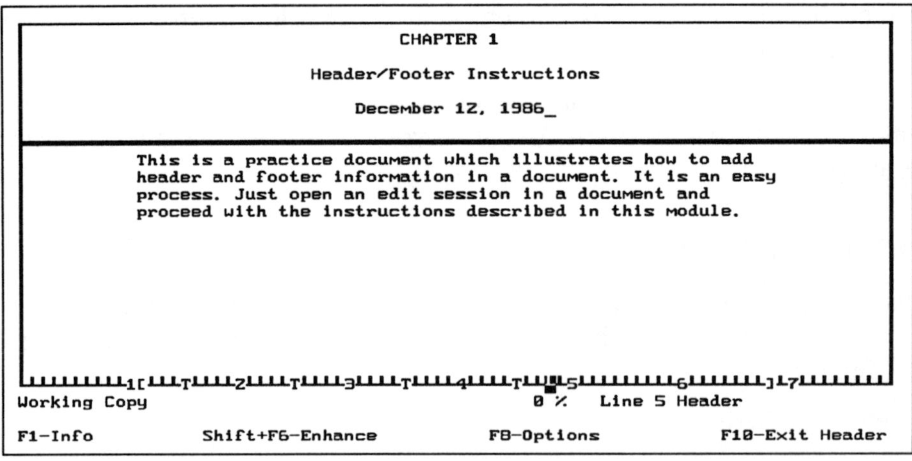

7. Press **F10**. The header window disappears, but the header remains displayed at the top of the screen. Document text is displayed below the header.
8. Press **F8** to display the Options Menu.
9. Type **F**. The footer window appears at the bottom of the screen.

10. Type the following footer information:

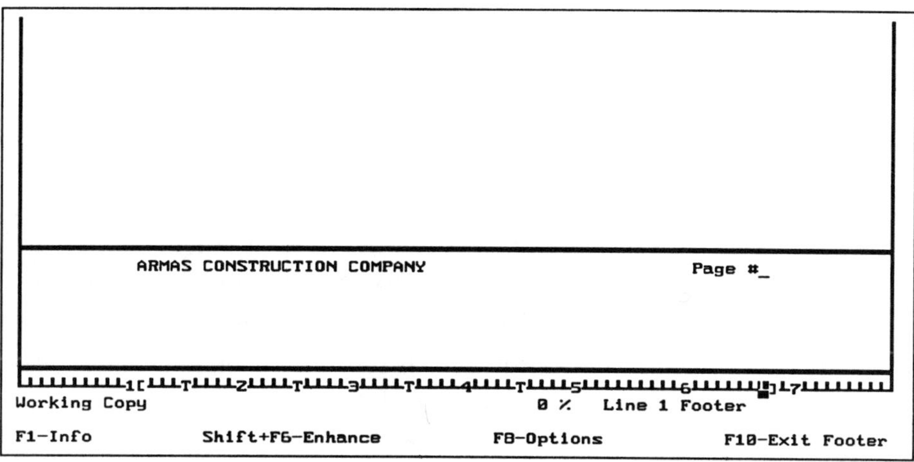

Note that a variable symbol of a pound sign (#) is entered as the page number. Q&A automatically counts the number of pages and replaces the symbol with the correct page number. Several # symbols can be used for varying the length of page numbers (ex. ### is used for a document having a page number count in the hundreds. To print the symbol # itself in the header or footer, type a backslash (\) delimiter before the # symbol (ex. \#).

11. Press **F10**. The footer is established and the cursor returns to its previous location in the document text.
12. Press **PgDn** and **PgUp** as necessary to move down or up on the document page and view the locations of the header and footer.
13. Return to the Q&A Main Menu without saving the document to disk.
14. Turn to Module 54 to continue the learning sequence.

Module 46
HELP — CREATE

DESCRIPTION

There are two ways to get help when using Q&A. One method is using "on-line" help. Using on-line help is discussed in Module 47. The other method is creating customized help to suit your specific needs. You can design help tips and messages that are meaningful to you and directly related to the databases that you create.

Up to seven lines of help information can be typed on each help screen. Each line can have up to 59 alphabetical or numerical characters typed within it. A help screen can be designed for every field in a database. Once designed, a help screen is always there to assist you when needed. This custom help option is accessible when either creating or revising a form.

As with on-line help, simply pressing F1 displays special the help screen information pertaining to the field where the cursor is located. Pressing F1 again displays the general on-line help screen if there is one available.

There is a HELP command that can be implemented through the Customize a File feature. The syntax for the command is:

@HELP(n), where n = a field. For the command to operate, you must have previously defined a help screen for the field (n) being queried.

The HELP command can be nested in IF/THEN statements to automatically display information should a file user enter incorrect data in a field.

Refer to Module 21 for detailed information about other customizing features for a file.

Creating on-line help is started at the Q&A Main Menu by selecting F to display the File Menu. At the File Menu, selecting D displays the Design Menu. Typing C to indicate that you want to customize a file initiates a filename prompt message. After entering a valid filename and pressing Return, the Customize Menu is displayed. Selecting D displays the Help Spec screen overlaying the form design for the specified file. The current field for which help can be created is highlighted. Pressing F8 highlights the next field for which help information can be entered. Pressing F6 backs up to the previous field, should you decide to make changes to previous help information.

It is not absolutely necessary to enter help information for every field on a form. You can enter help for only those fields that you choose. After entering the on-line help information, pressing F10 saves the help screens and returns display of the Customize Menu. Esc is pressed several times to return to the Q&A Main Menu.

Pressing F1 displays the standard Q&A help for a function if no custom help was previously created. If there is custom help for a field, pressing F1 displays the custom help; pressing F1 again displays the Q&A standard help.

APPLICATIONS

Creating customized help is a productive way to display reference information on the screen for users who may be unfamiliar with the database.

The same help information could be kept in a journal or notebook; however, it is more convenient to have that help installed on-line. Customized help is filed within Q&A automatically, stored at a location where help would actually be needed.

When designing a form and using restrictions for fields on a form, customized help is extremely valuable. You or your data entry personnel can easily retrieve the customized help information to have the restrictions displayed for each of the fields in question. Refer to Module 21 for detailed information about restricting field values on a form.

TYPICAL OPERATION

In this illustration, enter the File function, select Customize a file for a database, and create customized help for several fields on a form. Begin at the Q&A Main.

1. Press **Return** to select the File Menu.
2. Press **Return** to select the Design Menu.
3. Type **C**. A prompt message is displayed requesting the name of the file that you want to customize.
4. Type **CUSTOMER** and press **Return**. The Customize Menu is displayed.

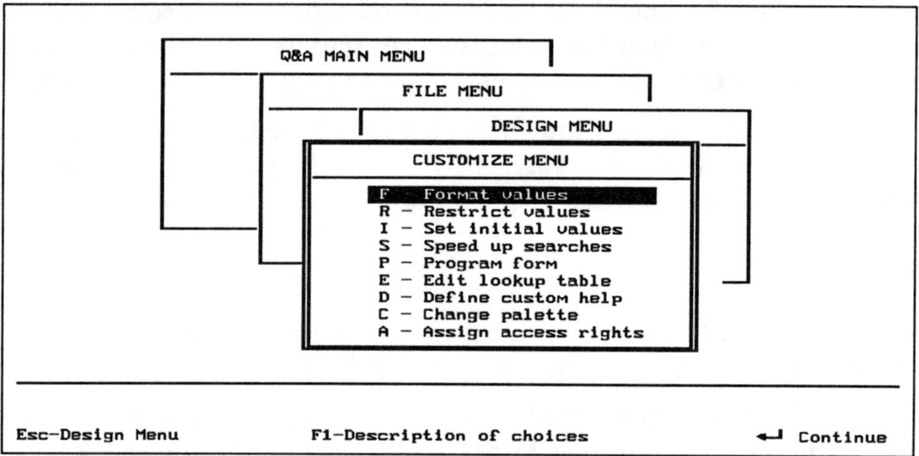

5. Type **D**. The first form for the specified file is displayed with a help window overlaying the basic form. The first field on the form is highlighted.

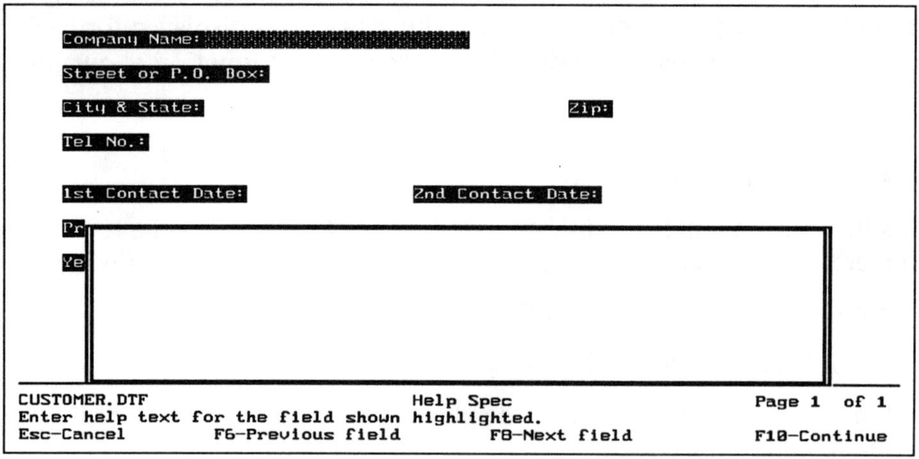

6. Type **The parent company to Warren Industries.** As you type, the information is displayed in the help window.

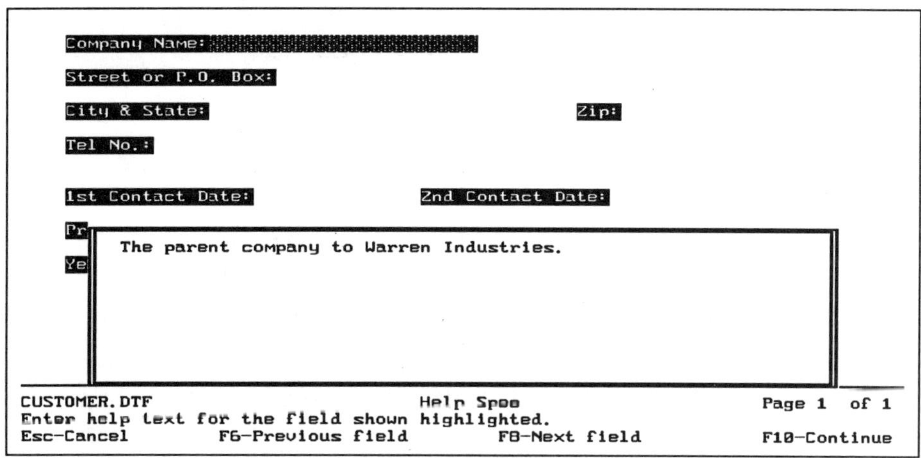

7. Press **F8** to move the cursor to the next field on the form. Again, a help window is displayed for you to enter customized help information pertaining to the highlighted field.

NOTE

To move back to the previous field, should you decide to change some information, simply press F6. The previous field is highlighted and the help window for that field is displayed.

8. Press **F8** and **F6** as necessary to step through the fields on the form, adding information where required.
9. Press **F10** to store the customized help that you have created for a particular database (form). The Customize Menu is displayed.
10. Return to the Main Menu.
11. Turn to Module 86 to continue the learning sequence.

Module 47
HELP — ON-LINE

DESCRIPTION

There are two means of getting help when using Q&A. An on-line help facility provides help menus. These help menus are accessed simply by pressing F1. This on-line help is available at all Q&A menus and at most other locations within Q&A's many functions.

Another help function allows you to create your own on-line help. You can design messages meaningful to you and directly related to the databases that you create. Refer to Module 46 for instructions for creating and using this unique facility.

At various locations within Q&A, there is more than one level of help available. When you press F1 and a help message is displayed, you will not know whether or not additional help is available. Pressing F1 a second time displays a second level of help. If this second level of help is not available, it will return you to the Q&A function or menu. To exit from help, just press Esc.

APPLICATIONS

On-line help is a convenient and quick way to display reference information on the screen when you need to know how to perform a certain task. It is much easier to use on-line help than to refer to printed information each time you want to refresh your memory about a function or operation.

TYPICAL OPERATION

In this illustration, request on-line help for menu functions. Select the File function and request help in using the displayed features. Select the design file feature and request help in using the feature. Begin at the Q&A Main Menu.

1. Press **F1** for help information about the Q&A Main Menu. Each selection on the Main Menu is displayed accompanied by a functional description.

CHOICE	DESCRIPTION	VOLUME
File	Create, fill out, and work with forms of information.	1
Report	Take information from your forms, sort and arrange it, print results in a table.	1
Write	Write and print documents.	2
Assistant	Teach your Intelligent Assistant (IA) about your forms then ask questions, generate reports, or change information using ordinary English.	1
Utilities	Set-up your printer, import/export data from other programs, DOS file facilities, etc.	2

CAUTION: Sudden loss or interruption of power can damage a data file. Never turn your machine off or reboot the system UNLESS you are at one of the main Q&A menus. If a power loss does occur, however, you can probably recover the file (see pg. U-65). Make frequent backups (pg. F-193).

Esc-Cancel

2. Press **Esc** to return to the Q&A Main Menu.
3. Type **F** to display the File Menu.
4. Press **F1** for help information about the File Menu. Each selection on the File Menu is displayed accompanied by a functional description.

CHOICE	DESCRIPTION	VOLUME 1, PAGE:
Design File	Create, edit and customize your forms for entering information.	F-13
Add Data	Fill out your forms, enter information.	F-31
Search/Update	Find specific forms, change them if required.	F-43
Print	Print some or all of your forms.	F-75
Copy	Copy your form design, data, or both.	F-177
Remove	Delete a group of forms.	F-187
Mass Update	Change information on a group of forms all at once.	F-189
Backup	Make a backup of your database. DO THIS OFTEN since sudden power loss can damage a database.	F-193

Esc-Cancel

5. Press **Esc** to return to the File Menu.
6. Type **D** (Design file). The Design Menu is displayed.
7. Type **D** (Design a new file). A prompt message is displayed requesting the name of the file to be designed.

8. Press **F1**. Help information is displayed describing how to design a new file, redesign a file, and customize a file.

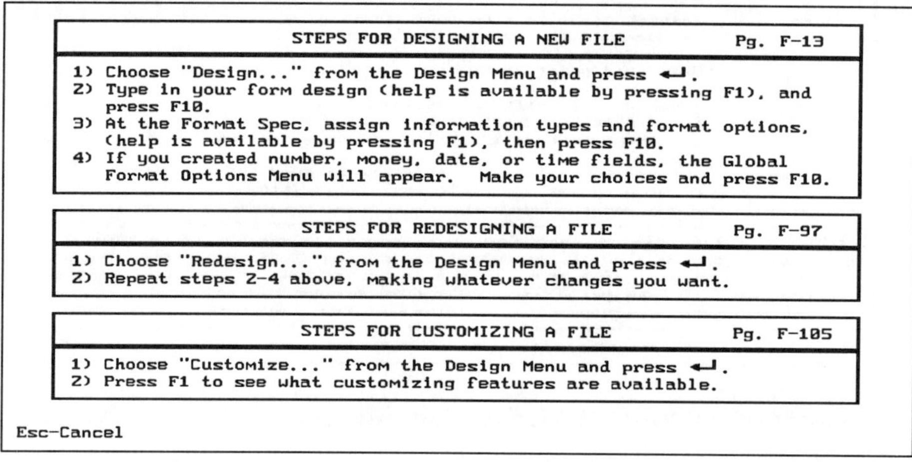

STEPS FOR DESIGNING A NEW FILE Pg. F-13

1) Choose "Design..." from the Design Menu and press ↵.
2) Type in your form design (help is available by pressing F1), and press F10.
3) At the Format Spec, assign information types and format options, (help is available by pressing F1), then press F10.
4) If you created number, money, date, or time fields, the Global Format Options Menu will appear. Make your choices and press F10.

STEPS FOR REDESIGNING A FILE Pg. F-97

1) Choose "Redesign..." from the Design Menu and press ↵.
2) Repeat steps 2-4 above, making whatever changes you want.

STEPS FOR CUSTOMIZING A FILE Pg. F-105

1) Choose "Customize..." from the Design Menu and press ↵.
2) Press F1 to see what customizing features are available.

Esc-Cancel

9. Return to the Main Menu.
10. Turn to Module 37 to continue the learning sequence.

Module 48
HELP THE ASSISTANT

DESCRIPTION

This module explains some of the things that you will need to do to help the Assistant should the Assistant have difficulty in complying with any of your requests.

There are some basic conditions that cause the Assistant to request your help. The following type of information or conditions result in a request for help.

- Ambiguous information, question, or statement.
- Impossible request. That is, a request for which there is no answer.
- Incomplete and/or contradictory request.
- Impossible or incorrect request to change a database.
- Use of words of which the Assistant is unaware or uninstructed.

Anytime you request your Assistant to perform a task that is questionable, a prompt message is displayed by the Assistant requesting your assistance. The messages are self-explanatory and your help is easily provided.

Often the Assistant's misunderstanding about words is simply caused by misspelled words in the request. These problems are easily corrected.

Other times, the Assistant simply does not have a particular word in its vocabulary. That is when you must teach the new word to the Assistant. Refer to the various modules in this book describing how to teach the Assistant.

When the Assistant encounters a word that it does not understand, a screen is displayed to inform you of the problem and to provide direction for the Assistant to take. Any word not understood is highlighted on the screen. Selections on the screen provide you with several options to take.

In the following encounter, Q&A does not know the word "ANIMALS." The selections on the screen are all self-explanatory.

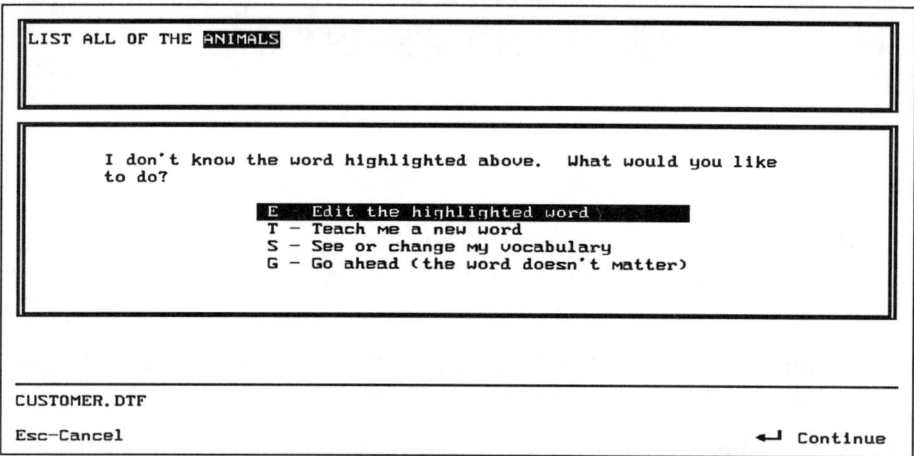

If you choose to teach the Assistant a new word, typing T displays a word-type screen.

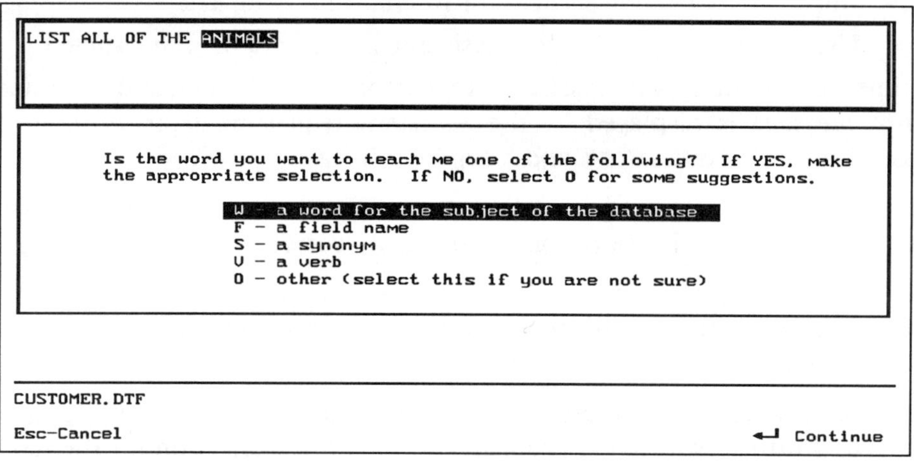

The options on this screen are also self-explanatory. Each selection displays screens similar to those covered in other modules. You will recognize them when they are displayed. However, if you select the S option to teach the Assistant a synonym, the following screen is displayed.

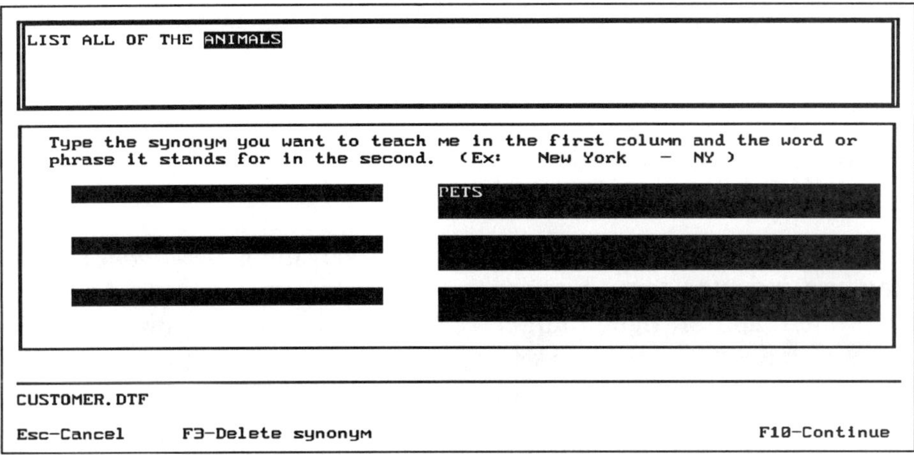

Notice that a synonym was entered: ANIMALS. A definition for that synonym was also entered: PETS.

If you enter the selection O, a help screen is displayed providing you with alternative actions.

APPLICATIONS

Helping your Assistant is an important aspect to getting the most from Q&A software and the data that you enter into databases.

TYPICAL OPERATION

A typical operation is not presented for this module because each incident that can arise is different and depends upon the database with which you are working. However, if the Assistant encounters any situation in which it has difficulty in proceeding with your request, it requests your help by displaying the screens previously discussed. By selecting one of the options on the screens that you think appropriate, help is rendered to the Assistant.

If you are not sure of which selection to choose, review the lesson modules which describe procedures for teaching the Assistant; these provide appropriate assistance to you.

Turn to Module 91 to continue the learning sequence.

Module 49
INDENT TEXT

DESCRIPTION

Another useful formatting tool used in word processing is the *indent text* feature. You can use indented text to enhance the appearance of your documents. A temporary left and/or right margin can be established at any time within a document by indenting to any tab setting or to any column. Tab settings are located on the format ruler at the bottom of the screen and are designated by the letter "T." Individual column locations are also located on the format ruler and are designated by small vertical marks.

Initializing a temporary left and/or right margin is accomplished by positioning the cursor at the selected tab or column, pressing F6, and selecting the appropriate choice on the prompt message. Pressing Esc cancels the prompt message if you decide to return to the document without setting temporary margins.

Once temporary margins are set for a new paragraph, all subsequent paragraphs typed retain those temporary margin settings. However, once the temporary margin settings are cleared, the original margins shown on the ruler line (indicated by [and]) control placement of text. If you return to a paragraph typed earlier in a document to make changes, the typed changes, including inserted text, conform to the temporary margins set for that paragraph.

APPLICATIONS

There are several forms of indenting text. Paragraph indents, which indent the first line of each paragraph, are a commonly used technique in creating a document. However, paragraph indents can be created more simply by pressing Tab on the first line of a paragraph to reach a tab setting where you want text to begin.

Hanging indents are another form of indenting text in a document. A hanging indent is one in which the first line of a paragraph is at the left margin and all of the following lines are indented to a specified tab setting. The following example shows hanging indents.

```
        This first line of text is positioned directly against the
            left margin. Remaining lines following are indented to
            the first set tab location. This is a good example of
            portraying a hanging indent.

        This next paragraph also has the first line of text placed
            against the left margin. This indent technique clearly
            provides visual separation of text._

Working Copy                                  0 %   Line 8 of Page 1 of 1

Esc-Exit  F1-Info  F2-Print  Ctrl+F6-Define Pg  F7-Search  F8-Options  ↑F8-Save
```

Hanging indents can be used to present a pleasing appearance of information or to emphasize text subordination. A familiar example of this type of indent is a basic outline.

Numbered or bulleted lists offer another use of intented text. The Typical Operation section in this module provides an example of using indented text for numbered lists.

In research papers or formal reports, text quoted from verbal or written sources is indented on the left and right margins. This technique emphasizes the text and distinguishes it from surrounding text.

By using the indent text feature, you can easily create bulleted and numbered lists, nested lists or paragraphs, paragraph indents, and hanging indents.

TYPICAL OPERATION

In this illustration, enter the Write function and open an edit session. Enter text into a Working Copy (blank screen) for a new document to practice using the various forms of indenting text. Begin at the Q&A Main Menu.

1. Type **W** to display the Write Menu.
2. Press **Return** to open a Working Copy for a new document.
3. Press **Tab** to indent the first line of text.
4. Type the following text:

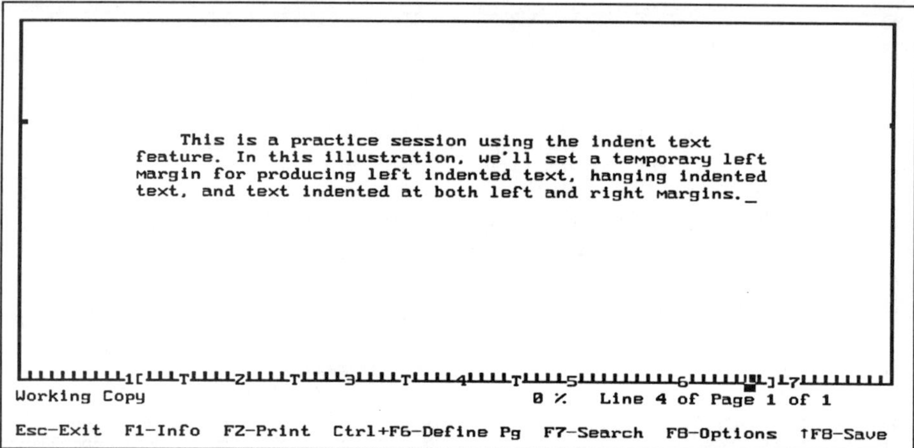

5. Press **Return** to ensure that the cursor is located at the left margin. Press **Return** again to insert a blank line.

6. Press **Right Arrow** to move the cursor to the column where you want the temporary margin. In this illustration, move the cursor five spaces to the right.

7. Press **F6**. A margin prompt message is displayed at the bottom of the screen.

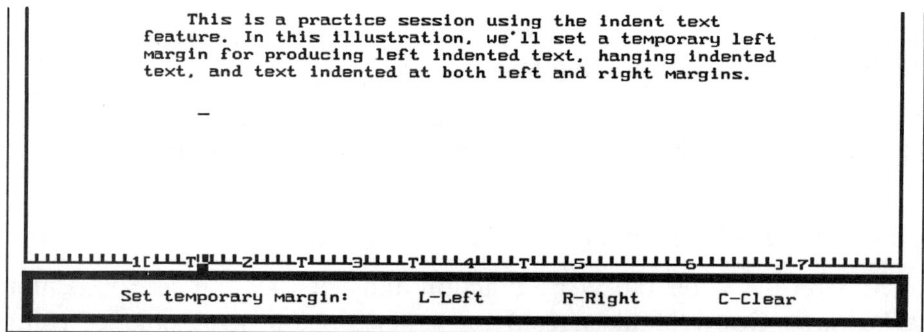

8. Type **L**. The left margin is set at the new location. A right arrow (>) on the format ruler at the bottom of the screen indicates the current location of the temporary left margin.

9. Continue typing the following text below the existing text.

```
     This is a practice session using the indent text
feature. In this illustration, we'll set a temporary left
margin for producing left indented text, hanging indented
text, and text indented at both left and right margins.

          This is the first paragraph of text indented from the
          left margin. Notice that each line typed indents to
          the new indent level._

Working Copy                              0 %   Line 8 of Page 1 of 1

Esc-Exit  F1-Info  F2-Print  Ctrl+F6-Define Pg  F7-Search  F8-Options  ↑F8-Save
```

10. Press **Return** to ensure that the cursor is located at the left margin. Press **Return** again to insert a blank line.
11. Press **Left Arrow** to move the cursor five spaces to the left (to the column at which the original margin was set) and press **F6**.
12. Type **L**. The left margin is moved to its original location. A left bracket ([) indicates the current location of the left margin.
13. Type the following lines of text on the screen below the existing text.

```
     This is a practice session using the indent text
feature. In this illustration, we'll set a temporary left
margin for producing left indented text, hanging indented
text, and text indented at both left and right margins.

          This is the first paragraph of text indented from the
          left margin. Notice that each line typed indents to
          the new indent level.

This paragraph illustrates the hanging indent feature
     where the second line is indented._

Working Copy                       Insert  0 %   Line 11 of Page 1 of 1

Esc-Exit  F1-Info  F2-Print  Ctrl+F6-Define Pg  F7-Search  F8-Options  ↑F8-Save
```

14. Press **Return** to move the cursor to the left margin. Press **Return** again to insert a blank line. Then, press **Right Arrow** to move the cursor to the right five spaces to position a temporary indent level.

15. Press **F6** and type **L**. The temporary margin is set five spaces to the right. A right arrow (>) indicates the current location of the temporary left margin.
16. Type the remainder of the text below the existing text.

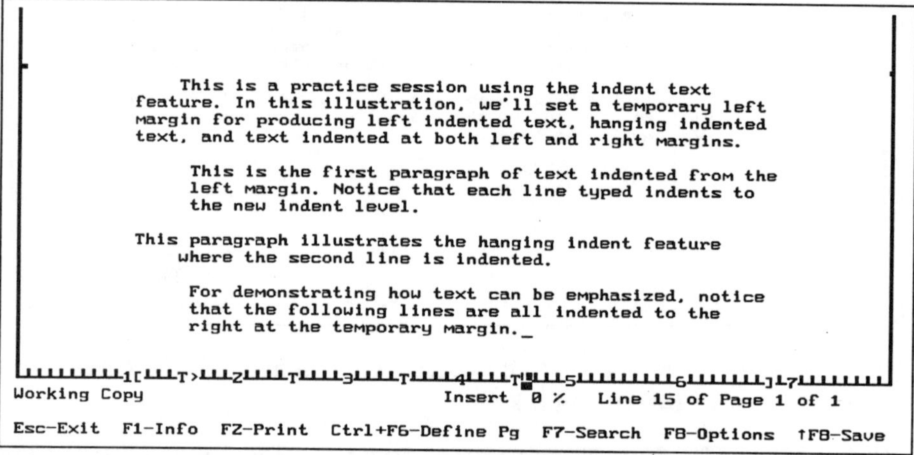

17. Press **Return** to return the cursor to the left margin. Press **Return** again to insert a blank line.
18. Leave the left margin set indented. Press **Right Arrow** until the cursor is located at the right margin. The right margin is denoted with a right bracket (]) on the format ruler.
19. Press **Left Arrow** to move the cursor five spaces to the left of the current right margin.
20. Press **F6** and type **R**. A temporary margin is set at five spaces left of the original margin. A left arrow (<) is displayed on the format ruler at the bottom of the screen, indicating the current temporary margin setting.
21. Type the following text and note the results.

```
          This is a practice session using the indent text
      feature. In this illustration, we'll set a temporary left
      margin for producing left indented text, hanging indented
      text, and text indented at both left and right margins.

           This is the first paragraph of text indented from the
           left margin. Notice that each line typed indents to
           the new indent level.

      This paragraph illustrates the hanging indent feature
          where the second line is indented.

           For demonstrating how text can be emphasized, notice
           that the following lines are all indented to the
           right at the temporary margin.

           This paragraph is an example of text that is
           indented on both right and left margins. A
           typical use of this technique is to emphasize
           text quoted from a verbal or written source._
LIIIIIIIII1[IIIT>III2IIIITIIII3IIIITIIII4IIIITIIII5IIIIIIIII6II< IIII]I7IIIIIII
Working Copy                              Insert  0 %   Line 20 of Page 1 of 1

Esc-Exit  F1-Info  F2-Print  Ctrl+F6-Define Pg  F7-Search  F8-Options  ↑F8-Save
```

22. Press **Esc** to return to the Write Menu.

23. Press **Esc** to exit from the Write function. A prompt message is displayed warning you that the Working Copy of the document has not been saved. The cursor is located at N - No.

24. Type **Y** to return to the Q&A Main Menu without saving the document to disk.

25. Turn to Module 25 to continue the learning sequence.

Module 50
IMPORT A DOCUMENT

DESCRIPTION

When *importing a document*, you insert an external document into the current document during an edit session. The external document must meet certain criteria to be accepted into Q&A as an imported document. Documents created in most common word processors that have been printed to disk (as print files), saved as ASCII files, or saved as text files can be imported into Q&A. For example, documents created in PFS:Write, IBM Writing Assistant, WordStar, Lotus 1-2-3 or Symphony, or Multimate can be imported into Q&A Write documents. DOS files and Basic programs can also be imported.

The import operation is fairly simple. While in an edit session, with a document displayed on the screen, position the cursor at the location that you want the imported document inserted. Pressing F8 displays the Options Menu. Selecting I designates that you want to insert a document. A prompt message is displayed asking you to type the document name that you want inserted.

You can press Return to display the names of the files stored to disk, or you can type the directory path and filename. Pressing Return displays the Import Document Menu. Selecting the type of document (i.e., ASCII, Lotus 1-2-3, etc.) completes the import operation and the imported document is displayed on the screen at the initial location of the cursor.

Importing an ASCII document imports the document with carriage returns embedded in the text.

Using the Special ASCII option imports the document and removes the carriage returns embedded in the text. This produces a document with word wrap and blank lines between paragraphs.

The WordStar selection imports the document as a true WordStar document.

The Lotus 1-2-3 or Symphony selection causes the Lotus range specification to display. From that screen you can select the spreadsheet range. Carriage returns are imported at the end of each spreadsheet row.

APPLICATIONS

A valuable feature of Q&A is the capability of inserting documents from other application and word processing software. This feature can save you time, especially if a document has already been created, perhaps in WordStar or Multimate, and you can use it in its existing form.

There is a wide variety of software in use today that creates documents and/or files in a data format readily acceptable by Q&A Write documents.

TYPICAL OPERATION

In this illustration, begin at the Q&A Main Menu, create a new document, and then select the location at which you want an imported document to appear. Import a document at the specified location.

1. Type **W** to select the Write Menu.
2. Press **Return** to display a Working Copy (blank) screen for a new document.
3. Type the following text:

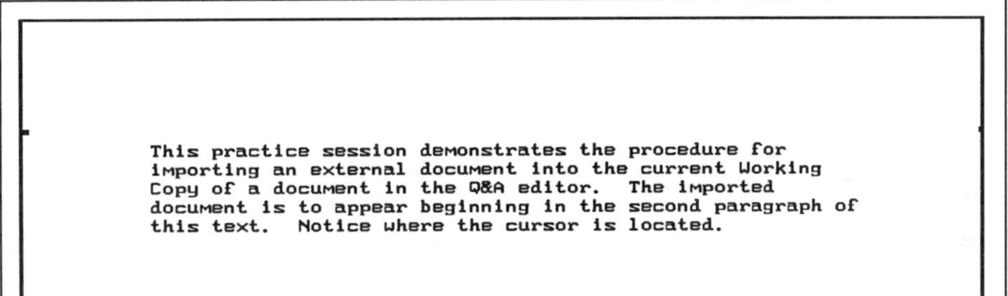

4. Press **F8** to display the Options Menu.

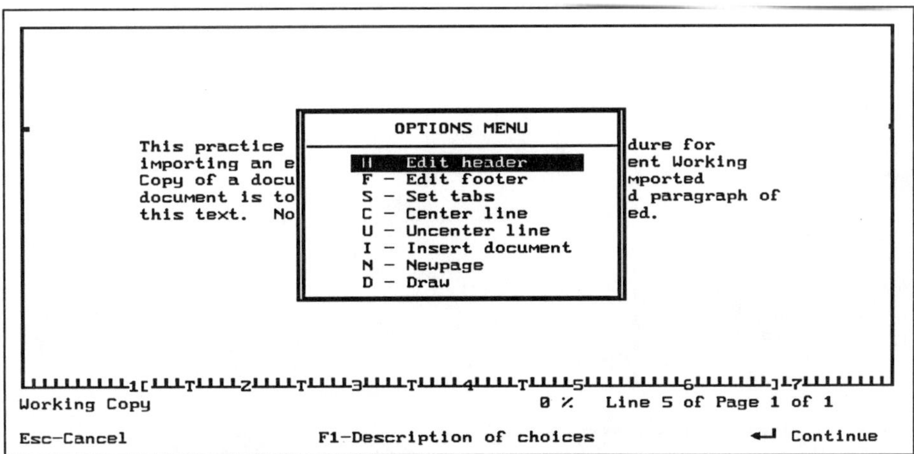

5. Type **I**. A prompt message is displayed requesting the name of the file to be imported. If you have forgotten the filename, press **Return** and a list of files stored to disk is displayed.

6. Type the name of any qualified file in response to the prompt message and press **Return**. The file can be an ASCII file, special ASCII file, a WordStar file, Lotus 1-2-3 or Symphony file, DOS file, or a Basic program file.

The Import Document Menu is displayed.

7. Type **A D**, **W**, or **L** (depending upon the type of document that you are importing). The document is inserted beginning at the cursor location. A typical example of importing a Basic program is shown:

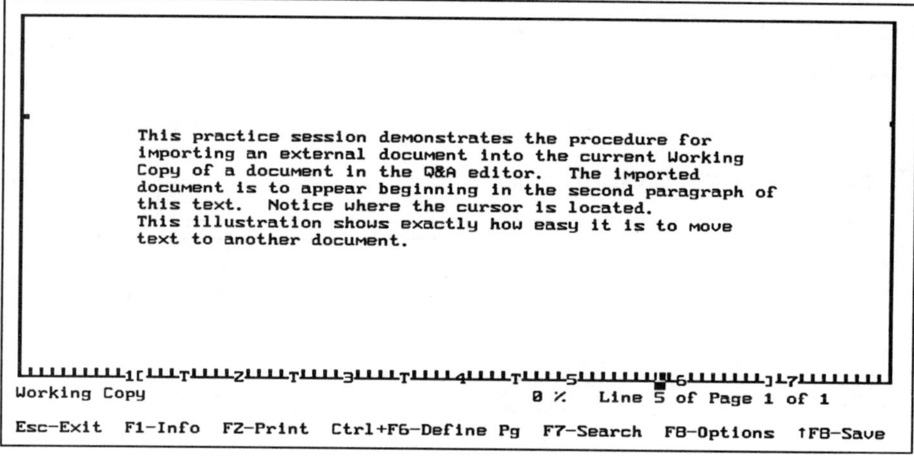

8. Return to the Q&A Main Menu without saving the document.

9. Turn to Module 66 to continue the learning sequence.

Module 51
IMPORTING FILES

DESCRIPTION

Q&A provides the capability to import data created by several other software packages. The importance of this capability is that many keystrokes, calculations, etc. can be saved and utilized within Q&A.

Some readily adaptable software includes dBASE II, III, or III Plus; Lotus 1-2-3, Symphony, PFS, and ASCII or DIF files. Even though a file may have been created by software other than those listed on the Import Data Menu, you may still be able to import the file into Q&A. In such cases, refer to the instruction manual for the originating software. Find instructions for converting the file to ASCII or DIF data format. Then use Q&A's Import Data Menu to perform the import operation.

IMPORTING dBASE, ASCII, or DIF FILES To import a dBASE file, as with a Lotus 1-2-3 file, you must have an existing Q&A file or have specifically created a Q&A file to receive the dBASE information.

Before a dBASE file can be imported into Q&A, the dBASE file must be converted to ASCII format. Once the dBASE file is converted to ASCII format, it can be imported into Q&A using the ASCII selection on the Import Menu.

Importing a dBASE file into Q&A enables you to convert your database system output to Q&A. All database information can be transferred to Q&A. In many cases, literally hours of data entry are eliminated because all data entered initially into dBASE is retrievable and convertible to Q&A. DIF files are imported in the same way as ASCII files. Remember to create a form that is compatible in structure to the original DIF source file before using the DIF import selctions of the Import Menu.

The Typical Operation section of this module guides you through a step-by-step dBASE import procedure.

IMPORTING LOTUS 1-2-3 When designing and creating an accepting Q&A file for Lotus 1-2-3, it is important to remember certain requirements. Each row in a Lotus 1-2-3 worksheet fits into a single Q&A form. Each cell in a Lotus 1-2-3 worksheet fits into a single field in a Q&A form. If you choose not to use the Merge Spec feature, the first cell in a Lotus 1-2-3 worksheet is assumed to be the first field in the accepting Q&A form. Each new row in the Lotus 1-2-3 worksheet begins a new Q&A form. As in the case of ASCII and DIF files, if there is more data in the Lotus 1-2-3 row than the accepting Q&A form can accommodate, the extraneous data is ignored by Q&A. Likewise, if there is less data in the Lotus 1-2-3 worksheet row than the accepting Q&A form expects, the extra fields in the Q&A form are left blank.

The Typical Operation Section of this module lets you practice importing a Lotus 1-2-3 file into Q&A.

IMPORTING PFS: When importing a PFS: File database into a newly created Q&A file, Q&A automaticlly creates a form design to receive the PFS: File database. When importing PFS: you must account for multi-line fields when applicable. When Q&A creates a form design, the Format Spec screen is displayed to allow you to specify the appropriate information type for each field on the form. You can import PFS: File database with or without merge specifications.

TYPICAL OPERATION

In this section, import a Lotus 1-2-3 and dBASE file into Q&A. Start at the Q&A Main Menu.

NOTE

The following activities require that you have one or all of the following programs and understand their use:

Lotus 1-2-3 (or Symphony)
dBASE II, III, or III Plus
The DOS COPY command

If you successfully complete the Lotus 1-2-3 or Symphony and dBASE activities, you may omit the DOS COPY procedure.

Lotus 1-2-3 (or Symphony) (Go to the dBASE activity of this exercise if you do not have Lotus 1-2-3 or Symphony software.)

1. Create and save a Lotus 1-2-3 worksheet that resembles the following one. Name it PRODUCE.WKS.

	A	B	C
1	Produce	Quantity	Cost
2	Artichoke	35	1.22
3	Cabbage	27	0.38
4	Orange	100	1.65

2. Start the Q&A program.
3. Type **F**; then type **D** to display the Design Menu. Type **D**, then type the filename n:**PRODUCE** and press **Return**. Note that n: is the disk drive designator.
4. Type the following field names and use ten spaces for each field length.

   produce: >**quantity:** >**cost:** >

5. Save the design by pressing **F10**.
6. Assign information types as follows and press **F10**.

Produce	**T**
Quantity	**N**
Cost	**M**

7. Accept the default option values by pressing **F10** twice to redisplay the File Menu. Press **Esc** to redisplay the Q&A Main Menu.
8. Type **U**. Then type **I** to display the Import Menu.
9. Type **L** for Lotus 1-2-3; then type n:**PRODUCE** and press **Return**. (The extension WKS is added automatically.) Notice that Q&A displays the PRODUCE.DTF filename for you.
10. Press **Return**; press **F10** in response to the Define Range menu. The Lotus worksheet is imported into the PRODUCE.DTF file and is now usable by Q&A.

dBASE II, III, or III Plus (Go to the DOS COPY activity if you do not have dBASE software.)

1. Create and save a dBASE database structure that resembles the following one. Name it PRODUCE.DBF.

Field	Field Name	Type	Width	Dec
1	PRODUCE	Character	15	
2	QUANTITY	Numeric	6	
3	COST	Numeric	6	2

2. Input the following information into the database.

Field Name	Rec. 1	Rec. 2	Rec. 3
Produce	**Bananas**	**Lettuce**	**Carrots**
Quantity	**10**	**500**	**350**
Cost	**1.79**	**0.24**	**.32**

3. From the dBASE dot prompt type **COPY TO PRODUCE SDF** to create an ASCII file named PRODUCE.TXT.
4. Quit the dBASE program and start the Q&A program.

NOTE

If you performed the Lotus 1-2-3 procedure, select the Utilities Menu and Import Menu and then go to step 6.

5. Perform steps 3 through 8 of the preceding Lotus 1-2-3 import procedure. Then return to step 6 of dBASE.
6. Type **A** for ASCII; then type n:**PRODUCE.TXT** and press **Return** in response to the Import from filename prompt.
7. Type n:**PRODUCE.DTF** as the Q&A filename and press **Return.**
8. Press **F10** in response to the Merge Spec screen. Notice that the data is imported for use with Q&A.

DOS COPY ACTIVITY

1. Use the DOS COPY command to create and save an ASCII file.
   a. Type COPY CON: PRODUCE.TXT and press **Return.**
   b. Type the information as shown; allow ten character spaces for each field of information. End the Carrots line by pressing **F6** (or Ctrl-Z) and **Return.**

```
Bananas        10,       1.79
Lettuce       500,       0.24
Carrots       350,       0.32 ^ Z
```

   c. Notice the message "1 File(s) copied" after you press Return.
2. Start the Q&A program.

NOTE

If you performed the Lotus 1-2-3 or dBASE procedure, select the Utilities Menu and Import Menu and continue with step 5.

3. Perform steps 3 through 8 of the preceding Lotus 1-2-3 import procedure.
4. Type **S** for Standard ASCII; then type n:**PRODUCE.TXT** and press **Return** in response to the ASCII filename.

5. Type n:**PRODUCE.DTF** as the Q&A filename and press **Return**.
6. Press **F10** in response to the Merge Spec screen. Press **F10** in response to ASCII OPTIONS. Notice that the data is imported for use with Q&A.
7. Turn to Module 35 to continue the learning sequence.

Module 52
INVISIBLE COLUMNS IN A REPORT

DESCRIPTION

When creating a report, it is possible to designate certain columns as invisible columns. These invisible columns can be used for sorting purposes or for performing calculations for a derived column. What is unique about invisible columns is that the column itself never appears on the report. Invisible columns are designated on the Column/Sort Spec screen with the special code of "I."

APPLICATIONS

The basic applications of invisible columns are sorting and calculating. These operations are performed using the values contained in the invisible columns. The results from the sorting or calculations can be produced in derived columns.

TYPICAL OPERATION

In this illustration, enter the Report function, proceed through the design of a report, and incorporate an invisible column for a report on the Column/Sort Spec screen for a single field. Exit from the operation or refer to an applicable module for printing the report. Begin at the Q&A Main Menu.

1. Type **R** to select the Report Menu.
2. Type **D**. A prompt message is displayed requesting the name of the database for which the report is to be designed.
3. Type **CUSTOMER** and press **Return**. A List of Reports screen is displayed. The list contains all previously designed reports for the database. If none have been previously designed, the screen is blank. The cursor is located at "Enter name:".
4. Type **INVISIBLE-COLUMN** and press **Return.** The Retrieve Spec screen for the database is displayed.
5. Press **F10**. All forms in the database are retrieved. The Column/Sort Spec Screen is displayed.

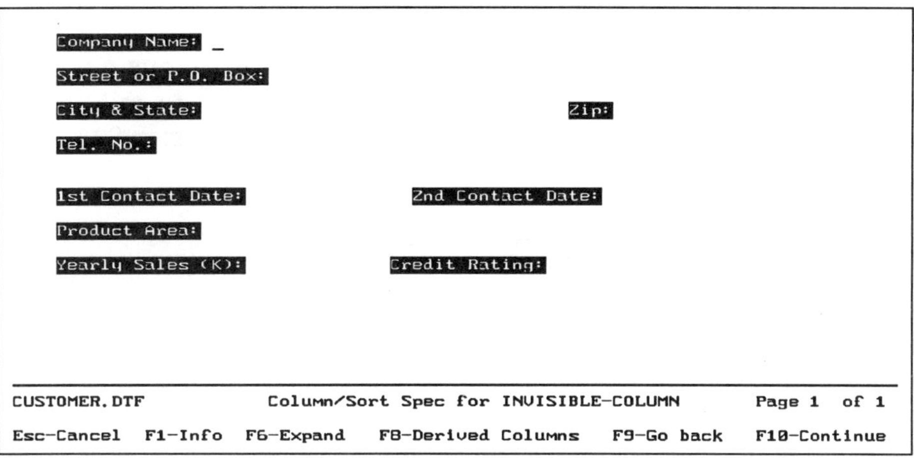

6. Move the cursor to each field on screen and type a number which designates the column in the report in which the information is to be printed or displayed. Select the "Yearly Sales" field as column 4 by typing **4** in the field.
7. Move the cursor to the Yearly Sales (K) column and type a comma (,) and a space following the number 4, **DS**, a comma (,), another space, and **I** (denoting an invisible column). The screen should be displayed as follows:

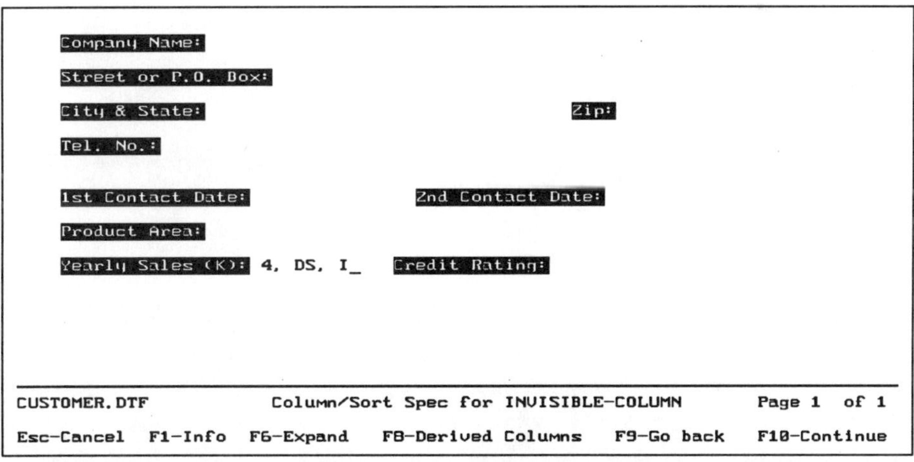

When this report is produced, the first column in the report is Company Name. The names are sorted in descending order by the values contained on the various forms in the Yearly Sales field.

The dollar values contained in the Yearly Sales field are not printed; they were designated as invisible columns.

8. Press **F10**. The Print Options Menu is displayed. For instructions on how to print a report, refer to Module 72. If you do not want to print the report, but want to return to the Q&A Main Menu, proceed to step 9.
9. Return to the Main Menu.
10. Turn to Module 87 to continue the learning sequence.

Module 53
JOIN DOCUMENTS

DESCRIPTION

Joining documents is similar to moving a document from disk into a document currently in an edit session. Within a document in the editor (called a *base document*), you can select the location where the embedded document is to be placed.

There are three commands that can be used to embed files stored on disk into a document when it is printed.

The *JOIN* command embeds another Write document into a base document.

The *SPREADSHEET* command embeds a Lotus 1-2-3 spreadsheet into the entire portion of a base document. Refer to Module 51 for detailed information on this process.

The *GRAPH* command embeds bit-map images or Lotus 1-2-3.PIC files (containing graphs) into a base document. Refer to Module 51 for detailed information on this process.

On the screen display, the embedded document from disk storage is never displayed. The JOIN (J) command indicates that the joined document is placed at a specific location when the base document is printed.

Joining documents involves inserting the name of any other Write document at any location in another Write document. The location of the insert is designated by the *JOIN* command. What you are actually doing is creating a print control file which properly merges all of the joined documents specified in a base document at the time of printing.

The process of joining documents is straightforward. From the Q&A Main Menu, enter the Write function and either create a base document or GET an existing document into the editor. Select the location where you want another document inserted and move the cursor to that location. Place the cursor at the beginning of a blank line. It may be necessary to insert a blank line in the base document to provide a place to type the JOIN command. Type the JOIN command preceded and followed by an asterisk (*). The syntax for the JOIN command is:

```
*JOIN drive/path/filename* or
*J drive/path/filename*
```

Where:

JOIN - designates that you want to perform the join document function.

drive - specifies the particular disk drive that contains the file in which the join document resides. If the document file is saved in a particular directory, you must specify the directory and path.

path - indicates a directory and/or subdirectory.

filename - indicates the exact name of the join document as it is stored on disk.

For example: `*JOIN A SAMPLE or *J a sample*`

As you can see from the example, the JOIN command can be abbreviated as "J."

If the document being joined to a base document is located on the preset drive, then specifying the drive is not required.

Any ASCII formatted non-Write document can be joined to a Write document. However, the ASCII non-Write document must have been printed to disk rather than saved to disk. For example, if you are joining a document created under WordStar, the WordStar document must have been printed to disk as a print file. Consequently, it has a filename extension of ".PRT" and the join will be successful when used.

Write documents can be joined with Reports as long as the Report has also been printed to disk rather than saved to disk. Keep this in mind when you are creating reports. If you think that there is a chance of wanting to join the report with a Write document some time in the future, you should not only save the report, but also print it to disk.

You can join as many documents as you want in a base document. In fact, the base document can be a control document or consist only of a series of JOIN commands defining an all encompassing document to be created when printed.

If you want to insert a full copy of a document in the editor, refer to Module 17; it describes the procedure for inserting a copy (and subsequent display of the text) of a document, stored on disk, directly into a document currently in an edit session.

APPLICATIONS

The JOIN command is useful in creating a document from standard paragraphs or statements previously stored on disk as individual files. It proves invaluable in creating contracts, leases, specifications, parts lists, composite customer lists, and specialized mailing lists.

TYPICAL OPERATION

In this illustration, begin at the Q&A Main Menu, enter the Write function and create two small documents saving each to disk. Create a base document which utilizes the JOIN command to compile a control file that prints each of the individual documents as if they were contained in the base document. Print the document by referring to Module 67 for instructions on how to print a document or exit from the document without saving it to disk.

1. Type **W** to select the Write Menu.
2. Press **Return**. A Working Copy (blank) screen for a new document is displayed.
3. Type the following text:

```
2.0 Mechanical Specifications

The equipment shall be contained in a stainless steel
enclosure.  Ventilation shall be provided to allow for at
least 2500 CFM of filtered air to circulate through the
enclosure...
```

4. Press **Return** twice to add space between paragraphs.
5. Press **Esc**. The Write Menu is displayed.
6. Type **S** (Save). A prompt message is displayed requesting the filename under which you want to save the document currently in the editor.
7. Type **MECHSPEC** and press **Return**. The document is saved to disk under the specified filename.
8. Type **C** to clear the document from the editor. A new document (blank screen) is displayed.

9. Type the following text:

```
3.0 Electrical Specifications

The equipment shall operate on 120 +5, -10 volts
alternating current.  Total power consumption shall not
exceed 30 amperes...
```

10. Press **Esc**. The Write Menu is displayed.
11. Type **S**. Type **ELECSPEC** and press **Return**. The document is saved to disk under the specified filename.
12. Type **C** to clear the document from the editor. A new document (blank screen) is displayed.
13. Type the following JOIN commands to create the base document:

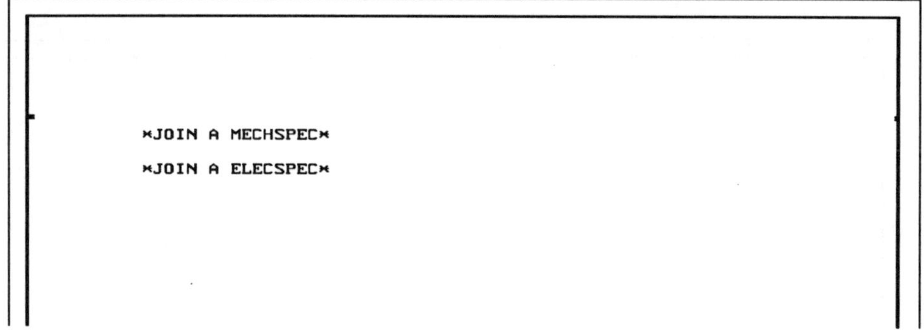

If your documents are saved in a directory (or subdirectory), you must specify the appropriate path and filename within the JOIN command. For example:

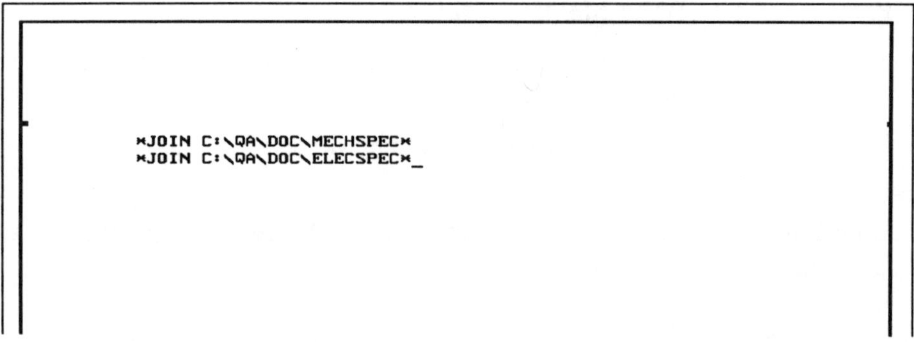

14. To save the document, press **Esc**, type **S** (Save) then type **JOIN** and press **Return** to name the file.

Refer the Module 67 for instructions on printing a document if you want to print this practice document. Otherwise, proceed to Step 15. The following is an example of the printout.

```
2.0 Mechanical Specifications

The equipment shall be contained in a stainless steel
enclosure. Ventilational shall be provided to allow for at
least 2500 CFM of filtered air to circulate through the
enclosure...

3.0 Electrical Specifications

The equipment shall operate on 120 +5, -10 volts
alternating current. Total power consumption shall not
exceed 30 amperes...
```

15. Return to the Q&A Main Menu.
16. Turn to Module 36 to continue the learning sequence.

Module 54
JUSTIFICATION — ON/OFF

DESCRIPTION

Text justification allows you to print a document with a uniform right margin. Each line of the document ends at the same position on the right margin. When you choose to have justification turned on, extra blank spaces are inserted between words to make all lines extend to the right margin. If your printer is capable of *microjustification*, spaces or portions of spaces are added to space out words on each line. Because of the microjustification process, your printer may operate somewhat slower.

Justification can be invoked for an entire document or for only parts of a document by using the JUSTIFY command.

Q&A's default setting is justification off. That is, a document is displayed and printed with a ragged right margin. This default is defined on the Print Options Menu. Refer to Module 67 for details on justifying text in a document being printed.

Remember, the justification commands are invoked only when a document is printed. The document text lines are not justified when the document is displayed on the screen.

JUSTIFICATION ON Justification is turned on using the command:

> *JUSTIFY YES* or
> *Justify Yes*
> or *JY Y*

Typing the command at the beginning of text justifies all following text until you turn justification off.

JUSTIFICATION OFF Justification is turned off using the command:

> *JUSTIFY NO* or
> *Justify No*
> or *JY N*

Typing the command at the end of justified text stops text justification. The JUSTIFY command does not occupy a line on the document page when printed. Nor does the command leave a blank line at its location in a document.

Another method of justifying text in a document is to set the JUSTIFY parameter on the Print Options Menu to YES. Refer to Module 67 for procedures describing how to select print options.

APPLICATIONS

Text justification on the right margin of a document is primarily used for enhancing document appearance. A smooth right margin, as opposed to a ragged right margin, is preferred by many people. Others believe that extra full space insertion between words spaces out the text too much. This is true in cases of lines having only a few words that contain many syllables. Q&A does insert full spaces between words to achieve line justification if your printer does not support microjustification. However, if your printer supports microjustification, only micro spaces are added. Thus, a more pleasing spacing of words and the overall layout is printed.

TYPICAL OPERATION

In this illustration, begin at the Q&A Main Menu, select the Write function, and begin an edit session with a Working Copy for a new document. Turn justification on and off in the document using the JUSTIFY command.

1. Select the Write Menu.
2. Press **Return** to display a Working Copy (blank) screen for a new document.
3. Type ***JUSTIFY YES*** on the first line and press **Return** twice.
4. Type the following text:

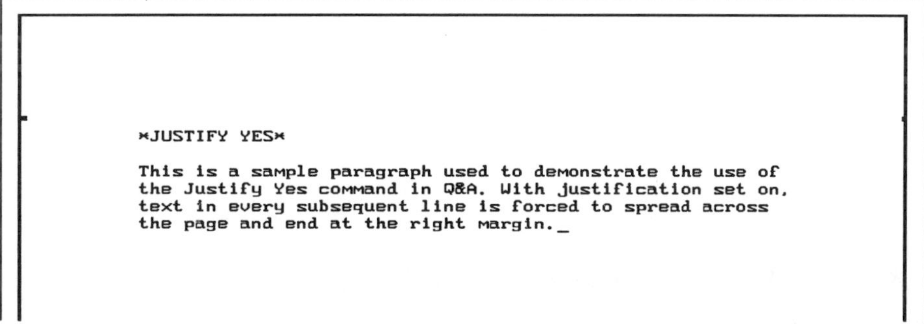

JUSTIFY YES

This is a sample paragraph used to demonstrate the use of
the Justify Yes command in Q&A. With justification set on,
text in every subsequent line is forced to spread across
the page and end at the right margin._

5. Press **Return** to place a carriage return after the paragraph that you have just typed.
6. Type ***JUSTIFY NO*** and press **Return** twice.

7. Now, type the following text:

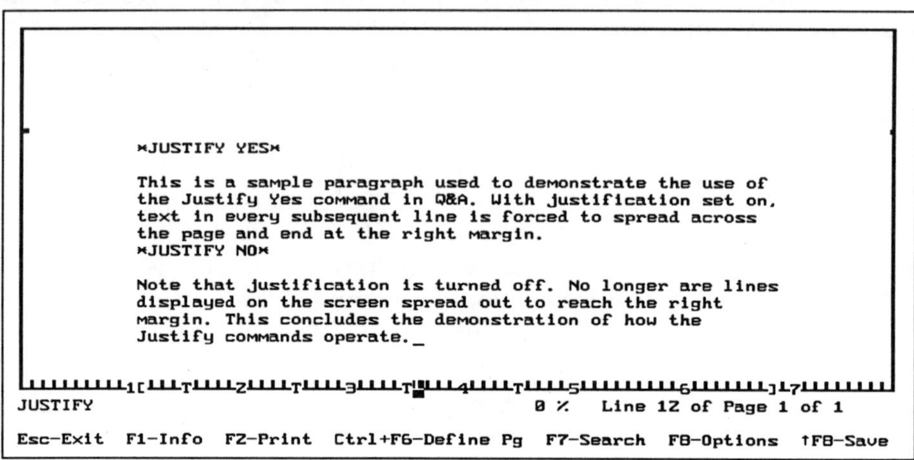

If you want to print the document, refer to Module 67. You can also set justification to ON at the Print Options Menu. However, notice that the embedded JUSTIFY commands overide that option during printing. The text prints as follows:

```
This is a sample paragraph  used to demonstrate the use of
the Justify Yes command in Q&A. With justification set on,
text in every  subsequent line is  forced to spread across
the page and end at the right margin.

Note that justification is turned off. No longer are lines
displayed on the screen spread out to reach the right
margin. This concludes the demonstration of how the
Justify commands operate.
```

8. Return to the Main Menu without saving.
9. Turn to Module 84 to continue the learning sequence.

Module 55
KEYWORD REPORT

DESCRIPTION

You can create a report based upon any designated keyword on a form in a database. When creating a keyword report, the keyword column must be the first column on the report. The *keyword* is designated by typing the code K on the Column/Sort Spec screen at the applicable field on the form; this field corresponds with the keyword that you want printed on a report.

For example, in a customer database a specialized product area could be designated as a keyword field. The following illustration depicts a form in a database with the "Product Area" field as the keyword field.

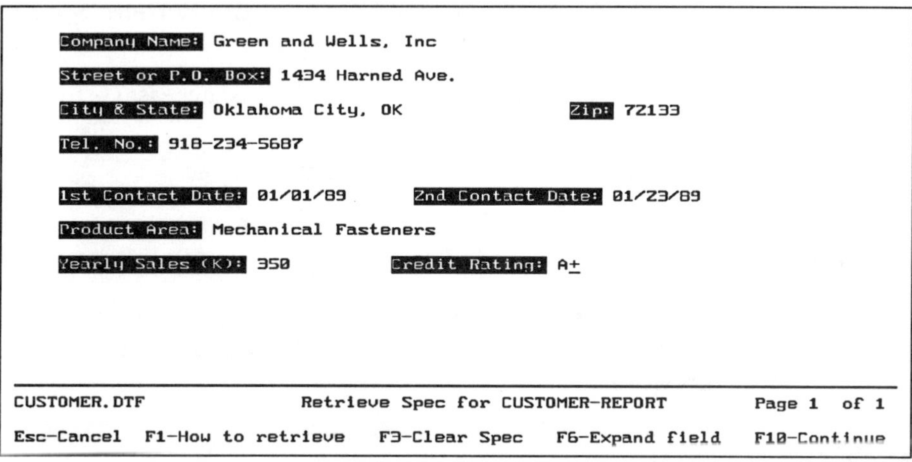

The Column/Sort Spec screen has a K typed on the form in the Product Area field. Notice in the example that the Product Area field is designated as the first column on the report, the Company Name field is the second column, and the Yearly Sales field is the third column.

```
Company Name: Z

Street or P.O. Box:

City & State:                                         Zip:

Tel. No.:

1st Contact Date:                 2nd Contact Date:

Product Area: 1, K

Yearly Sales (K): 3           Credit Rating:_

CUSTOMER.DTF          Column/Sort Spec for CUSTOMER-REPORT          Page 1  of 1
Esc-Cancel  F1-Info  F6-Expand   F8-Derived Columns   F9-Go back   F10-Continue
```

A keyword report can be restricted by using the Retrieve Spec screen to designate exactly which forms you want retrieved for creating the report. Pressing F10 at the Retrieve Spec screen retrieves all forms in the database. Entering the wildcard character "&" at the beginning of the keyword field on the Retrieve Spec screen retrieves only those forms having the keywords present.

When specifying more than one keyword in a field, it is necessary to separate keywords with a semicolon, for example:

> Product Area: mechanical fasteners; adhesives; castings

APPLICATIONS

Creating keyword reports provides you with the exceptional capability of automatically sorting information contained in a database by designated categories called "keywords."

TYPICAL OPERATION

When creating a report, designate the keyword field as the first column to appear in the report and type a K following the column specification on the Column/Sort Spec screen. When the report prints, fields on forms from the keyword field print as the first column on the report.

A keyword report is an option available to you when designing a report. To design a report, you must follow the instructions contained in Module 79. To create a keyword report, simply augment the directions contained in Module 87 with the additional information contained within this module.

Turn to Module 71 to continue the learning sequence.

Module 56
LOCATION/NAME FIELDS LESSON

DESCRIPTION

The Assistant must be taught which fields in a database identifying locations and which identify people's names. This module explains how to teach the Assistant this information.

To reiterate, the Assistant uses all of the information known about the various fields on a form (in a database) to provide you with concise information. To respond to requests involving locations (cities, towns, states, etc.) or people's names, you must define which fields contain these values.

At the Q&A Main Menu, selecting A displays the Assistant Menu. Typing T displays a prompt message requesting the name of the file for which you want to provide instruction to the Assistant. Entering any valid filename and pressing Return displays the Basic Lessons Menu.

Selecting option 3 - "Which fields contain locations" displays the form design for a specified database.

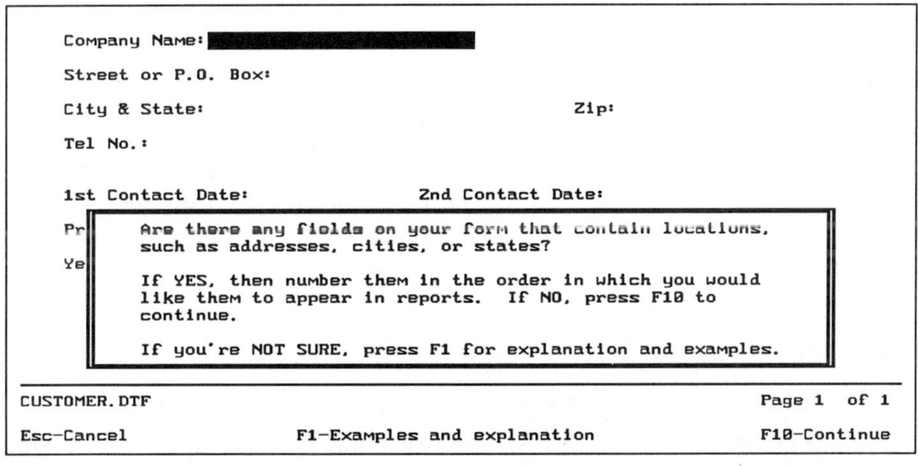

Selecting option 5 - Advanced lessons displays the Advanced Lessons Menu. The cursor is located at 1 - "What fields contain people's names." Pressing Return displays the following screen.

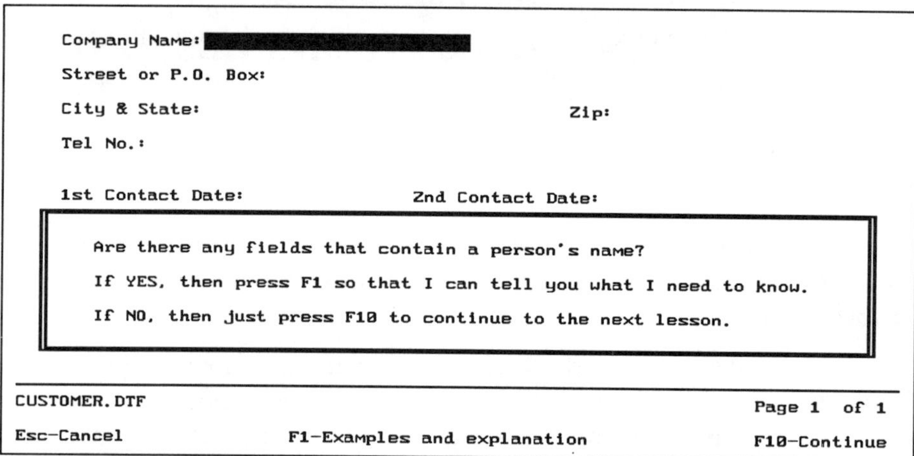

You indicate which fields pertain to locations simply by entering numbers 1, 2, 3, etc. in those fields. Be sure not to enter numbers in other fields (i.e., those fields which contain people's names or company names).

Pressing F1 displays a help screen that provides instructions on how to designate names on the form. Pressing F1 again returns the display of the form design. For either option, pressing F10 completes the lesson and displays the Basic Lessons Menu if you are identifying fields containing locations, or the Advanced Lessons Menu if you are identifying people's names.

APPLICATIONS

The Location/Name Field Lesson is important in that it is the only way you have to communicate to the Assistant the information needed to respond to your future requests. You must define those fields which contain locations and those fields which contain people's names. Once this is done, the Assistant can perform any task related to those fields.

TYPICAL OPERATION

In this illustration, enter the Assistant function, identify a location field and identify a person's name field in the database. Begin at the Q&A Main Menu.

1. From the Main Menu type **A**. The Assistant Menu is displayed.
2. Type **T**. A prompt message is displayed requesting the name of the file about which you want to teach the Assistant.
3. Type **CUSTOMER** and press **Return**. The Basic Lessons Menu is displayed.

4. Type **3**. The form design for the specified database is displayed.

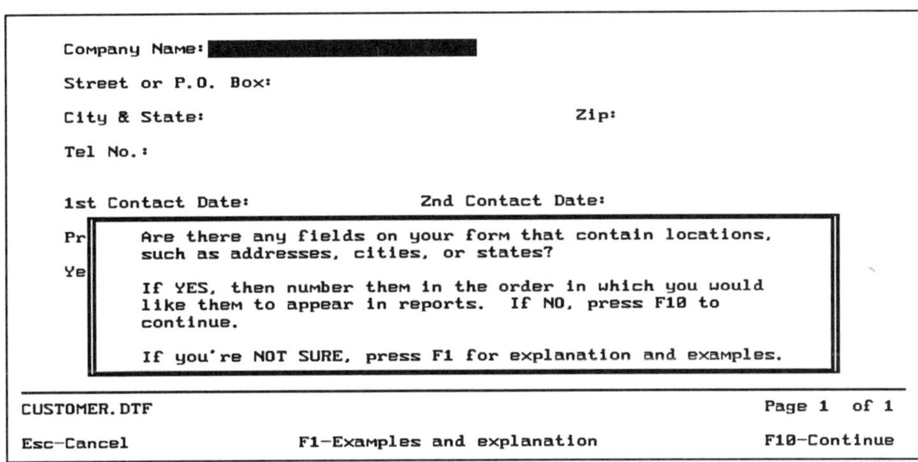
Company Name:

Street or P.O. Box:

City & State: Zip:

Tel No.:

1st Contact Date: 2nd Contact Date:

Pr

Ye

Are there any fields on your form that contain locations, such as addresses, cities, or states?

If YES, then number them in the order in which you would like them to appear in reports. If NO, press F10 to continue.

If you're NOT SURE, press F1 for explanation and examples.

CUSTOMER.DTF Page 1 of 1

Esc-Cancel F1-Examples and explanation F10-Continue

5. Press **Tab** to move the cursor to the "City and State" field.
6. Type **1** and press **Tab** to move the cursor to the "Zip" field.
7. Type **2** and press **F10**. You have identified two fields that contain locations. The Basic Lessons Menu is displayed.
8. Type **5**. The Advanced Lessons Menu is displayed. The cursor is located at 1 - "What fields contain people's names."
9. Press **Return**. The form design for the database is displayed. The cursor is located at the "Company Name" field.
10. Press **F1**. The Lesson Help Screen is displayed.

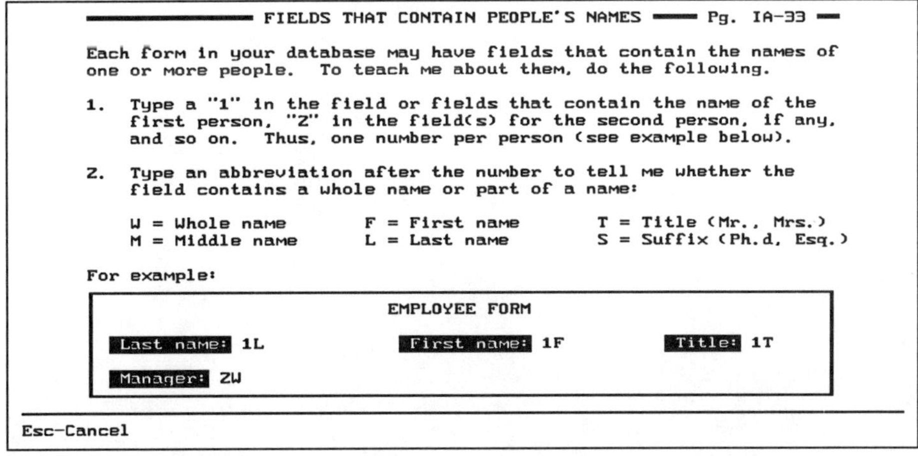
FIELDS THAT CONTAIN PEOPLE'S NAMES — Pg. IA-33

Each form in your database may have fields that contain the names of one or more people. To teach me about them, do the following.

1. Type a "1" in the field or fields that contain the name of the first person, "2" in the field(s) for the second person, if any, and so on. Thus, one number per person (see example below).

2. Type an abbreviation after the number to tell me whether the field contains a whole name or part of a name:

W = Whole name F = First name T = Title (Mr., Mrs.)
M = Middle name L = Last name S = Suffix (Ph.d, Esq.)

For example:

EMPLOYEE FORM

Last name: 1L First name: 1F Title: 1T

Manager: 2W

Esc-Cancel

11. Press **Esc**. The form design for the database is displayed.
12. Type **1W** in the "Company Name" field. You could also, at this point, move the cursor to any other field in the form design and identify other fields containing people's names.
13. Press **F10**. The collective fields ID box is displayed overlayed on the form design. Fields containing people's names are highlighted.
14. Type alternate names that you want to use for the persons identified. For example, customer, client, partner, etc.

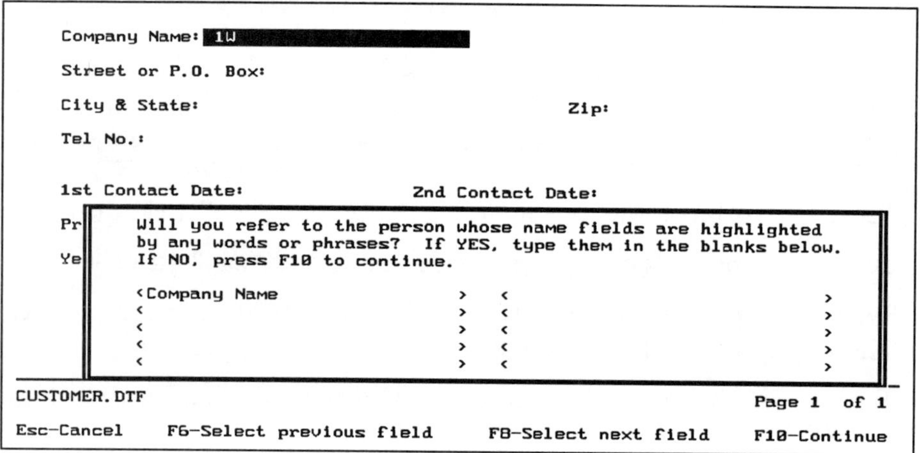

15. Press **F10**. The Advanced Lessons Menu is displayed.
16. Return to the Main Menu.
17. Turn to Module 5 to continue the learning sequence.

Module 57
MASS UPDATE OF FORMS

DESCRIPTION

The Mass Update feature is applicable to the Q&A File function for performing mass updating to existing forms. It permits you to do a global change to a specified group of forms. A *global change* is a change that is made to the specified forms all at once as opposed to making changes to each form individually.

Mass Updates is initiated from the Q&A Main Menu by entering the File function. On the File Menu, choosing the Mass Update selection displays a prompt message requesting the name of the file for the database being updated. The Retrieve Spec screen is displayed permitting you to determine which forms in a specified database are to be updated. When the retrieve specifications are entered, the Update Spec screen is displayed. This is actually where you indicate the update that is to be accomplished.

After entering the update specifications, pressing F10 begins the update process. A prompt message is displayed indicating the total number of forms being updated.

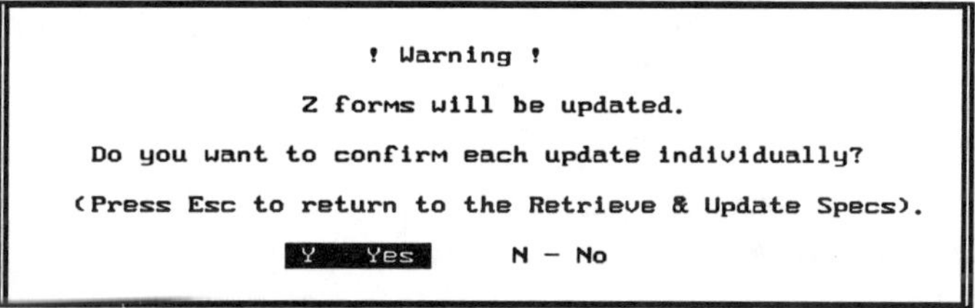

In this prompt, 2 is the total number of forms being updated by Q&A. By pressing N you are given the opportunity to update all of the selected forms without confirming the update of each as the update occurs. If you want to confirm the update to each individual form, pressing Y allows you this prerogative.

If you press Y, each form is displayed. Pressing Shift and F10 updates the displayed form. Pressing F10 alone causes the update not to occur and the next form to display. Pressing Esc cancels the update process and the File Menu is displayed. Pressing Esc again displays the Q&A Main Menu.

APPLICATIONS

One of the most useful applications for Mass Update is to perform recalculations of calculated data currently existing in a database. For example, in a sales organization, calculations defining bonuses or commissions can easily be adjusted automatically with a Mass Update.

In a wholesale operation offering a variety of discounts to customers, recalculation and adjustment of discount factors can be easily and rapidly modified. Maintenance to an existing database is simple and automatic.

In a real estate or property management business, status of listed properties can be maintained at a glance. Personnel files can be maintained to process salary updates, job title updates, or job description changes.

TYPICAL OPERATION

In this illustration, enter into the File function, specify a valid filename, and indicate all of the forms in the database that are to be retrieved for update. Enter the update specifications. Begin at the Q&A Main Menu.

1. At the Q&A Main Menu, the cursor is located at F - File. Press **Return**. The File Menu is displayed.
2. Type **M**, then type **CUSTOMER** and press **Return**. The Retrieve Spec screen for the specified database is displayed.
3. Press **F10**. Notice the change from the "Retrieve Spec" to "Update Spec" prompt at the bottom of the screen.

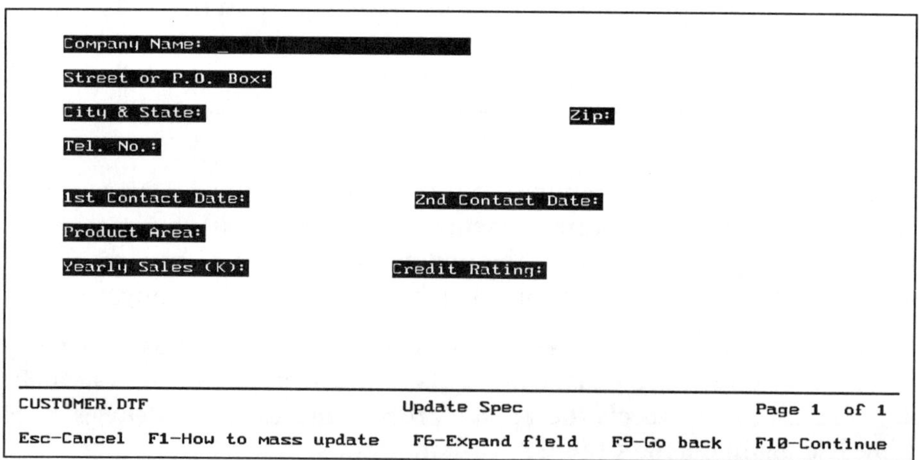

4. Press **Tab** to move the cursor to Product Area and type **#1 = "Sheet Metal Fabricator"**.
5. Move the cursor to Yearly Sales (K) and type **#2 = "135 +"**. These two entries indicate that all forms in the database are to be Mass Updated to embed the specified update values on every form in the database.

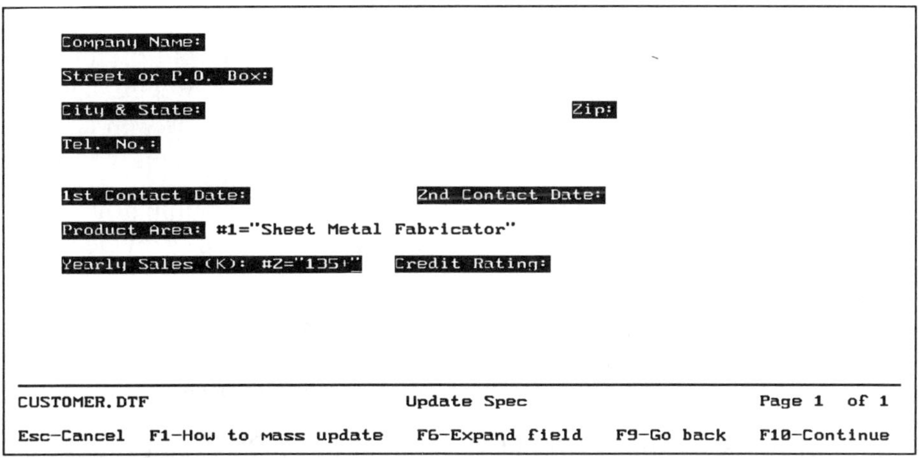

6. Press **F10**. A warning message is displayed indicating how many forms will be updated and giving you the option to confirm each update individually or permit a global mass update without your confirmation. The option Y - Yes is the default and is highlighted to prevent unintentional changes.
7. Select No; all forms are updated. Each form is rapidly displayed as it is updated. The File Menu is displayed after the update operation.
8. Press **Esc** to return to the Q&A Main Menu.
9. Turn to Module 21 to continue the learning sequence.

Module 58
MENU NETWORK

DESCRIPTION

Q&A is a *menu-driven* software application. That is, any major function that you want to perform is accessed through a Q&A menu or submenu. This kind of software architecture makes it very easy for the novice user, as well as extremely convenient for the advanced user.

A novice user can step through the menus and usually determine how to perform a function with the on-line help and the documentation provided with the software.

An advanced user, having frequently used the various Q&A functions, can rapidly access a function without having to refer to the documentation or access on-line help.

When you initiate Q&A by entering QA or qa at the DOS prompt (A>, C>, or D>), the Q&A Main Menu is displayed.

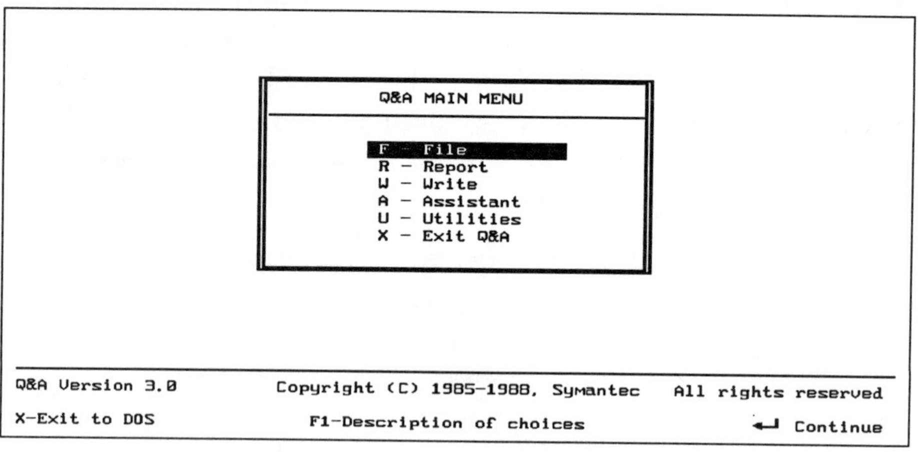

The main menu displays the six major functions that are available within Q&A. The following illustrations show the levels of submenus within each of the major functions.

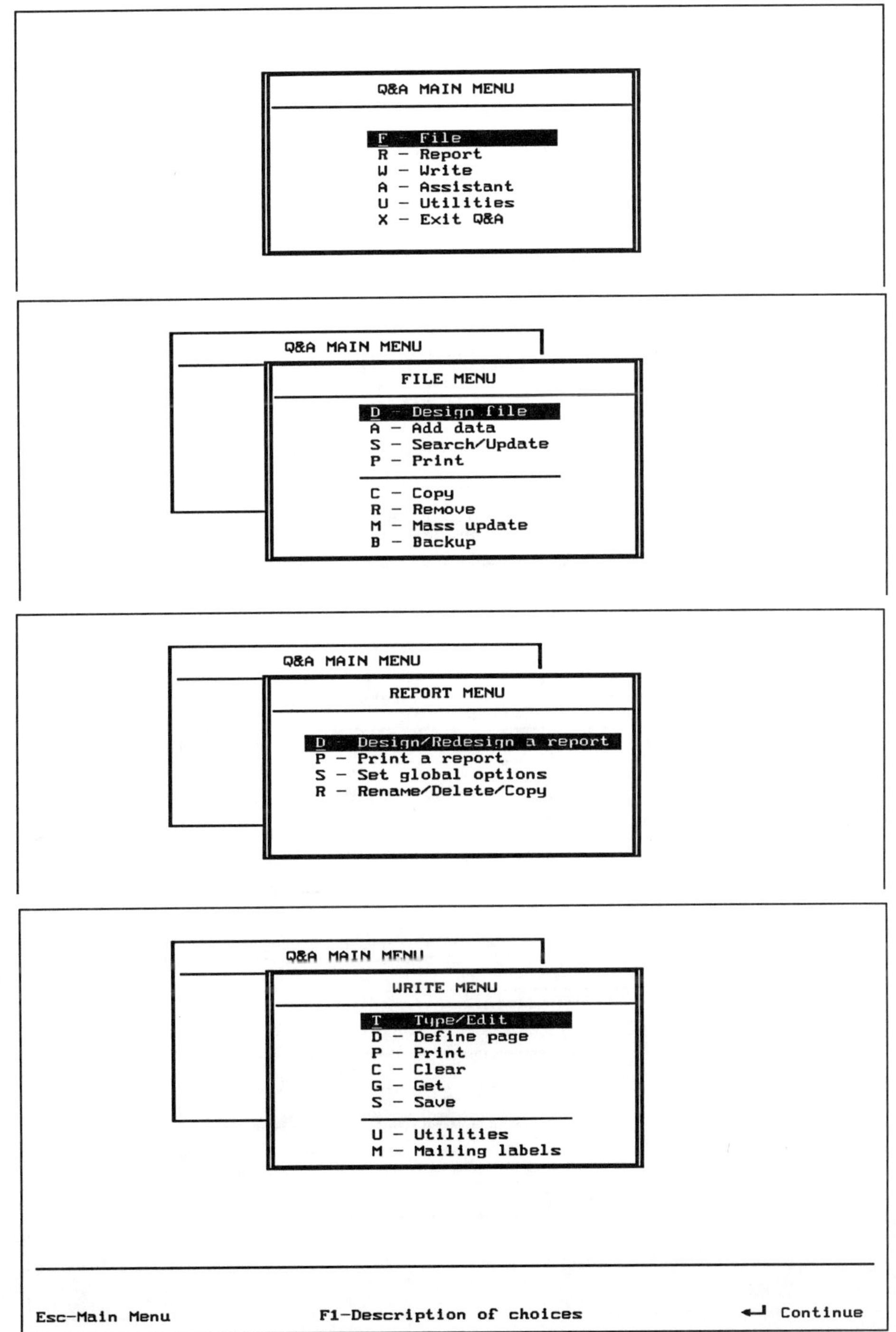
Q&A MAIN MENU
F - File
R - Report
W - Write
A - Assistant
U - Utilities
X - Exit Q&A
Q&A MAIN MENU
FILE MENU
D - Design file
A - Add data
S - Search/Update
P - Print
C - Copy
R - Remove
M - Mass update
B - Backup
Q&A MAIN MENU
REPORT MENU
D - Design/Redesign a report
P - Print a report
S - Set global options
R - Rename/Delete/Copy
Q&A MAIN MENU
WRITE MENU
T - Type/Edit
D - Define page
P - Print
C - Clear
G - Get
S - Save
U - Utilities
M - Mailing labels
Esc-Main Menu
F1-Description of choices
Continue

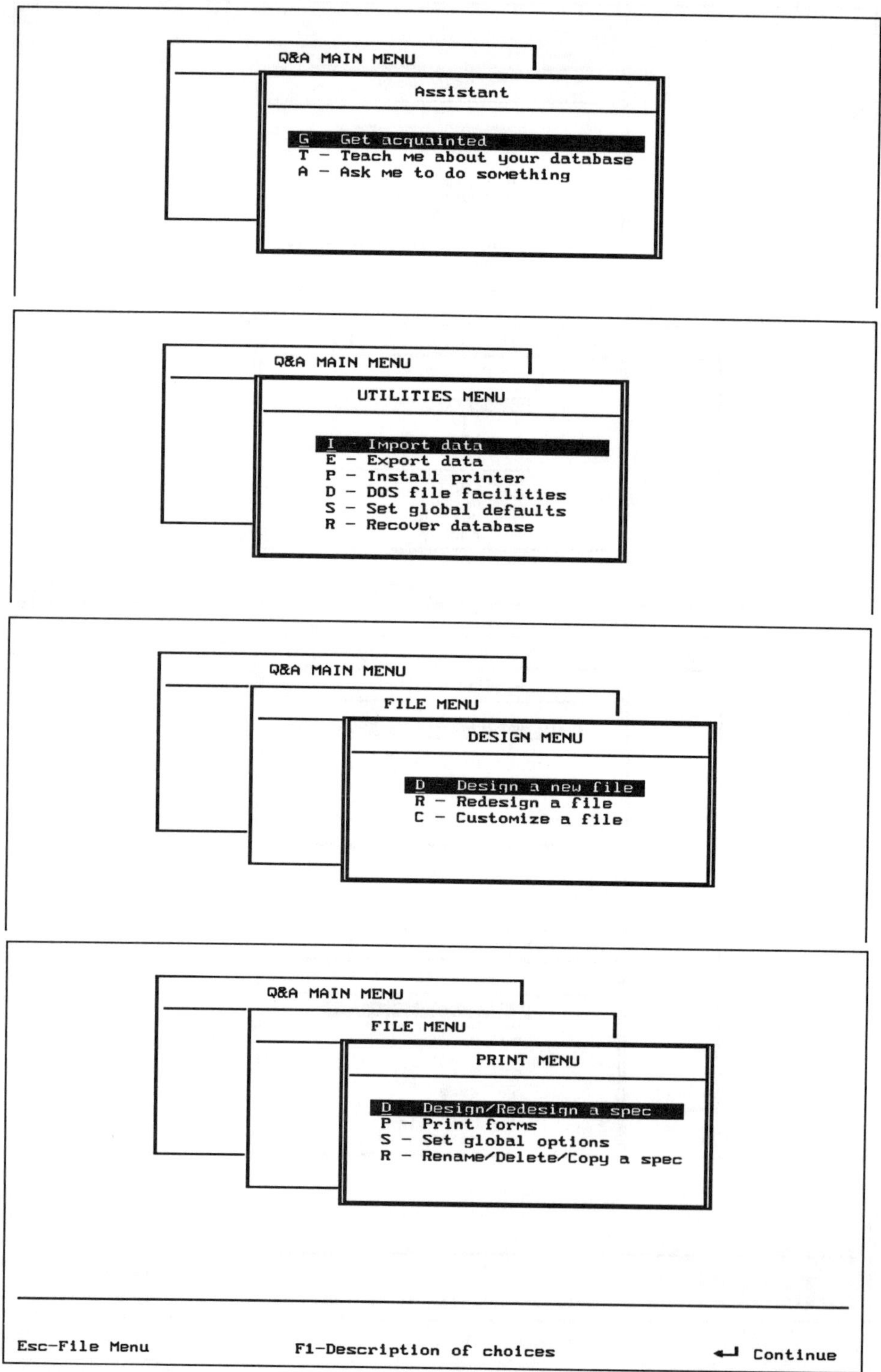
Q&A MAIN MENU
Assistant
G - Get acquainted
T - Teach me about your database
A - Ask me to do something
Q&A MAIN MENU
UTILITIES MENU
I - Import data
E - Export data
P - Install printer
D - DOS file facilities
S - Set global defaults
R - Recover database
Q&A MAIN MENU
FILE MENU
DESIGN MENU
D - Design a new file
R - Redesign a file
C - Customize a file
Q&A MAIN MENU
FILE MENU
PRINT MENU
D - Design/Redesign a spec
P - Print forms
S - Set global options
R - Rename/Delete/Copy a spec
Esc-File Menu
F1-Description of choices
Continue

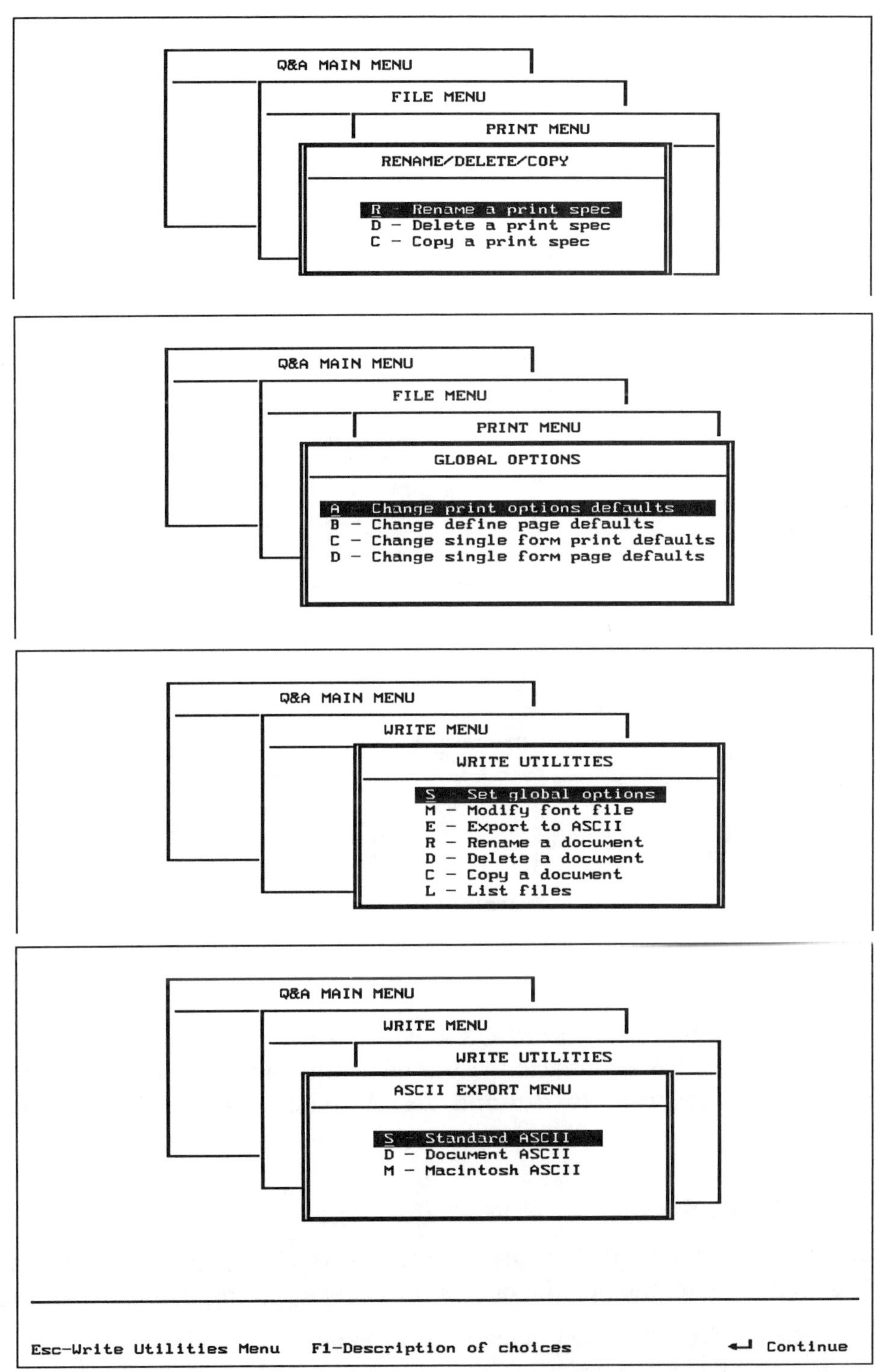
Q&A MAIN MENU
FILE MENU
PRINT MENU
RENAME/DELETE/COPY
R - Rename a print spec
D - Delete a print spec
C - Copy a print spec
Q&A MAIN MENU
FILE MENU
PRINT MENU
GLOBAL OPTIONS
A - Change print options defaults
B - Change define page defaults
C - Change single form print defaults
D - Change single form page defaults
Q&A MAIN MENU
WRITE MENU
WRITE UTILITIES
S - Set global options
M - Modify font file
E - Export to ASCII
R - Rename a document
D - Delete a document
C - Copy a document
L - List files
Q&A MAIN MENU
WRITE MENU
WRITE UTILITIES
ASCII EXPORT MENU
S - Standard ASCII
D - Document ASCII
M - Macintosh ASCII
Esc-Write Utilities Menu
F1-Description of choices
Continue

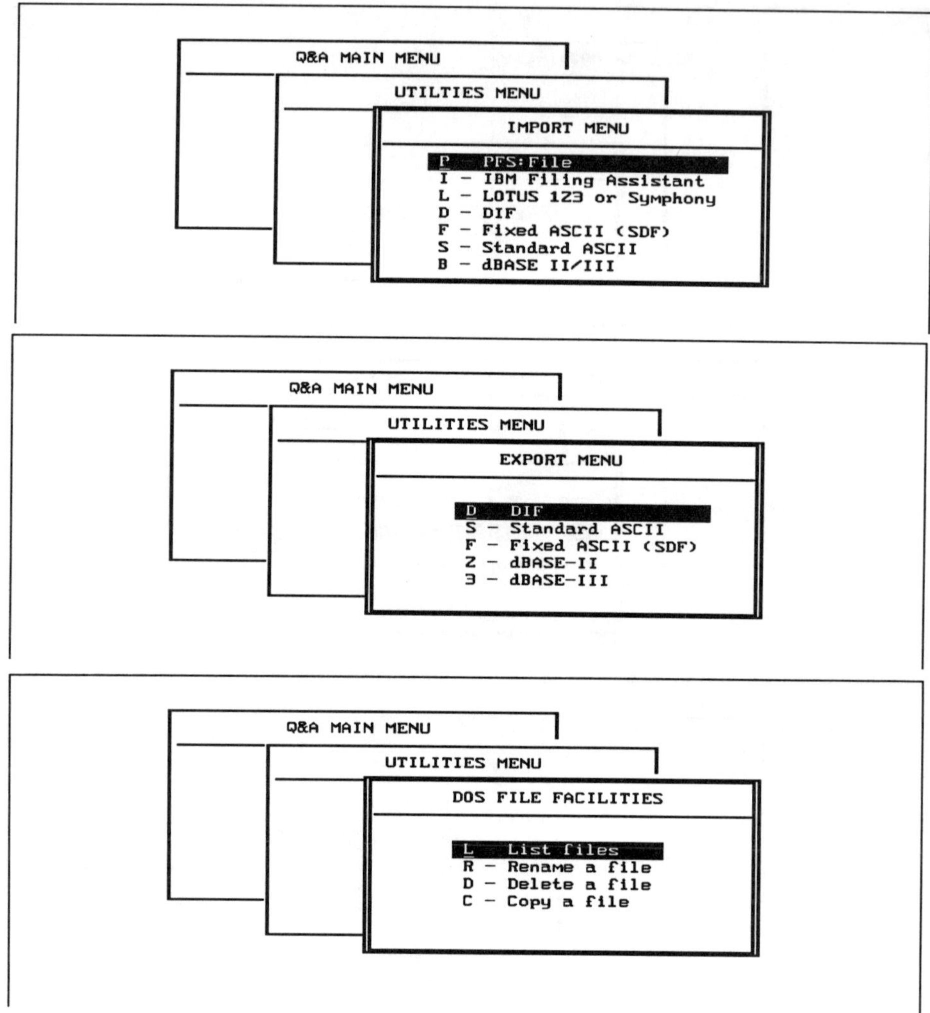

APPLICATIONS

To proceed to any function within Q&A you must do so through a menu or submenu. Use of menus eliminates the use of a command language. Command languages can be awkward to use and actual commands can be difficult to remember.

TYPICAL OPERATION

An illustration is not presented in this module. The module is presented primarily to provide a display of each of the menus in the menu network.

Turn to Module 20 to continue the learning sequence.

Module 59
MERGE DOCUMENT

DESCRIPTION

A *merge document* is one in which text, consisting of field information, from a supporting document is incorporated to produce a complete document. A base document is supplemented with information from a supporting document to create a merge document only when printed.

You can produce merge documents by joining information contained in a File database with a Write document.

For example, client names, addresses, etc. can be located in a Customer File database. A base letter intended for clients can be contained in a Write document. The client name, address, etc. information can be merged with the base letter to produce a personalized letter to each of the clients. With a single base letter and the individual information about each client, countless numbers of merge documents can easily be produced.

Before attempting to create a merge document refer to Module 37 (Form Design) and Module 40 (Form Redesign).

There are several steps required to produce a merge document.

- The File database containing field label information must either exist or must be created. The database contains all of the defined field labels that are used in a merge document.
- The base document must be created or exist in the Q&A Write function. The document integrates field labels as they are defined in the File database. This step is called creating the merge document.
- The merge document must be printed to produce the many individualized documents that comprise the total merge document. The merge document cannot be created and printed if either of the above two items are missing.

To create a merge document, begin with a Q&A Write document. Either create a Write document or use a previously created one that is already saved to disk. Insert the applicable field labels in appropriate locations throughout the text. The field labels are those defined in the File database. Separate the field label information from the document text using an asterisk (*) before and after each field label.

For example:

```
November 22, 1989

*client*
*address*
*city & state*   *zip*

Dear *client*:

Arrow Plumbing Manufacturing Company appreciates your
interest in our latest innovation of producing joint-free
household piping.

Working Copy                                  0 %   Line 11 of Page 1 of 1

Esc-Exit  F1-Info  F2-Print  Ctrl+F6-Define Pg  F7-Search  F8-Options  ↑F8-Save
```

The items enclosed in the asterisks are defined and contained in a File database. The letter is a base document created in the Write function.

Notice the way in which punctuation is placed in the salutation of the letter outside of the asterisk. See how the address is punctuated. Punctuation and spacing is critical in making your final printed letters. The date notation *@DATE(11)* prints the current date stored on your computer's clock. The format for this notation is: August 24, 1989

After the document is created, save it to disk as you would any other document.

USE ONLY DEFINED FIELD LABELS It is important that you refer to and use only field labels as they are exactly defined in the File database. Q&A attempts to use a field label reasonably close to what you want, but you can save time and effort by using exact field labels.

ARRANGING INFORMATION WITH THE (T) COMMAND When preparing a merge document you always want the file label information to conform with the general appearance of the text in which it is embedded. Information that may be contained in two or more lines in a File database can be forced to print on only one line. The (T) command permits this. For example, if a database contains the name and part number of a manufactured part on two separate lines and you want the information to print on a single line, the (T) command is used to accomplish the desired formatting. If the field label information appears as:

```
Part name: concentric spacer
  P/N 234567
```

using the (T) command in the base document sets up the information to print on a single line.

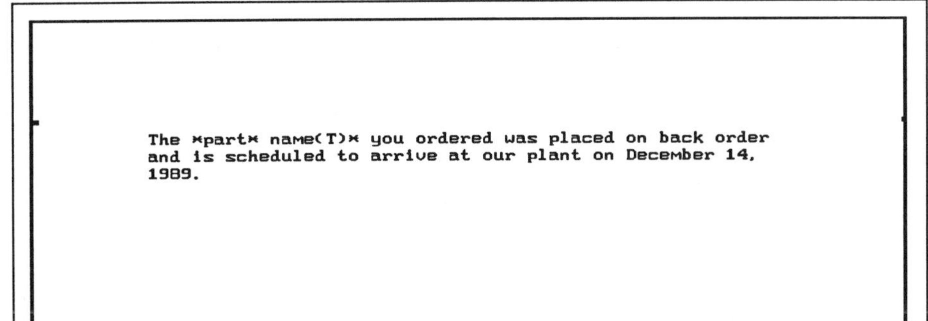
The *part* name(T)* you ordered was placed on back order
and is scheduled to arrive at our plant on December 14,
1989.

The merge document prints as:

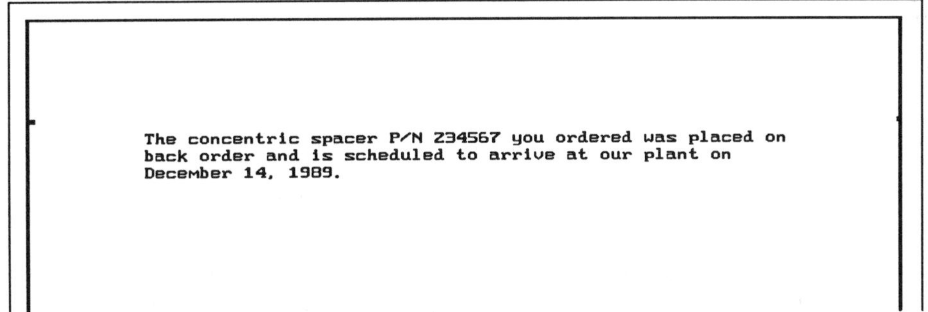
The concentric spacer P/N 234567 you ordered was placed on
back order and is scheduled to arrive at our plant on
December 14, 1989.

ALIGNING INFORMATION WITH THE RIGHT/LEFT JUSTIFY COMMAND

The right (R) and left (L) justify commands are used to control the position of field label information for tabular columns in a merge document.

For example, to left-justify a part number (consisting of 21 characters) and part price (consisting of 6 characters), separated by 6 blank spaces, you enter:

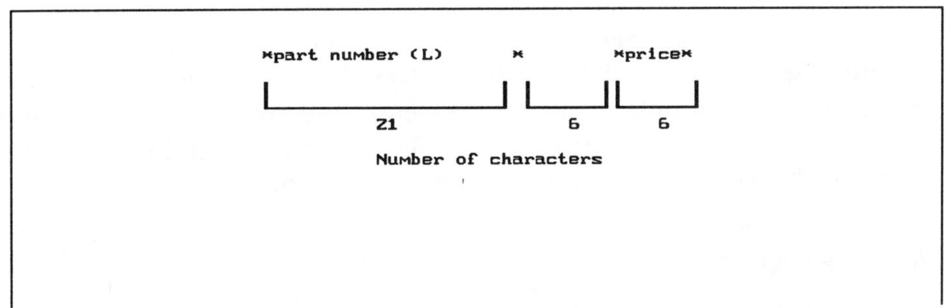

When using left justification, be sure to account for enough characters to match the number of characters in the field. If the field is larger than the number of spaces allowed for in the document, the field information is truncated.

To right-justify, the (R) command controls the length of merged information. Information is designated as right justified by using the (R) command immediately following the field label of the merge information and the closing asterisk. For example:

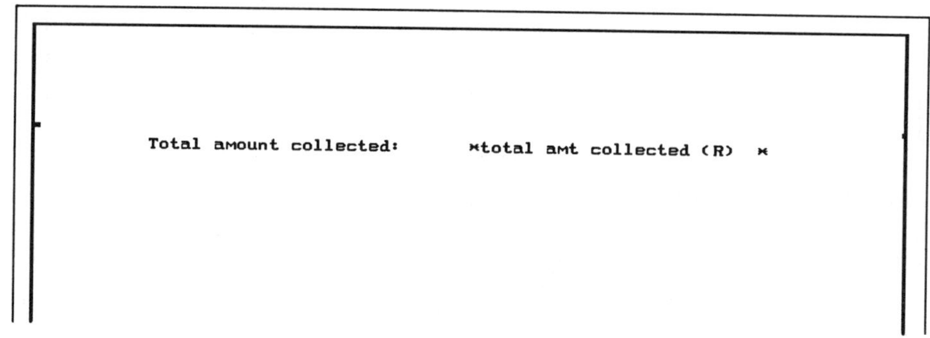

actually produces:

Total amount collected: 17,345.56

SUBSTITUTE FIELD LABELS You can use substitute labels if you cannot remember exact field labels as they actually appear in the database. When printing the merge document, the inconsistencies between actual field labels and substitute labels can be corrected.

It is a good idea to create your merge document (containing field labels enclosed by asterisks) and then print a copy for future reference.

APPLICATIONS

A merge document is extremely useful for preparing any type of document requiring the insertion of variable information from an existing file (form database). Letters, memorandums, announcements, advertising material, mailing labels, envelopes, client lists, telephone number lists and a multitude of other information can be easily created using a merge document.

TYPICAL OPERATION

In this illustration, prepare a base document in the Write function. Create a merge document containing field labels enclosed in asterisks where variable information is to be placed when the document is printed. After creating the base document, save it to disk with a filename MERGLTR. Begin at the Q&A Main Menu.

1. Select the Write Menu.
2. Press **Return** at Type/Edit to display a Working Copy (blank) screen for a new document.

Remember the practice database you created in the Sample Session called CUSTOMER? That database contains the following field labels:

```
Company Name:
Street or P.O. Box
City
State, Zip
```

These are not the only field labels in the database, but for this example, you may use these.

3. Type the following base document.

```
February 9, 1990
*Company Name*
*Street*
*City & State*  *Zip*

Dear Sirs,
This letter is to inform you of our latest...

Working Copy                                  0 %   Line 12 of Page 1 of 1
Esc-Exit  F1-Info  F2-Print  Ctrl+F6-Define Pg  F7-Search  F8-Options  ↑F8-Save
```

The document can be printed by referring to Module 67 for instructions or you can exit by proceeding to Step 7.

4. Press **Esc**. The Write Menu is displayed.
5. Type **S**. A prompt message is displayed requesting the name of the file to be saved.
6. Type **MERGLTR** and press **Return**.
7. Press **Esc** to return to the Q&A Main Menu.
8. Turn to Module 43 to continue the learning sequence.

Module 60
MOVE TEXT IN A DOCUMENT

DESCRIPTION

The ability to move text in a document is a valuable editing feature. Text is moved in blocks. You will recall from Module 7 that a block of text is a character, word, paragraph, or page of information.

To move a block of text, the text must be block selected (highlighted). Refer to Module 7 for a detailed description of block selection.

Moving the cursor to the beginning (or end) of the block of text to be moved and pressing Shift-F5 initiates the move operation by marking the beginning of the block of text. A message "Use the arrow keys to select the text you want to move, then press F10." is displayed at the bottom of the screen. The block of text is selected by using the cursor control keys to move the cursor across the text being selected. Text is highlighted as it is selected. F10 is pressed to end the block selection operation. Then, a message is displayed prompting you to move the cursor to where you want the selected text moved. When you move the cursor to the new desired location, pressing F10 completes the move of the block of text.

A unique feature of Q&A is that you also can obtain additional copies of the selected text. Moving the cursor to another location in the document and pressing Shift-F7 produces a copy of the text at the specified location. Each time you press these keys a copy is displayed at the cursor location.

The block selected text remains in memory and can be copied again and again (pressing Shift-F7) until you perform another block selection.

If another move, copy, or delete operation is performed, the lastest selected block of text remains in memory.

APPLICATIONS

Moving text in a document enables you to rearrange sentences, paragraphs, or pages within a document. You can move text in fractions of a second as opposed to the time required to manually retype the text at another location and then delete the text from its original location.

TYPICAL OPERATION

In this example, enter the Write function and move text from one location to another location in the same document. Enter the Write function and begin an edit session. Enter two paragraphs of text in a Working Copy for a new document. Move the second paragraph to a new location so that it becomes the first paragraph. Begin at the Q&A Main Menu.

1. Select the Write Menu.
2. Press **Return** to display a Working Copy (blank) screen for a new document.
3. Press **Return** twice to place two blank lines at the top of the page. Then, type the following text:

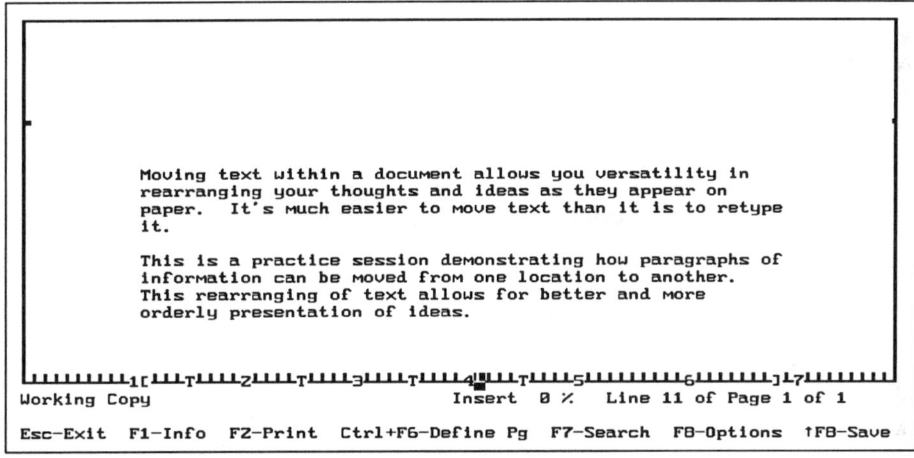

4. Press the arrow keys to place the cursor at the first character in the second paragraph.
5. Press **Shift-F5**. The block selection is initiated. The selected block of text is highlighted.
6. Press **Return** to move the cursor to the end of the second paragraph.
7. Press **F10**. The block selection operation is completed. The following message is displayed:

   `Move the cursor to the place you want the text moved, then press F10.`

8. Use the arrow keys to move the cursor to the blank line above the "M" in the first paragraph.

9. Press **F10**. The paragraphs are moved (rearranged). The cursor is located at the beginning of the moved block of text.

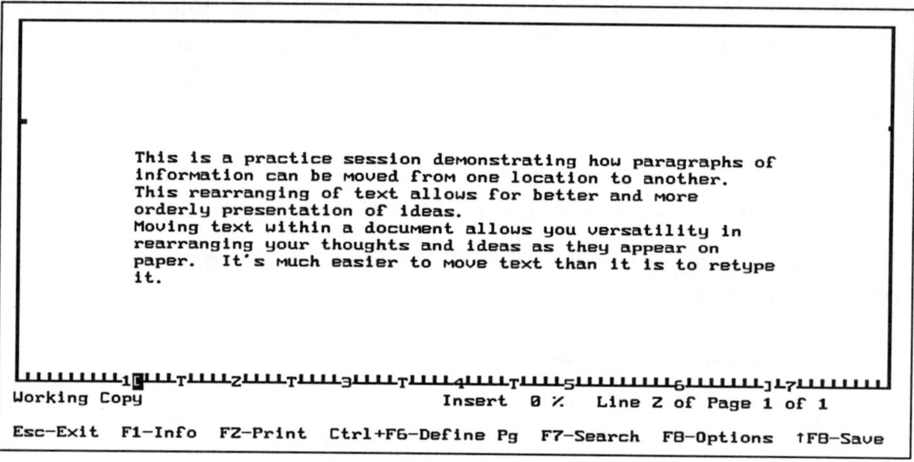

10. Return to the Main Menu without saving the document.
11. Turn to Module 61 to continue the learning sequence.

Module 61
MOVE TEXT TO ANOTHER DOCUMENT

DESCRIPTION

Moving text from one document to another allows you to freely transfer text. Unfortunately, you cannot move text from several documents into a single document by this method. Q&A permits only the selected text from one document to be moved to a second document. If you attempt to move even more text from a third document, the existing text in the receiving document is overwritten.

Moving text to another document is just as simple as most other Q&A operations. While in an edit session in a document, you select the block of text to be moved by placing the cursor on the first character of the block of text, moving the cursor through the text to highlight it, and pressing F10. A prompt message requests you to enter the filename to which the text is to be moved. Pressing Return moves the text to the specified document.

APPLICATIONS

The most widely used application of this function is to move large blocks of text to a Working Copy for new document. If only minor modifications are necessary, many hours can be saved by moving existing text to a new document and modifying it rather than typing it again.

TYPICAL OPERATION

In this illustration, enter the Write function and select a block of text to be moved to new document. The document to which text is moved is saved to disk. Begin at the Q&A Main Menu.

1. Open a new document and type the following text:

```
Move text from one document to another permits you to
easily capture existing text.  By capturing the text, you
do not need to retype any that can be reused or easily
modified to suit another purpose.

This illustration shows exactly how easy it is to move
text to another document.
```

2. Press **Ctrl-Home** to move the cursor to the first character in the first paragraph.
3. Press **Alt-F5**. Block selection is initiated. The selected block of text is the text to be moved to another document. A message is displayed at the bottom of the screen:

   `Use the arrow keys to select the text you want to move, then press F10.`

4. Press **Return** to move the cursor to the end of the first paragraph. Text is highlighted as it is selected.

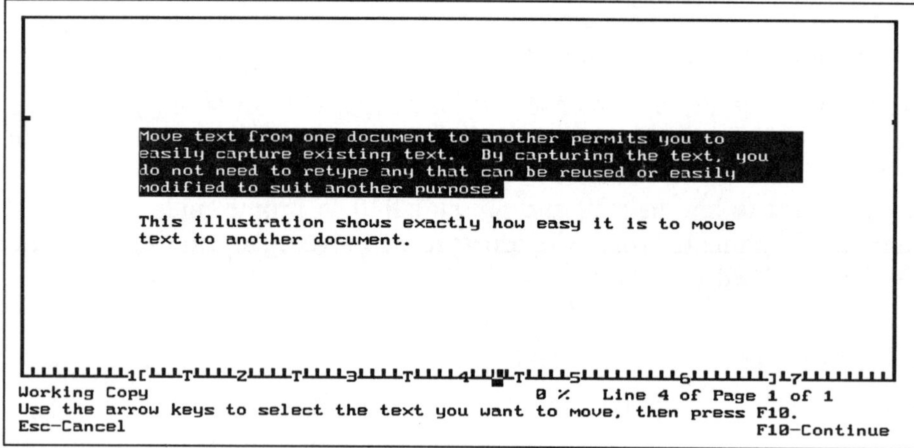

5. Press **F10**. A prompt message is displayed requesting the name of the document to which you want the text to be moved. The document should be a new document. Be sure to specify the correct directory path (ex., C:/QA/LTR).

NOTE

If you specify an existing document, a warning message is displayed indicating that the document already exists. The cursor is located at N - No. You can write over the existing document entirely by typing Y, or by leaving the cursor located at N - No and pressing Return to return to the previous prompt message.

6. Type **MVTXT** and press **Return**. The selected block of text is moved to the document named "MVTXT." The cursor is located in the original document at its last location. In this example, only the last paragraph remains displayed.

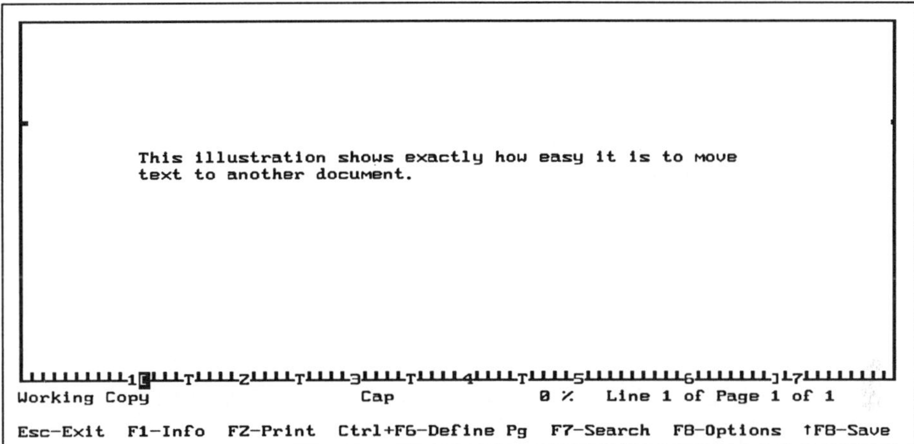

7. Return to the Main Menu without saving the document to disk. The new document receiving the moved text is saved in the specified file on disk.
8. Turn to Module 88 to continue the learning sequence.

Module 62
PAGE BREAK

DESCRIPTION

As you are typing a document in the Write function, page breaks occur automatically. The default for number of lines per page is 54 lines. However, you can control page breaks in a document by "hard coding" them on a page or when defining document page characteristics. Refer to Module 63 for a description on how to control the length of text contained on a page.

A page break is designated by a new page marker at the bottom of a page. The new page marker is displayed on each page that you have specifically designated a page break. A page break is indicated by two closely spaced horizontal parallel lines across the screen.

While in an edit session for a document, a page break can be specified by placing the cursor on the line that is to be the first line of the new page and pressing F8. Then, from the Options Menu you can select N (Newpage). Q&A designates a page break and places the cursor at the top of a new page. Text following the cursor is placed on the new page. Subsequent page breaks following the discretionary page break occur as previously defined unless you repeat the page break procedure later in the document.

To remove a page break, locate the cursor on the new page marker and press Del.

APPLICATIONS

Controlling the location of page breaks allows you to control the overall appearance of a document or form. You control the number of lines that appear on a specific page.

In many cases you may want a page of text or a table to be on a separate page. Discretionary page breaks permit you to customize your documents and forms.

TYPICAL OPERATION

In this example, enter the Write function, type a paragraph of text, then designate a line at which you want a page break to occur. Implement the page break and notice the results. Begin at the Q&A Main Menu.

1. Type **W**. The Write Menu is displayed. The cursor is located on T - Type/Edit.
2. Press **Return** to display a Working Copy (blank) screen for a new document.
3. Type the following text:

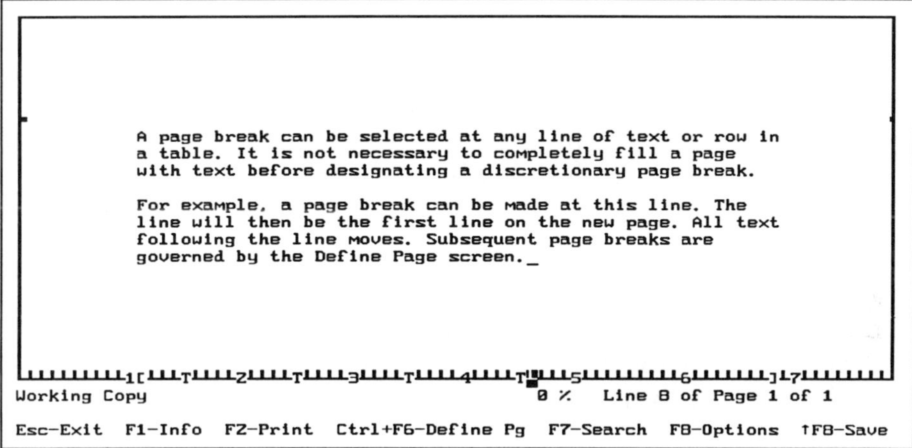

4. Locate the cursor any place on the first line of the second paragraph.
5. Press **F8** to display the Options Menu in a window over the text.
6. Type **N**. The page break (Newpage) is established with the designated line as the first line on the new page.

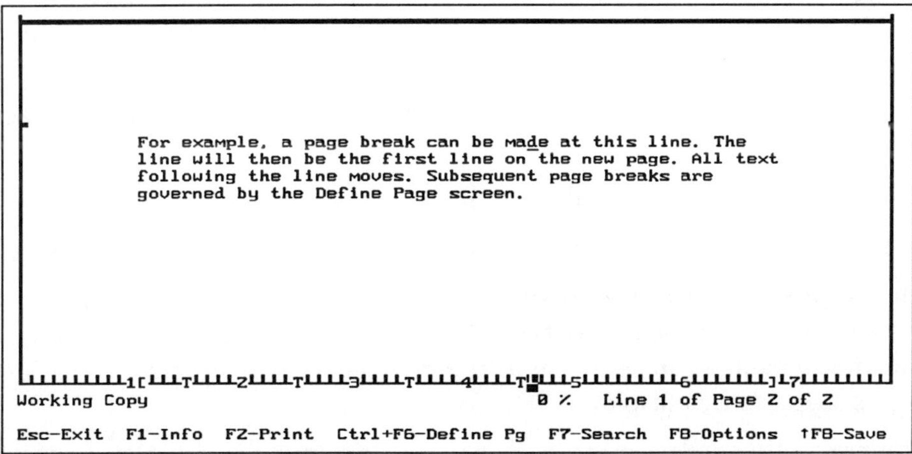

7. Return to the Main Menu without saving the document.
8. Turn to Module 45 to continue the learning sequence.

Module 63
PAGE LAYOUT FOR A DOCUMENT

DESCRIPTION

Defining the page layout for a document page in the Write function involves specifying the characteristics controlling the "look" of the page. These characteristics determine the overall appearance of each page in the document. Parameters that you can define for page characteristics include:

Left and right margins
Top and bottom margins
Page width and length
Characters per inch (cpi) when printed
Beginning page where header/footer is placed
Beginning page for page number

Certain default values are preprogrammed for each of these values for all new documents that you create. The default values may be easily changed; refer to Module 44 for instructions on changing global parameters using the Write Utilities Menu.

Values selected for page characteristics are reflected in each screen display of each page and in the printed document. The one exception is the "characters per inch" parameter. If you choose to select a compressed print (15 or 17 characters per inch) for text density, this compressed text mode is not displayed as compressed text on the screen.

Defining characteristics for page layout of a document is easy to do. You actually have two choices:

1. You can accept the default page layout values, or
2. You can define each characteristic for each document that you create.

To define page layout characteristics, a document must be in the editor. If there is not a document in the editor, type G at the Write Menu. Type the filename for an existing document in response to the prompt message, press Return, and the specified document is displayed.

If you are editing a document in an edit session, just press Esc to return to the Write Menu. Typing D at the Write Menu displays the Define Page Menu.

```
                         DEFINE PAGE

    Left margin: 10                  Right margin : 68
    Top margin : 6                   Bottom margin: 6
    Page width : 78                  Page length  : 66
    Characters per inch............:  10   12   15   17
    Begin header/footer on page #...:  1
    Begin page numbering with page #:  1

                  Page Options for Working Copy
Esc-Cancel       F1-Info        F2-Print Options          F10-Continue
```

Pressing Tab or Return moves the cursor to the locations for entering values. To change any value, just type over the displayed value and press Tab to move to the next location where you want to make a change.

Before attempting to change the "Characters per inch" value, refer to the User Manual for your printer to ensure that pitch sizes (10, 12, 15, or 17) are supported.

To change the "Characters per inch" value, use the Spacebar or Right/Left Arrow keys to make a change. Each time you press the Spacebar the cursor moves to the next selection.

When finished making changes on the screen, press F10. You are returned to the Type/Edit mode and into an edit session with the document. Once the document is saved to disk, the defined page layout is also saved for that particular document. The next time you edit or print that document, the saved defined page layout controls the appearance of each page.

If you do not save the document to disk, but exit to the Write Menu, the page layout settings that you made are lost and default page layout values remain in control.

APPLICATIONS

Overall document appearance is controlled by how you define page characteristics. Setting page characteristics permits you to establish the format appropriate for any document being created.

Changing margin settings and printer type size (pitch) go together. If you are planning to print a document in 10 pitch (10 characters per inch) on 8 1/2-inch wide paper, you will want a left margin setting at 1 and a right margin setting at

65. This provides for a 6 1/2-inch line of text with one inch of white space on both the right and left side of the page.

If you intend to print a document in 12 pitch (12 characters per inch) on 8 1/2-inch wide paper, you will want a left margin setting of 1 and a right margin setting of 78.

In either case, you may need to adjust the Print offset to adjust for 1 inch of white space at the left margin. Refer to Module 71 for instructions on how to set print options.

Determining top and bottom margins is also at your discretion. These margins are dependent upon the desired appearance for each particular document.

TYPICAL OPERATION

In this illustration, the objective is to reset all of the page characteristics for a document, except page length, differently from the default parameters displayed on the Define Page Menu. Change margins to 1 and 78, top and bottom margins to 4, page width to 80, and characters per inch to 12 (elite); begin header/footer to start on page 2; and begin page numbering on page 2. Begin at the Q&A Main Menu.

1. Type **W**. The Write Menu is displayed. The cursor is located on T - Type/Edit.
2. Press **Return** to display a Working Copy (blank) screen for a new document. You may begin typing a new document, or you may proceed immediately to setting a page layout. To set the page layout go to Step 3.
3. Press **Esc** to recall the Write Menu.
4. Type **D** to display the Define Page Menu. The cursor is located on the left margin default value.
5. Type **12** and press **Return**. The cursor moves to the right margin default value.
6. Type **78** and press **Return**. The cursor moves to the top margin default value.
7. Type **4** and press **Return**. The cursor moves to the bottom margin default value.
8. Type **4** and press **Return**. The cursor moves to the page width default value.
9. Press **Return** twice. The page width and page length values are left unchanged at 78 and 66 respectively. The cursor moves to 10 characters per inch.

10. Press **Right Arrow** twice to move the cursor to 12 and press **Return**. The cursor moves to the default page number where the header and footer are to begin printing.
11. Type **2** and press **Return**. The cursor moves to the default page number where page numbering is to begin.
12. Type **2** and press **Return**. The new page layout characteristics are defined. The cursor moves back to the top of the screen.

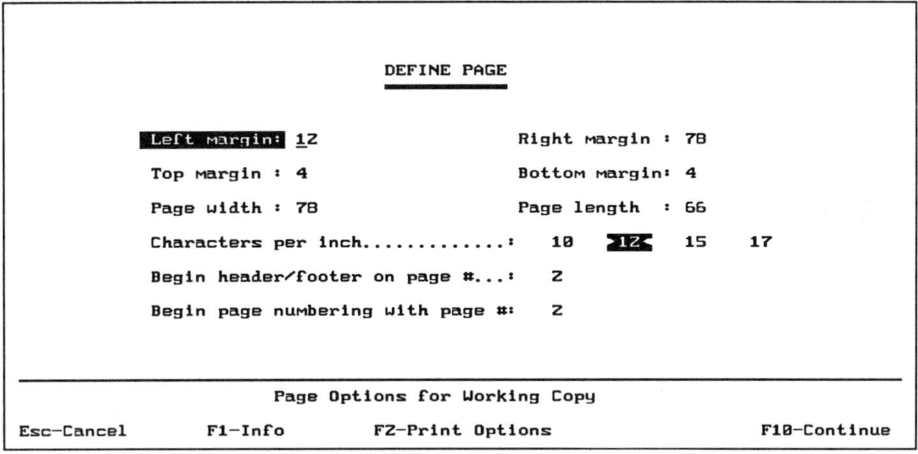

13. Press **F10** to complete page layout definition. The Working Copy of the document is displayed.
14. Return to the Q&A Main Menu without saving the document or the page layout for the document to disk.
15. Turn to Module 62 to continue the learning sequence.

Module 64
PERFORM TASKS USING THE ASSISTANT

DESCRIPTION

The Assistant can be used for a variety of tasks. Just about any task relating to your databases can be accomplished by the Assistant. It can retrieve information, change information contained in a database, perform calculations, and do a multitude of other tasks.

This module explains how to get the Assistant to perform a task. Beginning at the Q&A Main Menu, selecting I displays the Assistant Menu. Entering A places the Assistant in the "perform" mode. A display requests you to indicate the task you want to have performed.

Upon typing your request, the Assistant performs the specified task. If the Assistant does not understand what you want, it lets you know. If you have not taught the Assistant about a certain database or have not taught it certain vocabulary, it will let you know.

After your request has been answered, the request is erased from the Request Box and the Assistant waits for another request.

To restore the previous request, simply press Shift-F7. Pressing Esc displays the Assistant Menu. Press Esc again to display the Q&A Main Menu.

CREATING REPORTS When using the Assistant to create reports, there are several guidelines to follow.

1. Specify which fields on a form you want to appear on the report. When typing your request, use exact field names or synonyms previously defined to the Assistant.
2. Define in your request applicable selection criteria, so only information from appropriate forms is selected by the Assistant.
3. Accurately state in your request the sort criteria (e.g., by department, by salary, by job class, by ascending or descending order).
4. State exact field names that are to be used as column headings (e.g., Full Name, Department, Job Grade, Customer ID, Account Number).

RETRIEVING AND CHANGING FORMS As when creating reports, you must be explicit when retrieving and/or changing forms. The following guidelines will help you.

1. Include concise criteria in your request.
2. Provide the Assistant enough information to allow the request to be processed.
3. When changing forms, the Assistant displays the requested forms. Use the cursor movement keys to move the cursor to appropriate fields being changed.
4. If you use the Request Box to have the Assistant change a form, enclose all new information being added to a form in quotation marks.

APPLICATIONS

Having the Assistant perform tasks for you is one of the greatest advantages of having Q&A. Compared with just ordinary word processing, database, or spreadsheet software, this feature of Q&A is invaluable. Previously, you have been briefed on the various tasks that Q&A can perform for you.

The Assistant can perform tasks relating to answering questions for you. The questions can be posed as "What, Who, Where, or How many." Questions can be asked that result in a simple "yes" or "no" by the Assistant.

You can ask the Assistant to create new reports, run existing (defined) reports, create new forms, or manipulate/change/delete forms. The Assistant can perform calculations for you and answer combination or complex questions. When stating your requests, you can use crudely constructed sentences consisting of only partial sentences.

The Assistant can also create and use synonyms not previously defined on forms.

TYPICAL OPERATION

In this illustration, you may create any request or query for the Assistant. After practicing with several of your own requests, return to the Q&A Main Menu.

1. Type **A**. The Assistant Menu is displayed.
2. Type **A**. A prompt message is displayed requesting the name of the file for which you want to query for information.
3. Type **CUSTOMER** and press **Return.** The Assistant request box is displayed. The cursor is located in the request box.

4. Enter a question for the Assistant. Remember that the query must be related to the database. Practice with several requests or questions. Example: List company names.

NOTE

If you use an invalid field name, Q&A displays a help menu. Type T then type F to display field names of the selected database.

5. Return to the Q&A Main Menu.
6. Turn to Module 42 to continue the learning sequence.

Module 65
PERSONAL DICTIONARY UPDATE

DESCRIPTION

Q&A contains two spelling dictionaries that can be used to check the spelling in your documents. The *main dictionary* contains all of the built-in words. This dictionary cannot be edited to add, change, or delete words.

The second spelling dictionary is the *personal dictionary.* This dictionary contains the words that you personally add to suit your individual needs. As you work more with Q&A, you will continually update the personal dictionary by adding new words or deleting existing ones.

The personal dictionary can be updated in two ways:

1. By specifically accessing the dictionary file QAPERS.DCT and editing the contents.
2. By adding words to the dictionary during the spelling check of a document. Words can be added via the Spelling Menu which contains two "add to dictionary" options. Refer to Module 88 for detailed instructions.

UPDATING THE PERSONAL DICTIONARY FILE To update the personal dictionary directly by accessing the file QAPERS.DCT, you start at the Q&A Main Menu. Enter the Write function, type G, type the personal dictionary filename QAPERS.DCT, and press Return. The words in the dictionary are displayed in a Write document. Updating is performed by entering or changing words just as if you were in an edit session, typing words in any other Write document. Any words added must be positioned within the dictionary in alphabetical order. They can be typed in either upper or lowercase letters, but should be typed as they are normally used. Ensure that you press Return (Carriage Return) after each word. The carriage return is necessary for exporting the document as Document ASCII file when saving changes or additions to disk.

Exiting from updating the dictionary is done by pressing Esc to return to the Write Menu. Typing U displays the Write Utilities Menu. Typing E displays the ASCII Export Menu. Typing D (Document ASCII) on the ASCII Export Menu saves the updated dictionary to disk.

CAUTION

If you exit from editing the personal dictionary and do not export the document through U (Utilities) at the Write Menu, a message is displayed warning you that the changes just made have not been saved.

UPDATING THE PERSONAL DICTIONARY FILE DURING SPELL CHECK

Refer to Module 88 for instructions on how to update the personal dictionary while checking the spelling in a document.

APPLICATIONS

The ability to modify your personal spelling dictionary is a powerful feature making Q&A word processing a real convenience. You can customize your dictionary to fit your business or personal needs.

Once you add a word to the dictionary, it remains until you remove it. No longer do you need to "ignore" the word each time it is encountered during a spelling check.

In summary, the personal dictionary feature further promotes the word processing efficiency of Q&A.

TYPICAL OPERATION

In this illustration, begin at the Q&A Main Menu, get the personal dictionary file QAPERS.DCT, and import the personal dictionary file as an ASCII file without word wrap. Then, enter several words into the personal dictionary and exit to the Q&A Main Menu. The words entered remain saved in the personal dictionary file.

1. Type **W**. The Write Menu is displayed.
2. Type **G**. A prompt message is displayed requesting the filename (ex., Document: C:\QA_).
3. Type the personal dictionary filename **QAPERS.DCT** and press **Return**. The Import Document Menu is displayed. The cursor is located on A - ASCII.

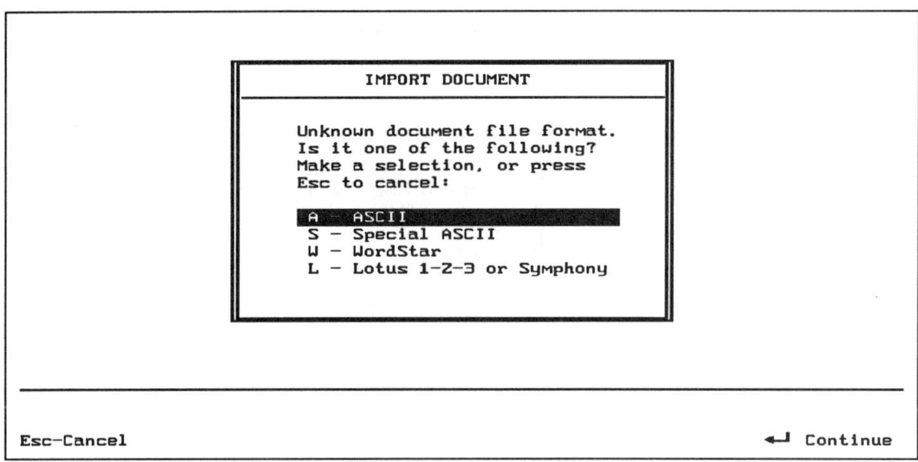

4. Press **Return**. The first page of the personal dictionary is displayed. Initially, upon accessing this file in an edit session, each page of the file is blank.

5. Type the following words in alphabetical order. Place each word on a separate line.

```
ASCII
DBASE
LOTUS 1-2-3
pfs:
Q&A
```

6. Press **Esc** to return to the Write Menu.

CAUTION

Do not type S (Save). The updated personal dictionary file, QAPERS.DCT must be saved to disk in the proper ASCII file format (Document ASCII).

7. Type **U**. The Write Utilities Menu is displayed.

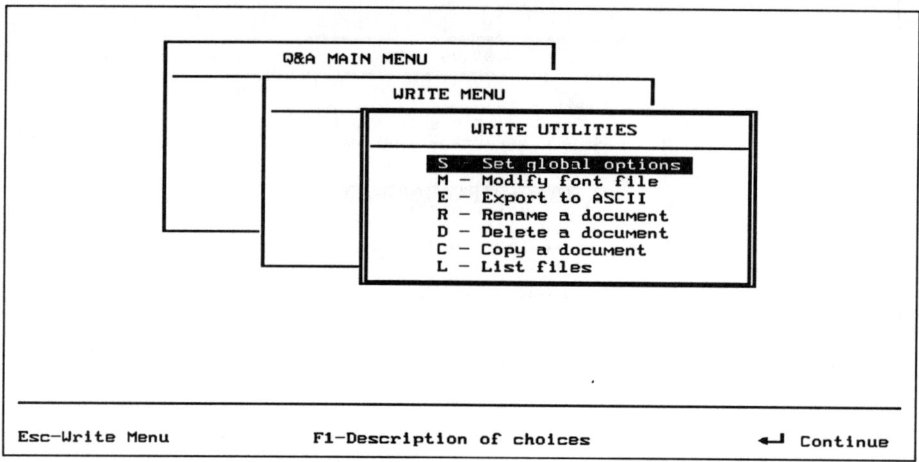

8. Type **E**. The ASCII Export Menu is displayed.

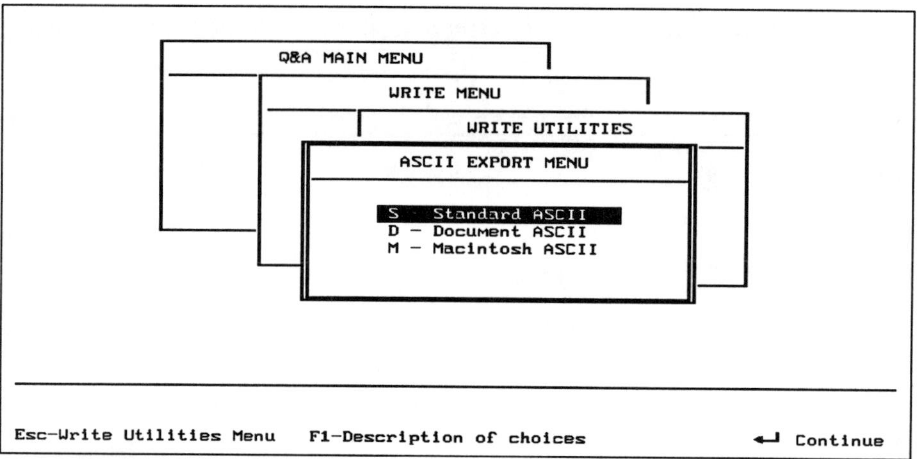

9. Press **Return**. A prompt message is displayed requesting the ASCII filename (ASCII filename: C:\QA\QAPERS.DCT).
10. Press **Return** to save the words entered in the document to the personal dictionary file. The ASCII Export Menu is displayed.
11. Return to the Q&A Main Menu.
12. Turn to Module 79 to continue the learning sequence.

Module 66
PRINT A BLOCK OF TEXT

DESCRIPTION

Any block of text consisting of a single line, several lines, or complete paragraphs can be printed. There is one restraint on printing blocks of text. Even if a selected block of text crosses defined page boundaries, the page boundary is ignored when the entire block of text is printed.

While in an edit session with a document, a block of text can be printed by first positioning the cursor either at the beginning or at the end of the text that you want selected.

Pressing Ctrl-F2 begins the block selection. A message is displayed directing you to use the arrow keys to select text and to press F10 when finished. The block of text is selected by moving the cursor through the text using any of the cursor control keys (e.g., arrow keys, Home, etc.). The text is highlighted as it is selected.

Make sure that your printer is turned on, that paper is installed, and that it is ready for printing. Press F10 and the selected block of text is printed. The Print Options Menu is not displayed during any part of this operation.

APPLICATIONS

There can be occasions when you want a printed copy of text to use as reference. Printing a block of text is an easy way to satisfy this need.

An alternative is to use the "screen print" feature available on most personal computers. For example, pressing Shift-PrtSc prints an exact duplicate of the entire screen display. One disadvantage is that the whole screen is printed. You may only want one or two short paragraphs printed and not the entire screen.

TYPICAL OPERATION

In this illustration, enter the Write function, type several blocks of text and then select a block of text to print. Invoke the print function to print the text. Exit from the document without saving it to disk and return to the Q&A Main Menu.

1. Open a new document and type the following text.

```
This practice session demonstrates the steps necessary to
print a block of text within a document.  The prerequisite
is having a document in the editor upon which you are
performing various edit functions.

By selecting a block of text and invoking the print
function, the specified text can be printed.

Working Copy                                    0 %   Line 7 of Page 1 of 1
Esc-Exit  F1-Info  F2-Print  Ctrl+F6-Define Pg  F7-Search  F8-Options  ↑F8-Save
```

2. Use the cursor navigation keys to move the cursor to the first character in the second paragraph (under the character "B"), then press **Ctrl-F2**. A message is displayed at the bottom of the screen requesting you to use the arrow keys to select text to be printed.

NOTE

You can use the arrow keys or other cursor navigation keys to move the cursor and highlight the block of text to be printed. Refer to Module 20 for information on the cursor navigation keys.

3. Press **Right Arrow** to move the cursor through the sentence. You can also press Return to select the entire sentence immediately. Notice that the selected text is highlighted. Ensure that power to your printer is turned on, that the printer is loaded with paper, and it is ready to print.
4. Press **F10**. The selected block of text is printed.
5. Return to the Main Menu without saving the changes.
6. Turn to Module 67 to continue the learning sequence.

Module 67
PRINT A DOCUMENT

DESCRIPTION

To print a document, your printer must be properly installed to match Q&A print parameters. Refer to Module 73 for printer installation procedures.

Most basic parallel printers operate with Q&A without the need of your setting any printer parameters. Q&A provides print enhancements such as underline, boldface print, and double strike.

Module 73 lists the common printers supported by Q&A and explains how to set printer parameters for parallel and serial printers.

The print facility provided is powerful. It incorporates print features found only in sophisticated word processing software. The print capability is extended to three of its major components: Write, File, and Report.

You may not print and edit simultaneously. When printing a document, you must wait until printing is completed before returning to an edit session with the document.

QUEUING A DOCUMENT TO PRINT If you have several documents to print, you can create a print queue document that contains several documents. The command used is: *QUEUE filename*

An example of a print queue document is:

```
*QUEUE PREFACE.DOC*
*QUEUE CHAPT1.DOC*
    .
    .
    .
*QUEUE CHAPT15.DOC*
*QUEUE INDEX.DOC*
```

Initiating the printing of the print queue document is done the same as with a single document. Use the print queue document filename when specifying the name of the file for printing.

To control the page on which each document is to print, you must define the page for each document individually. Refer to Module 63 for detailed instructions.

PRINTING A DOCUMENT A document must be brought into an edit session (using G - Get at the Write Menu) and it must reside in memory before it can be printed. Once the document has been brought into an edit session, it can be printed from the editor, or you can exit to the Write Menu and print it from the Write Menu.

A document is printed from the Print Options Menu.

```
                              PRINT OPTIONS

     From page.............:   1           To page.............:  2
     Number of copies......:   1           Print offset........:  0
     Line spacing..........:   Single     Double      Envelope
     Justify...............:   Yes  No
     Print to..............:   PtrA   PtrB   PtrC   PtrD   PtrE   DISK
     Type of paper feed....:   Manual  Continuous  Bin1   Bin2   Bin3   Lhd
     Number of columns.....:   1    2    3    4    5    6    7    8
     Printer control codes.:
     Name of Merge File....:

                       Print Options for HEADER
Esc-Cancel   F1-Info   Ctrl F6-Def Pg   F9-Save changes & go back   F10-Continue
```

Entries and selections on the Print Options Menu are used as follows:

FROM PAGE — Enter the range of pages that you want to print. Enter the first page number to be printed or press Return to begin at page 1.

TO PAGE — Type the page number of the last page in the range to be printed or press Return to print only the first page.

NUMBER OF COPIES — Enter the number for the total number of printed copies wanted. The maximum number is 999.

PRINT OFFSET — Enter the number of character spaces on the left margin to be skipped before printing is started. This feature allows you to align where printing starts on a page at the left side of the page. Positive numbers move text to the right. Negative numbers move text to the left.

LINE SPACING — Press Right or Left Arrow to select an appropriate choice: Single, Double, or Envelope. If you want to use more line spacing than double spacing, use the line spacing command embedded in the document. The command is *LS n*, where n = the number of line spaces.

JUSTIFY — Press Right or Left Arrow to select YES (for justified text) or NO (for unjustified text). You can also use either the *Justify Yes* or *Justify No* command within the document.

PRINT TO — Press Right or Left Arrow to select the printer port. It is possible to have a dot-matrix parallel printer attached to LPT1, LPT2, LPT3 . . . (Ptr A through Ptr E) depending upon how many parallel data ports your computer has. You could also have a serial printer, such as a daisy-wheel printer, attached to COM1 or COM2. You must select the port to which the appropriate printer is attached.

Selecting DISK indicates that you want a print file stored to disk. The Disk Print Menu is displayed.

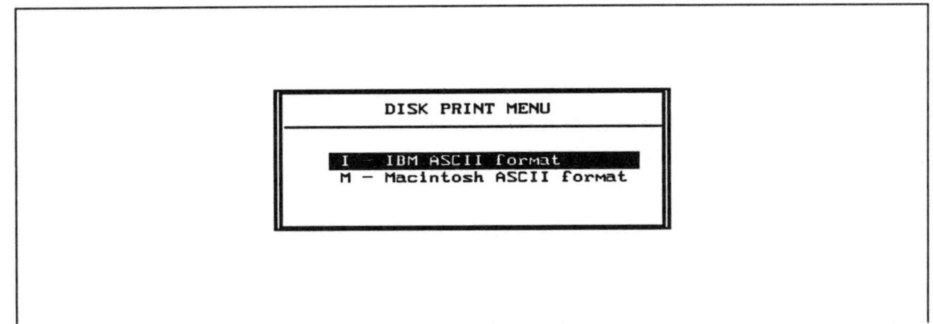

Selecting I - IBM ASCII format or M - Macintosh ASCII format displays a prompt message requesting the name of the file. A prompt message is displayed asking for the name of the disk file to which you want to print the document.

Pressing Return without entering a filename displays all files saved on disk. Entering the filename and pressing Return saves the file to disk. A message displays as the print file is being printed to disk.

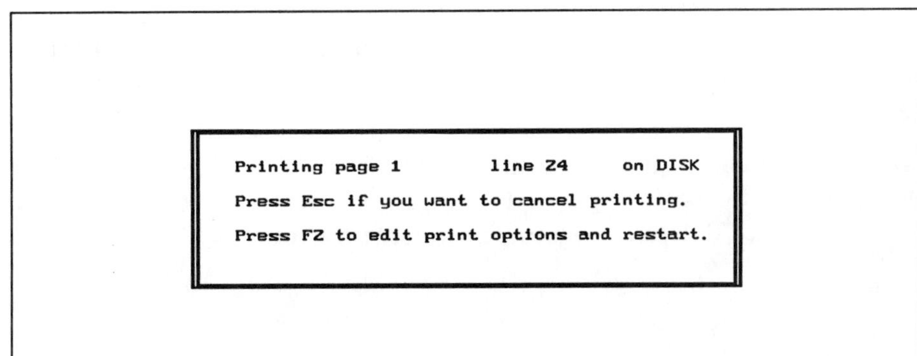

The Write Menu is displayed after print to disk is completed.

TYPE OF PAPER FEED — Press the Right or Left Arrow to select the type of paper feed that your printer has. Manual is selected for a sheet-fed printer. Continuous is selected for computer form paper. Bin 1, 2, 3, and Lhd (letterhead) feeds paper from various bins if your printer has the option. If Lhd is selected, letterhead paper is fed from Bin 1 for the first page of a document; subsequent pages of the document are printed on paper fed from Bin 2.

NUMBER OF COLUMNS — Use the Right or Left Arrow to select the number of columns into which the document text is to be reformatted.

PRINTER CONTROL CODES — Enter your printer's special effects codes (control codes) to permit printing effects such as compressed print, correspondence mode, data processing mode, etc. Type the decimal ASCII code for available selections provided by your printer. Separate the codes with a comma (ex., 14,27,71). Refer to the user's manual for your printer to select appropriate control codes. Leaving this selection blank results in standard (default) printing.

NAME OF Q&A MERGE FILE — If you are creating a merge document, enter the name of the Q&A database file. Refer to Module 59. Leaving this selection blank causes the document to print as if there is no merge document associated with the document to be printed.

Once entries and selections are made on the Print Options Menu, the document is printed.

Thus, print control is achieved by entering appropriate values (e.g., from/to page, number of copies, etc.) and making applicable selections (e.g., line spacing, justify, etc.) on the Print Options Menu.

APPLICATIONS

The use of the print feature is obvious — it provides you with a suitable paper copy of a document, report, or form. Print parameters that you set on the Print Options Menu allow you to control the overall appearance of the printed document.

You control how many pages you want to print. That is, you can print all pages in a document, only certain pages (a range of pages), envelopes, or merge documents. Module 70 details how to print merge documents.

TYPICAL OPERATION

In this illustration, enter the Write function, create a simple document, and then print the document to a printer connected to the LPT1 port.

1. Open a new document and type the following text:

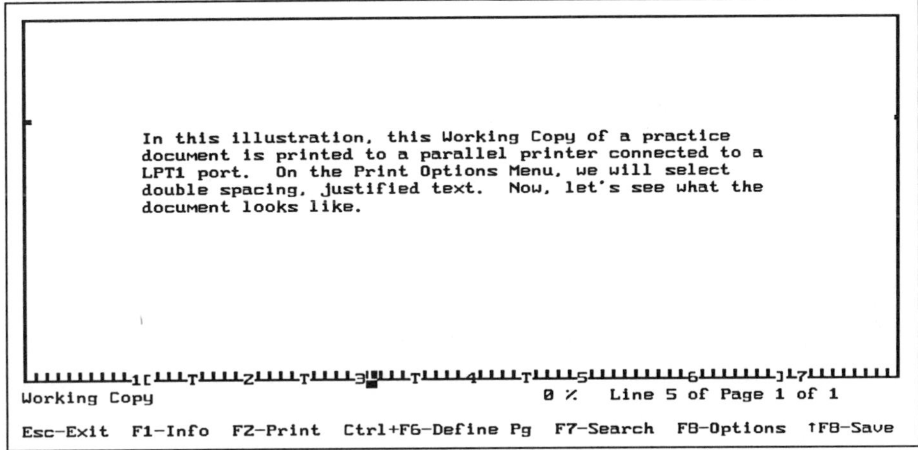

2. Duplicate the first page of the document several times by copying the paragraph as a block of text. Refer to Module 18 for instructions on how to copy text within a document.
3. Press **Esc**. The Write Menu is displayed.
4. Type **P** to display the Print Options Menu.
5. Press **Down Arrow** to move the cursor to Number of Columns.
6. Type **2** (two-column format). Accept the default values for all other values, unless you need to change a parameter to accommodate the requirements of your printer.
7. Press **F10**. A message is displayed indicating that printing is occurring. The document is printed single spaced, unjustified, in two columns. The Write Menu is displayed after printing is completed.
8. Return to the Q&A Main Menu without saving the document.
9. Turn to Module 68 to continue the learning sequence.

Module 68
PRINT A DOCUMENT WITH SPECIAL EFFECTS

DESCRIPTION

Q&A allows you to insert printer codes within document text. This feature allows you to designate special printing features to take effect when you print a document. Of course, this all depends upon the type and features of your printer.

Some special printing features include: bold print, shadow print, compressed print, normal print, expanded print, double-strike, variable pitch print, and various type fonts. Refer to the user manual for your printer to determine its capabilities.

Using this feature is not difficult. First, read the user manual for your printer. Take special note of the control codes for the printer. Often these control codes are contained in an appendix in the manual. The control codes are usually defined in ASCII, decimal, and hexadecimal code.

A typical example of an ASCII code is CR, designating a carriage return. A decimal code for the same function is 13 while the hexadecimal designation is OD. Print codes are designated to Q&A using ASCII codes.

While creating a Write document, indicate printer codes directly in the text of the document by typing an asterisk (*) followed by the word PRINTER and then the print codes. Multiple print codes must be separated by commas. The designation of special print codes is always ended with an asterisk. The word PRINTER can be abbreviated using only the character "P."

A generic example is: `*PRINTER code1,code2,code3,code4,. . .*`

A typical example is: `*PRINTER 29,49*`

With an Okidata printer, this example turns on compressed print (17.1 characters per inch) as designated by the ASCII code 29 and double strike (bold) with the code 49.

APPLICATIONS

This feature permits you versatility in dressing up the appearance of any Write document that you produce in Q&A. You are actually integrating macro programming with the word processing feature of Q&A.

TYPICAL OPERATION

In this example, enter the Write function and create a small document containing special print features. Follow directions in Module 82 to save the document. Use the instructions presented in Module 67 to print the document, or return to the Q&A Main Menu without saving the document to disk. Begin at the Q&A Main Menu.

1. Open a new document.

NOTE

The objective is to print compressed print and double strike. If your printer has this capability you can proceed with the example. If not, exit from the document by pressing Esc several times in succession until the Q&A Main Menu is displayed.

The ASCII codes indicated in the example are valid for an Okidata printer. Check your user manual for your printer to validate the proper code to use.

2. Type the following text.

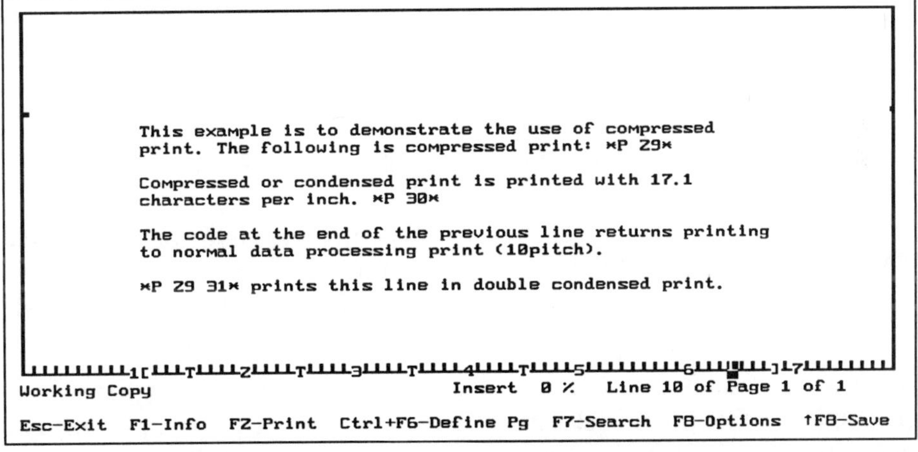

```
This example is to demonstrate the use of compressed
print. The following is compressed print: *P 29*

Compressed or condensed print is printed with 17.1
characters per inch. *P 30*

The code at the end of the previous line returns printing
to normal data processing print (10pitch).

*P 29 31* prints this line in double condensed print.

Working Copy                          Insert  0 %   Line 10 of Page 1 of 1
Esc-Exit  F1-Info  F2-Print  Ctrl+F6-Define Pg  F7-Search  F8-Options  ↑F8-Save
```

If you want to save the document refer to Module 82 for instructions; otherwise, go to Step 3. If you want to print the document, refer to Module 67 for instructions; otherwise, go to step 3.

3. Return to the Main Menu without saving the document.

4. Turn to Module 53 to continue the learning sequence.

Module 69
PRINT FORMS

DESCRIPTION

The options provided by Q&A for you to use for printing forms are extremely versatile. You can print any or all forms. All or only certain fields on forms in a database can be selected for printing. You also have the capability to arrange information contained in form fields in just about any layout on the printed page.

Printing forms is accomplished by entering the File function and selecting the Print option at the Print Menu. There are four options to select from this menu.

- Design/Redesign a Spec. This option defines and saves print specifications used when printing forms or portions of forms. Mailing labels can also be printed using this option.
- Print Forms. This option initiates the printing operation after you have designed a print specification for printing forms.
- Set Global Options. This option permits you to change print option defaults or change page defaults, single form print defaults, or single form page defaults.
- Rename/Delete/Copy Spec. This option gives you the capability to perform maintenance functions to Print Specs saved to disk. These maintenance functions include: renaming, deleting, or copying print specifications.

The first step you perform when printing a form is to design the print specification. Once a print specification is designed, you can use it, redesign it, or specify some other existing print specification for use in the printing operation. Refer to Module 38 for complete instructions on how to design print specifications.

From the Q&A Main Menu, the File Menu is accessed by entering the F selection. On the displayed File Menu, selecting the Print option displays a prompt message requesting the name of the file to be printed. Entering a valid filename and pressing Return displays the Print Menu. Selecting D on the Print Menu displays the print specifications for the database being printed.

If a print specification has not previously been designed for the database, the display is blank. If you are initially designing a print specification for the database, enter the name for the Print Spec. The Retrieve Spec for the database is displayed.

Enter the retrieve specifications that you want used as selection criteria and press F10.

Next, enter the Field Spec which defines how information is formatted on the printed page.

The last step is to enter the File Print Options and Page Options. The Print Spec is saved and you are ready to print forms.

APPLICATIONS

Printing forms is a way for you to retrieve any form exactly as it appears in the database or in a printed layout that you designate.

There are times when you will not want to create a special report just to retrieve information on a printed copy. This option of printing forms is an excellent alternative to designing a special report.

TYPICAL OPERATION

In this illustration, enter the File function and print all forms in a database. A print specification must have been previously designed using instructions presented in Module 38 before forms can be printed. Begin at the Q&A Main Menu.

1. Select the File Menu.
2. Type **P**. A prompt message is displayed requesting you to enter the name of the file containing forms to be printed.
3. Type **CUSTOMER** and press **Return**.

> **NOTE**
> A print specification must have been previously designed before you can proceed. If you have not designed a print spec for printing the database (refer to Module 38), press Esc to exit from this procedure.

4. Type **P** to select Print Forms. A list of print specs for the specified database is displayed.
5. Type **CLIENT** and press **Return**. A confirmation message is displayed. The cursor is located on "N - No."

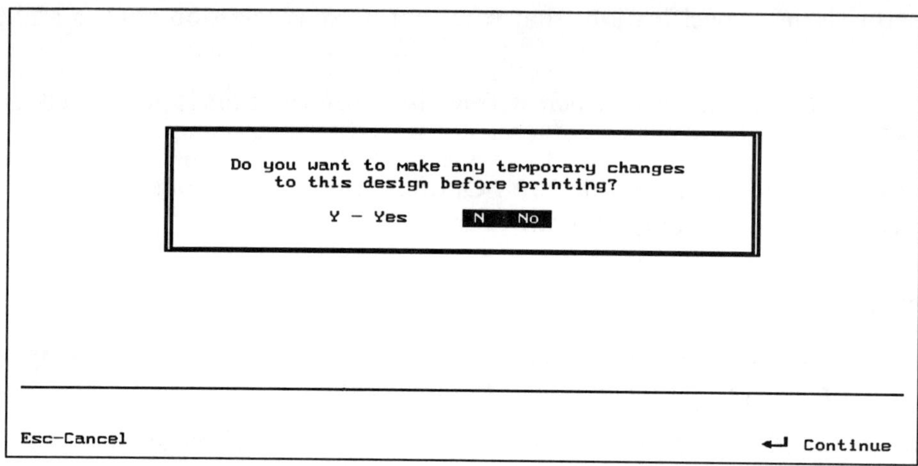

6. Press **Return**. The forms are printed. The Print Menu is displayed upon completion of the printing operation.
7. Return to the Main Menu.
8. Turn to Module 85 to continue the learning sequence.

Module 70
PRINT A MERGE DOCUMENT

DESCRIPTION

Printing a merge document encompasses the process of using a previously created base merge document and integrating it with information contained within a database (file of forms). The results are completed copies of documents each containing variable information retrieved from a database.

You can initiate printing of a merge document while in an edit session with the base document. Or, you can retrieve the base document using Get (G) at the Write Menu to bring the document into an edit session.

Pressing F2 while in the edit mode with the base document displays the Print Options Menu. After entering the print specifications and the name of the Q&A merge file, pressing F10 displays the Identifier Spec screen.

The Identifier Spec screen permits you to reconcile any substitute field labels used in the base document with actual field label names used in the database. If the field names in the database do not match those in the base letter, you can press Esc to return to the base document to make corrections.

You can press F8 to display the Identifier Spec screen for the merging database and make changes to ensure that the base document and the database field names match.

You can press F10, ignoring the mismatch of field names, and proceed with the operation. The results with this option are unpredictable. After entering identifier information, pressing F10 displays the Retrieve Spec screen.

On the Retrieve Spec screen you enter search and merge restrictions. You specify to Q&A which forms in the database to use with the base document. When finished entering the retrieve specifications, pressing F10 begins printing of the documents.

APPLICATIONS

Printing a merge document is the process of integrating information from a specified database into a base (merge) document that you have prepared. This process is the only way to achieve the merge operation. Otherwise, the database information and the base document remain completely separated and are never integrated into one document.

TYPICAL OPERATION

In this illustration, use a previously created base document called MERGLTR and a Q&A database named CUSTOMER to print merge documents. Begin at the Q&A Main Menu.

1. Select the Write Menu.
2. Type **G**, a prompt message is displayed requesting the name of the document being retrieved.
3. Type **MERGLTR** (or other base document) and press **Return**. The document is displayed.
4. Press **F2** the Print Options Menu is displayed.

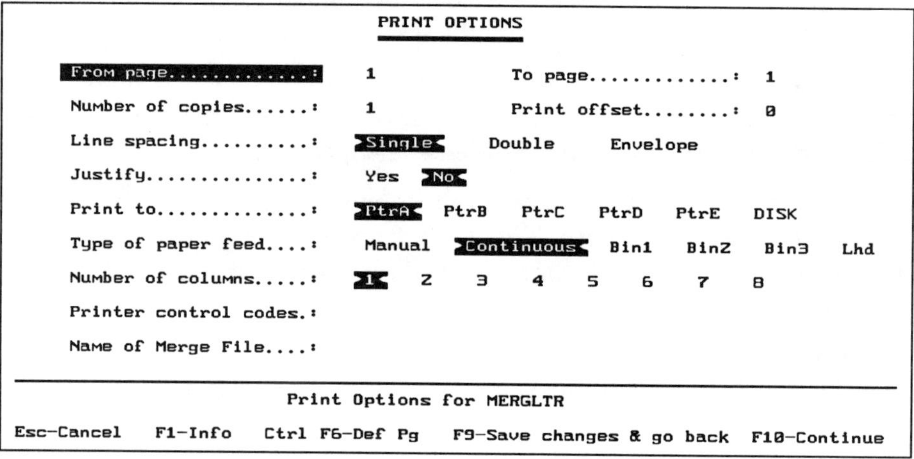

PRINT OPTIONS

From page.............: 1 To page.............: 1
Number of copies......: 1 Print offset........: 0
Line spacing..........: Single Double Envelope
Justify...............: Yes No
Print to..............: PtrA PtrB PtrC PtrD PtrE DISK
Type of paper feed....: Manual Continuous Bin1 Bin2 Bin3 Lhd
Number of columns.....: 1 2 3 4 5 6 7 8
Printer control codes.:
Name of Merge File....:

Print Options for MERGLTR
Esc-Cancel F1-Info Ctrl F6-Def Pg F9-Save changes & go back F10-Continue

Accept the default values displayed on the Print Options Menu. Since the base document (MERGLTR) is only one page in length, do not use the "From page" and "To page" print options.

NOTE

You may need to specify your "Print to" value (printer port, LPT or COM) depending upon how your printer is installed. Refer to Module 73 to determine the correct value to use.

5. Move the cursor to "Name of Merge File" and type **CUSTOMER**.
6. Press **F10**. The Retrieve Spec screen for the database is displayed. The Retrieve Spec screen is a replica of the form design for the database.

7. Press **F10** twice. Printing of documents begins. When printing is completed, the base document is displayed.

NOTE

If you want to print information only from selected forms, refer to Modules 16 and 29. Each contain instructions on how to select only certain forms.

8. Return to the Q&A Main Menu.
9. Turn to Module 6 to continue the learning sequence.

Module 71
PRINT OPTIONS FOR A REPORT

DESCRIPTION

There are various options that can be selected for Write function, File function, and Report function print options. Reports can be printed to the screen, disk, or paper. As well, report page format can be defined using features such as headers and footers.

PRINTING A REPORT ON THE SCREEN Selecting the option to print a report to the screen on the Report Print Options screen allows you to review a report on the screen before printing a paper copy. When viewing a report on the screen, you see the report formatted without headers or footers. You can view any report which is too large to fit entirely in the screen area by using the arrow keys on the numeric keypad to scroll across the screen or up and down in the report.

REQUESTING A SUMMARY REPORT To specify that you want a summary report for a database, choose YES in the Print totals only field on the Report Print Options screen. The result is that only column totals and subtotals are printed. No individual column entries from forms are listed on the report.

DEFINING A REPORT PAGE Another report print option that is available is the capability to define the size of the report page. When at the Report Global Options Menu, selecting D displays the Define Page screen. On this screen you can set page length, width, margins (top, bottom, left, and right), character density (characters per inch), page numbering, and header/footer information.

Other global options, such as format, print, and page options can be set at the Report Global Options Menu.

HEADERS AND FOOTERS Print options can be set up so header and footer lines print on each page of a report. A header or a footer or both can be set up to print on each page. You cannot have a header or footer or both only on certain pages.

Report title information, date, time, and page numbers are typical data that are contained in header or footer lines. To enter header and/or footer information, just type the information on the Define Page screen in the three blanks lines provided. Q&A provides you with the ability to position the text in a header or footer line. This locating text feature is controlled by use of exclamation points (!). For example, a header line typed as Report Number 345 ! Inventory Analysis

! @DATE left-justifies the wording "Report Number 345," centers the title "Inventory Analysis," and right-justifies the current date.

SAVING PRINT OPTION SPECIFICATIONS TO DISK After entering print specifications on the Define Page screen, pressing F10 saves the specifications to disk. A prompt message is displayed requesting you to decide if you want the report to print or if you want to return to the Report Menu.

If there is a problem with the specifications for your report, a warning message is displayed.

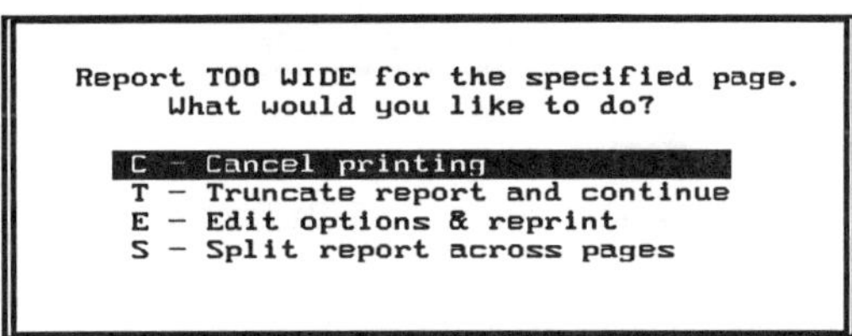

By resuming printing (selection R), you can see exactly what the problems are with your report. To correct problems with your report, you can then change column widths or headings, report margins, or the page setup.

APPLICATIONS

Viewing a report on your screen permits you to preview the report before printing a paper copy. Unfortunately, header and footer lines do not display on the screen.

Requesting a summary report enables you to limit the amount of information retrieved. There are occasions when you will be interested only in summary information.

Defining a report page provides you with the capability to exactly define the size of the report page, the number of characters printed per inch, and header and footer lines.

TYPICAL OPERATION

In this illustration, enter the Report function, go to the Column/Sort Spec screen, go to the Report Print Options screen, and finally to the Define Page screen to set up page characteristics. When finished, return to the Report Print Options screen. Begin at the Q&A Main Menu.

1. Type **R**. The Report Menu is displayed.
2. Type **D**. A prompt message is displayed requesting the name of the database for which a report is to be created.

3. Type **CUSTOMER** and press **Return**. A list of reports is displayed.
4. Type **CUSTOMER-REPORT** in response to the "Enter name:" prompt and press **Return**. The Retrieve Spec screen for the specified database is displayed.
5. Press **F10**. The Column/Sort Spec screen is displayed.
6. Press **F10**. The Report Print Options screen is displayed.

```
                         REPORT PRINT OPTIONS

Print to.........:      PtrA  PtrB  PtrC  PtrD  PtrE  DISK  SCREEN
Type of paper feed........:   Manual  Continuous  Bin1  Bin2  Bin3
Printer offset...........:    0
Printer control codes.....:
Print totals only.........:   Yes  No
Justify report body.......:   Left  Center  Right

CUSTOMER.DTF              Print Options for CUSTOMER-REPORT
Basic (Vanilla) Printer >>> LPT1
Esc-Cancel          F8-Define Page          F9-Go back          F10-Continue
```

7. Type in print option specifications. Refer to Module 72 for detailed instructions on how to complete screen information.
8. Press **F8**. The Define Page screen is displayed.

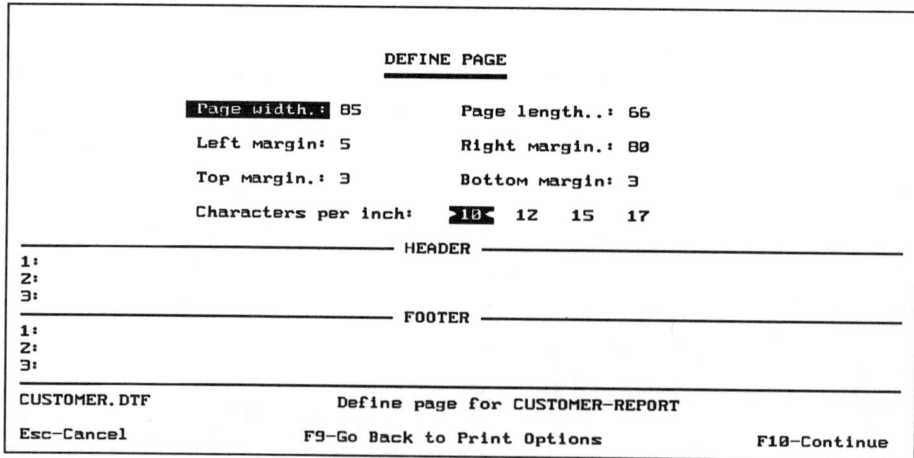

9. Press **Tab** to move the cursor to each item displayed on the screen. To change default values displayed on the screen, type over the value in each field and press **Return**. To specify characters per inch, press the **Spacebar** until the selection you want is highlighted.

10. Press **F9**. The Report Print Options screen is displayed.

    If you press F10, the report design is completed. You can proceed to print the report. Refer to Module 72 for instructions on how to print a report.

11. If you want to return to the Q&A Main Menu instead of printing the report, press **Esc**. A prompt message is displayed warning you that the report design has not been saved. The cursor is located on N - No.

12. Type **Y**. The Report Menu is displayed.

13. Press **Esc**. The Q&A Main Menu is displayed.

14. Turn to Module 72 to continue the learning sequence.

Module 72
PRINT A REPORT

DESCRIPTION

A previously designed and saved report is printed by selecting the Print a Report option on the Report Menu. You can print an existing report and make temporary changes to the report design before printing it or you can print a new report using a Report Print Spec once and not saving the specification to disk.

At the Q&A Main Menu, selecting the Report function displays the Report Menu. Selecting the Print a Report option initiates a prompt message requesting the name of the database that you want used for printing a report. After entering the database filename and pressing Return, a list of all reports designed for the specified database is displayed. To print an existing report, type the name of the existing report in response to the "Enter name:" prompt, and press Return. You are given the opportunity to print the report or to make temporary changes to the report specification.

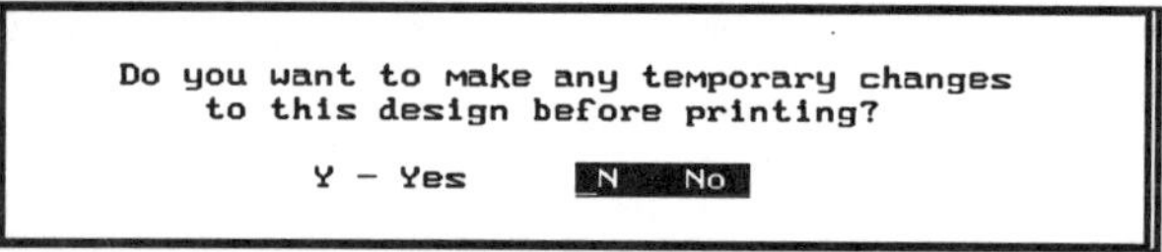

If you print the report without making temporary (one time) changes, accept the "No" default. Typing N and pressing Return causes Q&A to immediately start printing the report. Q&A performs the print operation using all of the existing specifications previously created for the report, including the Report Print Options specifications.

Typing Y causes Q&A to display all of the specifications and options screens for the existing report. You can make any necessary print specification changes before printing the report. This method creates a temporary or "one time" report print specification. Once the report is printed, the specification no longer exists. Refer to Module 79, Report Design/Redesign, for instructions on completing specification screens.

To print a new report, simply press Return without typing a report name. Q&A leads you through each specification screen used to design/redesign a report, but the report is designated as "New"; thus, the print specification created is used only once and discarded.

You can print the same report with different print and/or page options by pressing F2 while the report is printing. The print operation is stopped and the Report Print Options screen is displayed.

After you enter new print options on the displayed screen and press F10, Q&A prints the report.

APPLICATIONS

Even though you can display a report on your terminal screen, printing a report is the only way to get a copy of the report on paper. The printing function available in Q&A permits you to print a report using existing specifications or redesigned specifications. Furthermore, you can use the temporary specification feature to print a report once and discard the temporary print specification.

TYPICAL OPERATION

In this illustration, enter the Report Function and print an existing report to the screen. Begin at the Q&A Main Menu.

1. Type **R** to select the Report Menu.
2. Type **P**. A prompt message is displayed requesting the name of the database for which the report is being created.
3. Type **CUSTOMER** and press **Return**. A list of reports previously created for the specified database is displayed.
4. Type **CUSTOMER-REPORT** and press **Return**. A prompt message is displayed requesting you to decide if you want to make temporary changes before printing the report. You can also just press **Return** to create a "New" report.

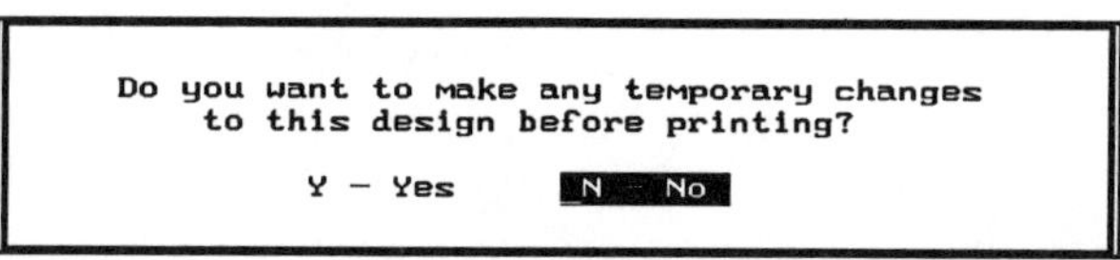

5. Type **Y**. The Retrieve Spec screen for the file is displayed.
6. Press **F10**. The Column/Sort Spec screen is displayed.

7. Press **F10**. The Report Print Options screen is displayed.
8. Press **Spacebar** to select "SCREEN" as the "Print to" option.

```
                         REPORT PRINT OPTIONS

  Print to..........:    PtrA   PtrB   PtrC   PtrD   PtrE   DISK  SCREEN
  Type of paper feed........:   Manual   Continuous   Bin1   Bin2   Bin3
  Printer offset............:   0
  Printer control codes.....:
  Print totals only.........:   Yes  No
  Justify report body.......:   Left   Center   Right

CUSTOMER.DTF              Print Options for CUSTOMER-REPORT
Print to screen.
Esc-Cancel         F8-Define Page          F9-Go back              F10-Continue
```

9. Press **F10**. The report is printed to the screen.
10. Return to the Q&A Main Menu.
11. Turn to Module 78 to continue the learning sequence.

Module 73
PRINTER INSTALLATION

DESCRIPTION

The printer installation feature offered by Q&A allows you to customize printing and special effects for documents and reports. Q&A is designed to function initially on a computer system with the assumption that a "no frills" basic printer is attached to the system.

If you have a printer capable of producing special effects such as variable pitch, boldface type, underscore, italic, typographic fonts, or other print enhancements, you will want to take advantage of those capabilities.

Printer installation is a utility feature accessed through the Utilities Menu via the Q&A Main Menu. Selecting P on the Utilities Menu displays the Printer Selection screen.

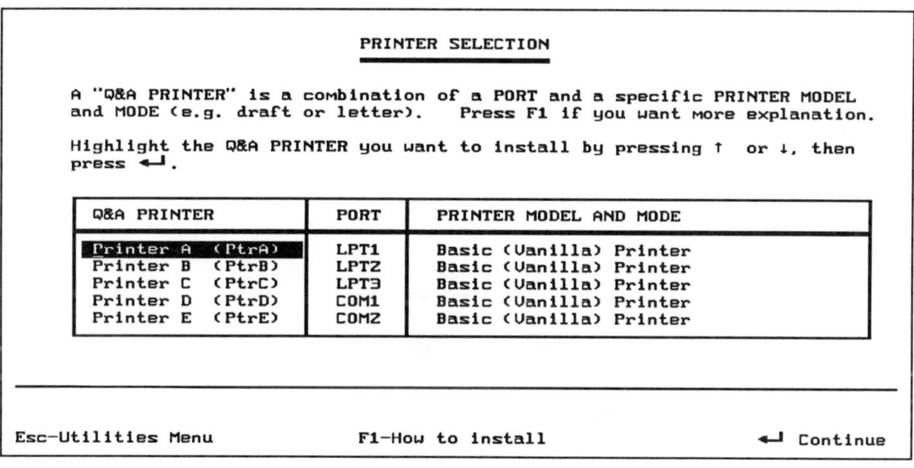

The Printer Selection Menu permits you to install up to five different printers in Q&A. Each printer installation is defined at a different port. Either parallel or serial printers can be accommodated by Q&A.

The ports available are: LPT1 through LPT3, and COM1 and COM2. LPT1 through LPT3 are reserved for parallel printers. COM1 and COM2 are reserved for serial printers.

Pressing the Spacebar moves you through the selections displayed on the screen. Pressing Return displays the Port Selection Menu screen. Pressing Return again displays a List of Printers screen. The following screen displays some of the names of printers that can be installed.

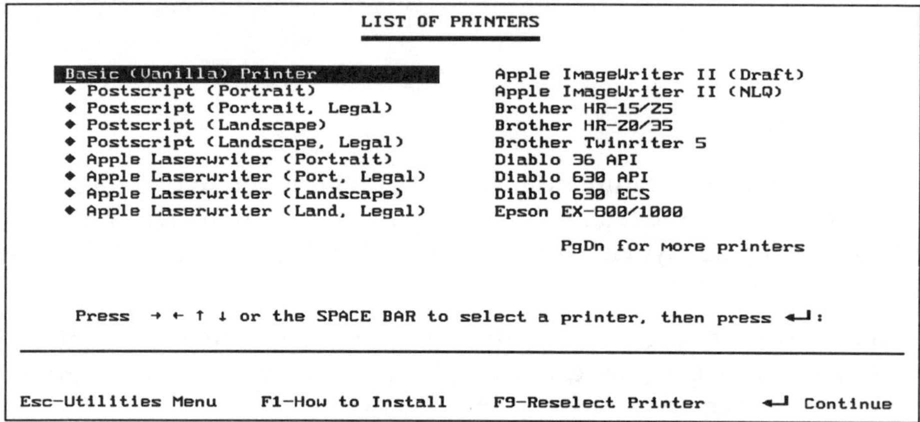

Pressing PgDn or PgUp displays more screens listing other printers.
Pressing the Spacebar selects the printer for Q&A to install.
Pressing Return displays the Special Printer Options screen.
Pressing F10 completes the installation. A message is displayed confirming the installation.

If you select a COM1 or COM2 port from the Port Selection Menu, a second screen is displayed.

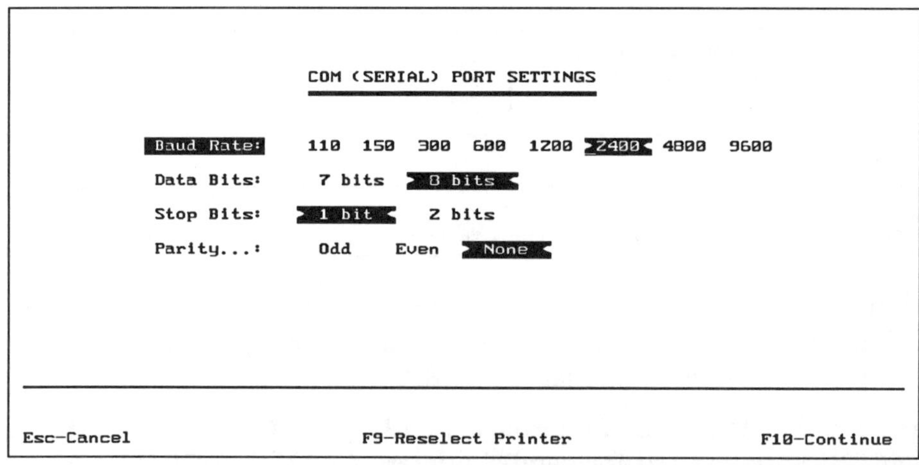

To install serial port settings for a serial printer, refer to the printer manufacturer's operation and installation manual for optimum settings.

Press the arrow keys, Tab key, or Spacebar to move through the fields on the screen. To choose a value, press Return.

Pressing F10 displays the Special Print Options screen, as with installing a parallel printer. Pressing F10 again installs the serial printer on a COM port. Pressing Return in response to the No prompt displays the Utilities Menu. Pressing Esc displays the Q&A Main Menu.

APPLICATIONS

The ability to install a commonly available printer lets you configure Q&A software for a number of popular printers. This allows you to choose printer capabilities and be assured that your printer is compatible with Q&A.

You have the option of selecting and using a printer model of your choice.

TYPICAL OPERATION

In this illustration, install an HP Laserjet (Portrait, Legal Size) printer on the LPT1 port on your computer system. If you have only one parallel port, it is designated as LPT1. Begin at the Q&A Main Menu.

1. Type **U**. The Utilities Menu is displayed.
2. Type **P**. The Printer Selection screen is displayed. LPT1 is highlighted. The cursor is located on Printer A (LPT1).
3. Press **Return** to display the Port Selection screen.
4. Press **Return** to display a list of printers.
5. Press **PgDn** to display another screen listing more printers. Highlight "HP Laserjet."
6. Press **Return** to select the printer. A confirmation screen is displayed.

If you are selecting another printer, use the arrow keys or the Spacebar to make your selection. Notice that a message about the selected printer is displayed.

7. Press **Return** to confirm the selection. The Special Printer Options screen is displayed.
8. Press **F10**. The printer is installed and a message is displayed to allow you to install another printer if you desire.
9. Return to the Main Menu.
10. Turn to Module 44 to continue the learning sequence.

Module 74
PROGRAM OVERVIEW

DESCRIPTION

Q&A is a popular word processing, database management, and Assistant software package for a number of reasons. First, it produces ASCII text document files making it compatible with most other popular word processing, database, and spreadsheet software. It has the ability to import other software files and to export files to the same software packages. Q&A can also produce spreadsheets having the same power and capabilities as dedicated spreadsheet software.

Q&A is compatible with most other software packages producing ASCII or DIF files, with dBASE files, IBM Filing Assistant, Lotus 1-2-3, and PFS:File.

Q&A can be used as a programming editor to write source code for various programming languages such as BASIC, Pascal, C, and Assembly Language.

It can also be used as a complete word processor. The word processing function is a sophisticated portion of this application software. Features such as copy, delete, move, global replace, justification, merge, and spell check are contained in Q&A. The Spell Check feature adds additional power to Q&A word processing. The main dictionary contains many commonly used words. You can add words to the personal dictionary to make the spell check function complete.

If your printer supports printing with a wide variety of typographic fonts, you can create documents that appear very impressive. Laser printers usually permit the printing of documents with typographic fonts (ex., PostScript printers). With all of these capabilities, it fully serves the many needs of a modern office. For the enthusiastic home computer user, it serves a variety of purposes.

Q&A PROGRAM FILES The following tables contain a list of Q&A program files as they are contained on individual 5 1/4-inch diskettes. All of these files should exist on the original distribution diskettes.

If you have 3 1/2-inch diskettes, there are only four diskettes containing all of the same files.

Q&A #1 Disk — Startup Disk The Startup diskette contains the programs that initially load Q&A into your computer's memory. It also contains the programs which permit you to branch out through the Q&A Main Menu to the major Q&A functions.

QA.COM QA1.EXE QAPRINT.CFG DELOLDQA.BAT
QA.DIS QAFILES EXE QAPRINT1.CFG

Q&A #2 Disk — File, Report, Write, and Utilities The second diskette contains the programs that permit operation of the major Q&A functions.

QAFR.OVL QAPRNDVR.OVL QAFRI.OVL
QAIA2.OVL QA.DIS

Q&A #3 Disk — Intelligent Assistant The third diskette contains programs that implement and control operation of the Assistant functions.

QANTA.OVL QAIA1.OVL QAIA2.OVL
QAFRI.OVL QA.DIS

Q&A #4 Disk — Write Function The fourth diskette contains programs pertaining to the write and spell functions.

QA.DIS QAPRNDVR.OVL QASPELL.OVL
QAWP.OVL QALABEL.OVL

Q&A #5 Disk — Proof The fifth diskette contains programs pertaining to the Q&A main dictionary and the online help facility

QASPELL.OVL QAMAIN.DCT
QA.DIS QAHELP.OVL

Q&A #6 Disk — Samples The sixth diskette contains various samples depicting typical uses for Q&A and the typographic font library.

EMPLOYEE.DFT EPSONLQ.FNT EMPLOYEE.IDX
TOSH321.FNT POST.FNT EMPLOYEE.DIF
PROPERTY.IDX PROPERTY.DTF KYOCERA.FNT
EPSONMRX.FNT EPSONFX.FNT HPLASERJ.FNT

Tutorial Diskette The seventh diskette contains tutorial programs. It also contains basic documents and files that are used in the tutorial process.

_FILE_0.DBD _FILE_3.DBD _FILE_6.DBD
_FILE_1.DBD _FILE_4.DBD _FILE_9.DBD
_FILE_2.DBD _FILE_5.DBD SG_MEM.COM
RT.EXE _MENU.DBD QATUTOR.BAT

A typical operation is not presented for this module. Its purpose is primarly for presenting information about the various Q&A files and their location on the different diskettes as shipped from the manufacturer.

Turn to Module 73 to continue the learning sequence.

Module 75
PROGRAMMING STATEMENTS

DESCRIPTION

Instructions can be contained at various locations on your forms in a database to provide for automatic processing. These instructions are given to Q&A using programming statements containing various programming words. Module 76 describes programming words available for use with Q&A.

APPLICATIONS

Entering programming statements on forms in a database widens the span of versatility available to you when using Q&A. Almost any possibility or any calculated result is at your fingertips. The capability to create programming statements makes Q&A far more sophisticated than most spreadsheet software.

Refer to Module 76 for a concise description of the programming words available for use in programming statements.

TYPICAL OPERATION

In this illustration, enter the File function and create a new database. Enter programming statements into some fields to perform calculations on a form. Begin at the Q&A Main Menu.

1. At the Q&A Main Menu, the cursor is located at F - File. Press **Return.** Type **D**. The Design Menu is displayed.
2. Type **D**. A prompt message is displayed requesting the name of the file to be designed.
3. Type **SALES**. A blank screen is displayed.
4. Type the following fields. Place a colon (:) after each name and enter the appropriate spaces noted in parentheses. Type a greater than (>) at the end of each line. Do not type the parentheses or the numbers within them. These are provided for you to know how many spaces to place in each field.

```
CUSTOMER: (20)                    >
QUANTITY: (10)          >
COST: (15)               >
TOTAL: (20)                 >

Order History
    1st Order: (10)      >
    2nd Order: (10)      >
    3rd Order: (10)      >

Average of Orders: (10)      >
Interest on Account: (10)      >
```

5. Press **F10** and type the following Information types in the designated fields:

CUSTOMER	**T**	2nd Order	**M**
QUANTITY	**N**	3rd Order	**M**
COST	**M**	Average of Orders	**N**
TOTAL	**M**	Interest on Account	**N**
1st Order	**M**		

6. Press **F10** again. The Format Options screen is displayed. Press **F10** to accept the values. The File Menu is redisplayed.
7. Type **D**. The Design Menu is displayed.
8. Type **C** for Customize and press **Return** to accept the filename SALES.DTF. The Customize Menu is displayed.
9. Type **P** for Program form. The Program Spec for the specified database is displayed.
10. Type the following information into each field to assign field numbers pressing **Return** after each field entry. Access the "Long field" option for those fields too small to hold the entire programming statement. The "Long field" option is accessed by pressing **F6**. Your screen should resemble the following.

```
CUSTOMER:#1
QUANTITY:#2
COST:#3
TOTAL:#4

Order History
    1st Order:#6
    2nd Order:#7
    3rd Order:#8

Average of Orders:#9=@AVG(#6,#7,#8)
Interest on Account:#10=.10*#3*1/12*#3*1/12
```

11. Press **F10** to save this design and redisplay the Customize Menu.

    Now that you have created a database and programming statements, perform the calculations. To do so, you must add data into the database.

12. Press **Esc** until the File Menu is displayed.
13. At the File Menu, type **A** and then press **Return** to accept the filename SALES.DTF. Notice that Form 1 of 1 appears at the bottom of the screen.
14. Type the indicated data so that your screen resembles the following. When you reach the programmed fields, do not type anything. Press **F8** to execute the programmed statement.

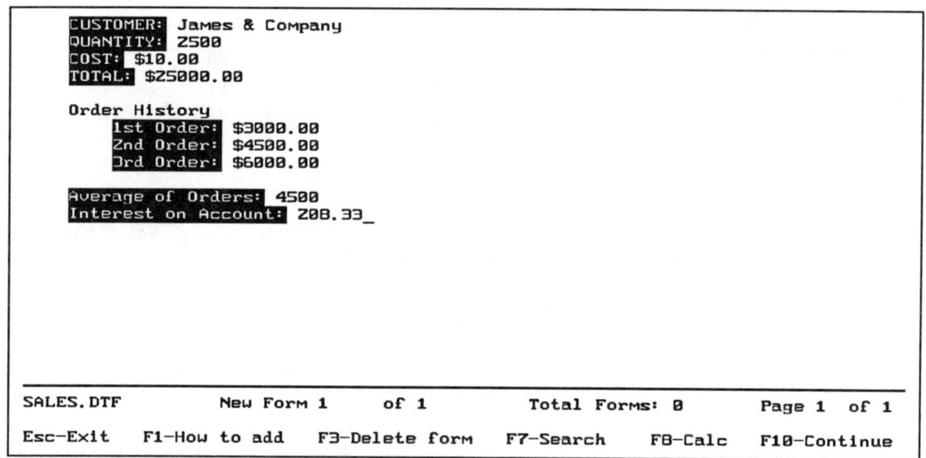

NOTE

You can continue adding data into forms and calculating them or proceed to the next step.

15. Press **Shift-F10** to save the document to disk. The File Menu is displayed.
16. Press **Esc**. The Q&A Main Menu is displayed.
17. Turn to Module 76 to continue the learning sequence.

Module 76
PROGRAMMING WORDS

DESCRIPTION

There are specific words used to program functions on Q&A forms. Each programming word is presented with a brief description of its function. There are several categories of programming words or functions. They include:

Date and Time Functions
Numbering Functions
Financial Functions
Mathematical Functions
Text or String Functions
Programming Commands
Form Entry and Exit Calculations.

DATE AND TIME FUNCTIONS

@DATE - Produces the current date provided your computer has an internal clock and the date is correctly set.

@TIME - Produces the current time provided your computer has an internal clock and the time is correctly set.

CONTEXT FUNCTIONS

@ADD - Executes a programming statement only when adding forms to a database.

@UPDATE - Executes a programming statement only when updating forms in a database.

NUMBERING FUNCTIONS

@NUMBER - Returns a specific number, one greater than the last number that was returned.

@NUMBER(N) - Returns a specific number "n" times greater than the last number that was returned.

FINANCIAL FUNCTIONS

@CGR(p,f,l) - Computes compound growth rate.

@FV(p,i,l) - Computes the future value of an annuity.

@PMT(p,i,l) - Computes a payment when principal, interest and length of the loan are specified.

@PV(p,i,l) - Computes the present value of an annuity.

MATHEMATICAL FUNCTIONS

@ABS(n) - Returns the absolute value of a number n.

@ASC(x) - Returns the ASCII decimal value of the character x.

@AVG(list) - Computes the average for values contained in a list of numbers.

@EXP(n,m) - Raises the number n to the m-th power.

@INT(n) - Produces the integer value for the expression n.

@MAX(list) - Produces the maximum of all values contained in a list.

@MIN(list) - Produces the minimum of all values contained in a list.

@NUM(x) - Returns the number represented by value of x.

@ROUND(n,m) - Rounds the number n to the number of decimal places equivalent to the number m.

@SGN(x) - Returns the algebraic sign of the number x.

@SQRT(n) - Produces the square root of the number n.

@STD(list) - Calculates the standard deviation for numbers contained in a list.

@SUM(list) - Produces the sum of the numbers contained in a list.

@VAR(list) - Produces the variance of numbers contained in a list.

TEXT OR STRING FUNCTIONS

@CHR(n) - Returns the ASCII character for the expression n.

@DEL(x,n,m) - Returns the expression x with m number of characters deleted from starting positon n.

@DITTO(list) - Returns the values from the list of fields in a previous form.

@FILENAME - Returns the name of the current file.

@HELP(n) - Causes created help for the field n.

@INSTR(x,y) - Returns the integer position of the first occurrence of the character y in string x.

@LEFT(x,n) - Returns the leftmost n characters in the expression x.

@WIDTH(n) - Returns the width of the field n.

@LEN(x) - Returns the length of the field x.

@MID(x,n,m) - Returns m number of characters from the string x, starting at the character n.

@MSG(x) - Produces the message x on the Message Line displayed on the screen.

@RIGHT(x,n) - Returns the rightmost n characters of the expression x.

@STR(n) - Returns the text value comprised of n number of characters in the expression x.

PROGRAMMING COMMANDS

LOOKUP - Finds the key in a lookup table and returns the corresponding value assigned to a field ID.

@LOOKUP - Finds the key in a lookup table and returns the corresponding value from one of the columns in a report.

@XLOOKUP - Finds the key for a Q&A database and returns a value from the file.

FORM ENTRY AND EXIT CALCULATIONS

Press F8 - Pressing this key displays the Entry/Exit Profile box.

APPLICATIONS

Programming words are used in constructing programming statements. These statements provide predefined actions that Q&A is to execute when certain conditions exist.

TYPICAL OPERATION

There is no typical operation for this Module. Refer to Module 75 for details on how to enter programming statements on a form.

Turn to Module 65 to continue the learning sequence.

Module 77
REMOVE A FORM

DESCRIPTION

Removing a form involves deleting one or more forms from a database file. It is recommended that you view the forms that are candidates for deletion before actually deleting them. The procedure described in this module permits viewing of forms. Refer to Module 96 for a more complete description of how to view forms.

The Remove a Form operation is as simple as most other Q&A functions. Selecting F at the Q&A Main Menu displays the File Menu. Selecting R, entering the name of the file containing forms to be deleted, and pressing Return displays the Retrieve Spec screen for the specified database. Pressing Return without entering the name of a file displays a list of all files stored on disk.

After you define the retrieve specification for forms in the database, Q&A displays the first form meeting the retrieve specification. View the first form displayed. Press F3 to remove it or press F10 to keep the displayed form and proceed to the next form.

If you do not indicate any retrieve specifications and press F10, Q&A removes all forms in the specified database. Before this happens, however, a warning message is displayed.

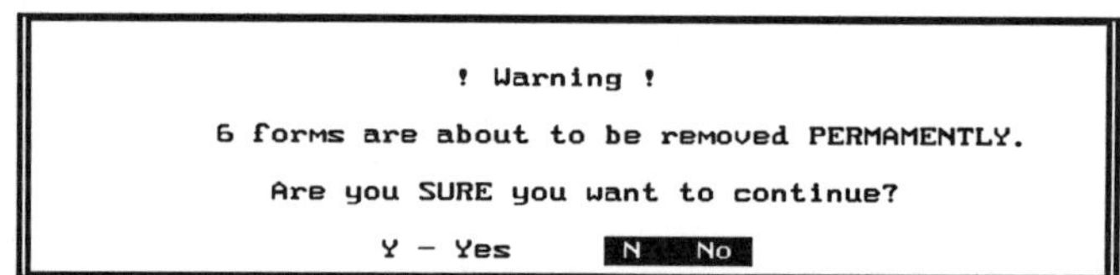

In this message, 6 is the number of forms that Q&A is going to permanently delete.

Choosing Yes deletes the number of forms indicated (6). Choosing No allows you to reconsider. Once forms are deleted, there is no way to recover the data.

APPLICATIONS

The process of removing forms is useful in allowing you to update your databases. It permits you to selectively delete database information. As information in your databases becomes obsolete or infrequently used, you can easily remove it and provide disk space for more relevant information.

In the process of removing forms, you first view and verify that you want to delete data before actually removing it from the database.

TYPICAL OPERATION

In this illustration, indicate the filename for the database with which you want to work. At the Retrieve Spec screen, proceed to the point where all forms in the database could be removed. However, in this illustration, the command to execute removal of all forms in the database will not be invoked. Forms in the example database are retained and the steps in the illustration return you to the Q&A Main Menu. Begin at the Q&A Main Menu.

1. Select the File Menu.
2. Type **R**. A prompt message is displayed requesting a filename for the database from which you want forms removed.

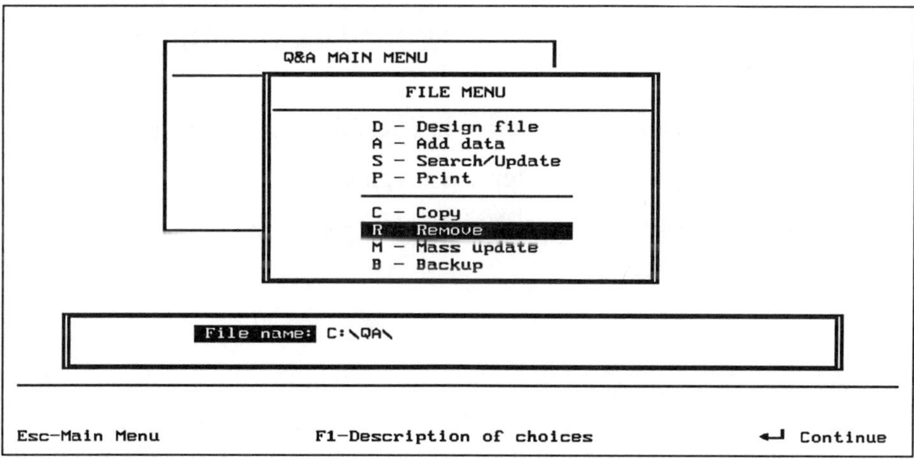

3. Type **INVNTRY** and press **Return**. The Retrieve Spec screen for the specified database is displayed.

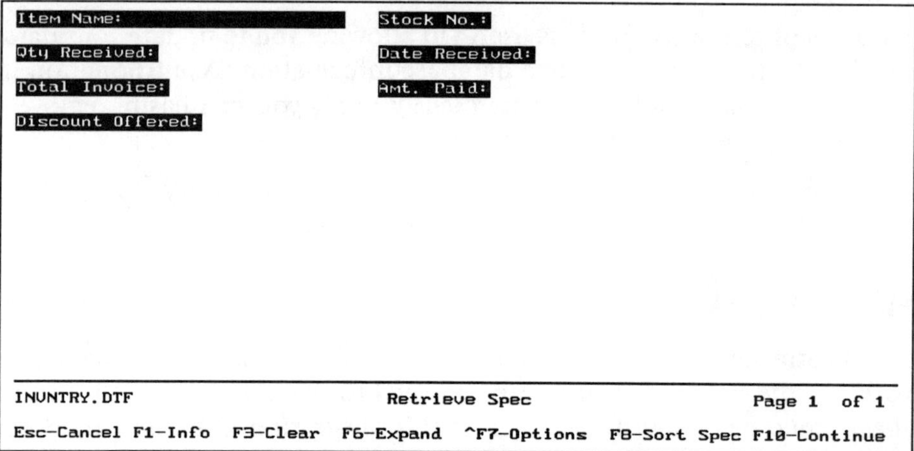

4. Press **F10** to remove all forms contained in the database. A warning message is displayed indicating the total number of forms to be permanently removed. It also requests that you confirm that you want to remove all of the forms. The cursor is located on N - No.

NOTE

If Y is typed, all forms are individually displayed very rapidly as each is removed. If N is typed, the remove operation is cancelled and the File Menu is displayed.

5. Press **Return** to cancel the removal. The File Menu is displayed.
6. Press **Esc**. The Q&A Main Menu is displayed.
7. Turn to Module 14 to continue the learning sequence.

Module 78
RENAME/DELETE/COPY

DESCRIPTION

Rename/Delete/Copy are applicable to the Write, File, and Report functions.

Rename	Assigns another filename for a Write document or Report.
Delete	Erases a Write document or Report design.
Remove	Deletes a Form file (database) in the File function.
Copy	Makes a duplicate of a Write document or Report.

The rename/delete/copy functions operate basically the same within each of the three functions. Use of rename/delete/copy within each Q&A function is briefly summarized in the following paragraphs.

RENAME/DELETE/COPY IN THE WRITE FUNCTION At the Write Menu, typing U displays the Rename/Delete/Copy Menu. Typing R, D, or C displays a prompt message requesting the name of the document upon which you want the specified function performed. If there was a document previously in the editor, the name of that document is displayed. Press Return if you want a function performed on that document. If not, type another document name over the displayed filename. Delete the document name on the prompt message by pressing the Spacebar. After entering a different document name, press Return.

If you are renaming or copying a document, a prompt message is displayed requesting the new name. If you are deleting a document, Q&A requests that you confirm your decision to delete the document.

After the requested function is performed, the Rename/Delete/Copy Menu is displayed. Pressing Esc returns you to the Write Menu.

REMOVE/COPY FOR FILE At the File Print Menu, typing R displays a prompt message requesting the name of the file to be deleted. You can press the Spacebar to delete the displayed filename in the prompt message and press Return to display all files stored on disk. The files are from databases having a DTF file extension. Q&A requests you to confirm your decision to delete the file.

Refer to Module 77 for detailed instructions on how to remove a form.

RENAME/DELETE/COPY IN THE REPORT FUNCTION Selecting R at the Report Menu displays a prompt message requesting the name of the report file. Pressing the Spacebar and Return displays all reports related to a specified database. Answering a prompt message with a filename for a database being renamed or copied displays the Rename/Delete/Copy Menu.

Pressing R, D, or C displays an appropriate prompt message requesting that a filename be entered. After completion of the operation, the Rename/Delete/Copy Menu is displayed. If you are deleting a report, Q&A requests confirmation from you that you want to proceed with the deletion.

APPLICATIONS

The rename/delete/copy function is convenient to use to rename/delete/copy a Write document, a Form, or a Report design. Renaming is used to provide a more concise name for a document, file, or report. Deleting effectively erases documents, forms, or report designs. Once deletion is performed, the document, file, or report design cannot be retrieved again.

TYPICAL OPERATION

In this illustration, delete a Write document. Begin at the Q&A Main Menu.

1. Type **W**. The Write Menu is displayed.

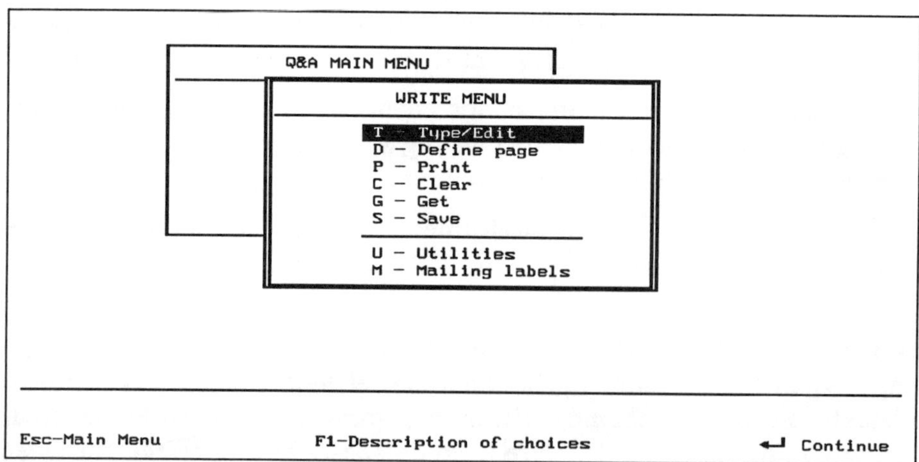

2. Type **U**. The Write Utilities Menu is displayed.

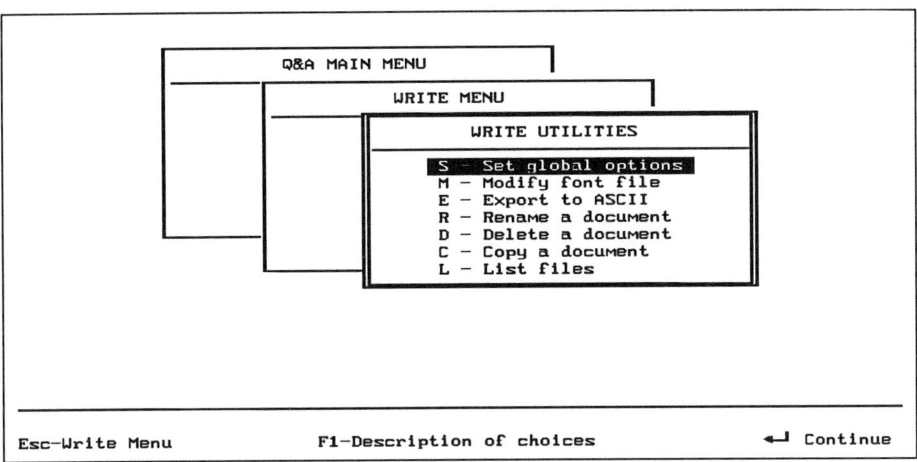

3. Type **D**. A prompt message is displayed requesting the name of the Write document being deleted.
4. Type the name of one of your practice documents and press **Return**. A message is displayed, requesting you to verify that you want to proceed with deleting the document.

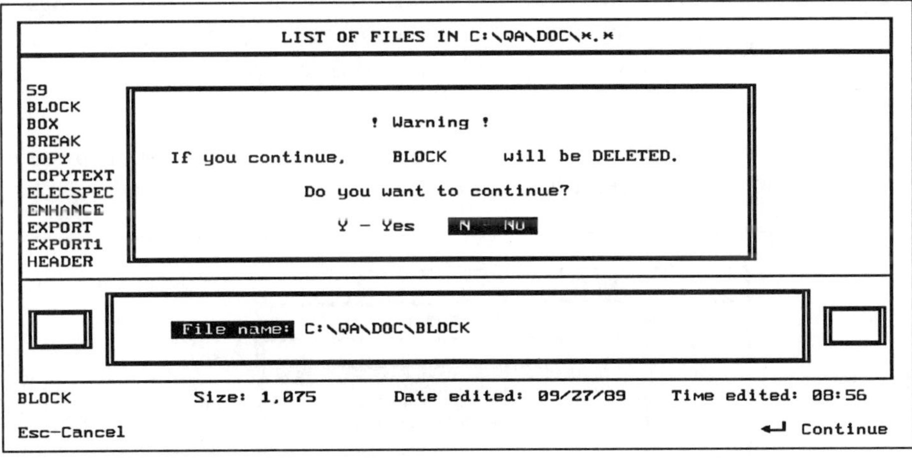

5. Type **Y**. The document is deleted and the Write Utilities Menu is displayed.
6. Return to the Q&A Main Menu.
7. Turn to Module 22 to continue the learning sequence.

Module 79
REPORT DESIGN/REDESIGN

DESCRIPTION

Designing or redesigning a report involves creating the layout for a report, choosing which of the forms from which you want information retrieved, setting up columns, and finally printing the report. Q&A retrieves information from any database that you specify, sorts it, and either displays it or prints it in the layout that you create.

Reports can be created for display on the screen or for printing on your printer. The information defining forms to be retrieved and the layout of the report are stored in the report print specification. The report print specification is saved and can be used later.

If you add or delete forms from a database, you can still use the same report print specification. The revised database is automatically usable by the report print specification and the defined parameters contained in the report print specification ensure that the report produced is consistent every time.

Column titles and width are set by Q&A; however, you can change these parameters to customize any report to fit your particular needs. For a single database, any modification to column widths and titles apply to all reports created for that database.

Entering the Report function is achieved from the Q&A Main Menu by selecting the R option; the Report Menu is displayed.

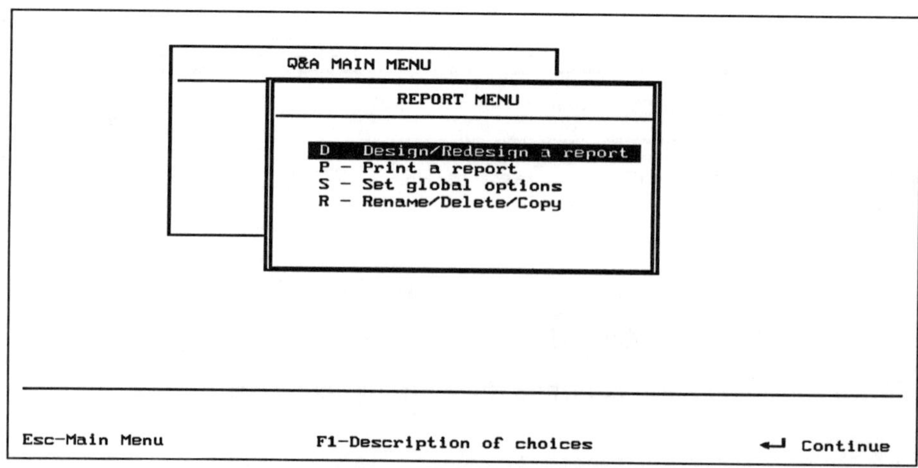

Selecting D initiates the design/redesign of a report. After entering the name of an existing database which is to be used in creating the report, Q&A prompts you to enter the name for the report. The name can be a maximum of 30 characters. Upon entering the report name, the Retrieve Spec screen for the database is displayed. On this screen, you specify which forms are to be retrieved for use in creating the report. After selecting the forms to be retrieved, the Column/Sort Spec screen is displayed. On the Column/Sort Spec screen, you enter codes to perform various operations. The possible operations include:

Sort information in a column
Perform calculations with a column
Specify where pages are to break in the report
Specify the inclustion of additional columns
Specify breaks in columns by date (day, month, or year)

Finally, you specify the print options to be used in printing the report. Printing can be directed to the screen, printer, or disk.

Redesigning a report is a process identical to designing a new report. When requested by Q&A to enter the name of the report, type the name of an existing report. Proceed as if you were creating a new report; make the necessary changes to redesign your existing report.

APPLICATIONS

There is no end to the list of applications for reports. You can take information contained in your databases and format it on the screen or on paper in any fashion. This capability provides you with a multitude of ways to analyze your data.

Salary analyses, inventory reports, student reports and records, personnel records, or customer contact lists can all be produced in any format that you want.

TYPICAL OPERATION

In this illustration, enter the Report function, set up a basic design for a report, retrieve all forms in a database, and set up the report columns. Begin at the Q&A Main Menu.

1. Select the Report Menu.
2. Type **D**. Type **CUSTOMER** and press **Return** in response to the prompt message requesting the name of the database for which the report is to be designed/redesigned. A prompt message is displayed requesting the name that you want to give to the report being created.

3. Type **CUSTOMER-REPORT** and press **Return**. Remember, the name can only be a maximum of 30 characters. The Retrieve Spec screen for the specified database is displayed.

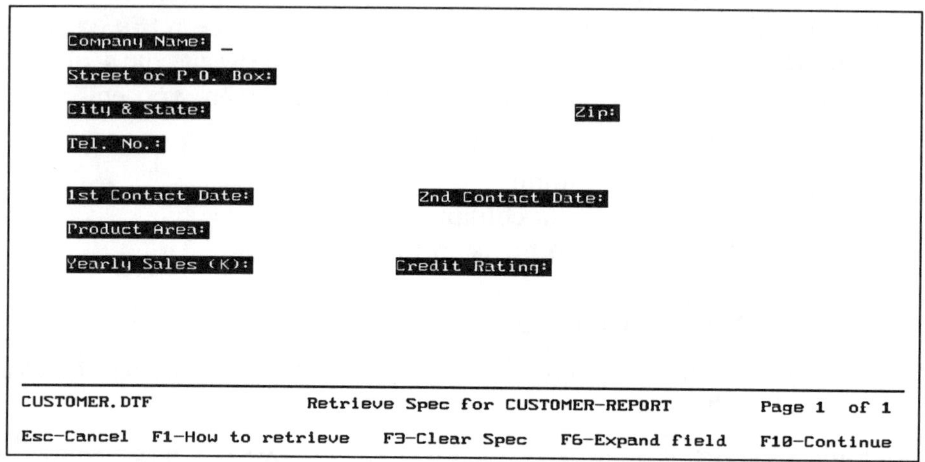

4. Press **F10**. All forms in the database are retrieved for information selection. The Column/Sort Spec screen is displayed.

To retrieve only certain forms in the database and extract information for the report, move the cursor to each field on the Retrieve Spec screen and enter a retrieve specification. For example, if you only want to retrieve those customers located in Chicago. Move the cursor to the "City" field and type "Chicago" in the field. Pressing F10 selects only those forms having a customer located in Chicago. You may enter as many retrieve specifications as wanted on the Retrieve Spec screen. However, only one specification may be entered for each field.

5. Press **Tab** to move the cursor to the field that you want to appear first on the report. Refer to the following example.

6. Type **1** in the field Company Name.

7. Repeat Steps 5 and 6, except type **2** for the second column, **3** for the third column, etc., until you have defined the order in which columns are to appear in the report.

```
Company Name: 1
Street or P.O. Box: 2
City & State: 3                                  Zip: 4
Tel. No.: 5

1st Contact Date: 6              2nd Contact Date: 7
Product Area: 8
Yearly Sales (K): 9            Credit Rating: 10

CUSTOMER.DTF          Column/Sort Spec for CUSTOMER-REPORT          Page 1  of 1
Esc-Cancel   F1-Info   F6-Expand   F8-Derived Columns   F9-Go back   F10-Continue
```

8. Press **F10**. The Print Options Menu is displayed. For instructions on how to print a report, refer to Module 72.
9. Press **F10**. The report print specification is saved to disk under the specified report name. A prompt message is displayed requesting you to decide if you want to print the report.

   Selecting Y prints the report. Selecting N exits from the operation and displays the Report Menu.
10. Press **Esc**. The Q&A Main Menu is displayed.
11. Turn to Module 13 to continue the learning sequence.

Module 80

RETRIEVE/CHANGE FORMS USING THE ASSISTANT

DESCRIPTION

Forms can be retrieved and even changed using the Assistant to perform both tasks. Module 64 describes how you can have the Assistant perform almost any task relating to your databases. A prerequisite is that you must have previously defined the vocabulary which you are using in making the request.

To retrieve a form, all that is necessary is that you make the request to the Assistant. Throughout this book, the sample database named "Customer" is used. For example, you can request the Assistant to retrieve forms from this database. From the Q&A Main Menu, selecting A displays the Assistant Menu. On the Assistant Menu, selecting A requests the Assistant to perform a task. Refer to Module 64 for detailed instructions on requesting that a task be performed. Typical requests that can be made are

List companies located in New York City
Display companies first contacted in July 1987
Give me all forms having a product area equal to sundries
Show forms with postal zip codes equal to 75074

Once a form has been retrieved, it is simple to change it when it is displayed on the screen. Using the cursor movement keys, move the cursor to the field that you want to change and overtype the field with new information.

You can also have the Assistant change information on a form for you. When requesting the Assistant to perform a task, type the request in the box displayed on the screen. Typical requests for changes to a form are

Change Green's address to "2354 St. Petersburg St."
Change all product areas to "undefined"
Remove all forms with 2nd Contact dates before January 15, 1985

Notice that the changed information is enclosed in quotation marks ("). Also note in the first example that the "period" actually belongs to the information being changed. Otherwise, do not include punctuation with the change.

APPLICATIONS

The possible applications for using the Assistant to retrieve and change forms for you are unlimited. Not only can changes be made to an isolated individual form, but global changes can also be made just as easily.

TYPICAL OPERATION

For this illustration, refer to instructions presented in Module 64. Specify a database filename to the Assistant. When the request box is displayed, make several requests of the Assistant to retrieve or change forms in the database.

Turn to Module 77 to continue the learning sequence.

Module 81
RETRIEVE A MACRO

DESCRIPTION

Retrieving a macro involves getting an existing macro from disk. The existing macro is one that was previously created. Module 24 describes how to define/redefine a macro. *Defining a macro* is creating a macro.

A macro can be retrieved from disk at any location in Q&A, that is, within any of the major functions (Write, File, etc.) as long as a prompt message is not being displayed.

Pressing Shift-F2 displays the Macro Menu.

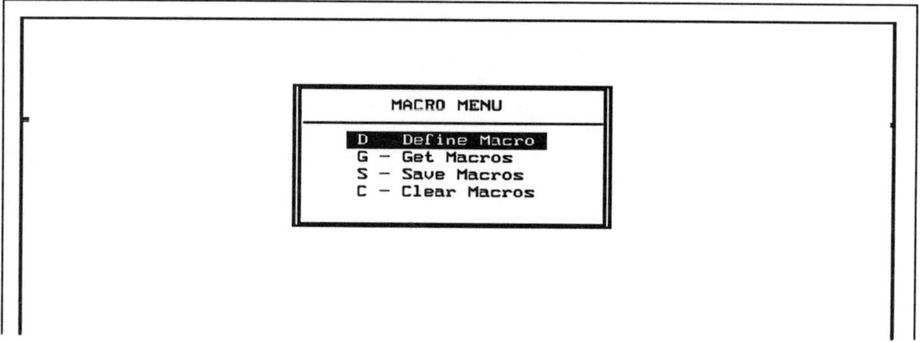

Typing G displays a prompt message at the bottom of the screen requesting the name of the macro file.

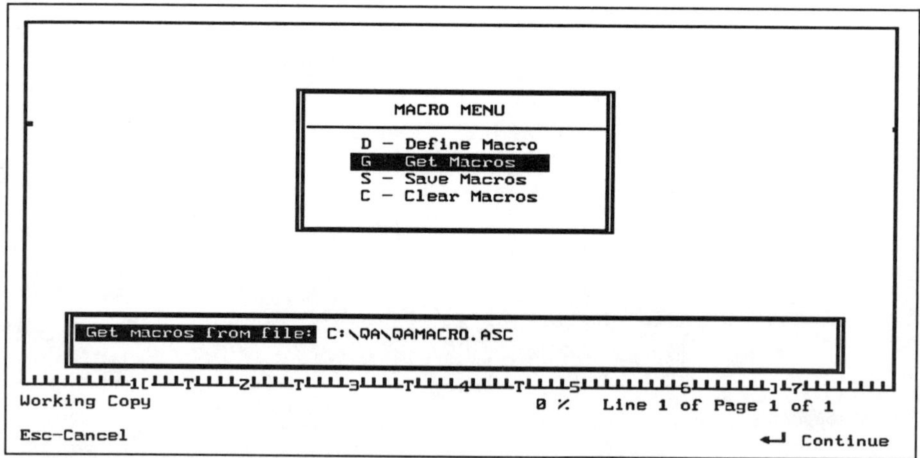

Typing the filename including the file extension and pressing Return gets the macro from disk and loads it into memory.

Only one macro file may be resident in your computer's memory at one time. However, a macro file can contain as many individual macros as you want to place in it. Putting a macro file into your computer's memory and then retrieving another macro file completely replaces the first macro file placed in memory.

A scheme in using macros is to define (create) macros and store them in a single file. This technique allows you to place all macros frequently used into memory and then to be able to access any of them for use.

Module 83 describes how to save commonly used macros in a macro file named QAMACRO.ASC. This file is automatically loaded into your computer's memory each time Q&A is started up. So, logically this is an excellent place to store frequently used macros.

In a file containing several macros, any errors (typically typographical errors) are identified to you by an error message.

APPLICATIONS

Saving macros that you create in the file QAMACRO.ASC ensures that each one is loaded into your computer's memory and each remains readily accessible for you to use. When this technique is employed, there is no need to retrieve a particular macro previously created.

However, if you save individually created macros into individual files, each time you want to use one of them you must retrieve the macro before it can be used. Consequently, the retrieval procedure described in this module is used.

Macros must be resident in your computer's memory before they can be used. The typical operation describes the only way to retrieve and place a macro into the computer's memory. The only exception is use of the QAMACRO.ASC file.

TYPICAL OPERATION

In this illustration, enter into the Write function and retrieve any macro previously saved to disk. After retrieving the macro, return to the Q&A Main Menu.

1. Type **W**. The Write Menu is displayed.
2. Press **Return**. A Working Copy (blank) screen for a new document is displayed.
3. Press **Shift-F2**. The Macro Menu box is displayed.

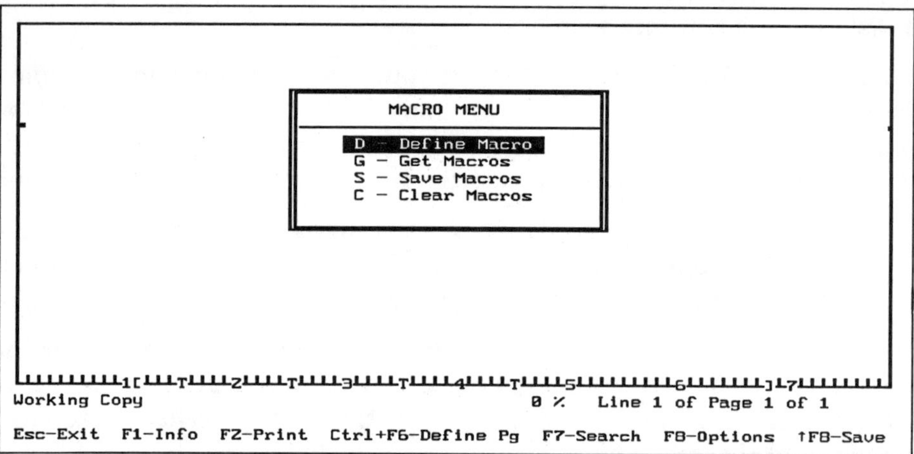

4. Type **G** A prompt message is displayed at the bottom of the screen requesting the name of the macro file. The default macro file QAMACRO.ASC is displayed in the prompt message.

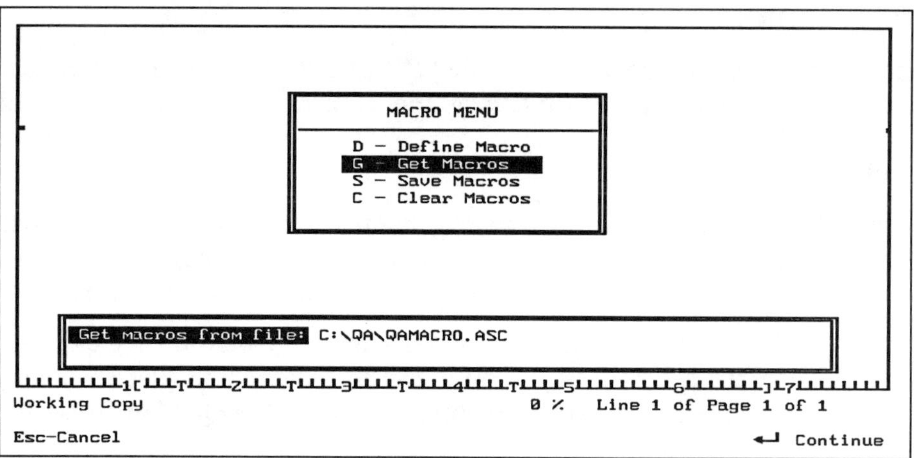

5. Type the filename for any macro that you had previously created or just press **Return** if QAMACRO.ASC is displayed. If you use one of your own macro files, remember to type the full name of the file including the file extension.

The macro created in Module 83 was assigned the macro identifier key: Ctrl-W.

Q&A brings the specified macro into the computer's main memory. The Working Copy for a new document is displayed.

You must remember the macro identifier keys (i.e., Alt, Ctrl, Shift, or Unshift plus a keyboard key) to use the macro.

6. Test the macro by pressing the macro keys. When macros are created you assign macro key identifiers (examples are: Ctrl-W, Ctrl-A, etc.). If you want to retrieve the macro defined in Module 83, recall the file QAMACRO.ASC and press Ctrl-W. The retrieved macro creates the following results:
7. Press **Esc**. The Write Menu is displayed.
8. Press **Esc**. A prompt message is displayed indicating that the changes made to the Working Copy of the document have not been saved.
9. Type **Y**. The Q&A Main Menu is displayed.
10. This is the last module in the learning sequence.

Module 82
SAVE A DOCUMENT

DESCRIPTION

Once a document is created you can save it to disk. It remains stored on disk until you are ready to make changes to it or to perform some other operation on the document. There are two ways to save a document to disk.

- Save a document while in the Type/Edit function during an edit session.
- Save a document by exiting from the Type/Edit function (edit session) to the Write Menu. At the Write Menu, select the Save (S) option.

SAVING A DOCUMENT DURING AN EDIT SESSION Saving a document during an edit session is initiated by pressing Shift-F8. A prompt message requests the filename under which the document is to be saved. If you have forgotten the names of documents saved to disk, you can press Return without entering a filename as requested. The following illustrates a typical screen display.

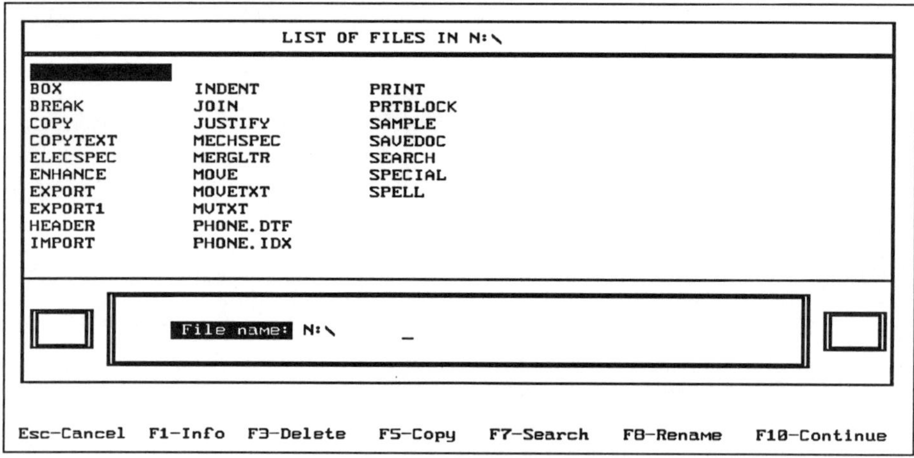

In this prompt, n is the applicable disk drive.

You can enter the filename at the bottom of the screen and press Return. The document is saved to disk under the specified filename. The Working Copy of the document is displayed after the save operation.

Later in the edit session, if you initiate the save feature, the document name is always displayed for you. Pressing Return saves the document to the filename displayed. By pressing the Spacebar, the displayed name is erased and you may type another filename. After pressing Return, the document is saved to the new filename.

SAVING A DOCUMENT FROM THE WRITE MENU Saving a document from the Write Menu is initiated by pressing Esc to exit from the edit session (the Working Copy). The Write Menu is displayed. At the Write Menu, selecting S displays a prompt message at the bottom of the Write Menu.

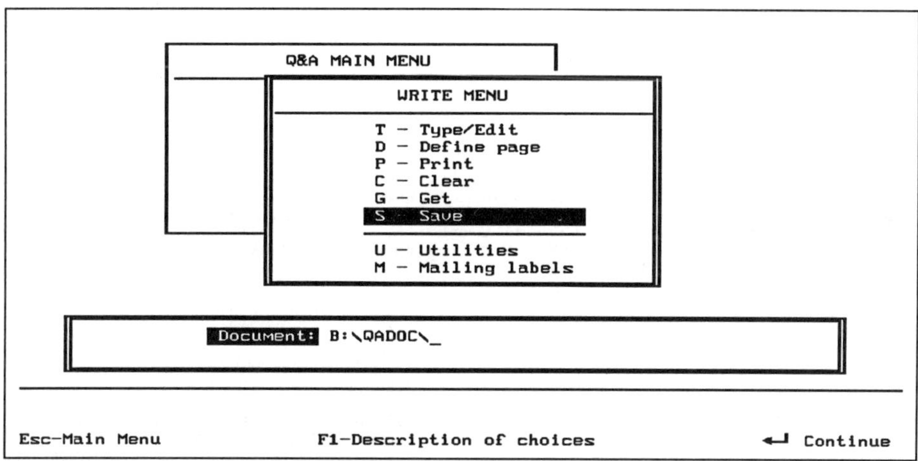

In this prompt, b is the applicable disk drive.

Entering the document filename and pressing Return saves the document to disk. A "Saving" message is displayed at the bottom of the screen. The Write Menu is displayed after the save operation is completed.

APPLICATIONS

At any time during text creation or the edit process, you may want to save your document to disk. This is a good technique to prevent potential loss of the document in case of a system or power malfunction. Using this method to save a document allows you to save the document to disk where it is safe without leaving the edit session.

The most commonly used filing method to save a document is to return to the Write Menu. Once you have completed a document, you are most likely to return to the Write Menu to perform other Write functions or to return to the Q&A Main Menu.

Once at the Write Menu, you can choose any of the Write functions.

TYPICAL OPERATION

In this example, begin at the Q&A Main Menu, enter the Write function, and create a new document. After typing the document, save it to disk under a specified filename.

1. At the Q&A Main Menu, type **W**. The Write Menu is displayed. The cursor is located at T - Type/Edit.
2. Press **Return** to display a Working Copy (blank) screen for a new document.
3. Type the following text:

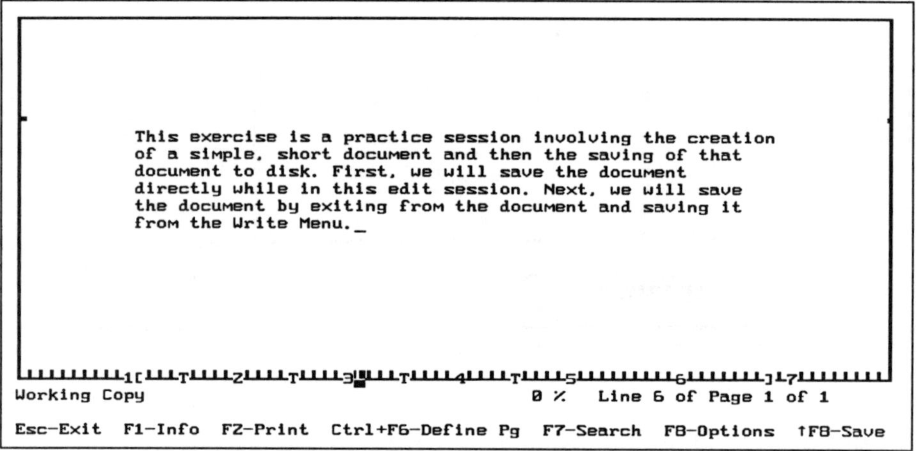

4. Press **Shift-F8** to save the document while still in the edit session. A prompt message requests you to enter the document name: Save as: C:\QA_.

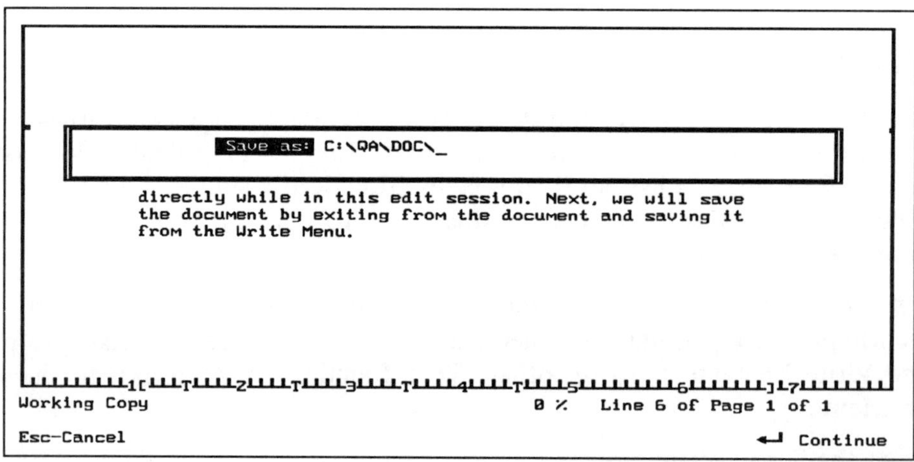

5. Type **SAVEDOC** and press **Return**. A "Saving" message is displayed at the bottom of the screen. The document is saved to the default disk drive.
6. After typing additional text in the document, press **Esc** to exit to the Write Menu.
7. Type **S**. A prompt message requests you to enter the filename. The previous filename entered is displayed in the prompt message. To see the names of all documents stored on the disk, press **Spacebar** (to erase the displayed filename), and press **Return** without entering a filename. The document names are displayed. You can save the document to a different filename at this point by typing over SAVDOC.
8. Type **SAVEDOC** and press **Return.** The document is saved on the default disk drive under the specified filename. The Write Menu is displayed.
9. Press **Esc** to return to the Q&A Main Menu.
10. Turn to Module 11 to continue the learning sequence.

Module 83
SAVE A MACRO

DESCRIPTION

In Module 24, you learned how to define and redefine a macro. A macro is placed in your computer's memory for use as long as Q&A is active or until you clear the macro. Once you leave Q&A, any defined macros created during the session are lost unless you save them. Q&A does not automatically save macros to disk.

To save a macro, press Shift-F2. The Macro Menu is displayed on the screen. Typing S causes Q&A to request you to enter the name of the macro.

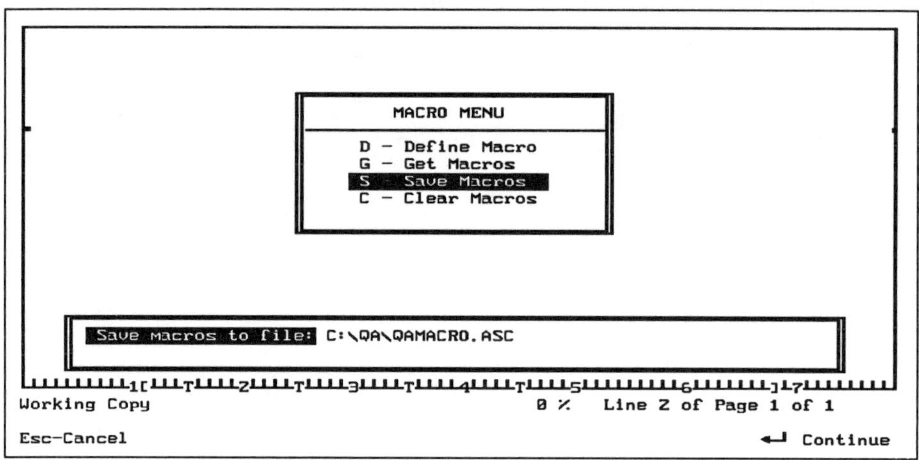

Q&A is designed with an existing macro file named QAMACRO.ASC. Its purpose is to provide you with a place to save your most frequently used macros. The big advantage of having this file is that each time you start up Q&A, it searches for the file and loads it into memory. Consequently, frequently used macros are resident in your computer's memory and ready for you to use. This eliminates the need to "Get" a macro each time you want to load it into memory during a session with Q&A.

If you define or redefine macros that you want saved in the QAMACRO.ASC file, you must specifically save the macros in the file. Q&A does not automatically save QAMACRO.ASC to disk.

A macro file holds many individual macros. You also can have as many macro files saved as disk space allows.

APPLICATIONS

Saving a macro is a vital part of making maximum utilization of the macro feature. Once you have taken the time to define a macro identifier and have laboriously entered a set of keystrokes, the macro is worth saving. This is especially true if you use the macro often.

Remember, save your macros to disk because Q&A does not automatically save macros to disk. Unfortunately, you are not prompted in any way when leaving Q&A to remind you to save any macros that you may have created during the session.

TYPICAL OPERATION

In this example, begin at the Q&A Main Menu, access the Write Menu, enter into an edit session in a Working Copy for a new document, create a macro, and save it to disk.

1. Type **W**. The Write Menu is displayed.
2. Press **Return**. A Working Copy (blank) screen for a new document is displayed.
3. Press **Shift-F2**. The Macro Menu is displayed. The cursor is located on D - Define Macro.
4. Press **Return**. A prompt message is displayed at the bottom of the screen requesting that you enter a macro key identifier.
5. Press **Ctrl-W**. This key sequence is now defined as the macro key identifier for the macro you will create. A small flashing square is displayed at the bottom right of the screen informing you that the macro sequence can be entered.
6. Type **Customer Name:**, press **Return**, type **Address:**, press **Return**, and type **City:**. The results should appear as shown in the following screen:

7. Press **Shift-F2**. A prompt message is displayed at the bottom of the screen requesting the name of the file to which the macro is to be saved. The File QAMACRO.ASC is the default.

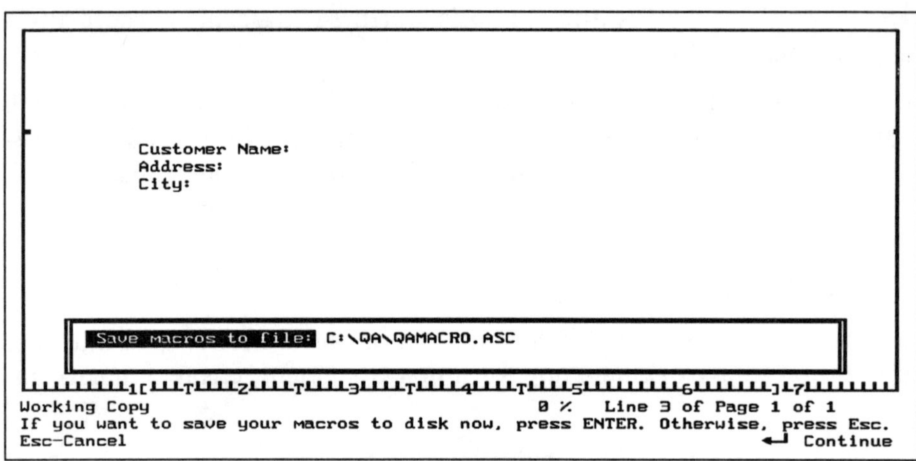

8. Press **Return**. The macro is saved to disk in the macro startup file, QAMACRO.ASC. Each time you start up Q&A, the macro will automatically be available for execution.
9. Test the execution of the macro by pressing **Ctrl-W**. The keystrokes contained in the macro are repeated beginning at the initial cursor location in the document.

If you are working in any function in Q&A and suddenly remember that you failed to save a macro just created, remember that the macro remains in the computer's memory until you exit from Q&A or specifically clear the macro from memory.

10. Press **Esc**. The Write Menu is displayed.
11. Press **Esc**. A prompt message is displayed indicating that the changes made in the Working Copy of the document have not been saved.
12. Type **Y**. The Q&A Main Menu is displayed.
13. Turn to Module 81 to continue the learning sequence.

Module 84
SEARCH/REPLACE TEXT

DESCRIPTION

From within a Write document, you can search or locate a specified character, word, or group of words ranging from one to 45 characters. The character, word, or group of words is called a *text string*.

SEARCH FOR TEXT The search for a text string begins from the current cursor position. It is important to move the cursor to the very beginning or top of your document if you are finding text which you want to replace throughout the document.

There are several options available.

- A search of a document can be performed just to locate a specified string of text.
- A search of a document can be performed to locate a specified string of text and permit you to replace that string of text with different text at your discretion.
- A search of a document can be performed to locate a specified string of text and automatically replace every occurrence of that text in the document with the option of seeing the replacement happening or not.

Searching for a string of text while editing a document is started by positioning the cursor where you want the search to begin. Pressing F7 displays a prompt message that requests the search information: word or string of text being searched, replacement word or string of text, and the method of search wanted. Methods available include:

Manual Finds the text string and allows you to decide if you want to replace it. This method would be used when only searching for text.

Automatic Finds all occurrences of a text string in a document and displays each occurrence as the replacement takes place. If a search is performed using this method, only a message is displayed indicating the number of occurrences encountered.

Fast Automatic Finds all occurrences of a text string in a document and replaces each without displaying each occurrence encountered. A message is displayed indicating the number of occurrences.

Typing the string of text in response to "Search for ..." and pressing Return indicates the text that is being searched for. Typing blank spaces for the replacement text in response to "Replace with:" indicates that only a search for text is being performed. Moving the cursor (with the Spacebar or Right Arrow key) to the method and pressing F10 begins the search request.

If Q&A cannot find a match for the string of text, it displays a message indicating so.

REPLACE TEXT If you want to replace a text string, type the text that you want as the replacement in the field designated "Replace with:" and press F10. Q&A finds the text and replaces it according to the method chosen. Press Esc at any time to cancel the search.

PRECAUTIONS When entering the string of text in response to the "search for..:" prompt, text is searched exactly as entered (i.e., if entered with all uppercase letters, initial uppercase letters, all lowercase letters). So, enter the exact string of text that you want to find.

REMOVING TEXT To remove a string of text, enter two periods (. .) in response to the "Replace with:" prompt. The string of text is deleted and subsequent text is moved forward.

WILD CARD SEARCH You can specify "wild cards" to represent a character or group of characters for a search. Wild card specifications are:

?	Wild card for any individual character
2 periods	Wild card for any group of characters

Examples of Wild Card searches are:

a?	Search is made to find any two-character word beginning with the character "a."
a. .	Search is made to find any word beginning with the character "a."
a????	Search is made for any five-character word beginning with the character "a."

A multitude of combinations with characters, ?, and .. can be made to handle wild card searches.

USING SEARCH/REPLACE TEXT TO GET WORD COUNT You can use the Search/Replace Text feature to actually count the total number of words contained in a document.

Pressing F7 displays the Search/Replace prompt message. Entering two periods (. .) in response to "Search for:," entering A for Automatic search, and pressing either F10 or F7 counts the words in the document.

A message: "Automatic search COMPLETED after n matches." is displayed. "n" is the total number of words counted in the document.

SEARCH FOR Q&A TEXT CONTROL CHARACTERS Every word processing software application embeds control characters that determine how the text is handled on the screen and when it is printed. You can search for the Q&A control characters by searching for characters noted in the following table.

Control Character	Function
@F1	Font 1
@F2	Font 2
@F3	Font 3
@F4	Font 4
@F5	Font 5
@F6	Font 6
@F7	Font 7
@F8	Font 8
@BD	Fold text
@CT	Center a line
@CR	Carriage return
@IT	Italic text
@NP	New page
@RG	Regular text (no enhancement)
@SP	Superscript text
@SB	Subscript text
@UL	Underlined text
@XO	Strikeout text

APPLICATIONS

The find/replace operation is a powerful word processing tool that lets you find every occurrence of a specified text string within any document. You can use the feature to locate known misspellings or to locate specific data within a document. The alternative to this automatic find operation is to manually scan a document. Manually scanning the document is time consuming, prone to error, and extremely unproductive.

Finding and replacing every occurrence of a string of text, called global find/replace, is an extremely powerful tool. Variable items such as names, quantities, or prices can be easily changed in standard forms or letters. If you are inclined to making a repetitive common typographical error, find/replace can be used to globally replace the error with correct information.

TYPICAL OPERATION

In this illustration, search for and locate all occurrences of a specified string of text. Then, locate and replace all occurrences of another string of text with a different text string. Finally, locate and replace all occurrences of a third string of text. Begin at the Q&A Main Menu.

1. Open a new document and type the following text:

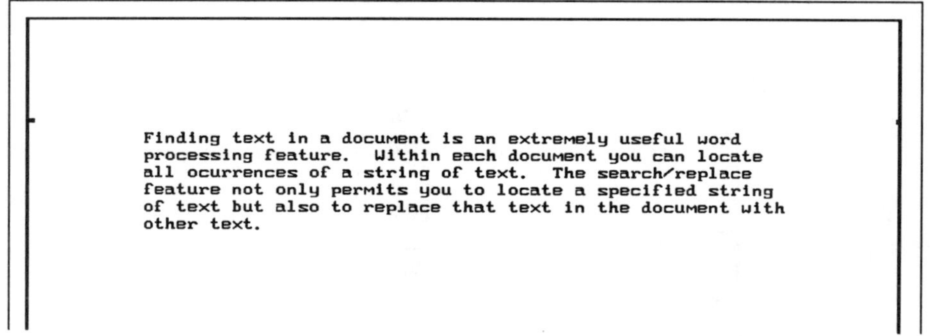

2. Press **F7** to initiate the search for a string of text. The following prompt message is displayed:

3. Type the word **document** and press **Return**. The cursor moves to "Replace with:"

4. Press **Return**, since you are not replacing the word "document" with another word. The cursor moves to the next option. "Manual" is the default. You have the option to step through the document and view each occurrence of the word.

5. Press **F10**. The document is displayed and the first occurrence of the word is located and highlighted. The following message is displayed at the bottom of the screen.

   `FOUND! Press F7 if search again, or Esc to cancel`

6. Press **Esc** to cancel the present search operation.
7. Press **F7**. Press **Down Arrow** to move the cursor to "Replace with:"
8. Type the word **file** and press **Return.**
9. Press **Spacebar** to move the cursor to Automatic and press **F10**.

A message is displayed at the bottom of the screen as the replacements are made. Finally, a message: "Automatic search and replace COMPLETED after n replacements" is displayed. "n" is the total number of occurrences of the string of text. Each occurrence of the string of text is replaced with the specified text. The cursor remains located at the first occurrence of the text string.

If there are several pages in the document, each page is displayed as an automatic search/replace is performed. If Fast automatic is used, only the completed message is displayed; the page where the search/replace was initiated remains displayed.

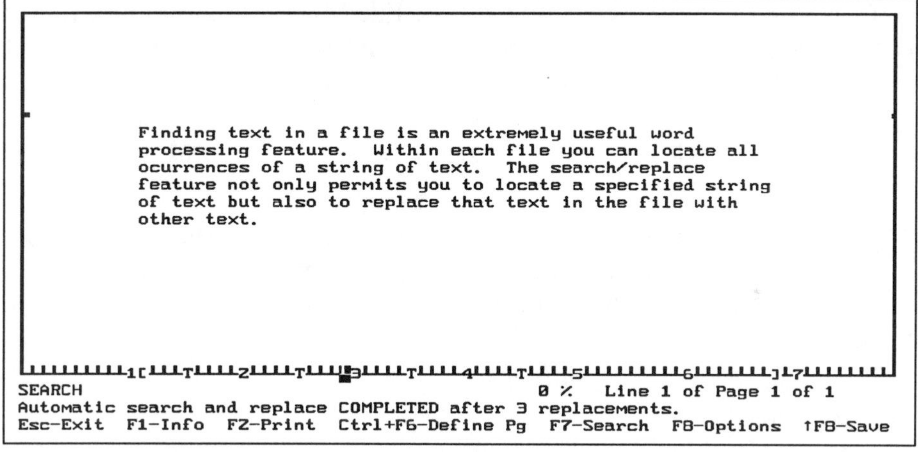

10. Press **Esc** once to end the search/replace and once to exit from the document. The Write Menu is displayed.
11. Press **Esc.** A prompt message is displayed indicating that the changes made in the Working Copy of the document have not been saved.
12. Type **Y**. The Q&A Main Menu is displayed.
13. Turn to Module 7 to continue the learning sequence.

Module 85
SEARCH/UPDATE FORMS

DESCRIPTION

The *Search* feature permits you to find and retrieve forms based on specific retrieve criteria that you specify. You can search a database and locate all forms or specify data ranges for individual fields using wildcard search operands (see Appendix C) to locate a particular individual form or locate groups of forms.

The *Update* feature permits you to change existing information contained in fields on forms.

The Search/Update function is initiated at the Q&A Main Menu by selecting F to enter the File function. Selecting S on the File Menu initiates a prompt message requesting the name of the file which you want scanned. Upon entering a valid filename, the Retrieve Spec screen for the specified database is displayed. You can page through each form in the database by pressing F10 or entering retrieve specifications to search for certain forms. Pressing Esc several times displays the Q&A Main Menu.

Another method to locate forms and make changes to them is by using the Assistant to actually retrieve and make changes to the forms. Refer to Module 80 for instructions on how to have the assistant retrieve forms and make changes to them for you.

APPLICATIONS

The Search/Update feature provides you with instant on-line capability of viewing all or specified forms. In addition, changes to existing forms can be made easily and quickly.

TYPICAL OPERATION

In this illustration, enter the File function, search an existing database, and update the first form in the series. Begin at the Q&A Main Menu.

1. Select the File Menu.
2. Type **S**. A prompt message is displayed requesting the name of the file being searched/updated.

3. Type **CUSTOMER** and press **Return**. The Retrieve Spec screen for the database is displayed. At this screen, you can enter specific retrieve information to retrieve only certain forms in the database.
4. Press **F8**. The Sort Spec screen is displayed. At this screen, you can enter specific sort information (sort codes) to retrieve forms in a sorted order.

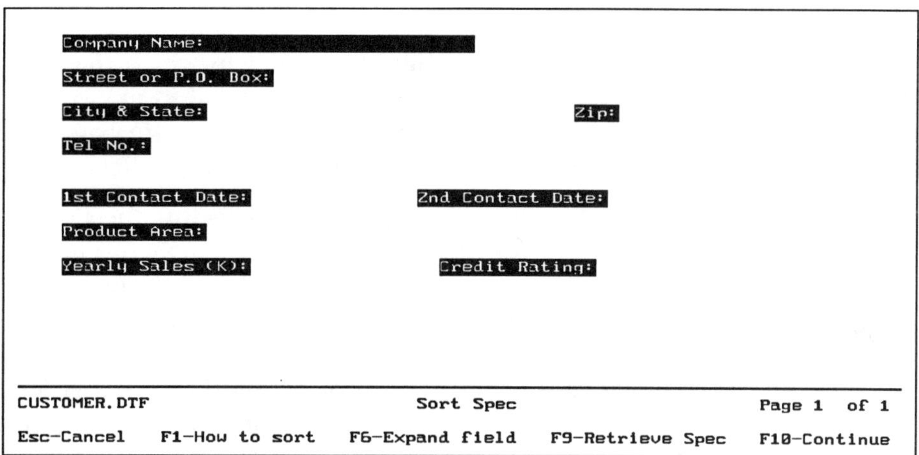

5. Press **F10**. The first form in the database is displayed. The cursor is located at the first field.

If you choose to enter retrieve and/or sort specifications in the preceeding steps, the first form complying with the criteria is displayed.

6. Type **Harrison** in the Company Name field and press **Return**. The new name entered is displayed.
7. Press **F6** to display a summary of up to 17 forms on the screen in a single display. **F7** may be pressed at anytime to display the Retrieve Spec screen should you want to enter retrieve criteria. Pressing **F10** redisplays the first form.
8. Return to the Q&A Main Menu.
9. Turn to Module 92 to continue the learning sequence.

Module 86
SORT FORMS

DESCRIPTION

Q&A retrieves forms from a database in the same order in which they were first entered. However, existing forms in a database can be sorted in any order before they are retrieved and displayed on the screen. Numerous levels are possible. These sort levels are based on a primary sort and secondary sorts.

From the Q&A Main Menu, sorting is accomplished by selecting the File function and choosing the Search/Update feature from the File Menu. After entering the filename for a database, the Retrieve Spec screen is displayed. Pressing F8 at the Retrieve Spec screen displays the Sort Spec screen. Moving the cursor to the field to be sorted and typing a sort specification defines sort criteria. Additional sort levels (secondary sorts) involve moving the cursor to another field to be sorted and defining a sort specification. As many secondary sort levels as desired can be accomplished. After all sort specifications are defined, pressing F10 starts the retrieval and sorting operation. After forms are sorted they can be viewed (refer to Module 92) or printed (refer to Module 69). Pressing Esc displays the File Menu. Pressing Esc again displays the Q&A Main Menu.

APPLICATIONS

Sorting of forms can be done to enable you to view database information in a specified order. The most useful application is to sort forms before printing them. Sorting enables you to configure the order of the printed or displayed output.

TYPICAL OPERATION

In this illustration, enter the File function, select a database, and conduct a primary sort on one of the fields in the database. Begin at the Q&A Main Menu.

1. Select the File Menu.
2. Type **S**; a prompt message is displayed requesting the name of the file to be sorted.
3. Type **CUSTOMER** and press **Return**. The Retrieve Spec screen for the database is displayed.

```
Company Name:
Street or P.O. Box:
City & State:                                    Zip:
Tel No.:

1st Contact Date:               2nd Contact Date:
Product Area:
Yearly Sales (K):                 Credit Rating:



CUSTOMER.DTF                     Retrieve Spec                    Page 1  of 1
Esc-Cancel F1-Info  F3-Clear  F6-Expand  ^F7-Options  F8-Sort Spec F10-Continue
```

4. To retrieve all forms for customers located in Dallas, Texas in the CUSTOMER database, move the cursor to the "City" field and type **Dallas**.
5. Press **F8**. The Sort Spec screen is displayed.
6. Press **Tab** or **Arrow** to move the cursor to the field whose contents you want sorted.
7. Type **1 AS** (for an ascending order sort) or **1 DS** (for a descending order sort). Ensure that you type a space between the numeral and the sort code.

If you were also performing secondary sorts, you would move the cursor to another appropriate field and type 2 followed by AS or DS. This operation is repeated (using 3, 4, 5, etc.) for the total number of secondary sorts that you want performed.

8. Press **F10**. The retrieve/sort operation is performed. After the sort is completed, the first form meeting the retrieve and sort criteria is displayed. Pressing F10 pages through the forms that were retrieved and sorted.

NOTE

If no forms were found, the following message is displayed.

```
No forms were found that meet your retrieve request.
   Do you want to check or change your request?
            Y - Yes         N - No
```

Refer to Module 92 for information on how to view multiple forms or to Module 69 for information on how to print sorted forms.

9. Return to the Q&A Main Menu.
10. Turn to Module 38 to continue the learning sequence.

Module 87
SORT REPORT INFORMATION

DESCRIPTION

Often when creating reports, you will want to sort information contained in the columns on a report. *Sorting* is arranging form information in a specific order of occurrence. Of course, you will actually sort the information contained in the fields on forms in the database before it is placed in a report.

When designing or redesigning a report, you can easily place the necessary sort codes on the Column/Sort Spec screen. Refer to Module 79, Report Design/Redesign for detailed instructions on how to go to the Column/Sort Spec screen. There are five basic sort codes. These codes are:

Sort Function	*Sort Code*	
Sort fields in ascending order	AS	(A to Z; and low number to high number)
Sort fields in descending order	DS	(Z to A; and high number to low number)
Cancel subcalculations for entries in this column	CS	
Cause a page break (start new page)	P	
Repeat values for entries in a sorted column	R	
Break/calculate when day changes	DB	
Break/calculate when month changes	MB	
Break/calculate when year changes	YB	

Once at the Column/Sort Spec screen for a database, pressing Tab moves the cursor to any field. A column ordering number must already have been typed in each of the columns for which you want to specify sort specifications. Immediately following the ordering number, typing a space or a comma (,) and then the sort code defines a sort specification. This process is repeated until all of the columns that are to appear on the report are coded for sort order.

It is not an absolute necessity that you sort columns. You can have information contained in a field on the forms in a database display or print exactly in the same order as the forms are ordered in the database.

Q&A is capable of producing reports having as many as 50 columns with 50 sort levels in a report.

If a field on a form is too small for you to type the sort code in the actual field, you can press F6. An editing line is displayed at the bottom of the screen on which you can type the sort code. After typing the sort code on the editing line, pressing F10 returns the cursor to the basic form. An arrow displays in the field, indicating that the field was too small to display the code.

When the value in a sorted column changes, a blank line is inserted and the next sort value is displayed or printed. For example, if you are printing a report listing cities or states, a break automatically occurs after each city and state. You can prevent these automatic line skips simply by entering the code CS where these column breaks occur.

You can also force page breaks to occur by typing the page break code, P, in the field where you want the corresponding break to occur in a report (for example: 1,AS,P). The character "P" causes the page break.

To enter page break codes, use Tab to move the cursor to any field to be included in a report as a sorted column. These fields already have previously entered sort codes (e.g., AS, DS) in them. Press End to move the cursor to the end of the field. Then, type a space or a comma (,) and a P. Repeat this procedure for each numbered field for which you want a new page started.

It is easy to have Q&A repeat all values in a sorted column. Normally, Q&A displays a value only once in a sorted column. For example, if a column contains a list of cities, each time a different city is printed, the remainder of the same column does not repeat the same city name. However, you can have values repeat within a column (e.g., city, state, or other repetitive value). The repeat function is invoked by typing R on the Column/Sort Spec screen in any field included in a report as a sorted column.

APPLICATIONS

The capability to sort column information provides you with the means to create diversified reporting techniques. Sorting in ascending or descending order is essential in most reporting functions.

Breaking columns and page break codes permits you to create innovative reports for just about any need you may have.

Repeating values within a column in a report can be used to enhance readability of your reported information.

TYPICAL OPERATION

In this illustration, enter sort codes, enter a new page code, and enter the repeat code in the Column/Sort Spec screen for a database. Use these instructions in conjunction with those described in Module 79 for designing or redesigning a report. They are as follows:

1. At the Q&A Main Menu, select the Report Menu. Type **D** for Design/Redesign a report, type **CUSTOMER** for the practice database. and press **Return**.
2. Type **CUSTOMER-REPORT**, and press **Return** for the name of the report. At the Retrieve Spec screen, press **F10** to display the Column/Sort Spec sreen. A typical Column/Sort Spec screen is:

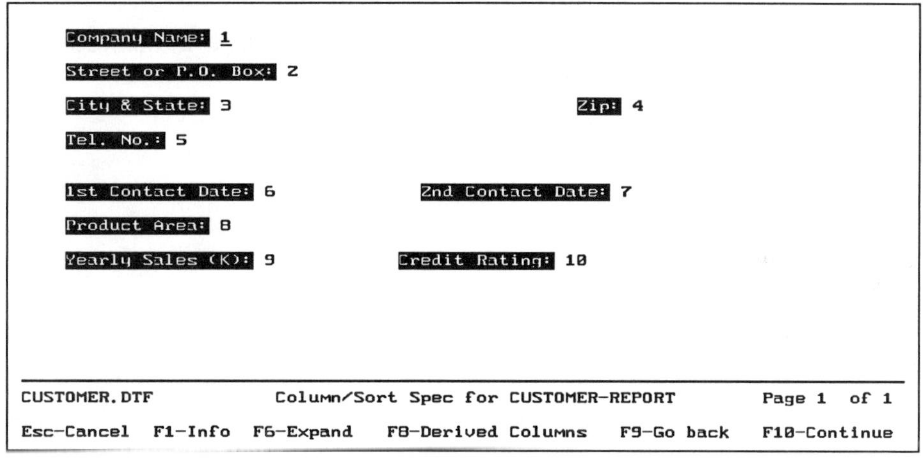

Entering Sort Codes

1. At the Column/Sort Spec screen, press **Tab** to move the cursor to any field having a column ordering number (e.g., AS or DS).
2. Immediately following the ordering number, type a blank space or a comma (,).
3. Repeat Steps 1 and 2 for each field designated as a numbered field (i.e., field to appear in a report).

Entering New Page Codes

1. At the Column/Sort Spec screen, press **Tab** to move the cursor to any field having a column ordering number. (e.g., AS or DS).
2. Press **End**. The cursor moves to the end of the field.
3. Type a space or a comma (,) and **P**.
4. Repeat Steps 1 through 3 for each field designated as a numbered field (i.e., a field to appear in a report).

Entering Repeat Value Codes

1. At the Column/Sort Spec screen, press **Tab** to move the cursor to any field having a column ordering number. (e.g., AS or DS).
2. Press **End**. The cursor moves to the end of the field.
3. Type a space or a comma (,) and **R**.
4. Repeat Steps 1 through 3 for each field designated as a numbered field (i.e., a field to appear in a report).
5. Turn to Module 55 to continue the learning sequence.

Module 88
SPELL CHECK

DESCRIPTION

Q&A provides a Spelling Check program that checks the spelling of any Write function document that you prepare. In addition, the spelling check locates any repeated words that may have been typed in error. For example, "the the" in a document would be located and pointed out as being incorrect.

Not only does Q&A have a dictionary file containing commonly used words, but it also has a personal dictionary available. The personal dictionary is reserved for you to enter special words that are specific to your personal needs or business. Refer to Module 65, Personal Dictionary Update, for instructions on how to add words to your personal dictionary.

The Spelling Check program contains a built-in dictionary file of words. A program compares the words in a document to the words in the dictionary file. When the Spelling Check program is invoked, words found in a document that do not match the words in the dictionary file are flagged. This indicates that the words are either misspelled, a typographical error has occurred, or the word is not contained in the dictionary file.

A word flagged as being incorrect is highlighted on the screen. You are then given a chance to choose (through a menu selection) whether you want to view a list of all possible spellings, ignore the word found and continue checking, add the word to the personal dictionary and continue checking, or add the word to the personal dictionary and stop.

There are two ways to check the spelling in a document.

SPELL CHECKING AN ENTIRE DOCUMENT While in an edit session with a Write document, press Ctrl-Home to move the cursor to the first character in the document. The Spelling Check is activated by pressing Shift-F1. Each word in the document is compared to the dictionary file and the personal dictionary. The Spelling Check is made progressively through each word in the document.

If a repeated word is found, a message indicates that condition; you can press F3 to delete the repeated word or press Return to continue.

NOTE

If you do not place the cursor at the first character in the document, text preceeding the cursor location is not spell checked.

Once spelling is checked in a document, Q&A will not recheck the spelling on the same document unless edit changes (additions, deletions, etc.) are made to it.

SPELL CHECKING A SINGLE WORD While creating or editing a document, you can check spelling of any word on the spot. Position the cursor on or immediately after the word and press Ctrl-F1. The spelling of the selected word is checked and a message is displayed at the bottom of the screen indicating whether spelling is correct or not.

In any of the above alternatives, if a word is found that is not in the dictionary file or the personal dictionary, the Spelling Menu is displayed.

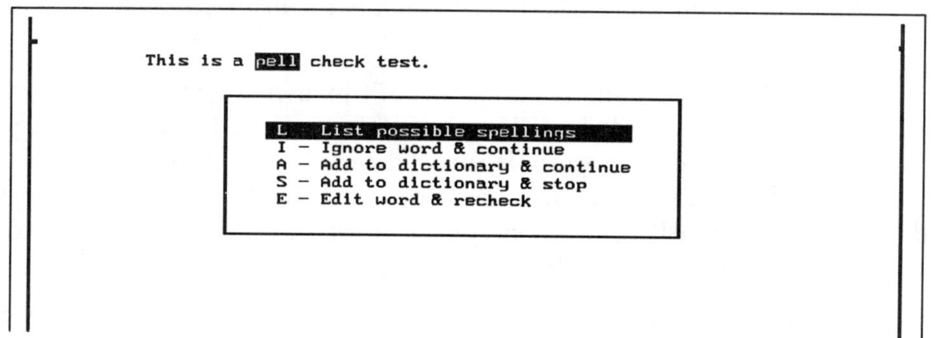

At the indication of a misspelled word, type one of the options displayed on the Spelling Menu and press Return or Esc to cancel the Spelling Check.

If a selection is chosen, the applicable operation as indicated on the Spelling Menu is performed. If Esc is pressed, Spelling Check is cancelled and you are returned to the edit session for the document.

The options indicated on the Spelling Menu are self-explanatory. If you choose to list possible spellings of a word, Q&A displays a short list of words closely resembling the spelling of the word that is highlighted in the document. The misspelled word can be replaced with one of the words on the displayed list by typing the corresponding number and pressing Return. If the correct spelling is not displayed on the list, press Esc to return to the edit session. You may manually correct the word while in the edit mode.

If you choose to add a word to the dictionary and continue to the next word (or stop), the word is added to your personal dictionary.

APPLICATIONS

Being able to check any document for correct spelling of every word is invaluable. This feature saves time in proofreading the documents you create. The added feature of being able to create your own personal dictionary customizes Q&A to suit your individual needs.

TYPICAL OPERATION

In this illustration, enter the Write function, open a new document, and type text indicated in the example. Next, Spell Check the document. List possible spellings for several words. Begin at the Q&A Main Menu.

1. Open a new document and type the text shown in the following screen. Be sure to type it exactly as shown. The text intentionally contains misspelled words.

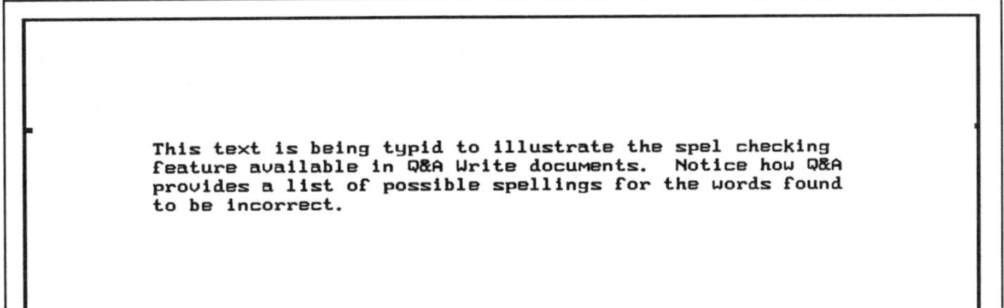

2. Press **Ctrl-Home** to move the cursor to the first character in the document.

3. Press **Shift-F1** to activate the Spelling Check. The first misspelled word is located. The word "typid" is highlighted and the Spelling Menu is displayed. The cursor is located at "Selection: L."

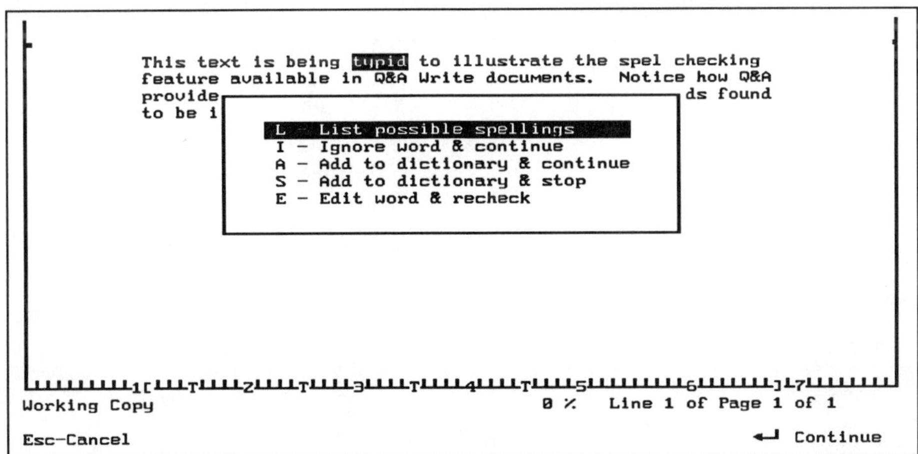

4. Press **Return**. The following list of possible spellings is displayed:

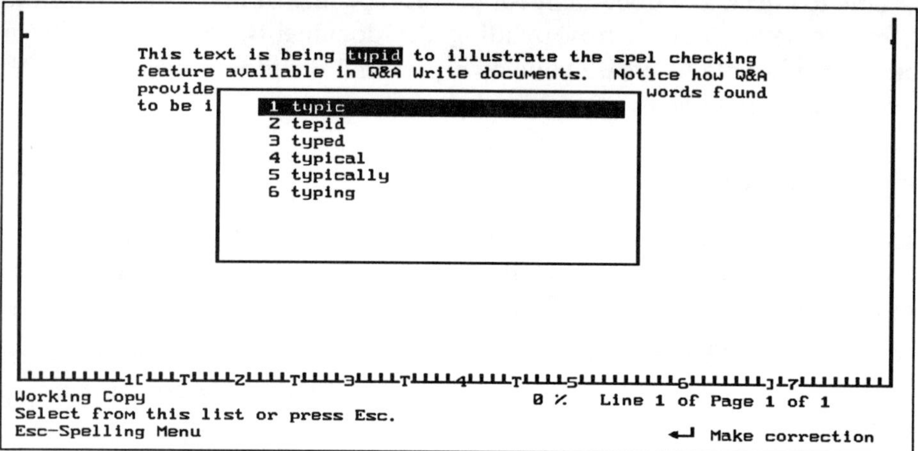

5. Type **3** to select the word "typed" and press **Return**. The misspelled word is corrected and the next misspelled word is found and highlighted. The cursor is located at: L - List possible spellings.
6. Press **Return** and a list of possible spellings is displayed. Item number 1 is the correct word spelling.
7. Type **1**.
8. Press **F3** to delete the repeated word. Spell checking continues until completed; a message is displayed at the bottom of the screen indicating that the spelling check is completed. The cursor returns to the first character in the document.
9. Return to the Q&A Main Menu without saving the document.
10. Turn to Module 50 to continue the learning sequence.

Module 89
TAB SETTINGS

DESCRIPTION

There are two types of tab settings that are available in the Q&A Write function: standard (typewriter) tabs and decimal or align tabs. The same tab setting feature is also available for you to use in form design or redesign.

STANDARD TABS Setting, using, and clearing standard tabs are necessary functions related to word processing. The *standard tabs* are called *text tabs.* Tabs permit you to customize the page layout of a document. You will use the paragraph indent tab to indent the first line of each paragraph and frequently use other tabs to set up tabular information.

Q&A allows you to change the position of a tab, thus making tabs that are called variable tabs. However, as you enter an edit session on a new document, notice the default tab settings on the format ruler at the bottom of the screen. *Default tabs* are those programmed into Q&A software. They are always displayed as you enter an edit session in a new document.

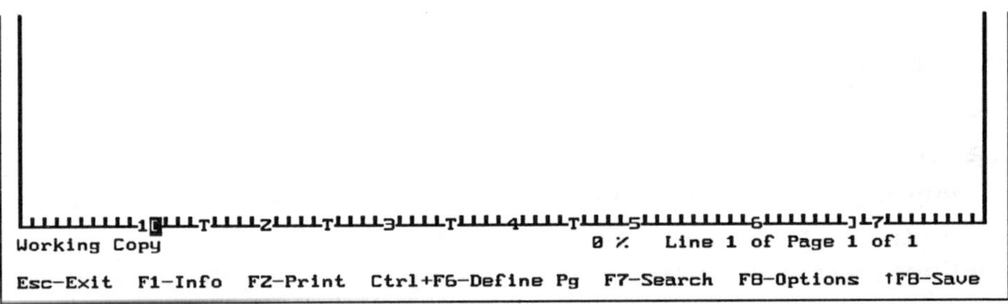

Positions of default tabs are indicated by the letter T at each tab location.

DECIMAL TABS A *decimal tab* automatically aligns decimal points contained in numbers. As you type decimal numbers in vertical columns in a document, the decimal points are automatically aligned vertically. The decimal tab feature is not only related to word processing, but also is critical in spreadsheet preparation, forms, and reports, used with Q&A.

As you are typing numbers in a document and tab to a decimal tab position, the numeral characters move from right to left as they are typed. When a decimal (.) is typed, the decimal is automatically aligned under the decimal tab on the format ruler.

The letter D is displayed on the format ruler to designate a decimal tab.

Tabs are set in the Type/Edit mode by first pressing F8 to display the Options Menu, then typing S (Set tabs). The cursor moves to the format ruler line.

MOVING THE CURSOR ON THE FORMAT RULER LINE Using the arrow keys to move the cursor across the format ruler at the bottom of the screen is a simple technique. When the cursor is located at a column position where you want a tab setting, type T for a standard tab or type D for a decimal tab.

The following key combinations can also be used to make you more proficient.

Key	*Moves the Cursor*
Right Arrow	One space right
Ctrl-Right Arrow	Five spaces left of cursor
Left Arrow	One space left
Ctrl-Left Arrow	Five spaces right of cursor
Home	1st space right of left margin
End	1st space left of right margin
Tab	Next tab on format ruler line
Shift-Tab	Previous tab on format ruler line

Pressing F10 sets the tabs permanently for the document. The cursor moves back to its original position in the document text. When the document is saved to disk, the tab settings are also saved.

DEFAULT TAB SETTINGS Default tab settings are at 5, 15, 25, and 35 from the left margin. To set different default tab settings, refer to Module 44 for procedures on setting global parameters.

CLEARING TAB SETTINGS Any tab setting or default tab setting can be deleted while working in an edit session with a document by displaying the Options Menu, selecting S, moving the cursor to the setting using the arrow keys or key combinations previously described, and pressing either Spacebar or Del.

APPLICATIONS

Text tab settings are used just as standard typewriter tabs are used to indent the first line of each new paragraph or to align columns of text when creating tabular information.

You can to set tabs to correspond to printed output. Text tabs set at every five spaces correspond to 1/2-inch spacing for 10-pitch (10 characters per inch) printing. If you are using 12-pitch type (12 characters per inch), set text tabs at every six spaces. This corresponds to 1/2-inch tab spacing for 12-pitch printing.

Decimal tabs are a pleasure to have when typing tables or financial documents with many columns of decimal fractions. When typing numbers (such as dollars and cents), tabbing to the decimal tab and typing the number causes the number and decimal to align automatically.

A decimal tab can be used to create "flush-right" text. This technique can enhance a report title page. Once you tab to the decimal tab setting and enter text, the text characters move to the left until you press Return to move down to the next line. Pressing Return terminates the decimal tab function.

An example of flush-right text is:

FINAL REPORT
FEASIBILITY STUDY
Advanced Parts Inventory System

TYPICAL OPERATION

In this illustration, begin at the Q&A Main Menu. Enter the Write function and the Type/Edit mode. In a Working Copy of a new document, erase the default tab settings and set new text tabs at 20 and 40 and a decimal tab at 60 on the format ruler. Exit from the document without saving the document or tab settings to disk.

1. Type **W.** The Write Menu is displayed.
2. Press **Return.** A Working Copy (blank) screen for a new document is displayed.
3. Press **F8** to display the Options Menu.

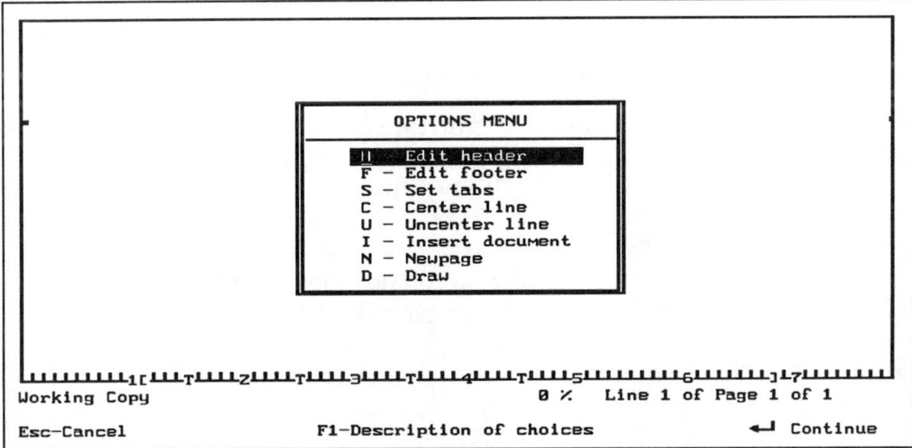

4. Type **S**. The cursor moves to the format ruler at the bottom of the screen.

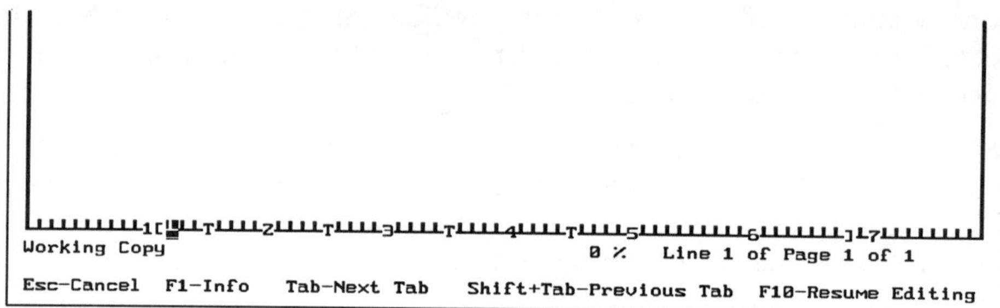

5. Use the arrow keys or press **Tab** to move the cursor to each tab setting (indicated by a T on the format ruler) and press **Spacebar** or **Del** at each location. The default tabs are erased (cleared).
6. Press the arrow keys to move the cursor to 20 and 40 on the format ruler line, typing **T** at each location.
7. Move the cursor to 60 on the format ruler and type **D**

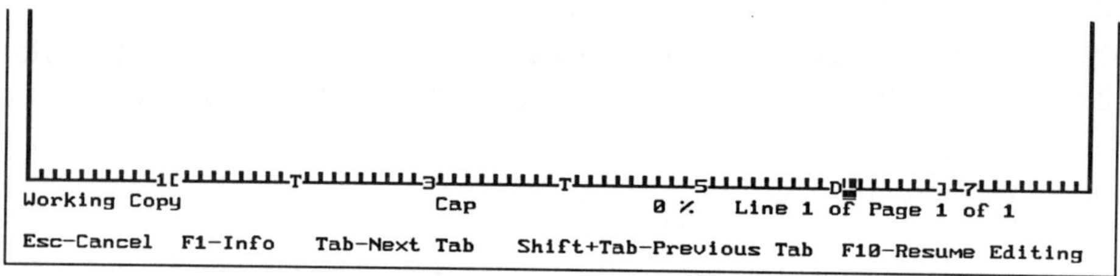

8. Press **F10** or **Return** to exit from the format ruler line. The cursor moves to the text area of the Working Copy for the document. Text tab settings are now set at 20 and 40; a decimal tab setting is now set at 60 on the format ruler.
9. Press **Esc**. The Write Menu is displayed.
10. Press **Esc** twice. Since text was not typed into the Working Copy of the document, the Q&A Menu is immediately displayed.

NOTE

If you typed text in the practice document, a prompt message is displayed warning you that the document has not been saved to disk.

11. Turn to Module 49 to continue the learning sequence.

Module 90
UNITS OF MEASURE LESSON

DESCRIPTION

Units of measure is an important topic that you will want to teach the Assistant. Q&A permits you to identify to the Assistant all of the common units of measure frequently used in numeric fields in your databases. Each field on a form for which the unit of measure applies is identified with a string of number symbols (#). Thereafter, should you inquire for information relating to units of measure, the Assistant is able to respond with correct answers.

Typical units of measure are:

inch	each	cup	teaspoon
foot	dozen	ounce	tablespoon
yard	gross	pint	cup
rod		quart	
mile		gallon	
millimeter		barrel	
centimeter			
decameter			
meter			
kilometer			

Teaching the Assistant about units of measure is done by first selecting A on the Q&A Main Menu. The Assistant Menu is displayed. At this menu, selecting T indicates that you want to teach the Assistant about a database. A prompt message is displayed requesting the name of the form (database) to which the lesson applies. Upon entering a valid filename, the Basic Lessons Menu is displayed.

Selecting option 5 displays the Advanced Lessons Menu. Selecting option 2 on the Advanced Lessons Menu displays the lesson screen overlayed on the form design for the database. Each numeric field contains a series of number symbols (#). Using the cursor movement keys to direct the cursor to applicable numeric fields and entering the desired unit of measure comprises the lesson for the Assistant. Pressing F8 moves the cursor forward to the next field. Pressing F6 moves the cursor backward to the previous field. Pressing F10 completes the Units of Measure Lesson and displays the Basic Lessons Menu. Pressing Esc twice returns you to the Q&A Main Menu.

Fields on a form that are designated monetary fields are measured in currency by Q&A. Refer to the Print Options screen for currency options (U.S. dollars or British pounds)

If a form does not contain any numeric fields, you are not allowed to enter any units of measure values. A message is displayed informing you of the condition:

```
                    ! Stop !

Units of measure are for NUMBER fields only, and none
of the fields on your form have that information type.
See Vol. 1, page F-107 of your manual if you want to
see how to change information types.

             Press ←┘ to continue
```

If you have fields that are supposed to be numeric fields, but are incorrectly identified as to their information type, change the form information types on the form. Refer to Module 6, Assign/Change Form Information Types.

APPLICATIONS

For the Assistant to accurately comply with your requests, the Assistant must be informed of every possible fact pertaining to a database. Teaching the Assistant all of the units of measure that are used on a form is extremely important.

TYPICAL OPERATION

In this illustration, give the Assistant the Units of Measure Lesson. Since the procedure is a fairly simple operation, only the general details that apply to any database are presented. Begin at the Q&A Main Menu.

1. Select the Asistant menu.
2. Type **T**. A prompt message is displayed requesting the name of the database for which you want to provide instruction.
3. Type **INVNTRY** and press **Return**. The Basic Lessons Menu is displayed.
4. Type **5**. The Advanced Lessons Menu is displayed.
5. Type **2**. The form design for the specified database is displayed with the cursor located at the first numeric field.

Assigned numeric fields are displayed with number symbols (#) filling the field. Each numeric feild is highlighted, and the following message is displayed over the form design.

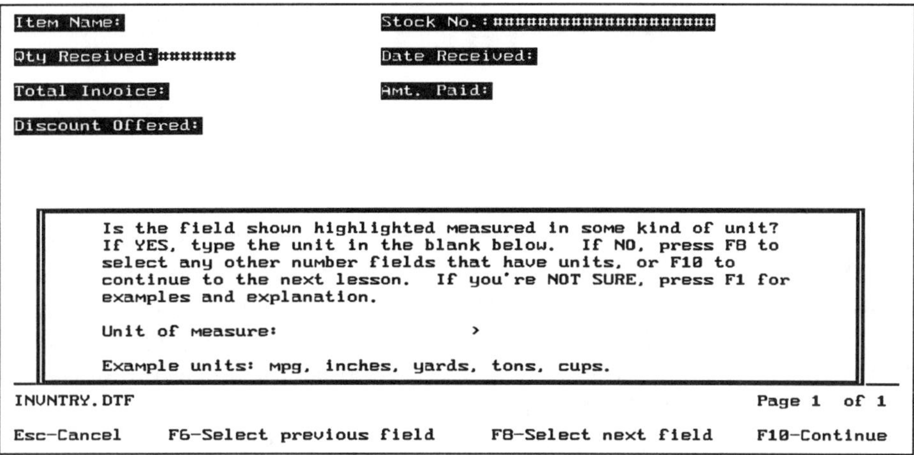

6. Press **F8**. The cursor is located at the "Qty Received" field. Type **gross** and press **F8**. The unit of measure is recorded for the field and the cursor moves to the next numeric field. You can continue moving through the fields by repeating this step for each numeric field.
7. Press **F10**. The units of Measure Lesson is completed. The Advanced Lessons Menu is displayed.
8. Return to the Q&A Main Menu
9. Turn to Module 3 to continue the learning sequence.

Module 91
UPDATE THE ASSISTANT

DESCRIPTION

Occasionally it is necessary to update the Assistant. As you make changes to the various databases that you have created, the Assistant becomes outdated and is no longer informed of the latest contents of your databases, of any new fields that you have added to forms, of alternate names recently assigned to fields, and more. This module explains how to update the Assistant; updating makes current information available to the Assistant.

Updating the Assistant should be a regularly scheduled event. Any or all of the lessons described in this book can be used to update the Assistant. Lessons included are:

Advanced Adjectives Lesson	Module 3
Advanced Verbs Lesson	Module 4
Alternate Field Names Lesson	Module 5
Data Base Lesson	Module 22
Form Fields Lesson	Module 39
Location/Name Fields Lesson	Module 56
Units of Measure Lesson	Module 90

Updating the Assistant is initiated by selecting A on the Q&A Main Menu.

Selecting T on the Assistant Menu displays a prompt message requesting the name of the file for which you want to provide instruction to the Assistant. Entering a valid filename and pressing Return displays the Basic Lessons Menu. Refer to each of the referenced modules for complete instructions on how to teach, or in this case reteach, the Assistant about an individual topic. Updating the Assistant is reteaching it the new contents of your databases.

Updating the Assistant does take time depending upon the size of the database. However, it is an important step to ensure that the Q&A Assistant performs for you.

APPLICATIONS

The only application for updating the Assistant is simply keeping the Assistant current as to all information contained in your databases. You do not need to instruct the Assistant about all information contained in your databases. If you have taught the Assistant the information once, all you need do is teach the new information or changes made to databases since the last lessons. For example, if you have redesigned forms to contain more locations or persons' names, you need only to repeat those particular lessons.

TYPICAL OPERATION

The operation of updating the Assistant consists of performing the steps contained in each of the individual lessons for the Assistant. In this illustration, begin at the Q&A Main Menu and select the Assistant function. From the Basic Lessons Menu, you can select any of the lessons to update the Assistant.

Before beginning any lesson to update the Assistant, make a backup copy of your databases. Refer to the DOS manual for your computer for instructions on how to make a backup copy of your data.

1. Select the Assistant Menu and type **T**. A prompt message requesting the name of the database for which you want to provide instruction is displayed.
2. Type a valid filename and press **Return**. The Basic Lessons Menu is displayed.

Four basic lessons can be executed from this menu. To select additional lessons, proceed to the next step. Lessons described in individual modules in this book describe detailed instructions on how to teach the Assistant.

3. Type **5**. The Advanced Lessons Menu is displayed. An additional four lessons can be executed from this menu.
4. Press **Esc** several times to move through the menus returning you to the Q&A Main Menu.
5. Turn to Module 93 to continue the learning sequence.

Module 92
VIEW MULTIPLE FORMS

DESCRIPTION

There are two ways in which forms may be viewed on the screen. You can easily view forms by either method.

- View each form completely and individually.
- View the highlight information for up to 17 forms on each screen display.

VIEW COMPLETE FORMS To view entire forms, begin at the Q&A Main Menu. Select the File function. Once the File Menu is displayed, choose the Search/Update feature. Type the name of the file containing the database that you want to view. Enter the appropriate retrieve specifications on the Retrieve Spec screen or choose to view all forms in the database by pressing F10 at the Retrieve Spec screen. You can also specify a sort specification that causes forms to be displayed in a particular order.

Page through the forms by pressing F10. Exit from the viewing mode by pressing Esc to return to the File Menu. Press Esc again and the Q&A Main Menu is displayed.

VIEW HIGHLIGHTS OF FORMS To view the highlight information for up to 17 forms on each screen display, begin at the Q&A Main Menu. Select the File function. Select the Search/Update feature from the File Menu. Type the name of the file containing the database that you want to view. Enter the appropriate retrieve specification on the Retrieve Spec screen or choose to view all forms in the database by pressing F10. To view the first highlight screen, press F6.

Each row on the screen display represents one form. The list on the screen corresponds to the order of the forms in the database.

Pressing Esc displays the File Menu. Pressing Esc again displays the Q&A Main Menu.

APPLICATIONS

Having the capability to view database information on forms that you have created is extremely helpful. This feature can be used to rapidly retrieve important data, preview information, or view data so that you can keep abreast of what is in your files.

This view feature can be easily adapted for use with telephone lists or even a tickler file. A tickler file can contain reminder information that salesmen or agents refer to regularly to recall pertinent facts about their customers or prospective buyers.

TYPICAL OPERATION

In this illustration, enter the File function and choose the Search/Update option on the File Menu. When the Retrieve Spec screen is displayed, press F10 to view individually each form contained in the file. Begin at the Q&A Main Menu.

1. Select the File Menu and type **S**. A prompt message is displayed at the bottom of the screen requesting the name of the file that you want to view.
2. Type **INVNTRY** and press **Return**. The Retrieve Spec for the specified file is displayed.

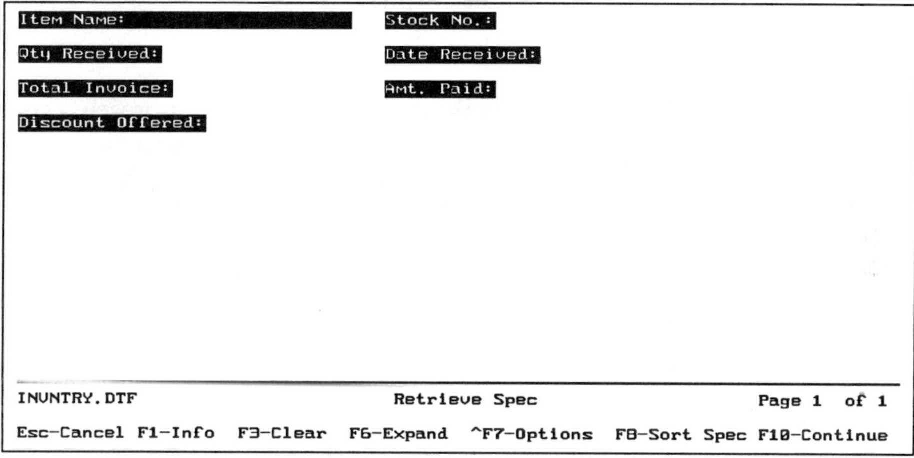

3. Press **F10**. A "Searching/Working" message is displayed at the bottom of the screen. The first form in the file is displayed.
4. Press **F10** to display the next form. The form number (e.g., 1, 2, 3, etc.) is displayed at the bottom of the screen.

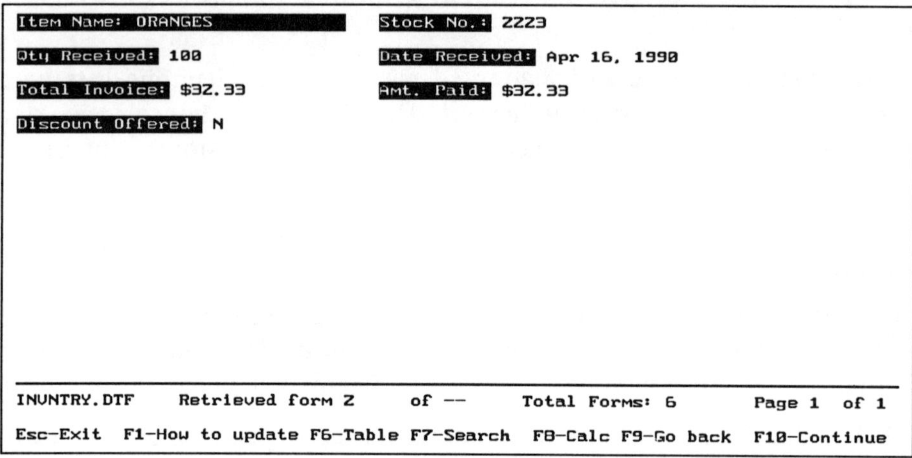
Item Name: ORANGES
Stock No.: 2223
Qty Received: 100
Date Received: Apr 16, 1990
Total Invoice: $32.33
Amt. Paid: $32.33
Discount Offered: N

INVNTRY.DTF Retrieved form 2 of -- Total Forms: 6 Page 1 of 1
Esc-Exit F1-How to update F6-Table F7-Search F8-Calc F9-Go back F10-Continue

NOTE

As you view forms by pressing F10, each time you proceed to the next form, remember that pressing F9 displays the previous form.

5. Press **F9** to return to the first form in the database.
6. Press **F6**. A form highlights table is displayed. This screen presents summary information for 17 forms at a time. Pressing the Spacebar moves the highlighting line down the screen. When the highlighting line reaches the bottom of the screen, the screen scrolls to display the next line of information.
7. Return to the Q&A Main Menu.
8. Turn to Module 80 to continue the learning sequence.

Module 93
VIEW VOCABULARY

DESCRIPTION

The vocabulary built into Q&A for the Assistant is impressive in itself. However, the capability to add additional vocabulary words specifically related to your personal, business, or occupational needs makes the Assistant a formidable force. The vocabulary that Q&A understands through the Assistant stands alone. That is, it is completely independent of any single database. It spans all databases and files or forms that you create.

There are three categories of vocabulary available to the Assistant: built-in words, field names, and synonyms. Q&A permits you to view the vocabulary within each of these categories. Built-in words are locked firm in the Q&A vocabulary and cannot be altered or deleted. Built-in words are categorized into verb functions: display, calculate, search/sort, and edit. Field names are the names of fields on forms that you provide to the Assistant. The field names are directly related to specific fields defined on forms. Module 39 describes how to teach the Assistant these words. Synonyms are alternate words that you have placed in the vocabulary. Module 5 explains how to teach the Assistant alternate field names and synonyms.

To view vocabulary words, enter the Assistant function from the Q&A Main Menu. At the Assistant Menu, select the "Ask me to do something" option and enter a filename to set Q&A into the "do something" mode. The Assistant must review the database if this is the first request made for that database. Pressing F6 allows you to select which vocabulary words you want to view.

APPLICATIONS

As you use Q&A more, you will be increasing the vocabulary available to the Assistant. From time to time, you will want to check to see if a certain word or synonym is contained in the vocabulary. Viewing the vocabulary permits you to check the words.

At times, it may be necessary to change a field name or synonym, perhaps to adapt to the most recent usage in new files that you have created.

The most important aspect of being able to view vocabulary is that you have readily available the complete list of all words that the Assistant uses to perform designated tasks. The vocabulary words in Q&A are not mysteriously hidden in a file or some obscure location in a printed manual. They are at your fingertips. You can always access the vocabulary.

TYPICAL OPERATION

In the following illustration, select the Assistant function. Then ask the Assistant to "do something." Enter a filename and press Return. When the Assistant is ready for you to ask it to do something, initiate viewing vocabulary by pressing F6. View the built-in vocabulary. Begin at the Q&A Main Menu.

1. Select the Assistant Menu. Type **A**, type the name of any existing file, and press **Return**. If the database has not been previously reviewed by the Assistant, it could take a few minutes for Q&A to perform the review operation. Then, the following screen is displayed:

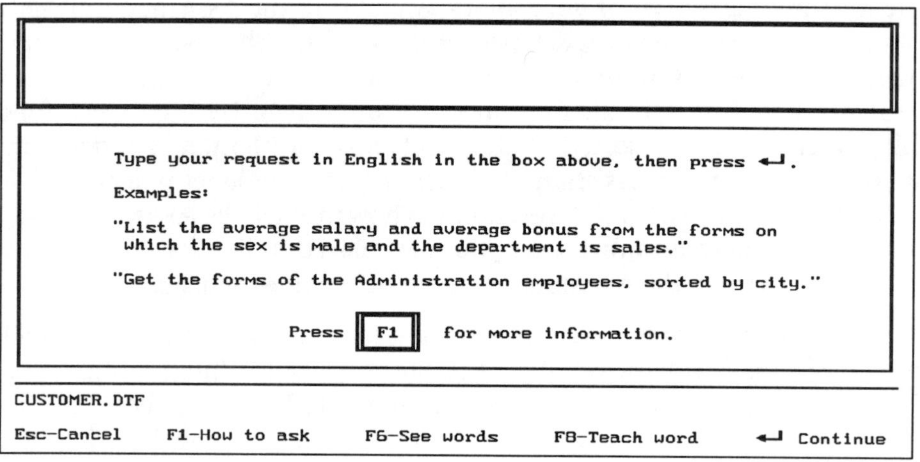

2. Press **F6**. The following screen is displayed with the cursor located at B - Built-in words.

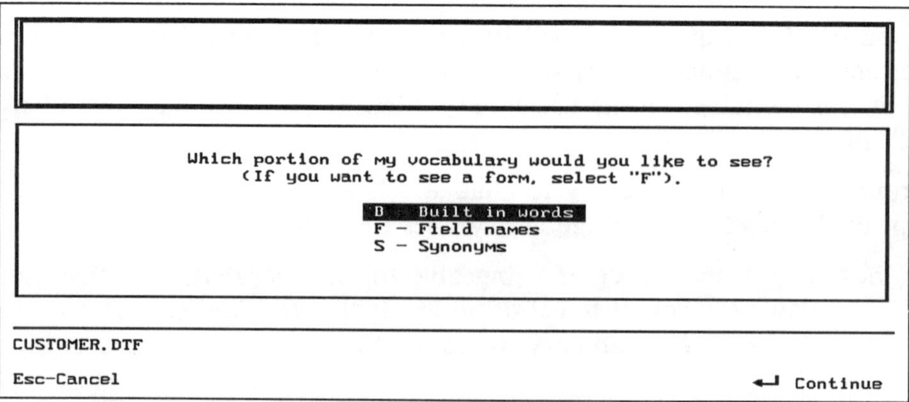

3. Press **Return**. The first page of the built-in vocabulary is displayed.
4. Press **PgDn**. The last page of the built-in vocabulary is displayed.
5. Press **Esc** to return to the screen displayed in Step 2.
6. Press **Esc**. A blank "Ask me to do something" screen is displayed.
7. Press **Esc** again. The Assistant Menu is displayed.
8. Press **Esc**. The Q&A Main Menu is displayed.
9. Turn to Module 51 to continue the learning sequence.

Appendix A
TERMS AND DEFINITIONS

Alternate Field Name Another name for a field that is different than the field label. The alternate field name is used in Assistant functions.

ASCII A standard computer coding system for text characters and control characters. The acronym for American Standard Code for Information Interchange.

Back-up Copy A copy of a file or diskette that is created to protect against loss of information if the original file or diskette is damaged.

Base Document The primary document created in the Write function. Used with the merge feature to create merge documents.

Block of Text A character, word, sentence, paragraph, complete page, or entire document identified to Q&A to be copied, moved, or deleted.

Calculation Statement Coding placed in fields on a form to instruct Q&A to perform the specified calculation. The calculation can be performed manually or automatically when you create or revise forms.

Clearing a Document Removing the Working Copy of a document from the editor. Editing changes made during the current editing session are not saved to disk.

Clear a Macro Remove a macro from computer memory.

Column Break The location in a sorted report column where a value changes. Q&A skips a line at column breaks.

Column/Sort Spec The screen used in Report functions to specify which fields are to be used by Q&A to create columns in a finished report.

COM Option Specified on the Print Options screen to direct printed data to a serial printer port, modem, or other serial device.

Composite Name A collection of name fields taken as a unit in the Assistant function.

Customized Help Help features created by a Q&A user. Custom help displays messages about the Add, Search, or Update features when using the File function.

Database A collection of information contained in forms within Q&A. A database is stored on a diskette or hard disk and identified by a filename.

Database Administrator The person who creates and manages databases. Responsible for assigning passwords to database users, setting requirements for data entry values, and assigning database access rights to users.

Data File A database stored in memory or on diskette or hard disk.

Decimal Tab A tab that controls decimal point placement when typing decimal fractions. Decimal tabs are frequently used in tables having numbers that must be lined up around a decimal point.

Define Page The screen used to set printed page layout in the Write function. Page dimensions, margins, type size, are typical layout specifications.

Default Tab A standard typewriter or decimal tab preprogrammed on the format ruler in a Working Copy of a document. Default tabs are set at 5, 15, 25, and 35 (from the left margin).

Degrees of Comparison Pertaining to adjectives having comparison relationships. The three degrees of comparison are: positive, comparative, and superlative.

Delete The process of removing information from a document or form.

Derived Column A column generated by calculations performed within another column in a report.

DIF The acroynm for Data Interchange Format. An industry standard for coding and ordering of information.

Document File A file containing word processing.

DOS File Facilities Special functions normally only available from the DOS prompt (A, B, or C). These functions include listing a directory (file list) or setting the default directory.

Edit Session Entering the Write function, selecting Type/Edit, and displaying a Working Copy (blank) screen of a document initiates an edit session.

Editing The processing of adding, deleting, or changing the existing text within a document or form.

Editor A synonym for the Type/Edit feature in the Write function. Used to create and edit word processing document files.

Empty Synonym A synonym that is not acknowledged by the Assistant.

Enhancement A way to emphasize printed type. Examples are bold, italic, or underlined type.

Field A name for a field label and its associated information blank in the File function. The field label identifies the type of information to be placed in the information blank.

Field ID An identification used to mark and set the order of fields for programming forms. A field can be calculated or referenced by a programming statement or formula, but it must first have a field ID.

Field Tag A special code used by Q&A to connect a label with its field. These tags are displayed on the screen when you redesign a form in the File function.

File A collection of data stored on diskette, on hard disk, or in computer memory

Filename A name specified for a file. A filename can contain a maximum of eight characters plus an optional extension.

Filename Extension A suffix to a filename consisting of a period (.) and any three characters.

Font A typographic character set used by most laser printers.

Footer Repetitive information that is positioned at the bottom of each document page. A footer can contain a date, page number, version number, or document name.

Form The equivalent to a record in a database. A form is comprised of information for each field label when created using the Form Design feature.

Form Design The collection of form fields and labels that are displayed in a specific pattern on the screen.

Format Options The screen that is displayed after the Format Spec screen in the File function when fields are identified as type D (date), N (number), or M (money).

Format Spec The screen on which you identify to Q&A the information type of each field on a form.

Free Form Style Displaying or printing a form without respect to any specific location requirements for the data involved.

Get a Document Retrieve a document or form from storage on disk.

Global Change Making a change in a document or on a form for every occurrence involved. (e.g., replacing the word can't with cannot at every location in a document).

Header Repetitive information that is placed at the top of each document page. A header can contain a date, page number, version number, or document name.

Indent Text Used in word processing to indicate the beginning of paragraphs. The process of locating the first line of text several spaces to the right of the left margin.

Insert The process of embedding a character, word, or paragraph at a specified location in a document. Characters or words can also be inserted on forms.

Identification Column A column that contains values identifying the forms from which the information was taken in a report.

Identifier Spec The screen displayed in the Print feature of the Write function during mail merge. It is used to match field labels used in a merge document having identical field labels in a database.

Import a Document Move a document from another software package into an existing Q&A document.

Infinite Loop A condition occurring when programming statements perform the same repetitive operation without leading to a solution or result.

Information Blank The blank space allocated in a form field immediately following the field label.

Information Type The code defining the type of information contained in an information blank. Examples are numeric or alphabetical.

Invisible Column A column used in the Report function that is not displayed or printed in a final report, but is used for calculations and reference only.

Join a Document Combine an existing document contained in the Q&A editor with another document that is resident on disk.

Justify To arrange information in a document making the left and/or right margins evenly line up. Used in the Write function and implemented using the Justify ON/OFF feature.

Key Assignment Line The line displayed at the bottom of screens that defines the function key operations currently available.

Key Column The first column in a lookup table in the File function.

Keyword An information type designated for a field in the File function that facilitates search operations. A word or phrase in a keyword field.

Label The name placed before the information blank for each field on a form in the File function.

LAN A Local Area Network. Usually consists of several personal computers interconnected which allows for complete communication among them.

Lookup Table A table containing values commomly used in information blanks on forms in a database. The lookup table allows for automatic insertion of values onto forms in the File function.

LPT Option Specified on the Print Options screen to direct printed data to a parallel printer port or other parallel device.

Macro A sequence of keystrokes programmed to execute when a single key or two-key combination is pressed.

Macro File A file containing one or more individual macros.

Macro Identifier The single key or two-key combination that activates the macro operation.

Mailing Label Dimensions Characteristics for mailing labels:

Height - Distance from the top edge of the label to the top of the following label.
Left Margin - Distance from the left edge to the position where text is printed on a line.
Right Margin - Distance from the right edge to the position where text printing stops on a line.
Width - Horizontal distance between edges of the label.
Top Margin - The number of lines from the top edge of the label to the first line of text.
Bottom Margin - The number of lines from the bottom edge of the label to remain blank.

Main Dictionary A complete set of commonly used words that is contained with the Q&A dictionary. The main dictionary is set in the software and cannot be modified.

Mass Update The process of automatically changing information on forms at one time. The update is performed on a "global" basis.

Merge Document A base document that is typed once in the Write function, but can be used (printed) many times and automatically inserts variable information in merge fields.

Merge File The variable information used with a merge (base) document.

Merge Spec The screen on which you specify fields that are to be copied from one database to another and the order in which the copy is to be made. This screen is displayed while in the File function and a copy operation is initiated.

Message Line The bottom line of the Q&A screen on which system messages are displayed.

Microjustification A function available in some printers. The adding of increments of space between words and/or characters to facilitate producing text that is right justified.

Network Administrator A person who manages the Local Area Network. Responsible for assigning user identification codes, manages required data backup, and controls data security.

Navigation Moving the cursor across the screen and in a form or document.

Order Number The number typed in fields in the File and Report functions to indicate the order in which a column is to display in a report. The order number also indicates where a copied field is to be placed in another database.

Page Coordinate Set The line number corresponding to the row and the character position (column number) on a page on the Field Spec screen in the File function.

Palette The foreground and background color characteristics for the display screen.

Password A special word that must be entered on the keyboard before access to a database is allowed.

Path Name The convention for identifying a specific diskette, hard disk, subdirectory, and filename.

Personal Dictionary The user created dictionary within Q&A. User can add, delete, or modify words contained in the personal dictionary.

Pivot Character The character on which the cursor is located when a block operation is initiated in the Write function. The pivot character indicates the beginning or end of a block that is to be copied, deleted, or moved.

Precedence The order in which an operation is performed. For example the order in which a formula is read to produce a calculation.

Preset Value A default value used by Q&A if a value is not typed. A value assigned by Q&A to an information blank.

Primary Sort The initial sort upon which other sort operations are dependent.

Print Options The screen on which print specifications are entered by the user. Print options include destination, line spacing, and number of copies for the printed document or file.

Print Queuing Scheduling the printing of files in a predetermined order.

Print Spec The retrieve, sort, field, and print specifications for forms in the File function.

Printer Control Code The ASCII value controlling special effects for a printer. Printer control codes are entered on the Print Options Menu.

Printer Offset The value on the Print Options Menu that aligns the print head of the printer to the right or left of the default starting position.

Programming Statements Defined operations that are entered on forms to control the updating of fields and the order in which data is entered.

Range The specified limits within which a search operation is to be performed. The method of indicating a block of cells being imported from a Lotus 1-2-3 or Symphony spreadsheet.

Read/Write Assigned levels of access to a database. Some users are assigned only Read authorization to a database by the Database Administrator; others are assigned both Read and Write authority.

Redesign a Form Perform an edit on a form design to add, delete, or modify fields, field labels, or field locations.

Report The collection of data from specified forms in a database. A report is printed or displayed as a table in the Report function.

Request Box The box displayed at the top of the screen in which requests are typed for the Assistant to perform some action.

Retrieve Spec The screen on which retrieve criteria for forms are entered. The retrieve criteria are used in search operations.

Ruler Line The line at the bottom of the screen that indicates column positions, tab locations, and page margins.

Save Store information on diskette.

Select Choose an option on a menu.

Status Line The line at the bottom of some screens that indicates the current status of a document or file.

Subcalculation A secondary calculation performed in the Report function.

Subvalue A value that results from a subcalculation.

Summary Report A report that displays only totals and subtotals.

Synonym An alternate word or phrase representing another word or phrase.

Update Spec The specified criteria for updating information on forms in the File function when the Mass Update feature is used.

User Identification (ID) A word that identifies an individual user to the system in a network environment.

Wild Card A character or series of characters translated by Q&A to represent another character or group of characters.

Working Copy A document in the Write fuction that is contained in the active editor, has not yet been named, and has not been saved to disk.

Appendix B
SPECIAL Q&A VOCABULARY AND RESTRICTIONS

SPECIAL VOCABULARY

There are certain special words that are contained in the Assistant's vocabulary. The following is a list of these words with their corresponding meanings.

Word	*Description*
Alpha	Abbreviation for alphabetical
Best	Superlative signifying highest
Better	Comparative signifying higher
Between	Signifying a range from a lower value to a higher value. Always specify the lower value first, followed by the higher value.
Blank	Indicating no value
Cut	Indicating to decrease
Delete	Signifying to erase
Poorly	Signifying a low value
Respect	Meaning: With respect to. Also abbreviated as WRT
Set	Indicating to make
Top	Superlative signifying the highest
WNEC	Also expressed as: With no extra columns. Either the abbreviation or the expression is used when requesting the Assistant to produce a report.
WNIC	Also expressed as: With no identification columns. Either the abbreviation or the expression is used when requesting the Assistant to produce a report.
WNRC	Also expressed as: With no restriction columns. Either the abbreviation or the expression is used when requesting the Assistant to produce a report.

Q&A RESTRICTION SPECIFICATIONS

When typing retrieve specifications in the File and Report functions, certain special symbols and words are used. The following is a list of these special symbols and words with corresponding descriptions.

Symbol or Word(s)	*Description*
BEGINS WITH or	First letter(s) is/are
STARTS WITH BETWEEN	Contained within the specified limits
BOTTOM	At the minimum
CONTAINS	Has as a part of; has within, the specified letter(s)
EARLIEST	First or earliest date
ENDS WITH	Last letter(s) is/are
GREATEST	Superlative signifying the highest number
LATEST	Superlative for last or most recent date
LEAST	The lowest number
MATCHES	Equivalent to a value expressed in a retrieve specification
NOT	Negates the term immediately following
TOP	At the maximum
=, IS, or EQUAL	Is equal to; is an exact match; equivalent to
>, IS GREATER THAN, or IS AFTER	Greater than; alphabetized after (can be used with calendar dates)
<, IS LESS THAN, or IS BEFORE	Less than; alphabetized before (can be used with calendar dates)
> =, IS GREATER THAN OR EQUAL TO, or IS ON OR LATER THAN	Greater than or equal to (can be used with calendar dates)
< =, IS LESS THAN OR EQUAL TO, or IS ON OR BEFORE	Less than or equal to (can be used with calendar dates)
/=, IS NOT, or IS NOT EQUAL TO	Not equal to (can be used with calendar dates)

Appendix C
SEARCH CRITERIA

The following values are restrict values used in the Search/Update function. The table lists information types, the applicable Restrict Value symbols, and definitions for the symbols.

Symbol	*Definition*
x	equal to the value of x
=x	equal to x
/x	not equal to the value of x
=	empty
/=	not empty
x	equal to the value of x
=x	equal to the value of x
>x	greater than the value of x
<x	less than the value of x
> =x	greater than or equal to the value of x
< =x	less than or equal to the value of x
>x..<y	greater than the value of x and less than the value of y
x..<y	greater than or equal to the value of x and less than the value of y
>x..y	greater than the value of x and less than or equal to the value of y
MAXn	n highest values
MINn	n lowest values
x..	greater than or equal to the value of x
..x	less than or equal to the value of x
x..y	values x through y
x	begins with the value of x
..x	ends with the value of x
x..y	begins with the value of x and ends with the value of y
..x..	includes the value of x
?	the value of any character
..x..y..z	includes the values of x, y, and z (in order)
..	Any group of characters (or correctly formatted values)
/..	incorrectly formatted values
/	literal character after the character "/"
x;y;z;	or the value of x or y or z
&x;y;z	

Appendix D
Q&A IN A NETWORK ENVIRONMENT

Q&A software and databases can be used on Local Area Networks (LANs). Refer to the documentation provided with your Q&A software for the local area networks that are compatible.

USER ACCESS

Q&A databases can be set up for multiple user access. Instructions on how to set up users in this environment are provided in the Network Administrator's Guide provided with Q&A software.

WHEN IS A Q&A NETWORK PACK REQUIRED?

A Q&A Network Pack is necessary if you want to put the Q&A software on a network file server and have several users access the Q&A software simultaneously. A single registered copy of Q&A can be installed on a file server; however, only one user can access the software at any one time. This pack is not necessary if each user has a registered copy of the Q&A software on his computer, but is accessing Q&A databases from a network file server.

A single Network Pack supports four users. A second pack supports seven users, and a third pack supports ten users. Afterwards, each pack increases the number of users by three.

ADVANTAGES OF A CENTRALIZED FILE SERVER

LANs normally have a centralized file server on which all database information is stored. With such an environment, the following advantages are apparent:

1. Every user has access to all data on the file server.
2. Users can share printers, plotters, scanners, etc.
3. Database integrity is easy to maintain. Regular backup of the data is usually handled by the Network Administrator.
4. Data in the databases is always the latest information and readily available to all users.

MULTIPLE USERS ACCESSING Q&A DATABASES

Access to databases is controlled by passwords. If a user is using a database and others attempt to access the same database, the subsequent users have "read" access only at that time. When the first user releases the database another user has "write" access to the database.

The rules governing shared and locked file functions in Q&A are extensive and detailed information provided with the Q&A software documentation should be studied carefully.

PRINTING IN A NETWORK ENVIRONMENT

Q&A captures a report, forms, or a document at the point in time a print request is entered. Other users can be changing the database while the request print is uninhibited, and the integrity is valid for the point in time that the request was issued to the printer.

ACCESS CONTROL

Access rights to databases are entered through the File function, Customize Menu. Selecting A on the menu permits the Database Administrator to assign access rights. The Access Control screen contains various parameters permitting the Database Administrator to define the access profile for each user in the LAN.

Selecting D permits the Database Administrator to set shared mode access. A Declare Sharing Mode screen allows the Database Administrator to define concurrent use of databases in a multi-user environment.

USER PASSWORDS

User passwords for access to databases are assigned through the Access Control screen. Passwords can be assigned to databases and can also be removed or changed. These functions are usually performed by the Network Administrator in a LAN environment.

A user can enter a password for initial entry into the Q&A Main Menu. This password can also be changed by the user.

Appendix E
MAILING LABELS

Mailing labels are created from within the Write function. The software accommodates creation of mailing labels using may common brands. The following screen illustrates common labels that you can use with the Q&A software.

John B. Goode
11503 South Main St.
Peoria , IL 42613

CREATING MAILING LABELS

Mailing labels can be created from the Write function by accessing the Mailing Label screen. After selecting the label size that matches your labels, pressing F10 displays a label with merge fields for name, address, city, and postal zip code.

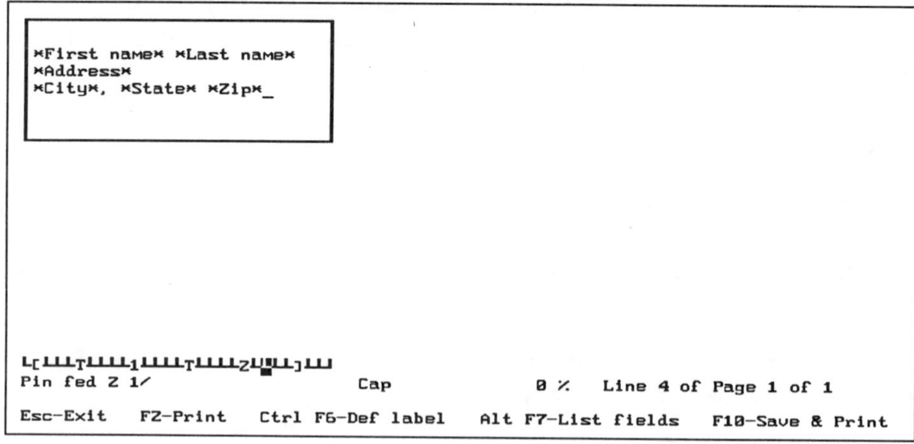

You can edit the label just as if it were a Write document. Pressing Alt-F7 displays a prompt requesting a database name. Entering the filename and pressing Return displays a list of field names from the database.

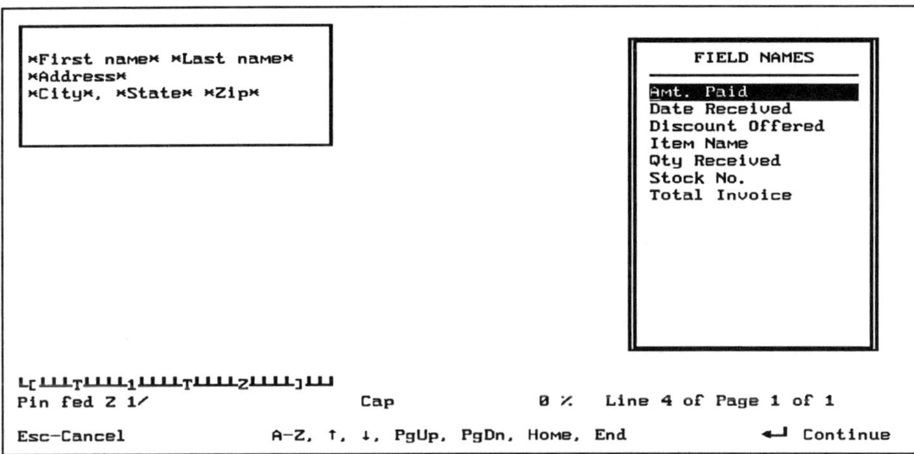

Fields from the list can be added to the label or can replace existing text on the displayed label. Pressing Shift-F8 saves the label to disk. Pressing F10, saves the label to disk and displays the Mailing Label Print Option screen. The label can be saved under its original name or under a new name consisting of up to 32 characters.

PRINTING MAILING LABELS

Up to eight labels can be printed across a page. To print labels, press F2 at the Define Label screen or while editing a label; the Mailing Label Print Options screen is displayed.

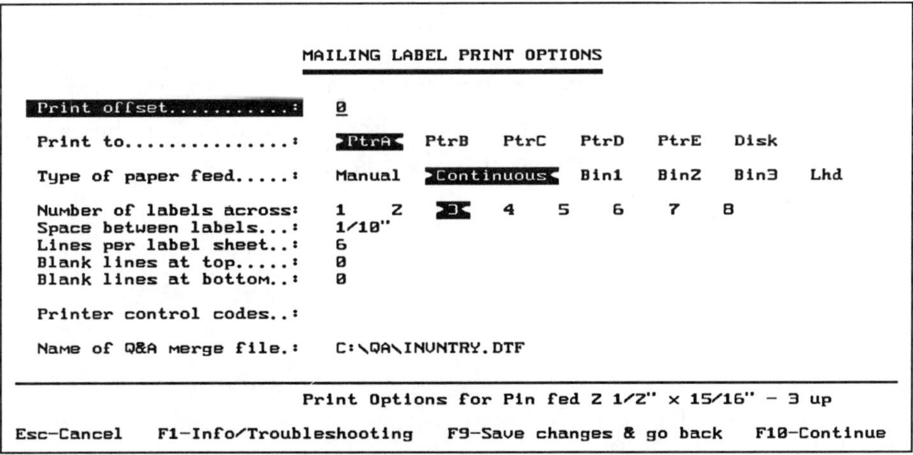

Any field on the screen can be changed. Pressing F10 displays the Retrieve Spec screen for the database. You can selectively retrieve forms or press F10 and retrieve all forms in the database.

If field names on your labels do not match field names in the specified database, a warning message is displayed and you have the opportunity to make necessary corrections.

DEFINING A NEW LABEL

If your mailing label does not match any of the existing labels defined in the Q&A software, you can define your own. From the Write Menu, selecting M displays the list of available labels. Typing the name of any label and pressing Return displays the Mailing Label screen. Pressing Ctrl-F6 displays the Define Label screen.

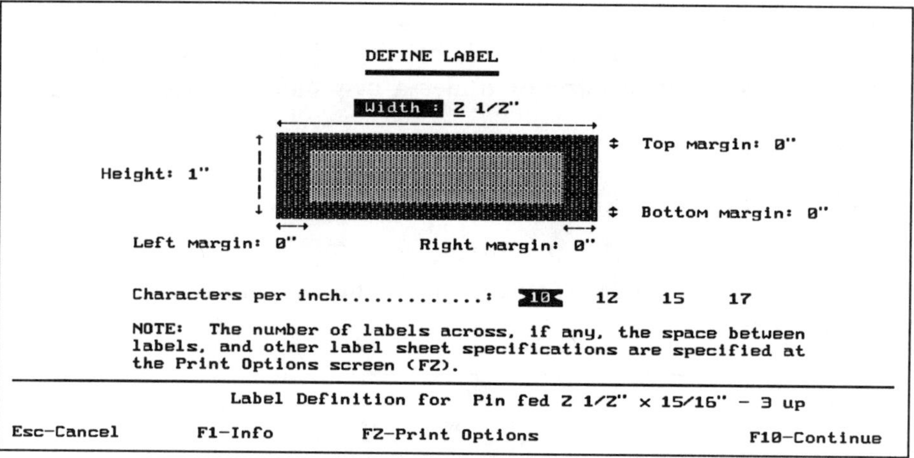

On this screen you can type over the existing dimensions to define the exact label that you want. Pressing F10 displays the Mailing Label screen. You can proceed to printing labels from here.

Appendix F
Q&A EXERCISES

1. About this Book
   a. What features does Q&A combine into its single software package?
   b. If you are learning Q&A, what sequence should you follow to go through this book?
   c. For what kind of user is this book designed?
   d. What kind of disk drive system is recommended for using Q&A most efficiently?
2. Sample Sesson
   a. Name the major purpose of the checklist.
   b. Describe the organization of the Recommended Learning Sequence Checklist.
3. Advanced Adjectives Lesson
   a. What is the purpose of the Advanced Adjectives Lesson?
   b. What are the three degrees of comparison?
   c. Is it necessary to assign adjectives to every numeric or money field?
   d. Through which Q&A Main Menu function is the Advanced Adjectives Lesson accessed?
4. Advanced Verbs Lesson
   a. Define a "verb" and explain what verbs permit the Assistant to do?
   b. What is a regular verb ending? Give examples.
   c. Through which Q&A Main Menu function is the Advanced Verbs Lesson accessed?
5. Alternate Field Names Lesson
   a. Define alternate field name.
   b. Give the main reason for using alternate field names.
   c. Can duplicate field names be assigned to fields that are related?
   d. How can assignment of alternate field names be helpful to your business?
6. Assign/Change Form Information Types
   a. Name the information type automatically assigned to each field by Q&A.
   b. For what major Q&A function is assigning form information types important?
   c. What are the purposes for assigning information types to form fields?
   d. Through which Q&A Main Menu function is the Assign/Change Form Information Types feature accessed?
7. Block Selection
   a. What is a block of text?
   b. For what purposes are blocks of text marked?
   c. How do you know that a block of text has been selected or marked?
   d. Within which major Q&A function are blocks of text selected?

8. Calculate in a Report
   a. In which columns on a report can calculations be performed?
   b. What is the purpose of column calculation codes? Give several examples.
   c. How can subcalculation codes be canceled?
   d. Through which screen are column calculation codes entered?
9. Center/Uncenter Text
   a. When can the line centering feature be used?
   b. Describe how to center an existing line of text.
   c. Through which menu is line centering canceled?
   d. Within which major Q&A function is the Center Text feature used?
10. Change the Screen Palette
    a. Within which major Q&A function is the Change Palette feature used?
    b. Through which File function menu is the Change Palette feature accessed?
    c. How many color combinations are available through the Change Palette feature?
    d. Can selected colors for database forms be changed later?
11. Clear a Document
    a. Name some purposes for clearing a document.
    b. Once deciding to clear a document, do you have the opportunity to change your choice? Explain.
12. Clear a Macro
    a. Within which major Q&A functions can a macro be cleared?
    b. What are the two ways in which a macro can be cleared?
    c. Explain what clearing a macro involves?
13. Column Headings/Width for a Report
    a. What does Q&A automatically use as column headings for reports?
    b. What is the maximum number of lines that can be used for a heading?
    c. Through which screen are column headings and/or widths created or changed?
14. Copy a Enter Database to Another Database
    a. Describe the two procedures used to copy a database design.
    b. Within which major Q&A function is the Copy a Database Design feature used?
    c. What is one reason for copying a database design?
15. Copy a Form Design
    a. Why would you want to copy a form design?
    b. When performing the copy operation, can you view the names of files existing on disk to aid in your copy selection?
    c. What are the two functions displayed on the Copy Menu?
16. Copy Forms From One Database to Another Database
    a. Name the options that are available through this copy feature.
    b. What do retrieve specifications allow you to do?
    c. What do merge specifications allow you to do?
    d. Describe the three restrictions that must be observed when using this copy feature.
    e. What is the alternate method for copying an entire database to another database?

17. Copy Text to Another Document
    a. When must be copy operation be performed?
    b. Can blocks of text from several documents be copied into a single document? Explain.
18. Copy Text Within a Document
    a. Explain how text is selected for the copy operation.
    b. How can duplicate copies of a block of text be made? What combination keystroke can be used?
    c. Explain how this copy feature can help you be more productive in your work.
19. Create a Report Using the Assistant
    a. List the four requirements for the information that must be provided to the Assistant for a report to be created.
    b. Through which Q&A Main Menu function is a report created?
    c. Explain the consequences of using vocabulary of which the Assistant is unfamiliar.
    d. Are there prerequisite lessons that must be given to the Assistant before a report can be created? Explain.
20. Cursor Movement
    a. What is the purpose of the cursor?
    b. How can you recognize the cursor?
    c. What are the navigation keys?
    d. Explain why moving the cursor is an important operation.
21. Customize a File
    a. Name some customizing features.
    b. What is the purpose of creating indexed fields?
    c. Describe how field format values affect a form.
22. Database Lesson
    a. Why is the Database Lesson essential?
    b. What items in the database does the Assistant search for and review?
23. Default Directory
    a. Describe the purpose of the Q&A Default Directory feature.
    b. What are the default settings for Q&A directories for a floppy disk drive system?
    c. What is a good reference to use to find instructions on how to define and use directories and paths?
24. Define/Redefine a Macro
    a. What is a macro?
    b. When can a macro be used? Explain.
    c. What process is involved in defining a macro?
    d. Cite some cautions to observe when identifying a macro.
    e. When in an edit session in word processing, what keystrokes display the Macro Menu Box?

25. Delete Text
    a. Explain what deleting text involves and some delete options that are available in Q&A.
    b. Explain how deleted text in a Working Copy of a previously saved document can be retrieved.
    c. Describe how the combination keystroke, Shift-F4, is executed.
26. Derived Columns in a Report
    a. What is the purpose of derived columns in a report?
    b. How are calculations performed in derived columns?
    c. What is the maximum number of derived columns allowable in a report?
    d. Describe the order of precedence for calculations in derived columns.
27. DOS File Facilities
    a. Through which Q&A Main Menu function is the DOS File Facilities feature accessed?
    b. Name the common DOS functions.
    c. Describe the function of each DOS function.
28. Draw Lines/Boxes
    a. Within which major Q&A function is the Draw Lines and Boxes feature used?
    b. Name some typical applications for utilizing the drawing capabilities provided by Q&A.
29. Edit a Form
    a. What is the first step performed to edit a form?
    b. Explain how the Retrieve Spec screen is used when editing forms.
    c. What effect does editing forms have on the status of your database?
30. Edit Lookup Table
    a. What kind of information is contained in an Edit Lookup Table?
    b. What are the components in an Edit Lookup Table?
    c. What programming word is used in conjunction with an Edit Lookup Table?
    d. What is the maximum number of items that can be contained in an Edit Lookup Table?
31. Editing a Macro
    a. Within which major Q&A function are macros created?
    b. What are the components of a macro?
    c. What is the purpose of editing a macro?
32. Enhance Document Text
    a. Name the five enhancements that can be made to document text.
    b. What is the purpose of using enhanced text in a document?
    c. Describe the enhanced text process when creating a document.
    d. How does enhanced text display on the screen?
    e. For what kind of text is italics type customarily used?
33. Enter Data on a Form
    a. What does entering form data involve?
    b. How can a form field be left blank?
    c. Define editing a form?
    d. How can field information from a previous form be duplicated in the current form?

34. Enter/Edit Document Text
    a. What is another name for the Type/Edit function?
    b. What is an edit session?
    c. What functions are involved in editing test?
    d. Describe how an edit session is initiated.
35. Export Data
    a. Define exporting data.
    b. List the common data formats.
    c. Through which Q&A Main Menu function is the Export Menu accessed?
    d. What advantage does exporting data provide?
36. Export a Document
    a. What is exporting?
    b. What are the two options available when exporting a document?
37. Form Design
    a. What is the purpose of designing a form?
    b. Name the procedures required to design a form.
    c. What should be considered when you create a filename for a design?
38. Form Design/Redesign Print Criteria
    a. What does defining print specifications involve?
    b. What are the two types of specification styles that are available? Define each.
    c. Name a typical application for free-form style.
    d. For what purpose is coordinate style primarily used?
39. Form Fields Lesson
    a. What is the purpose of the Form Fields Lesson?
    b. Through which Q&A Main Menu function is the Form Fields Lesson accessed?
    c. What is the limit for the number of fields identified on a form?
40. Form Redesign
    a. Name one important step to take before attempting to redesign a form.
    b. What is a field tag? What is its purpose?
    c. Name some form design specifications that can be changed.
    d. Give some examples of information types.
41. Function Keys
    a. Where are the function keys defined within Q&A?
    b. List some of the function keys and define their purpose.
    c. What is the purpose of function keys?
42. Get Acquainted with the Assistant
    a. How are commands communicated to the Assistant?
    b. Name three tasks that the Assistant can perform.
    c. How many words are contained in the Assistant's vocabulary?
43. Get a Document
    a. Explain what getting a document means.
    b. Through which Main Menu function is the Get a Document feature accessed?
    c. List the two ways in which a filename can be selected when you are getting a document.
    d. Name some other software packages from which Q&A can retrieve documents.

44. Global Parameters
    a. What are global parameters?
    b. List some typical global parameters.
    c. Within which Q&A major function are global parameters used?
    d. Through which Write function menu are global parameters accessed?
45. Headers/Footers
    a. Describe the purpose for using headers and footers.
    b. Explain how headers and footers are used in combination.
    c. Through which Write function menu is the Headers and Footers feature accessed?
46. Help, Create
    a. Name two help features available within Q&A.
    b. How many lines of help information can be typed on a help screen? How many characters can be typed on each line?
    c. Which function key is used to display help information?
47. Help, On-Line
    a. If a second level of help information is available, which function key is pressed to access it?
    b. Which key is pressed to exit from the On-line Help feature?
48. Help the Assistant
    a. List three conditions that can cause the Assistant to request your help.
    b. If the Intelligent Assitant encounters a word that it does not understand, what are the four options that you can take?
49. Indent Text
    a. How are tab settings indicated on the format ruler displayed at the bottom of the screen?
    b. What is a hanging indent?
    c. Describe some typical applications for indenting text.
    d. Explain what temporary margins are and how they control text being typed.
50. Import a Document
    a. What is importing a document?
    b. Through which Q&A Main Menu function is the Import a Document feature accessed?
    c. How is importing documents into Q&A advantageous?
51. Importing Files
    a. Through which Q&A Main Menu function are documents imported? Explain.
    b. Name some other kinds of documents that can be imported.
    c. Explain how merge specifications can be used when importing documents.
    d. Describe the features of the Q&A file accepting an imported file.
52. Invisible Columns in a Report
    a. Do invisible columns appear on a report? Explain.
    b. On which screen are invisible columns created? What special code is used?
    c. Give a typical use for invisible columns.

53. Join Documents
    a. What is joining documents?
    b. Write two versions of the command used to join documents.
    c. What is a base document? Explain.
54. Justification On/Off
    a. What does justification, set to ON, permit you to do in a document?
    b. What is the default for justification in Q&A?
    c. Write two versions for the justify command to set justification to ON.
    d. Describe another method for justifying text in a document without using the justify command.
55. Keyword Report
    a. Where must the keyword column appear on a report?
    b. What code designates a keyword field on the Column/Sort Spec screen?
56. Location/Name Fields Lesson
    a. Describe the purpose for the Location/Name Fields Lesson.
    b. Through which Assistant Menu function are locations and names taught to the Assistant?
    c. Name and define the abbreviations used to tell the Assistant about name fields.
57. Mass Update of Forms
    a. To which major Q&A function is the Mass Update feature applicable?
    b. What is one of the most useful applications for using the Mass Update feature?
    c. Define global change.
58. Menu Network
    a. What are the major functions available through the Q&A Main Menu?
    b. What does menu-driven mean?
59. Merge Document
    a. What is a merge document?
    b. List the steps necessary to produce a merge document.
    c. Explain the use of asterisks ald2*2) in a base document.
    d. What is the purpose of the I command?
    e. What is the purpose of the R command?
    f. Why would you want to use the Merge Document feature?
60. Move Text in a Document
    a. What operation must first be performed before text can be moved in a document?
    b. What advantages does moving text in a document provide to you?
    c. What keystroke completes the move of a block of text?
61. Move Text to Another Document
    a. Can text from several documents be moved to a single document? Explain.
    b Explain why block selection of text is an important part of moving text to another document.
62. Page Break
    a. What is the default for the number of lines per page?
    b. How is a page break designated?
    c. How can a page break be deleted?

63. Page Layout for a Document
    a. List the page characteristics that can be defined for a document page.
    b. Name the one selectable page characteristic that is not displayed on the screen.
    c. What are the two ways in which page characteristics can be defined?
    d. Explain how page characteristics defined for a document can be saved.
64. Perform Tasks Using the Assistant
    a. Explain how you initiate a request to the Assistant to perform some task.
    b. List the guidelines to follow when using the Assistant to retrieve and change forms.
65. Personal Dictionary Update
    a. What is the personal dictionary?
    b. What are the two ways in which the personal dictionary can be updated?
    c. Name the file that contains the personal dictionary.
66. Print a Block of Text
    a. Explain what happens to the page boundary when printing a block of text that crosses the page boundary.
    b. What is a typical application for printing a block of text?
    c. What is the advantage of printing a block of text rather than using the "screen print" feature available on most personal computers?
67. Print a Document
    a. Which type of printer operates without the need to set printer parameters?
    b. List some print enhancements available in Q&A.
    c. Is it possible to print and edit simultaneously?
    d. Through which Q&A Main Menu function is printing a document accessed?
68. Print a Document with Special Effects
    a. What is a major dependency for printing special effects in a document?
    b. Name the special printing features that are available.
    c. What is a prime source of reference for printer control codes?
    d. List the forms in which control codes are defined.
    e. Write the syntax for issuing special print codes.
69. Print a Form
    a. Name some of the options available when printing forms that make this feature extremely versatile.
    b. Describe the three options that are selectable from the Print Menu for printing forms.
    c. What is the first step to perform when printing a form?
70. Print a Merge Document
    a. What does printing a merge document encompass?
    b. What are the two ways to initiate the printing of a merge document?
71. Print Options for a Report
    a. What is the one unique option available when printing a report?
    b. What is a Summary Report?
    c. What parameters are specified on the Define Page screen?
    d. List the options that are available for printing a report.

72. Print a Report
    a. Through which Q&A Main Menu function is the Print a Report feature accessed?
    b. Describe the options displayed on the Print Options screen.
73. Printer Installation
    a. Through which Q&A Main Menu function is the Printer Installation feature accessed?
    b. What options are displayed on the Port Selection screen?
    c. What is the maximum number of printers that can be installed for use with Q&A?
    d. What is the port designation for parallel printers? For serial printers?
    e. If installing a serial printer, what are the serial port parameters that must be specified?
74. Program Overview
    a. What feature makes Q&A files compatible with most other popular word processing, database, and spreadsheet software?
    b. List the names of the Q&A diskettes and briefly what kind of files are contained on each.
75. Programming Statements
    a. Which keyboard characters designate the beginning of a programming statement?
    b. Where may programming statements be entered on a form?
76. Programming Words
    a. List and describe the purpose of at least three programming words.
    b. List and describe the purpose of at least two programming words that move the cursor.
    c. Programming words are used to construct what kind of statements?
77. Remove a Form
    a. Explain what removing a form involves.
    b. Through which Q&A Main Menu function is a form deleted from a database?
    c. Once deleted, can forms be retrieved again? Explain.
78. Rename/Detele/Copy
    a. Define each function: Rename, Delete, and Copy.
    b. Describe in which major Q&A functions Rename, Delete and Copy are used.
79. Report Design/Redesign
    a. What does designing a report involve?
    b. Name some operations that can be coded on the Column/Sort Spec screen.
    c. How is redesigning a report similar to creating an original design for a report?
80. Retrieve/Change Forms Using the Assistant
    a. Through which Q&A Main Menu function can a form be retrieved?
    b. Write a typical request to the Assistant to change a field on a form.
81. Retrieve a Macro
    a. Where are macros stored when not being used?
    b. When can a macro be retrieved?
    c. Name the options displayed on the Macro Menu Box.
    d. How can macros be used to imporve your productivity?

82. Save a Document
    a. Describe the two ways to save a document.
    b. Through which Q&A Main Menu function is a document saved?
    c. Which menu is displayed after the save operation is completed?
83. Save a Macro
    a. Does Q&A automatically save macros to disk?
    b. Where is a macro placed for use as long as Q&A is active?
    c. Why would you want to save each macro that you create?
84. Search/Replace Text
    a. What is the maximum number of characters which you can search?
    b. What are the options available when searching for text in a document?
    c. Explain how to use the search feature to get a word count for a document.
85. Search/Update Forms
    a. Describe the Search feature.
    b. Describe the Update feature.
    c. Through which Main Menu function are the Search and Update features accessed?
86. Sort Forms
    a. In what order does Q&A retrieve forms from a database?
    b. Describe how forms are sorted.
    c. What are the two basic sort levels?
87. Sort Report Information
    a. Define sorting.
    b. List at least three sort functions and the applicable sort code for each.
    c. What can be done if a field on a form is too small for you to type the sort code in the actual field?
88. Spell Check
    a. How many dictionaries are contained in Q&A? Explain the purpose of each.
    b. What are the two ways in which spelling can be checked in a document?
    c. List the options displayed on the Spelling Menu.
89. Tab Settings
    a. What are the two types of tab settings that are available?
    b. Describe the use of each type of tab setting.
    c. How are tab settings displayed on the screen?
    d. Through which menu is the Set Tabs feature accessed?
    e. Explain how tabs are cleared.
90. Units of Measure Lesson
    a. List some common units of measure.
    b Through which Q&A Main Menu function is the Units of Measure Lesson accessed?
    c. How are fields designated as monetary fields measured by Q&A? Explain.
91. Update the Assistant
    a. What is the purpose of updating the Assistant?
    b. Name some of the other lessons that are important in updating the Assistant.
    c. Name the options displayed on the Assistant Menu.

92. View Multiple Forms
    a. Name and describe the methods that can be used to view forms.
    b. What is the maximum number of forms for which highlight information can be viewed on a single screen?
    c. Name typical uses for viewing forms.
93. View Vocabulary
    a. What are the three categories of vocabulary available to the Assistant?
    b. Through which Q&A Main Menu function is the View Vocabulary feature accessed?

Index